Collaborative
Therapy

Julia,
Wishing you the best
in the next phase of
your journey - you
are doing important
work.

Diane Gehart
WAMFT 2012

Collaborative Therapy

Relationships *and* Conversations *that make* a Difference

Edited by **Harlene Anderson and Diane Gehart**

Routledge
Taylor & Francis Group
New York   London

Routledge is an imprint of the
Taylor & Francis Group, an informa business

Routledge
Taylor & Francis Group
270 Madison Avenue
New York, NY 10016

Routledge
Taylor & Francis Group
2 Park Square
Milton Park, Abingdon
Oxon OX14 4RN

© 2007 by Taylor & Francis Group, LLC
Routledge is an imprint of Taylor & Francis Group, an Informa business

Printed in the United States of America on acid-free paper
10 9 8 7 6 5 4 3 2

International Standard Book Number-10: 0-415-95327-8 (Softcover) 0-415-95326-X (Hardcover)
International Standard Book Number-13: 978-0-415-95327-6 (Softcover) 978-0-415-95326-9 (Hardcover)

Visit the Taylor & Francis Web site at
http://www.taylorandfrancis.com

and the Routledge Web site at
http://www.routledgementalhealth.com

To the memory of our beloved colleagues
whom we lost to tragic deaths during the creation of this book:
Gianfranco Cecchin, Judy Elmquist, and Glen Gardner.

About the Editors

Harlene Anderson, Ph.D. (U.S.), is a cofounder of the Houston Galveston Institute in Houston, Texas, and the Taos Institute, in Chagrin Falls, Ohio. She is the author of *Conversation, Language, and Possibilities: A Postmodern Approach to Therapy*, in addition to numerous journal articles and book chapters on postmodern collaborative therapy. Harlene is recognized internationally as being at the leading edge of the development and linkage of a postmodern philosophy and collaborative practices in therapy, supervision, teaching, and business consultation. She lives in Houston, Texas with her husband H. David Shine.

Diane Gehart, Ph.D. (U.S.), is an associate professor in the Marriage and Family Therapy Program at California State University–Northridge and coauthor of *Theory-Based Treatment Planning for Marriage and Family Therapists: Integrating Theory and Practice*. Diane has authored numerous articles on postmodern and collaborative therapies, qualitative research, mindfulness, and Buddhist philosophy. She has a private practice in Thousand Oaks, California.

Contributors

Jukka Aaltonen, M.D., Ph.D. (Finland), professor of family therapy, Department of Psychology, University of Jyväskylä, Finland.

Birgitta Alakare, M.D. (Finland), chief of psychiatry, Western Lapland Health District, Finland.

Tom Andersen, M.D., Ph.D. (Norway), professor of social psychiatry, Institute of Community Medicine, University of Tromsø, Norway, and editor, *The Reflecting Team in Action: Dialogues and Dialogues about the Dialogues.*

Jennifer Andrews, Ph.D. (U.S.), faculty member, Department of Counseling and Family Studies, Loma Linda University, California, and cofounder of Master'sWorks Productions, which produces training videos for marriage and family therapy.

Saliha Bava, Ph.D. (U.S.), associate director of Houston Galveston Institute, Houston, Texas, and adjunct faculty at Our Lady of the Lake University-Houston.

Alejandra Cortés, M.D. (Mexico), primary care physician and psychotherapist in Mexico City and founder of the Mexican Association for Eating Disorders.

Klaus G. Deissler, Ph.D. (Germany), cofounder of the Marburg Institute, German Association for Family Therapy, International Society for Systemic Therapy, German Systemic Society, and Langenfeld Institute. He is cofounder and editor of *Kontext,* editor of *Zeitschrift für systemische Therapie,* and author of *Phil und Sophie auf der Couch: Die soziale Poesie therapeutisher gespraeche.*

Debbie Feinsilver, M.S. (U.S.), clinical associate, Houston Galveston Institute, Houston, Texas.

Elena Fernández, M.A. (Mexico) cofounder of Grupo Campos Elíseos, a training institute in Mexico City and faculty member of the Houston Galveston Institute, Houston, Texas.

Glen Gardner, Ph.D. (U.S.), professor and chair of psychology, Our Lady of the Lake University-San Antonio, Texas, and faculty member, Houston Galveston Institute, Houston, Texas.

Kenneth J. Gergen, Ph.D. (U.S.), Mustin Professor of Psychology, Swarthmore College, Massachusetts, and cofounder of the Taos Institute, Chagrin Falls, Ohio. His major works include *The Saturated Self, Realities and Relationships,* and *An Invitation to Social Constructionism.* Many acknowledge Gergen as the dean of social constructionism.

Mary Gergen, Ph.D. (U.S.), professor of psychology and women's studies, Pennsylvania State University; division head of psychology for the Commonwealth College Philadelphia, PA; and cofounder of the Taos Institute, Chagrin Falls, Ohio. Her major works include *Toward a New Psychology of Gender* and *Impious Improvisations: Feminist Reconstructions in Psychology.*

Kauko Haarakangas, Ph.D. (Finland), chief psychologist, Western Lapland Health District, Finland.

Lynn Hoffman, M.S.W. (U.S.), family therapy historian living in Easthampton, Massachusetts and author of numerous publications including the books *Foundations of Family Therapy, Exchanging Voices,* and *Family Therapy: An Intimate History.*

Patricia Koch, Ph.D. (U.S.), codirector of Cuente Conmigo, a training, supervision, and research group in Austin, Texas.

Susan B. Levin, Ph.D. (U.S.), executive director and faculty member, Houston Galveston Institute, Houston, Texas, and adjunct faculty member, Our Lady of the Lake–Houston M.S. Psychology Program.

Sylvia London, M.A., (Mexico), cofounder of Grupo Campos Elíseos, Mexico City; faculty member, Psychology Department, Universidad de las

Americas, Mexico City; and faculty member, Houston Galveston Institute, Houston, Texas.

Marsha McDonough, Ph.D. (U.S.), codirector of Cuente Conmigo, a training, supervision, and research group in Austin, Texas.

Sheila McNamee, Ph.D. (U.S.), professor and chair of communications, University of New Hampshire; cofounder, the Taos Institute, Chagrin Falls, Ohio, and coeditor of *Therapy as Social Construction* and coauthor of *Relational Responsibility: Resources for Sustainable Dialogue.*

Eileen Murphy, M.S. (U.S.), clinical associate, Houston Galveston Institute, Houston, Texas.

Tony Neugebauer, M.A. (U.S.), assistant professor and clinical supervisor, Department of Psychology at Our Lady of the Lake University–San Antonio, Texas, and clinical director of Community Counseling Service, the university's clinical training facility.

Peggy Penn, M.S.W. (U.S.), supervising faculty member and former director of training and education, Ackerman Institute for Family Therapy, New York, N.Y. She is the author of *So Close* and coauthor of *Milan Systemic Family Therapy: Conversations in Theory and Practice.*

Irma Rodríguez-Jazcilevich, M.A. (Mexico), faculty member, Houston Galveston Institute Houston, Texas, and Grupo Campos Elíseos and Universidad de las Américas, both in Mexico City, Mexico.

Sallyann Roth, M.S.W. (U.S.), founding associate, Public Conversations Project; faculty member, Family Institute of Cambridge, Massachusetts; consultant to the interpersonal skills component of the Harvard Negotiation Project at Harvard Law School.

Jaakko Seikkula, Ph.D. (Finland), senior assistant in psychology, University of Jyväskylä, Finland, and professor, Institute of Social Medicine, University of Tromsø, Norway.

Sally St. George, Ph.D. (U.S.), codirector of the Family Therapy Program, Kent School of Social Work, University of Louisville, Kentucky.

Margarita Tarragona, Ph.D. (Mexico), professor, Psychology Department, Universidad de las Americás, Mexico City; faculty member, Houston Galveston Institute, Houston, Texas; and cofounder of Grupo Campos Elíseos, Mexico City.

Judit Wagner, M.S.W. (Sweden), part-time faculty member, University of Kalmar Social Work; private practice in Sweden; and consultant, Kalmar Prison and Probation Administration, the Kalmar Health Care Administration, welfare and child psychiatry clinics, and the Swedish Feldenkrais Pedagogues.

Dan Wulff, Ph.D. (U.S.), codirector, Family Therapy Program, Kent School of Social Work, University of Louisville, Kentucky.

Table of Contents

About the Editors   vii

Contributors   ix

Preface: HARLENE ANDERSON AND DIANE GEHART   xvii

PART 1   An Invitation to Collaborative Therapy: Relationships
          and Conversations That Make a Difference   1

Collaborative Therapy Then and Now

1   A Postmodern Umbrella: Language and
          Knowledge as Relational and Generative,
          and Inherently Transforming   7
          HARLENE ANDERSON

2   Historical Influences   21
          HARLENE ANDERSON

3   Dialogue: People Creating Meaning with
          Each Other and Finding Ways to Go On   33
          HARLENE ANDERSON

4   The Heart and Spirit of Collaborative Therapy:
          The Philosophical Stance—"A Way of Being" in
          Relationship and Conversation   43
          HARLENE ANDERSON

Other Voices: Netting and Expressing

5   The Art of "Withness": A New Bright Edge   63
     LYNN HOFFMAN

6   Human Participating: Human "Being" Is the Step
     for Human "Becoming" in the Next Step   81
     TOM ANDERSEN

PART 2   The Therapy Room   95

7   Listening Voices   99
     PEGGY PENN

8   Hearing the Unheard: Advice to Professionals
     from Women Who Have Been Battered   109
     SUSAN B. LEVIN

9   You Make the Path as You Walk:
     Working Collaboratively with People
     with Eating Disorders   129
     ELENA FERNÁNDEZ, ALEJANDRA CORTÉS,
     AND MARGARITA TARRAGONA

10   Honoring Elders through Conversations
     about Their Lives   149
     JENNIFER ANDREWS

11   Collaborating with Parents and Children in
     Private Practice: Shifting and
     Overlapping Conversations   167
     MARSHA MCDONOUGH AND PATRICIA KOCH

12   Creating Space for Children's Voices:
     A Collaborative and Playful Approach to
     Working with Children and Families   183
     DIANE GEHART

PART 3   Beyond the Therapy Room   197

In Social and Institutional Settings

13   Trialogues: A Means to Answerability and
     Dialogue in a Prison Setting   203
     JUDIT WAGNER

14   Open Dialogue: An Approach to
      Psychotherapeutic Treatment of
      Psychosis in Northern Finland   221
      KAUKO HAARAKANGAS, JAAKKO SEIKKULA,
      BIRGITTA ALAKARE, AND JUKKA AALTONEN

15   The Development of a Collaborative Learning and
      Therapy Community in an Educational Setting:
      From Alienation to Invitation   235
      SYLVIA LONDON AND
      IRMA RODRÍGUEZ-JAZCILEVICH

16   Collaborative Therapy and Supervision in
      a Psychiatric Hospital   251
      SYLVIA LONDON AND MARGARITA TARRAGONA

17   Women at a Turning Point:
      A Transformational Feast   269
      DEBBIE FEINSILVER, EILEEN MURPHY,
      AND HARLENE ANDERSON

18   Dialogues in a Psychiatric Service in Cuba   291
      KLAUS G. DEISSLER

In Education, Supervision, and Research

19   Relational Practices in Education:
      Teaching as Conversation   313
      SHEILA MCNAMEE

20   From the Theory to the Practice of Inquiring
      Collaboratively: An Exercise in and
      Clinical Example of an Interviewee-Guided
      Interview   337
      SALLYANN ROTH

21   Curious George: Interview with a Supervisor 351
      GLEN GARDNER AND ANTHONY NEUGEBAUER

22   A Collaborative Approach to Research
      and Inquiry   367
      DIANE GEHART, MARGARITA TARRAGONA,
      AND SALIHA BAVA

Never-Ending Possibilities

23   Collaboration without End: The Case of the
      Positive Aging Newsletter   391
      MARY GERGEN AND KENNETH J. GERGEN

24   Collaborating as a Lifestyle   403
      SALLY ST. GEORGE AND DAN WULFF

Index   421

Preface

Collaborative Therapy: Relationships and Conversations That Make a Difference brings together a rich and diverse collection of applications, innovations, and expansions of many postmodern assumptions. It includes the work of a wide variety of professionals from varied disciplines, contexts, and cultures, who detail what they actually do in their everyday practices. It demonstrates and documents the versatility and extension of the postmodern collaborative approach to the domains of therapy with individuals, couples, families, and groups, as well as its application in larger social arenas such as education, research, organizations, communities, businesses, and other kinds of relationship systems.

We are honored to have an image created by Mexico City artist Sara London for the cover of *Collaborative Therapy*. Sara has been the resident artist for the International Summer Institute (ISI) for the past nine years. The ISI is an international learning community that convenes each summer in Mexico. Its shifting membership is a kinship of people interested in postmodern philosophical assumptions and practices. During the week Sara generates art inspired by the people and activities—the relationships and conversations.

She titled the cover image "Red En*redando*." In Spanish red is the word for "net, netting, and network" and enredando is "entangling." Red En*redando* depicts the soul of this book. In Sara's words the image symbolizes

> Net, netting, networking: conversations and relationships provide threads that create a net that holds the members of the community and allows them to connect, entangle, and venture beyond the familiar and explore new possibilities.

&

For over 25 years, I (Harlene) have sustained an interest in the accounts of the successful and unsuccessful therapy experiences of clients, practitioners, and students. The expertise of those most intimately involved cannot be overemphasized. What I have learned from their collective observations has influenced the development of a postmodern collaborative approach that, in my experience, is congruent with a societal trend that values, invites, and incorporates consumers' perspectives of what is important to them in their daily lives, and their participation in product design, implementation, and evaluation. These voices have confirmed a view of human beings as resilient, as desiring and striving toward healthy, successful relationships and qualities of life, and as having the potential and ability to contribute to the good of society.

What I have learned from clients has also led me to question familiar therapy concepts such as "universal truths," knowledge and knower as independent individuals, language as representative, and that the word "holds" the meaning. These concepts risk placing human behavior into narrow frameworks of understanding, promoting discourses of pathology and dysfunction, seducing therapists to create and endorse hierarchical expert–nonexpert structures, and creating a professional world of knowing and certainty. Alongside this questioning, I became increasingly interested in a body of ideas that I now place under what I call a "postmodern umbrella," though it is difficult to find a term that adequately specifies the assumptions held by this body of ideas.

Postmodernism, as we, the editors, use the term, refers to an interdisciplinary metaphor within the social sciences that calls for skepticism and critical questioning of our knowledge constructs and particularly the assumed relevance of universal social and psychological knowledge to human behavior and the complexity of contemporary human life. A central thread running through various postmodern perspectives including social construction, contemporary hermeneutics, and dialogue theories is an emphasis on the pervasive and defining role of language (spoken and unspoken forms of communication and expression) in the lives of human beings and in how we perceive or know our world.

This emphasis indicates a move from the traditions of language as representative and objective and knowledge as discoverable and individually constructed to language and knowledge as relationally created processes and products. It specifies a move to language as inventive and central in forming our knowledge and the construction of knowledge as a dialogical process—a dynamic and fluid process in which, for instance, meaning, understanding, and reality are attributions communally created within particular cultures and shaped and reshaped in language. Transformation, therefore, is inherent in the creative and inventive aspects of language.

Postmodern therapies locate themselves within this dialogical movement in the social sciences in general and psychology in particular.

My treasured colleague, the late Harry Goolishian, and I began developing our collaborative approach in the 1970s while we were at the University of Texas Medical Branch in Galveston. Its roots, however, can be traced back to the traditions of the Galveston group's early Multiple Impact Therapy (MIT) clinical research project, described by Robert Sutherland of the Hogg Foundation for Mental Health as "fresh and hopeful" (MacGregor, Ritchie, Serrano, Schuster, & Goolishian, 1964, p. viii). Since Harry's death in 1991, I have continued to develop and expand the approach that we then called "collaborative language systems" (Anderson & Goolishian, 1987, 1988). I now simply refer to it as collaborative therapy.

I first fully described and discussed the approach in my book *Conversation, Language, and Possibilities: A Postmodern Approach to Therapy* (Anderson, 1997). The emphasis then and still is on a philosophy of therapy instead of a theory of therapy. Philosophy is a more fitting descriptor: for centuries philosophers and ordinary citizens have continually puzzled over commonplace ongoing questions about human life such as self-identity, agency, mind, relationships, and futures. Conversely, theory informs agreed-upon knowledge that, in turn, informs methods; for instance, it creates types and categories of people and methods that, in turn, are then applied across the types and categories. In other words, methods are applied to people as members of a group. Collaborative therapy is not a method that is applied to people; it is about finding ways to move toward and to speak *with* a person "in the moment."

As the number of postmodern and related philosophical and theoretical contributions to psychotherapy literature grows so, too, do postmodernism's appeal and recognition of its relevance. Many of these writings suggest practical applications, yet there are gaps in the literature between theoretical explications and in-depth accounts of the many forms of everyday practice that flow from it. The purpose of *Collaborative Therapy* is to provide a means to bridge these gaps. Its aim is also to illustrate the application and never-ending possibilities of postmodern collaborative assumptions beyond the therapy room to social and institutional settings, to education, supervision, research, business environments, and to our lives.

The primary contexts of my practices to date have included the Houston Galveston Institute and the mental health organizations, clinical and training programs, and business organizations that I have consulted with around the world. The Institute is a nonprofit clinical, teaching, consultation, and research center whose clients are mostly referred by public and community agencies (e.g., child protection services, juvenile and adult justice systems, women's shelters, and schools) and clients who are often mandated to therapy. Our learners are practicing professionals such as therapists and teachers and supervisors of therapists as well as masters, doctoral, and postdoctoral level interns.

I am fortunate to be part of an ever-growing international community network of scholars, practitioners, educators, consultants, and students who are part of the dialogical movement mentioned above. Its members are occupied with a similar challenge: how can our work have relevance in our fast-changing world and, especially, for people's everyday lives. Not all, though, identify themselves primarily as collaborative therapists nor do they place their guiding assumptions under the same postmodern umbrella that I currently do. Some use descriptors such as dialogical therapy, discursive therapy, conversational therapy, relational therapy, open dialogue therapy, and postmodern therapy.

Aside from what we call ourselves, we connect and engage in enriching discussions with each other at learning venues and conferences around the world, as well as through e-mail and the Web. Some of these venues include among others: the International Summer Institute that Harry and I began more than 25 years ago and that I now convene each summer in Mexico along with my colleagues from Grupo Campos Elíseos, as well as international guests; the Houston Galveston Institute Symposiums; the North Norway conferences that Tom Andersen organized for many years; the Open Dialogue network and conferences organized by Jaakko Seikkula and Tom Andersen; the numerous Taos Institute activities; the Marburg Institute Summer Academy; the Taos Institute–Tilburg University doctoral program in social construction; Lois Shawver's Postmodern Therapy Listserv; and the Postmodern Participants Conference.[1] People all over the world are collaborating with each other: therapists in the United States with those in Norway, supervisors in Hong Kong with therapists in Canada; supervisors in Sweden with colleagues in Mexico; educators in South Africa with students in Canada; students in the United States with students in Mexico—and the examples go on and on. And each, through this international community network, continues to expand and enrich our practices and, most importantly, improve our lives.

Of great consequence, what I realized in cocreating this book is that collaborative therapy is in the hands of this worldwide community. All of us participate in its deepening and broadening and share responsibility for its future evolution and for its ethics.

The telling of my story involved the process of thinking and writing, of reading and rewriting my words, and of being in numerous rich conversations with the book's contributors. It has been immensely inspiring and generative. I found that some ideas that used to excite me such as "evolutionary systems," "therapy systems as language systems," and "the problem creates the system instead of the system creates the problem" have fallen from my descriptive vocabulary. Some ideas and concepts are no longer relevant, and some like problem organizing systems are so much a part of my fabric that I do not purposely think about or highlight them. At times, I recreate history as I remember it, and at other times, I create new ideas about my current assumptions and work. Undoubtedly, I would tell this story differently at another point in time and context. I hope that my account invites you—the reader—to join with me and others in conversations and that you keep in mind that the collaborative approach illustrated in this book has many expressions and will continue to evolve, just as the world in which we live does.

Though I extended the invitations to the authors, the idea for this book was Diane's. She approached me and said, "There needs to be a practice book for collaborative therapy. Therapists need it, students request it, and educators are eager for it." That was four years ago. She was extremely patient and diligent as I was occupied with so many commitments in my life that kept taking precedence over the book. For her initiative, patience, and diligence I am grateful.

I appreciate the time and efforts of numerous people who helped with reading and editing the chapter manuscripts, including Our Lady of the Lake University (OLLU) students Kristen Mauro, Adrienne Albright, and Glen Hilton, and OLLU graduates Nancy Baxley and Colleen Paxton. I am deeply indebted to Greg Fenberg, a student at the University of Houston–Clear Lake who did a yeoman's job with numerous chapters and formatting the manuscript. And, lastly, to my dear colleague Sylvia London whose comments and suggestions for my introductory chapters were quite valuable. Most of all, I express my enormous respect for each author and my deep gratitude for their generosity, the engaging conversations that I have had with them, and for being my colleagues.

Harlene Anderson
Houston, TX
January 2006

When you sit down to read *Collaborative Therapy: Relationships and Conversations That Make a Difference* you are joining a rich and on going dialogue between collaborative practitioners from around the world. This dialogue, which occurs through conferences, workshops, publications, e-mails, Websites, and chance meetings, has formed a vibrant and evolving community of therapists, theorists, educators, students, and professionals from various disciplines. This community is passionate about their work and the difference it makes in their professional contexts, as well as their personal lives. As Sally St. George and Dan Wulff describe in Chapter 24, there is no way to do this work and not have it transform one's personal life.

I (Diane) was first introduced to collaborative therapy at the Annual Conference of the Texas Association for Marriage and Family Therapy in 1993; I was a doctoral student at St. Mary's University in San Antonio at the time. When I heard Sue Levin and the faculty of the Houston Galveston Institute speak, I knew that I had finally found a therapy approach that could work for me. Having studied Buddhist philosophy in a prior graduate program, I had learned to view reality as constructed, people as inherently sane, and suffering with deep compassion. Up to that point in my education, no other therapy approach came close to honoring such a worldview. And it is fair to say, I fell in love.

I dedicated the remainder of my doctoral studies to learning more about collaborative therapy and postmodern ideas. I gathered together a group of students from St. Mary's to make a monthly trek to Houston for an externship with Harlene at the Houston Galveston Institute. My doctoral dissertation research (Gehart & Lyle, 1999) examined the lived experience of change from the perspective of therapists working from this approach and their clients. The clients and therapists in my study emphasized how working in this way supports and strengthens the dignity and humanity of each person involved. It awakens us to the fullness of our lives.

I began my academic career in 1997 at California State University-Fresno, where I was the only faculty member in their family therapy program who was trained as a marriage and family therapist and the only one familiar with either systemic or postmodern ideas. This context challenged me to expand my practice of collaboration to working with colleagues who did not understand what I did or what I meant when I used words like "construction," "meaning," or "dialogue." In graduate school, my enthusiasm for these ideas frequently caused me to speak as though collaborative therapy were the "best" therapy approach, which shut down dialogue with my peers rather than invite it. In Fresno, I learned how to be collaborative in professional dialogue with peers as well as in session and how to appreciate the value of multiple voices in the broader context of my discipline.

In 2004, I accepted a position at California State University–Northridge, where I now work with colleagues who have various orientations and a strong commitment to collaboratively working together. Again, I am the only faculty member working from a formal collaborative approach, yet the department has a remarkable commitment to working in a collaborative way—a reminder to me that these practices are not owned by any one person but grow out of relationships and community.

My understanding of this approach and its applications continues to evolve as I meet others working with these ideas, learn about developments in and outside of psychotherapy, and apply these ideas in my classroom and practice. I am continually amazed and awe-struck at how this philosophical stance can be applied in almost any context, and although the forms may look vastly different—a prison, hospital, classroom, playroom—the process is the same. This approach does not offer a miracle cure, but it consistently inspires compassion, humanity, and creativity—and I believe nothing is more important in the therapy process.

In fall of 2001, I approached Harlene with the idea of editing a book that showcases the many ways these ideas have been put into practice. The idea came from my students asking to learn more about the examples I would use in class about colleagues whose work I had learned about at conferences in the States and abroad. Over the past 4 years, the idea has grown to include the voices of over 30 colleagues from 6 countries. Each chapter shares how collaborative therapy and related ideas have been put into action to make a difference in psychotherapy, education, research, and the community. I was frequently moved to tears and humbled as I read about the profound impact these ideas have had in people's lives, often ending extraordinary suffering and creating hope where there was none before.

The evolution of this book has been an amazing journey. I am especially grateful to Harlene for her guidance and mentoring in the process. Her attention to language was remarkable and inspiring. Most of all, I have appreciated her leadership in clarifying and furthering the evolution of these ideas. It has been a highlight of my career to work with her on this project. I would also like to thank Randy Lyle, my former professor, colleague, and dear friend, who encouraged and supported me, especially during the early phase of this project. In addition, I sincerely appreciate the contributions of Lori Granger-Merkle, my former student, who dedicated numerous hours to editing chapters from foreign authors; for her work was superb. Diana Pantaleo, my dearest friend and colleague, has provided feedback on the work and supported me throughout; my gratitude is endless. And, finally, I would like to thank the many students and colleagues who have served as my teachers in the collaborative process and its potentials.

I look forward to participating in the conversations and adventures *Collaborative Therapy: Relationships and Conversations That Make a Difference* inspires.

Diane Gehart
Northridge, CA
January 2006

Endnote

1. Many of these venues can be found on the Web through the following sites and their links: www.harleneanderson.org, www.talkhgi.com, www.taosinstitute.org, and www.masterswork.com.

Reference

Gehart, D.R., & Lyle, R.R. (1999). Client and therapist perspectives of change in collaborative language systems: An interpretive ethnography. *Journal of Systemic Therapy, 18,* 78–97.

PART 1

An Invitation to Collaborative Therapy: Relationships and Conversations That Make a Difference

As our world shrinks, globalization and technology are catalyzing social, cultural, political, and economic transformation. With an associated, ever-increasing spotlight on democracy, social justice, and human rights, the importance of the people's voice, singular or plural, becomes further relevant to how we respond to the unavoidable complexities inherent in these transformations and the effects on our individual and communal lives. The shifting circumstances and increasing complications of contemporary life challenge us to reassess the relevance of the traditions of our social and psychological theories and our practices for social and personal change, including how we conceptualize the people we work with, their problems, and our role with them. This challenge calls for creative yet pragmatic and effective ways to address the ever more multifaceted nature of human experience and to work across a multiplicity of cultures and values. My professional career has been devoted to an evolving philosophy and practice of therapy that has benefit with respect to theses challenges. It is a never-ending journey.

My collaborative approach has evolved over the past three decades, alongside this challenge and the questions that accompany it. My approach is one among others being developed by kindred scholars and scholar practitioners who collectively share an interest in therapy as a relational and dialogic activity (Tom Andersen, Kenneth Gergen, Lynn Hoffman, Lois Holzman, Sheila McNamee, Peggy Penn, Jaakko Seikkula, Lois Shawver and John Shotter).

All of us have been largely influenced by the writings of thinkers such as Mikhail Bakhtin, Gregory Bateson, Jacques Derrida, Jean-Francois Lyotard, Lev Vygotsky, and Ludwig Wittgenstein among others. The above authors variously use the terms *collaborative, dialogical, open-dialogue, conversational, constructionist, relational,* and *postmodern* when referring to therapy. I dare to say that these authors refer to their respective work more as an "approach" to, or as "assumptions" about, therapy rather than a theory or a model. I also dare to say that none of these therapy perspectives is held above others as a meta- or better approach. Those of us who are proponents of these therapies or what Lynn Hoffman refers to as "the art of withness" (Chapter 5 this volume) have found that these perspectives offer us as practitioners and educators, along with our clients and students, opportunities to broaden and deepen our options, possibilities, and capacities for effective action. Or, as Wittgenstein would say, the ability to go on and, I would add, "as human beings with one another."

Writing the introductory chapters for this book has been like creating a collage—reviewing snapshots of the highlights of the theoretical and philosophical developments that I encountered along the way to my collaborative approach. I had to decide which ones to select and where to place them. There was always the chance that I might pause too long at one snapshot and bypass a significant one. There is the risk that in putting my words in print, others might take them to be carved in stone. What is important is that this is an endless journey.

Collaborative Therapy: Relationships and Conversations That Make a Difference has three parts. Part 1 has two sections: The first section, Collaborative Therapy Then and Now, provides an overview of the evolution, assumptions, and characteristics of collaborative therapy. It highlights the practical and performative nature, setting the tone for the chapters in parts 2 and 3 that follow. I begin in Chapter 1 with a discussion of postmodern, social construction, and contemporary hermeneutics and discuss how, combined, they influenced the ideas central to my approach: *collaborative relationships* and *dialogical conversations*. I also review the influence of the narrative metaphor, the significance of thinking in terms of "person(s)-in-relationship" instead of individual(s), and the notion of self-agency. In Chapter 2, I go back in time and talk about the historical roots of collaborative therapy; in Chapter 3 I expand on the notion of dialogue, highlighting listening, hearing, and speaking and their relevance to dialogue. I then share tips for enhancing dialogue. In Chapter 4 I present the *philosophical stance* that is the heart and spirit of collaborative therapy and its characteristics. I also discuss the effectiveness of collaborative therapy and address the question "What's next?" Both Chapters 2 and 4 expand on ideas presented in Chapter 1.

In the second section, "Other Voices: Netting and Expressing," the first four chapters are supplemented by two scholar practitioners and dear colleagues: Lynn Hoffman and Tom Andersen. For decades, each has been at the forefront of the epistemological and practice development and the critical analysis of the "ideological shift" that this book is about. Each is, as am I, occupied with an ever-present inquiry: How can therapy have relevance for people's everyday lives, and what is this relevance? Hoffman, in Chapter 5, continues to earn her reputation as family therapy's historian and soothsayer. She establishes "a train of forebearers" and "distinguished ancestors" through which she sees the field currently and develops her prediction for its future direction. She refers to the community of therapy practices such as the ones described in this book and discusses some of the authors' works, specifically, as having "an elusive quality" called "withness" that is "represented by those special kinds of conversation . . . that give us our bearings in the matter of social bonds." In Chapter 6, Andersen's dialogical perspective, as Hoffman suggests, takes the "world of the senses more into account." He concentrates on the importance of the "not-spoken," the body movements that accompany the spoken word: they cannot be separated. Andersen's wisdom, compassion, and humbleness has influenced therapists around the world, and notably in the area of social justice.

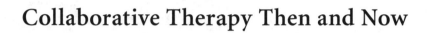

Collaborative Therapy Then and Now

A Postmodern Umbrella: Language and Knowledge as Relational and Generative, and Inherently Transforming

HARLENE ANDERSON

My introduction to postmodern thinking flowed from my interest in contemporary hermeneutics, dialogue, and social construction. The thread that connects these three perspectives is a similar viewpoint of knowledge and language: a viewpoint that places central importance on the concepts of language and knowledge as relational and dialogical activities that give meaning and understanding for making sense of our lives and navigating our worlds. Combined, hermeneutics, dialogue, and social construction, and postmodern assumptions offer a broad challenge to the culture of the helping professions. They invite us to examine and reimagine the traditions and the practices that we have assumed in this inherited culture. These traditions include the ways that we "understand" a person and attribute meaning to their words and actions, develop descriptions of them that are arrived at from that understanding, relate to them, and our role in the relationship with them.

I begin this chapter with a description of my current postmodern umbrella. I then backtrack and trace my view of social construction and contemporary hermeneutics, and the relationship between them. Lastly, I discuss the ideas of narrative, person-in-relationship, and self-agency.

A Postmodern Umbrella

Postmodern is a term that refers both to the late-20th-century movements in art and architecture, and in contemporary French philosophy. Broadly speaking, I use *postmodern* to refer to a family of concepts that have developed among scholars within some social science and natural science disciplines that call for an ideological critique—a questioning perspective—of the relevance and consequences of foundational knowledge, metanarratives, and privileged discourses, including their certainty and power for our everyday lives. Specifically, postmodernism challenges these fundamental and legitimizing Truths with a capital "T" and the foundations on which they are generally based. Mainly, it challenges the truth and centrality of individual knowledge, an objective knowable world, and language as the carrier of truth (Gergen, 2001). The truths and the assumptions that flow from them are inherent in our everyday lives, and we often take them with passive acceptance or unwittingly for granted.

Although the postmodern family includes some diverse traits, the notion of knowledge and language as relational and generative is an important and consistent one that runs throughout it. This notion markedly contrasts with the Western tradition of individualism: the individual as an autonomous knower who can create or discover knowledge that can be passed on to others. Knowledge, in this tradition, represents an objective reality that is observer-independent: the knower is separate from that which he or she observes, describes, and explains. It is fixed and tangible. In this tradition, knowledge is conveyed in language and language can correctly represent knowledge. Language represents or mirrors Truth. It is an outward description of an internal process.

Knowledge

Postmodernism takes a quite different perspective of knowledge: knowledge is socially constructed; knowledge and the knower are interdependent; and all knowledge and knowing are embedded within history, context, culture, language, experience, and understanding.[1] Postmodern advocates, therefore, that we entertain truth with a little "t." Dispensing with the notion of absolute truth and taking a position of plurality does not imply nihilism or solipsism. It simply suggests critical reflection of our truths, keeping all truths open to critique, including postmodernism as well.

Equally important, postmodern favors local knowledge, knowledge developed within a community of people in which they actively engage in its development. Local knowledge might be thought of as participatory knowledge or relational knowing as opposed to objective or observer-independent knowledge. As such, the knowledge will have relevance and utility for its participants. Perhaps another way to think about local knowledge is that it is a dialogical reality. This is particularly pertinent to research. The traditional research emphasis is on the outsider observing and studying the subject, looking for similarities and patterns from which theoretical knowledge is created and which can then be used to describe and know a person or multiple persons as a member of a group or classification. The knowledge, subsequently, is used to support and explain actions such as categorizing and predicting. Such knowledge can be thought of as the privileged, dominant, or authoritative discourse that postmodern holds in question. Postmodern shifts the emphasis to the inside inquirer; focus is centered on learning about the first-person-lived experience and about the uniqueness of it instead of similarities and patterns. Difference is valued.

We can only know the world through our experience; we cannot have direct knowledge of it. We continually interpret our experiences and interpret our interpretations. And, as such, what we create (e.g., knowledge) is fluid, continually evolving, shifting, broadening, and changing. Thus, there is no finality to our knowledge—our meanings, understandings, or realities. What we create, we create with each other. Knowledge is not an individual activity or passive process: knowledge cannot be sent to or received by another.

Language

From a postmodern tradition, language (i.e., any means by which we communicate or express ourselves or respond to others—spoken and unspoken) is the primary vehicle through which we construct and make sense of our world. As philosopher Richard Rorty (1979) suggests, language does not mirror the truth. Philosopher Ludwig Wittgenstein (1953) similarly suggests that language is not an outward description of an internal process and does not describe accurately what actually happens. More exactly, language allows a description and attribution of meaning to what happens. Language gains its meaning and its value through its use: the meaning of a word, for instance, is in its use. We are always in the process of trying to understand and search for meaning. The process and the search itself create meaning. Language in this perspective is the vehicle of the process and search through which we try to understand and create meaning—knowledge about our world and ourselves. Language thus limits and shapes our thoughts and our expressions.

What is created in and through language (e.g., realities such as knowledge, truth, and meaning) is multiauthored among a community of persons. The reality that we attribute to the events, experiences, and people in our lives does not exist within the thing or person; instead, it is socially created within a particular culture and is continually shaped and reshaped in language. What is created, therefore, is only one of multiple and, perhaps, infinite possibilities. Language, therefore, is fluid and creative. Like Gergen, I do not suggest that nothing exists outside linguistic constructions; whatever exists simply exists irrespective of linguistic practices (Gergen, 2001). As indicated in my discussion of social construction, my focus is on the meaning of these existences and the actions they inform, once we begin to describe, explain, and interpret them.

Language, Knowledge, and Words

Both Wittgenstein and the Russian philosopher Mikhail Bakhin take a dialogical approach to language and knowledge and to words. Social psychologist John Shotter (2005) refers to Wittgenstein's dialogical approach to language: " … language as primarily rooted in people's embodied, dialogical activities, in their social activities, and not as grounded either in their minds or in the worlds around them" (p. 182). Shotter (2004, 2005) also exemplifies Wittgenstein's perspective on language and words with the following quotes, "Only in the stream of thought and life do words have meaning" (2005, p. 123), "the meaning of a word is its use in the language" (2004, p. iii), and "let the use of words teach you their meaning (2005, p. 6). Bakhtin's (1981) view of words is similar, "The word is born in dialogue as a living rejoinder within it; the word is shaped in dialogic interaction with an alien word that is already in the object. A word forms a concept of its own object in a dialogic way" (p. 279). In these views, words are not the things nor do they represent the objects of which they refer. We are always struggling with each other to understand the words we use, their meanings. We are always foreigners trying to learn the native's local language.

Transformation

By transformation, I refer to the continual newness in our lives such as knowledge, expertise, meaning, identity, and futures that is inherent in the inventive and creative aspects of language. I prefer the word "transformation" or "transform*ing*" instead of the word "change." "Change" in the psychotherapy field often has the connotation of lineal or circular causality; in other words, one person changing another or a person changing from one thing to another. In the view of knowledge and language discussed above, causality regarding human thought and action is not possible: One person cannot unilaterally determine another's response, perception, interpretation, or behavior. Information does not objectively exist; it is an observer punctuation. Each person uniquely interprets and responds to what appears to be information. Information, like an observer, cannot influence a system in a predetermined way. This view of causality fits with

Gregory Bateson's (1972) idea that change is an epistemological error and Humburto Maturana's (1978) idea that instructive interaction is impossible. A therapist, therefore, is not a causal agent or an agent of change. Whether we think of it as changing or transforming, it is something that people do with each other—it is relational.

"Transforming," for the current lack of another word, permits me to keep in mind that we are never at a standstill; our meanings, our bodies, and so on are always in motion (e.g., altering, developing, evolving), from the moment of birth to death. And, there is always a sense of continuity in it; we do not change, for instance, from one person to another, but as new and different identities come forward, we remain who we have been and are, while at the same time we are becoming. Most important, because "it" (again, whether the word preference is "changing" or "transforming" is preferred) is always occurring, it is often slow and unnoticed.

"Transforming" permits me to be ever mindful of the fluid nature of language. It also permits me to be hopeful: to appreciate that human beings are resilient, that each person has contributions and potentials, and that each person values, wants, and strives toward healthy successful lives and relationships. (This does not mean that each person is successful in these endeavors.) This hopefulness is also characteristic of the above therapies that I mentioned and is similar to psychologists Mikhail CsikszentMihalyi and Martin Seligman's (2000) emphasis on positive psychology as more promising than deficit-based psychology.

Social Construction

To step back a bit in time, the keen interest that Harry Goolishian and I had in social construction, particularly the writings of Kenneth Gergen, flowed naturally from our earlier interest in hermeneutics. When Harry met Ken at an American Psychological Association meeting in the early 1980s, they sealed a bonded camaraderie and had various opportunities for rich exchange that ended prematurely with Harry's death. I am fortunate, however, to carry on this tradition of exchange.

As with the postmodern umbrella that I place it under, social construction takes a skeptical stance regarding established truths and is concerned with the power and authority that these truths award. From a social construction perspective, the universal and taken-for-granted truths that we inherit in our world are not inevitable; they are not fixed or stable. Instead, truth such as knowledge is a communal construction. Ideas or self-identities, for instance, are authored in a community of persons and relationships. Social construction places emphasis on the activity and product of social exchange; the emphasis is not on locating the origin, as this would be impossible.

Social constructionism, hence, concerns itself with the way that people arrive at their descriptions, explanations, and understandings of themselves and their world. It is not concerned with the literalness of the thing or idea itself, but with the meanings attributed to it. Take "bullying" for example. A focus would not be placed on whether the physical and verbal action of what we call bullying exists, but the meaning that we give to it. The meanings that we attribute to the things, the events, the people in our lives, and to our selves, are arrived at through the language used by (and between) persons—through social dialogue, interchange, and interaction between people. From this perspective, reality represents a human functional adaptation: humans as experiencing subjects and observers who construct and interpret reality and the world they live in.

Meanings are contingent. They are contingent on context: the relational, historical, and linguistic domains in which behaviors, feelings, emotions, understandings, and so forth are communal constructions. Their construction occurs within a plurality of ever-changing complex webs of relationships and social processes, and within local and broad discourses. As Gergen (1994) put it, the basis of meaning is contextual and is continually negotiated across time (p. 66).

Social constructionism moves beyond the social contextualization of behavior and simple relativity. It suggests that there are possibly infinite ways to describe, explain, understand, or value the various aspects of our world. This does not mean that anything goes. Instead, it calls for taking a critically reflective stance, considering the implications of accepted assumptions, and not having blind trust in them.[2]

Sometimes the terms *social constructionism* and *constructivism* are used interchangeably, but the latter differs from the former. Constructivism[3] historically concentrates on the notion of the autonomous individual and the individual constructing mind and not on the social. Although both reject the notion that the mind reflects reality and advance that knowledge is a construction, social constructionism moves beyond the constructivist notion of individual authorship to multi- or plural authorship. As discussed above, it emphasizes the social process of constructing and the communal and interactional context in which the process occurs. As well, the mind, from a social construction perspective, is relational and the development of meaning is discursive in nature. Shotter (1993b), who is particularly occupied with the self–other relationship and the ways in which people spontaneously coordinate their everyday activities with each other, refers to "conversational realities." He is concerned with what it is like to be a particular person living within a network of relations with others, a person positioned or situated in relation to others in different ways and at different times. He calls this self–other dimension of interaction *joint action*, suggesting that "all actions by human beings involved with others in a social group in this fashion are dialogically or responsively linked in some way, both to previous, already executed actions and to anticipated, next possible actions" (Shotter, 1984, pp. 52–53).

Inherent in the perspectives of understanding as an interpretive process, and the relational and communal development of knowledge and meaning, are the ideas of multi- or plural authorship, the promise of multiple realities, and the possibilities of newness that can emerge from dialogue. These ideas gave my colleagues and me a new language for describing our clinical experiences of how stories are told and retold and of how new versions or new meanings of old ones emerge from these tellings and retellings.

Relational Hermeneutics[4]

In the early 1980s, we began to have an interest in contemporary hermeneutics. Somewhat simultaneously, largely influenced by hermeneutics, we became uncomfortable with the cybernetic systems theories—the bedrock of family systems therapies that had guided our work for years. Though the notion of observing systems brought in the observer as part of the description, overall, cybernetic theories offered a mechanical-oriented metaphor, not a people-oriented one. Hermeneutics provided a view of understanding as an interpretive process and brought in persons as active participants in constructing their worlds and not as depersonalized objects of study.

Hermeneutics is concerned with understanding and interpreting the meaning of the other (or a text or discourse). In this view "understanding is always interpretive, there is no uniquely privileged standpoint for understanding" (Hoy, 1986, p. 399). The search for understanding and meaning is a generative process in that the search itself creates understanding and meaning. Hence, true understanding and final interpretation of an event or a person can never be reached. Each account is only one version of the truth. Likewise, each account is influenced by what the interpreter brings to the encounter. Each interpreter, each member of a social exchange, brings and contributes his or her history, beliefs, assumptions, intentions, and current linguistic practices in which he or she lives to the exchange and the reading. Hermeneutics cautions that it is important to be aware of these preunderstandings and to beware how they prejudice each member's participation in the development of meaning as he or she interacts with the other. Ideally, preunderstandings would be intentionally suspended or sidelined, but this is impossible. (I discuss how this ideal is approximated in a natural way when I talk about the dialogical process in Chapter 3.)

From a hermeneutic perspective, a person can never fully understand another person, know what is purportedly behind their words,[4] or know their intention and meaning. This is impossible. The process of understanding is relational and dialogical; it is a two-way joint activity—a dialogue with self and others—as each person is open to the other and tries to grasp the other's meaning. The process of understanding is "the process of immersing ourselves in the other's horizon" (Anderson, 1997, p. 39). It is through this action of immersion—this quest for understanding the other person's meaning, this quest to make sense of the familiar and unfamiliar—that the horizons are fused (Gadamer, 1975). The events and experiences in our lives, including our self-identities (emphasis on the plural) and our understandings of them, are created by individuals in conversation and action with others and with themselves. We participate in creating what we think or believe we understand or know about the other and ourselves. Furthermore, in this generative process of trying to grasp meaning, as indicated above, something different from that which is trying to be understood is produced. Hermeneutics "assumes that problems in understanding are problems of a temporary failure to understand a person's or group's intentions, a failure which can be overcome by continuing the dialogic, interpretive process" (Warneke, 1987, p. 120).

Hermeneutics places emphasis on language as playing a central role in the development of meaning. Language is the "medium within which we move and understand ourselves and the world from various perspectives" (Wachterhauser, 1986, p. 31). The emphasis is on language as a medium and not as a tool or instrument. Shared meanings emerge through language that enable us to be in conversation with each other (and ourselves) and develop mutual understandings. According to Gadamer, "language has its true being only in conversation, in the exercise of understanding between people" (Wachterhauser, 1986, p. 31). It is relational. This latter is similar to Wittgenstein's assertion, mentioned earlier, that the meaning is not in the word, but that words gain their meaning through their use.

For me, the primary influence of hermeneutics was an appreciation (a) of what the interpreter brings to the interpreting process and the meanings produced; (b) that interpretation is a relational process, the extension of a focus on the individual to a focus on between people; (c) that in the process of trying to understand, something else is/can be fashioned; and (d) of the role of language in understanding. Hermeneutics also influenced our ideas about the "unsaid" and the "not-yet-said" in therapy: Through being in language, through trying to understand, "the development, through dialogue, of new themes and narratives and, actually, the creation of new histories" emerge (Anderson and Goolishian, 1988, p. 381). As we placed emphasis on our attempts to learn about the other person's views and to understand them, we experienced that in the participatory two-way process of articulating and trying to understand a view that something happened, the view altered, new ones emerged, and some dissolved—for our clients and us. Also around this time, we began to think that this process of understanding occurred in a metaphorical "space" between us. As well, being immersed in this process of understanding helped us have an appreciation of uncertainty and a trust that the process would lead to yet-known possibilities. The most significant shift that hermeneutics influenced was a shift away from thinking in terms of human systems as cybernetic systems to thinking of "human systems as linguistic systems" (Anderson & Goolishian, 1988, 1989; Anderson, 1997). We determined that as language systems, humans are meaning-making systems; therapy, thus, is one kind of language or meaning-making system.

Social construction theory (Gergen, 1985, 1994, 1999) added emphasis to the influence from hermeneutics, especially the relational aspect of meaning-making from a hermeneutic perspective and extended beyond it. Though hermeneutics places primary focus on the nature of understanding and social construction places emphasis on the nature of knowledge, both share the viewpoint that these truths are situated in history, culture, and tradition and are arrived at through dialogue and conversation.

Parallel to our interest in postmodern and related philosophies was an attraction to the narrative metaphor. The 1991 Narrative and Psychotherapy Conference organized by the Houston Galveston Institute highlighted this attraction and explored the role of narrative in psychotherapy theory and practice.[5] This was our introduction to John Shotter who was keenly interested in the way people spontaneously respond to and coordinate their everyday activities with each other through dialogue and bodily activities. Through Shotter, we developed a deeper understanding of Wittgenstein and were introduced to authors such as Bakhtin, Billig, Vygotsky, and Voloshinov. From this time on, we became increasingly openly critical of the traditions of psychotherapy, particularly its deficiency-based language, its tradition of classifying people, and its confidence in the therapist's "knowing" (Anderson and Goolishian, 1988). We gained even more respect for people's local knowledge and their first-person narratives. (I talk about the related influential clinical experiences in Chapter 2.) Also within this time frame, Kenneth Gergen, Lynn Hoffman, and I collaborated on our "Is Diagnosis a Disaster" paper (Gergen, Hoffman, & Anderson, 1995).

Narrative, Persons-in-Relationship, and Self-Agency

The Narrative Metaphor[6]

The narrative or story metaphor is an important dimension of hermeneutic, social construction, postmodern, and related philosophies.[7] Narrative is a form of discourse, the discursive way in which we organize, account for, give meaning, understand, provide structure, and maintain coherence to the circumstances, events, and experiences in our lives (Anderson, 1997; Goolishian & Anderson, 1994, 2002). Our narratives, including our descriptions and our vocabularies constitute our understanding of human nature and behavior. Narrative is a metaphor for a process; it is not a template or map for understanding, interpreting, or predicting human behavior. Narratives are created, experienced, and shared by individuals in conversation and action with one another and with oneself. Language (in its broadest sense) is the vehicle of the narrating process. We use language to construct and attribute meaning to our stories and its limits constrain what can be expressed and how it can be expressed.

As Gergen (1994) suggests, "Stories serve as communal resources that people use in ongoing relationships" (p. 189). They form, inform, and reform our sources of knowledge and views of reality. Stories are not accomplished facts; rather, they are stories in the process of being made, of evolving. Narrative and story become the way we imagine alternatives and create possibilities, and the way we actualize these options. They are the resource of transformation.

A narrative never represents a single voice; the narrator is a multiauthored polyphonic self. Harry Goolishian and I (Goolishian & Anderson, 1996, 2002) discussed the self as a storyteller in a relational process of . . . .

> . . . being and becoming, through language and storytelling. . . . [T]his makes the nature of self and our subjectivities intersubjective phenomena . . . [T]he changing web of narratives is a social product of social exchange and practice, dialogue and conversation . . . . [W]e are never more than the coauthors of the identities we construct narratively. . . . We are always as many potential selves as are embedded in the conversations. (Goolishian & Anderson, 2002, pp. 221–222)

In this view, the self is a "dialogical-narrative" self and identity is a "dialogical-narrative" identity.

The Individual as a Person-in-Relationship

Though there are distinctions among "postmodern" scholars about the notion of the individual and self, they share a similar bias. Each brings the individual and the relationship to the forefront, redefining individual and relationship, including: (a) the interrelated ideas of dialogical relational selves, narrative identity, self-agency, and action; (b) the abandonment of the self as bounded and knowable and the dichotomy of socially layered systems such as individual and family; and (c) the narrator as an multiauthored polyphonic self.

The newly defined "individual" as "person(s)-in-relationship" is now dialogical and relationally (linguistically and socially) created. The individual in this view is always engaged in conversational becoming, constructing and reconstructing, and shifting identities through continuous interactions with others (Anderson & Goolishian, 1988a; Goolishian and Anderson, 1994, 2002). We are continually forming and performing "I." Hence, we are always as many potential selves and identities as are embedded within and created by our conversations. As "individuals," we are persons-in-relationships.

As self, or "I," does not exist outside of language and discourse, there is no inner core or fixed tangible self. The individual, including individual rights and responsibility is not lost; instead, individual and responsibility are conceived differently. As persons-in-relationship or nonsolitary selves, we are confronted more, not less, with issues of responsibility. Nor does the narrative or socially constructed multiple self result in a fragmented self; "the multiplicity of the self does not result in fragmentation, because it is *the same I* that is *moving back and forth* [italics are my emphasis] between several positions" (Hermans et al., 1992, pp. 28–29).

Placing the person(s)-in-relationship (Anderson, 1997, p. 234) shifts, as Gergen (1994) suggests, the attention from the individual actor to coordinated relationships. This has significant implications for the way that we think about the people that we meet in therapy (the subject of the inquiry) and about ourselves (the inquirers). The notion of the relational individual transcends individual and relationship dichotomies inherent in layered social-systems frameworks such as individual–family, family–therapist, and individual–collective behavior. This challenges the restrictive definition of family therapy and its narrow concept of relationship by redefining the domain and focus (Anderson & Goolishian, 1988; Anderson, 1994, 1997; Anderson, Goolishian, & Winderman, 1986). That is, it challenges the familiar "what," "who," and "means" of inquiry—what is examined, who is the inquirer/describer, and what are the means of examination and description.

The Dialogical–Relational Self and Agency

Self-agency refers to a sense of competency or ability to perform or take action, to have choices, and to participate in the creation of choices. Self-narratives can create identities (meanings) that permit or hinder a sense of self-agency (Anderson & Goolishian, 1988a; Goolishian, 1989; Goolishian & Anderson, 1994). In therapy, we meet people whose problems can be thought of as emanating from social narratives and self-definitions or self-stories that do not yield choices or that blind a person to choices. The purpose of therapy becomes to help people participate in the telling and retelling of their first-person narratives. The therapist does not direct the narrative account, does not choose which account should emerge, does not privilege one account over another, and does not determine which account is the truest, most useful, or preferred. In other words, the therapist is not a narrative expert or editor. The therapist's role is to invite and foster a dialogical space and process, remaining open to the unexpected newness that will emerge. In this process, self-identities (meanings) transform to ones that permit self-agency (action or a sense that action is possible), varied ways of being, and multiple possibilities regarding the life circumstances we sometimes think of as problems. Meanings and actions cannot be separated.

Later, in Chapter 4, I will come back to the postmodern notions of knowledge and language and the heart and spirit hallmark of collaborative therapy: the "philosophical stance." I will then also detail the characteristics of the stance.

Endnotes

1. When I speak of knowledge here, I am referring to so-called social knowledge and the associated meanings. I am not referring to scientific facts or knowledge about objects but the meaning that we attribute to the facts or the objects.
2. See Gergen, 1999, Hacking, 1999 and Shotter, 1993 for fuller discussions of social construction.
3. Constructivism has its roots in mathematics: " ... mathematical objects do not exist until they have been built up by proofs of their existence ... constructed by mental operations (Hacking, 1999, p. 46).
4. Saliha Bava suggested that I was talking about "relational hermeneutics."
5. From this perspective, the idea that something is behind words or actions does not fit; there is nothing hidden to discover.
6. We invited Tom Andersen Kenneth Gergen, John Shotter, and Rachael Hare-Mustin to participate with us in this exploration.
7. My ideas about narrative, self, and identity are influenced by authors Beneviste, Bruner, Gadamer, Gergen, Harré, Rorty, and Shotter, among others.
8. I use narrative and story interchangeably.

References

Anderson, H. (1994). Rethinking family therapy: A delicate balance. *Journal of Marital and Family Therapy, 20*, 145–150.

Anderson, H. (1997). *Conversation, language and possibilities: A postmodern approach to therapy.* New York: Basic Books.

Anderson, H. & Goolishian, H. (1988). Human systems as linguistic systems: Evolving ideas about the implications for theory and practice. *Family Process, 27*, 371–393.

Anderson, H. & Goolishian, H. (1989). Conversations at Sulitjelma: A description and reflection. *American Family Therapy Association Newsletter.* Spring. *35*, 31–36.

Anderson, H., Goolishian, H., & Winderman, L. (1986a). Beyond family therapy. *Journal of Strategic and Systemic Therapies, 5*, i–iii.

Anderson, H., Goolishian, H., & Winderman, L. (1986b). Problem determined systems: Towards transformation in family therapy. *Journal of Strategic and Systemic Therapies, 5*, 1–13.

Bakhtin, M. (1981). *The dialogic imagination: Four essays by M.M. Bakhtin.* (M. Holquist, Ed., and C. Emerson & M. Holquist, Trans.) Austin: University of Texas Press.

Bateson, G. (1972). *Steps to an ecology of mind.* New York: Ballantine Books.

Beneviste, E. (1971). *Problems in general linguistics.* (M. Meck, Trans.) Coral Gables, FL: University of Miami Press.

Bruner, J. (1986). *Actual minds, possible worlds.* Cambridge, MA: Harvard University Press.

Bruner, J. (1990). *Acts of meaning.* Cambridge, MA: Harvard University Press.

Gadamer, H.-G. (1975). *Truth and method*. (G. Burden & J. Cumming, Trans.) New York: Seabury Press.
Gergen K.J. (1985). The social constructionist movement in modern psychology. *American Psychologist, 40*, 255–275.
Gergen, K.J. (1994). *Realities and relationships: Soundings in social construction*. Cambridge, MA: Harvard University Press.
Gergen, K.J. (1999). *An invitation to social construction*. Thousand Oaks, CA: Sage.
Gergen, K.J. (2001). Psychological Science in a Postmodern Context. *American Psychologist, 56*, 803–813.
Gergen, K.J., Hoffman, L., & Anderson, H. (1995). Is diagnosis a disaster: A constructionist trialogue. In F. Kaslow (Ed.), *Handbook of relational diagnosis* (pp. 102–118). New York: John Wiley & Sons.
Goolishian, H. (1989). *The self: Some thoughts from a postmodern perspective on the intersubjectivity of mind*. Unpublished manuscript.
Goolishian, H. & Anderson, H. (1994). Narrativa y self. Algunos dilemas posmodernos de la psicoterapia [Narrative and self: Some postmodern dilemmas of psychotherapy]. In D.F. Schnitman (Ed.), *Nuevos paradigmas, cultura y subjetividad* (pp. 293–306). Buenos Aires: Paidos.
Goolishian, H. & Anderson, H. (1996). Narrative e self: Alguns dilemmas pos-modernos da psicoterpia, por. In D. Schnitzman (Ed.), *Novas paradigmas, cultura e subjetividade* (pp. 191–200). Porto Alegre: Artes Medicas.
Goolishian, H.A. & Anderson, H. (2002). Narrative and self: Some postmodern dilemmas of psychotherapy. In D.S. Friedman (Ed.), *New paradigms, culture and subjectivities*. New York: Hampton Press.
Hacking, I. (1999). *The social construction of what?* Cambridge, MA: Harvard University Press.
Harré, R. (1979). *Social being: A theory for social psychology*. Oxford: Basil Blackwell.
Harré, R. (1983). *Personal being: A Theory for individual psychology*. Oxford: Basil Blackwell.
Hermans, H.J.M., Kempen, H.J.G., & Van Loon, R.J.P. (1992). The dialogical self: Beyond individualism and rationalism. *American Psychologist, 47*, 23–33.
Hoy, D.C. (1986). Must we say what we mean? The grammatological critique of hermeneutics. In B.R. Wachterhauser (Ed.), *Hermeneutics and modern philosophy* (pp. 397–415). Albany, NY: State University of New York Press.
Maturana, H.R. (1978). Biology of language: Epistemology of reality. In G. Miller & E. Lenneberg (Eds.), *Psychology and biology of language and thought* (pp. 27–63). New York: Academic Press.
Rorty, R. (1979). *Philosophy and the mirror of nature*. Princeton, NJ: Princeton University Press.
Seligman, M.E.P. & Csikszentmihalyi, M. (2000). Positive psychology: An introduction. *American Psychologist, 55*, 5–14.
Shotter, J. (1984). *Social accountability and selfhood*. Oxford: Blackwell.
Shotter, J. (1993a). *Conversational realities: Constructing life through language*. London: Sage.
Shotter, J. (1993b). *Cultural politics of everyday life*. Toronto: University of Toronto Press.
Shotter, J. (2005). *Wittgenstein in practice: His philosophy of beginnings, and beginnings, and beginnings*. London: KCC Foundation.
Wachterhauser, B.R. (Ed.) (1986). Introduction: History and language in understanding. In *Hermeneutics and modern philosophy* (pp. 5–61). Albany, NY: SUNY Press.
Warneke, G. (1987). *Gadamer: Hermeneutics, tradition and reason*. Stanford, CA: Stanford University Press.
Wittgenstein, L. (1953). *Philosophical investigations*. (G.E.M. Anscombe, Trans.) New York: Macmillan.
Wittgenstein, L. (1981). *Zettel* (2nd. ed.), G.E.M. Anscombe & G.H.V. Wright (Eds.). Oxford: Blackwell.

CHAPTER 2

Historical Influences

HARLENE ANDERSON

My journey toward a collaborative approach spans three decades and has involved the reflexive nature of theory and practice. Several theoretical and philosophical perspectives and clinical circumstances have influenced my approach along the way. I highlight and summarize some of these to help the reader appreciate that I did not just one day wake up in this postmodern therapy world. I begin with my version of the story of the roots of the approach that were planted years before I joined the Galveston group. I then give a synopsis of the significant clinical experiences that influenced a search for new languages to describe and understand our work. I follow this clinical account with discussions of key metaphors that I have tagged as precursors to the influence of hermeneutics, social construction, and postmodern ones.

Multiple Impact Therapy

My entrance into postmodern therapy dates back to 1970 when I took a position in the pediatric department at the University of Texas Medical Branch in Galveston, TX. Shortly after my arrival, I heard about the family seminar in the psychiatry department, taught by Harry Goolishian and his colleagues. I did not know how fortunate I was at the time; I had stepped into one of the pioneering efforts in family therapy: Multiple Impact Therapy (MIT). I did not know how the contagious enthusiasm for family therapy that I caught would influence my future. Importantly, neither could I guess that the ingenious, provocative, and intellectual Harry Goolishian would become my mentor and friend. Years later, I realized in retrospect, and with created memory, that the threads of the meandering path that Harry and I would take toward our collaborative approach could be traced back to MIT (Anderson, 1997, 2000, 2001).

Roots

MIT was a short-term, family-centered approach created to work with adolescents from a variety of ethnic and socioeconomic groups with severe psychiatric problems. It was a collaborative, collective, and collegial effort in which a multidisciplinary team worked intensely with adolescents, their families, and relevant others in their lives (e.g., significant members of the extended family and community professionals such as a counselor, priest, or football coach) over a 2 to 3-day period. Its development was inspired by the challenge of the dueling realities of family members, which were then thought to be mirrored by the professionals. The team believed that the differing realities of the family members and the relevant system members could be collected and integrated; in turn, this integrated problem picture would help the team have a truer reality of the problem and consequently a more effective diagnosis and treatment for their adolescent population. As the medical school hospital was a state facility, the patients, as they were called, were often prior treatment failures, and many were referred to the hospital because they could not afford private treatment.

The team, usually three colleagues serving as the therapists and a fourth acting as a consultant to the team, would first meet with each other to exchange impressions and information about the identified patient and his or her family members. The team next met with the patient, family members, and the relevant others. In this meeting, or *conference* as they called it, the team began to explore each person's definition of the problem, including their ideas about its etiology, symptoms, and previous treatment, and their expectations of treatment. The conference, usually lasting for 2 hours, was followed by each team member meeting with a subsystem—parental, sibling, and community professionals. The consultant rotated through the subsystem conferences, often sharing the focus of the other conversations. The consultant was also present during the team's planning and debriefing meetings. Over the next 2 to 3 days, there were various conferences with varying membership. The membership of each conference and the topic of its conversation were addressed on a conversation-by-conversation basis, instead of being determined ahead of time. For instance, one therapist might meet with one family member while two therapists met with the rest of the family and the community professionals. At any point in time, the two memberships might overlap or flow into some other configuration.

Theoretically and pragmatically, the MIT colleagues aimed to help a family grow as it confronted the crisis of its adolescent member by capitalizing on the rapidity of change possible in the adolescent years and the family to achieve a self-rehabilitating process (Macgregor, Ritchie, Serrano, Schuster, McDanald, & Goolishian, 1964). They held the assumption that "If the family itself can become a partner in therapy, more energies are released for the task at hand" (MacGregor et al., p. viii). An important focus was the relationship among the team members. This focus was influenced by the communications theory research by Don D. Jackson and his colleagues in Palo Alto, CA, as they sought to understand and reduce internal professional communication problems. MIT was described by Robert Sutherland[1] as "fresh and hopeful," having "far-reaching implications for the training of therapists" and having "many implications for [a] new social theory" (MacGregor et al., pp. viii–ix).

As with other early pioneering family therapies, MIT developed out of clinical experiences and the inability of familiar psychotherapy theories and practices to meet the demands of challenging clients. Also like other early efforts, the theoretical explanations about problems and therapy came later as clinicians searched to describe, understand, and explain their work.

Threads

I trace the threads of my collaborative approach back to some of the key assumptions and characteristics of MIT, including: (a) the team valued the importance of the individual and their relational systems; (b) the team believed that human creativity and ingenuity were boundless; (c) the team's role was to mobilize the resources of the family and community members rather than to be the resource expert; (d) the team believed in the importance of self-reflection and self-change, and in learning together with the family; (e) the team valued a multiplicity and diversity of voices; (f) the team believed that it was important to understand a different point of view rather than dismiss or judge it; (g) team members openly probed and analyzed each other's views in front of the family; (h) the team valued live training and supervision with trainees working alongside experienced therapists; (i) the team did not think that they empowered the family but instead helped them find and use their inherent potentials; and (j) "team" was a concept broader than the number of therapists in the therapy room or behind a mirror.

The team's preferred behavior is also notable: (a) the team thought of itself as a modeler of healthy communication, especially modeling disagreement without losing respect for each other;[2] (b) team members, with the consultant's help, continually checked-in with each system member to make sure members understood each perspective; (c) family and community members were invited to outline in their own words their views of the immediate crisis, and the patient was invited to participate in this recapitulation and to make needed corrections; (d) one therapist would summarize what the team had learned and a second therapist would respond to the summary by reflecting on it; and (e) team members were aware that their open way of being with families might be different from their previous experiences with other professionals saying, "Most families are unaccustomed to this novel interchange" (p. 6). You will notice below and in Chapters 3 and 4 how these assumptions, characteristics, and behaviors evolved over the years as they were influenced by our continuing experiences and searches to find new descriptive language.

The MIT approach was part of an emerging paradigmatic shift at the edge of the psychotherapy field. The shift represented a move from viewing human behavior as intrapsychic phenomena to seeing it in the context of interpersonal relationships, namely, the family. The family became the chief subject of inquiry and explanation for an individual's problem. Family therapists adopted various systems theories as their explanatory metaphors. This shift influenced psychotherapy theory and the education of therapists as well.

Going back and reading about the MIT project was like going into a dusty attic and learning about your ancestry. When you look at this work and realize the time in which it was produced, it was incredible. It was a therapy ahead of its time. I pause here to highlight some aspects of its theoretical footing, to show the threads that held through time, to honor it, and to share it with those not familiar with it.

Clinical Shifts: From Hierarchical Strategy to Collaborative Inquiry

Historically, the Galveston group always had an interest in the early work of David Jackson and Gregory Bateson and later the work of the Mental Research Institute (MRI) associates in Palo Alto. Soon after I joined the group, an interest developed in the MRI's use of language—their radical move away from traditional therapy methods in which the therapist taught the client the therapist's language to a focus on the therapist learning the client's language. By language, the MRI associates referred to words and phrases as well as to beliefs, values, truths, and worldviews. Put very simply, if the therapist could learn to speak the client's language, in the broadest sense, then the therapist's interventions, assignments, and so forth could be placed in the client's language. As a result, therapy would be more successful and resistance less likely.

We purposely set about to learn our clients' everyday ordinary language in the MRI sense. Overtime, as we continued in this quest, our therapy began to take an unpredictable turn that would eventually lead us to new theoretical interests and a new therapy paradigm. (See Anderson 1997 and 2000 for a fuller discussion of these clinical shifts and their implications.)

We became genuinely immersed in and inquisitive about our clients' stories. We spontaneously became more focused on maintaining coherence within a client's experience and committed to being informed by their story. That is, we less and less tried to make sense of our clients' stories from our therapist sense-making maps. Instead, we became absorbed in trying to understand the sense that clients made of things from their maps. Consequently, in this effort to learn and understand more about what they said—for example, their stories and views of their life situations—our questions began to be informed by what was just said or what we later described as coming from within the local conversation, instead of being informed by preknowledge brought in from the outside.

We learned that a family did not have a language. Family members, of course, shared some language—a necessity for any group to have continuity over time. But the family itself did not have a language nor did it have a belief or a reality: its individual members did. Each member had his or her language and had what seemed to be multiple distinctive ones as well.[3] For instance, each had his or her description of the problem and its solution, as well as a description of the family and expectations of therapy. And, often a member would have multiple descriptions and not necessarily compatible ones. There was no such thing, therefore, as "a" problem, "a" solution, or even "a" family for that matter. There were at least as many descriptions of these as there were system members (including non-family system members). We were fascinated by these differences in language, especially the distinctions in descriptions, explanations, and meanings attributed to the same event or person. We sensed that somehow these differences were valuable and held possibilities, though at the time we did not know in what way. We gave up trying to negotiate or blur differences or strive for consensus and instead let them be.

We listened differently. We became intensely interested in each person and his or her version of the story and found ourselves intensely listening and talking to each person one at a time. We discovered that while we were talking with one person that the others seemed to listen in a way that was new to us. They listened attentively and nondefensively, seemingly eager to hear more of what the other was saying and being less apt to interrupt, correct, or negate the other. We understood this in a twofold way: First, we conveyed in our words and actions that we were sincerely interested in and respected what each person had to say, giving ample time to, and trying to understand, each. Thus, the storytellers did not have to work so hard to try to get us to understand or convince us of their version of the story. Second, the familiar story was being told and heard differently from before. Clients would remark that though they had heard the other's story before, somehow it was different this time. As one person put it, it was as if the content was the same but somehow the pieces were assembled differently. Through this new assemblage, people had an altered sense of their experiences and each other. New ways of understanding their life struggles and relationships, for them and for us, seemed to evolve as a natural consequence of this new way of talking and listening. We did not purposefully try to influence their stories or their sense-making.

We learned and spoke the client's everyday ordinary language. We found that when we talked with our colleagues about our clients that we tended to naturally present them in terms of their stories, their descriptions, and their words instead of in our usual professional language. We less and less used reproduction professional descriptions, explanations, and diagnoses. For instance, when we presented our patients in hospital staff meetings, we used their everyday ordinary language instead of our professional language to describe them. Our students noted that when we told the client's story using the client's words that the students felt it captured the humanness and uniqueness of each client, making them and their situation come alive. As the "specialness" of each client emerged, the sameness receded. (We would later think that the only way to approximate the richness of another person's voice and to respect the authority of it was to invite it instead of trying to re-present it.)

We bracketed our preknowledge and focused on the client's knowledge. As our concentration on the client's story and our value of it grew, so did our interest in their knowledge and expertise on their lives. This increased notice of the client's knowledge spontaneously began to allow more room for it in the therapy and to make our therapist knowledge and content expertise less important. We became more tentative about our knowledge: our sense-making maps and biases, our opinions about how families ought to be, how narratives ought to be constructed, and which narratives were more useful. Our knowledge seemed to have less relevance and faded into the background. When we did offer it, we found ourselves presenting it in a tentative and provisional manner. That is, we wanted our clients—as well as ourselves—to be able to discuss, doubt, and challenge it.

We moved from a one-way inquiry toward a mutual inquiry. As we immersed ourselves in learning our client's language and meanings in the manner that we were developing, we realized how our clients and we were spontaneously becoming engaged with each other in a mutual or shared inquiry. In other words, what began as a relationship—wherein the client was the teacher and the therapist was the learner—soon and naturally shifted to a partnered process of coexploring the problem and codeveloping possibility. Therapy became a two-way conversational give-and-take process in which we jointly explored, discussed, and questioned. Consequently, the storytelling process became more important than the content or the details. We began to focus on the conversational process of therapy and on how we could create a facilitating space for it.

We no longer needed interventions. As we learned about a client's language and meanings, we spontaneously began to abandon our expertise on how people ought to be and ought to live their lives. We found, for instance, that we did not need to use this expertise to create in-session or end-of-session interventions. When we examined what we thought were individually tailored therapist-designed interventions, we discovered that they were not interventions at all in the usual sense. That is, although we thought we were using interventions, we were not. The ideas and actions that we once thought of as interventions became new possibilities that materialized in the therapy conversation inside the therapy room and were not brought in by us as an outside expert. And, as the client had participated in the conception and construction of the possibility, the newness was more coherent with the family and its members' logics.

We entertained uncertainty. Combined, these experiences left us in a constant state of uncertainty. We began to appreciate and value this sense of unpredictability, which in a strange way provided feelings of freedom and comfort. We learned that we did not have to know. What we later came to refer to as "not-knowing" liberated us from being content or outcome experts. We did not need to edit clients' stories or realities. We were comfortable that our knowledge was not superior to that of our clients. In turn, our not-knowing perspective allowed an expanded capacity for imagination and creativity. Not-knowing became a pivotal concept and would mark a significant distinction between our and others' ideas about therapy. (Not-knowing is discussed in Chapter 3.)

We became more aware of the reflexive nature of our practicing and teaching. We began to notice our students' voices differently—their remarks, questions, and critiques. Their voices forced new ways of thinking about describing and understanding our work. Students often commented on the positive way we spoke about our clients. They described our manner and attitude as respectful and humble. They were amazed at our excitement about each client and how we seemed to like those clients that others might judge as socially abhorrent or believe were immoral. They were surprised by how many of our mandated referrals actually came to the first therapy session and continued in therapy. They were puzzled that our therapy looked like "just having a conversation." In an effort to describe our approach to therapy, a student once wondered, "If I were observing and did not know who the therapists were, I wonder if I could identify them?"

We moved from behind the mirror. Traditionally, family therapy teams were organized in a hierarchical and dualistic manner. The team behind the mirror was in what is often thought of as a metaposition, believing that team members could observe more correctly and quickly than those in the therapy room. The team members had private conversations that the family, and sometimes the therapist, was not privileged to hear. They combined their multiple voices, creating consensus hypotheses, interventions, and questions and funneled these to the family via the therapist. With this team preselection, the family and the therapist lost the richness of the multiplicity of views. So, when clients would question the messenger or want to know why the team said "x," we would invite the team from behind the mirror to come into the therapy room. This coming out was also influenced by the growing numbers of visiting therapists who came to observe our work, often asking what the clients thought of our kind of therapy. In response, we suggested to them that they should pose that question to the client not us. So, with the clients' permission, we invited the visitors into the room, calling them "visiting therapists." Together, these "going public" acts dissolved some of the artificial boundaries between the team, the therapist-in-the-room, and the client, and led to a sense of openness and unity as well.

For learning purposes, we preferred two-person student therapists in-the-room teams for at least two reasons. One, we wanted to discourage the idea that the student behind the mirror could know more or sooner. Two, we wanted the students to learn to feel free to share their silent thoughts. For instance, they could talk with each other as the client listened.

In summery, our interest in language as a strategic-like tool waned as our new experiences of being in language with our clients took over. In the end, we knew, as did our MIT forefathers, that our clients were the heroes and heroines of their own lives.

Though at the time we were inspired by constructivists such as von Foerster, von Glassersfeld, and Maturana and tried to translate some of the ideas of scientists such as Bohm and Prigogene to the therapy arena, we especially wanted to learn about other views of language. We read contemporary hermeneutic thinkers like Gadamer, Habermas, and Heidegger. We read philosophers such as Derrida, Kuhn, Merleau-Ponty, and Rorty, and later Wittgenstein, Bakhtin, and Vygotsky. In one way or another, all challenged (1) the notion of language and knowledge as representational, (2) the individual knower as autonomous and separate from the object observed, described, and explained, (3) that the mind can act as an inner mental representation of reality or knowledge, (4) the notion of reality or knowledge as fixed, a priori, or empirical fact independent of the observer, and (5) that language can correctly represent knowledge.[4]

Shifting Metaphors

Social Systems Metaphor

In the early 1980s, Harry Goolishian began to challenge the relevance of the hierarchically layered Parsonian-like social systems view in family therapy, describing it as an "onion theory" (Goolishian, 1985; Anderson and Goolishian, 1988). Like the layers of an onion, from its core outwards, the individual is encircled by the family, the family by the larger system, the larger system by the community, and so forth. Each layer is subordinate to and controlled by the surrounding layer in the service of its own requirements—for maintenance and order. In this view, social systems are objectively defined and are independent of the people involved and of the observers. This onion-like social theory contextualizes behavior, naming what should be fixed—the social structure and organization—and thus supports the notion of psychopathology. In this framework, with encircled relationships based on role and structure, the duality of the individual and the individual-in-relationship (e.g., with the family) is maintained. The therapist is an independent external observer who is hierarchically superior to the system. Therapy informed by this view risks bumping the container of the pathology up a level, for instance, from individual to family or family to professional system. Nothing has really changed.

We had a long history since the early MIT days of including members of the client's family, social, and professional system in therapy (Goolishian & Kivell, 1981). We did not think about this practice theoretically, however, until we realized how often family therapy bumped the level of blame. This led to questioning the onion theory and to developing an alternative way of understanding broader familial and professional systems and contexts and their relationships to therapy. Others in the family therapy field explored these contexts as well and referred to them as the ecological system, the larger system, the meaningful system, and the relevant system.

Evolutionary Systems: Process Determines Structure

Coinciding with the questioning and abandonment of the onion theory was an interest in the concept of evolutionary systems in biology and physics. The concept represented movement away from the notions of homeostasis and causation (both linear and circular) associated with cybernetic theories. Systems were viewed as evolutionary, nonequilibrium, nonlineal, self-organizing, and self-recursive networks that are in a constant state of change that is random, unpredictable, and discontinuous. This constant state of change leads to higher levels of complexity: "This view of evolutionary systems emphasizes process over structure and flexibility and change over stability" (Dell & Goolishian, 1981, p. 442). As Harry and our colleague Paul Dell radically suggested, applying these concepts to human systems implied that neither therapy nor the therapist could unilaterally amplify one fluctuation over another or determine the direction of change (Dell & Goolishian, 1979; Dell, 1982). When therapists surrender this hierarchy and dualism they realize that they are an active part of a mutual evolutionary process, they do not and cannot control the system. That is, a therapist cannot intervene to determine the outcome or the "ongoingness" (Dell & Goolishian, 1981, p. 444) of the system's evolution. Coincidently, as Bateson (1977) cautioned, the word "change" is an epistemological confusion; a system does not change. Change and system are observer punctuations; the observer is part of each. This was the beginning of separating ourselves from the pragmatists in family therapy who strove to change others. We invited colleagues Luigi Boscolo, Gianfranco Cecchin, Lynn Hoffman, and Humberto Maturana, among others, to our 1982 Epistemology and Psychotherapy Conference to join us in exploring these theories that were developing outside the psychotherapy discourse that we felt had some applicability to therapy.

This concept of a mutual evolutionary process combined with our continued interest in language, first from a hermeneutic perspective and later from a social construction one. Over time, we moved from using the mechanic-like cybernetic and onion-like social system metaphors as ways to think about human systems. And, our view of therapy shifted away from understanding a therapy system as a collective, contained entity that acts, feels, thinks, and believes. Instead, we had moved toward thinking of a therapy system as people who have coalesced around a particular relevance (problem-determined or problem-organizing system); when the relevance for coalescing "dis-solves," the system dissolves (problem-dis-solving systems). We began to conceptualize human systems as linguistic systems—as fluid, evolving communicating systems that exist in language. The therapy system was simply one kind of language system. (*See* Anderson, Goolishian & Winderman, 1986; Goolishian & Anderson, 1987; and Anderson & Goolishian, 1988 for fuller discussions of these shifts and the idea of problem-determined/problem-organizing/problem-dissolving systems.)

Endnotes

1. Sutherland was the director of the Hogg Foundation, which funded the MIT project.
2. I currently speak of "being public" which is discussed in Chapter 4. A major difference between being public and the MIT actions is that I would not have an intent such as modeling.
3. Later we decided, thinking relationally, that it is even impossible for a person to have his or her own language.
4. To learn more about the influence of these authors and their ideas, see Anderson, 1997.

References

Anderson, H. (1997). *Conversation, language and possibilities: A postmodern approach to therapy.* New York: Basic Books.

Anderson, H. (2000). Becoming a postmodern collaborative therapist: A clinical and theoretical journey, Part I. *Journal of the Texas Association for Marriage and Family Therapy, 5,* 5–12.

Anderson, H. (2001). Becoming a postmodern collaborative therapist: A clinical and theoretical journey, Part II. *Journal of the Texas Association for Marriage and Family Therapy, 6,* 4–22.

Anderson, H. & Goolishian, H. (1988). Human systems as linguistic systems: Evolving ideas about the implications for theory and practice. *Family Process, 27,* 371–393.

Anderson, H., Goolishian, H., & Winderman, L. (1986a). Beyond family therapy. *Journal of Strategic and Systemic Therapies, 5,* i–iii.

Anderson, H., Goolishian, H., & Winderman, L. (1986b). Problem determined systems: Towards transformation in family therapy. *Journal of Strategic and Systemic Therapies, 5,* 1–13.

Bateson, G. (1972). *Steps to an ecology of mind.* New York: Ballantine Books.

Dell, P. & Goolishian, H. (1979). Order through fluctuation: An evolutionary epistemology for human systems. Paper presented at the Annual Scientific Meetings of the A.K. Rice Institute, Houston, TX.

Dell, P. & Goolishian, H. (1981). Order through fluctuation: An evolutionary epistemology for human systems. *Australian Journal of Family Therapy, 21,* 75–184.

Goolishian, H. (August 1985). Beyond family therapy: Some implications from systems theory. Paper presented at the Annual Meeting of the American Psychological Association, Division 43, San Francisco, CA.

Goolishian, H. & Anderson, H. (1987). Language systems and therapy: An evolving idea. *Psychotherapy, 24,* 529–538.

Goolishian, H. & Kivell (Anderson) H. (1981). Planning therapeutic interventions so as to include non-blood related family members in the therapeutic goals. In A.S. Gurman (Ed.), *Questions and answers in the practice of family therapy.* New York: Bruner/Mazel.

MacGregor, R., Ritchie, A.M., Serrano, A.C., Schuster, F.P., McDanald, E.C., & Goolishian, H.A. (1964). *Multiple impact therapy with families.* New York: McGraw-Hill.

CHAPTER 3

Dialogue: People Creating Meaning with Each Other and Finding Ways to Go On[1]

HARLENE ANDERSON

Over the years, I have had a sustained interest in client voices—their experiences and descriptions of successful and unsuccessful therapy, and of therapists who were helpful and not so helpful. I have interviewed and consulted with clients, therapists, and students in my local setting and around the world. I frequently ended my conversations with them asking, "What advice do you have for therapists?" These voices and their responses to this question have significantly influenced my understanding of therapy and my approach to it. If I had to sum it up, I would say that clients spoke of what I now think of as "relational conversations." They described particular ways that therapists listened, heard, and spoke—indicating therapists' manners, actions, and responses communicated to clients that they were important and respected and that what they had to say was worth hearing. What I learned highlighted the significance of the relationship in dialogue and partly influenced the heart and spirit of my approach, a therapist's "way of being," which I call a "philosophical stance." I will address the philosophical stance in Chapter 4. But, first I will discuss the role of dialogue and the importance of listening, hearing, and speaking to it in a relationship and a conversation, beginning with a question that is influenced by these client voices and that is always present: *How can practitioners therapists create the kinds of conversations and relationships with their clients that allow all participants to access their creativities and develop possibilities where none seemed to exist before?*

Central in hermeneutics, social construction, and postmodern philosophies is the notion of dialogue. Dialogue in early Greek society referred to *dia* ("through") and *logos* ("word"). It referred to social exchange and the generation of meaning and understanding through it. I use "dialogue" similarly, to refer to a form of conversation: talking or conversing with another or with oneself toward a search for meaning and understanding. I place emphasis on the "doing with." Participants engage with each other in a mutual or shared inquiry: jointly pondering, examining, questioning, and reflecting. In and through this dialogic search, meanings and understandings are continually interpreted, reinterpreted, clarified, revised, and created. As newness in meanings and understandings emerges, possibilities are generated for thought, feeling, emotion, expression, and action. True dialogue cannot be other than generative. In other words, as I mentioned earlier in Chapter 1, transformation is inherent in dialogue. I also place emphasis on the importance of having a "space" for dialogue in which people can connect and talk with each other. As I also mentioned in Chapter 1, I think of it as a metaphorical space that the client and therapist occupy together and in which dialogue occurs.

A search for understanding is not to seek the undiscovered but to look at the familiar with scrutiny, with new eyes and ears, to see and hear it differently, to understand it differently, to articulate it differently. The challenge is that sometimes we are so accustomed to the familiar that we miss the anomaly, the usually unnoticed, or the unarticulated expression (e.g., a movement, a glance). Interestingly though, in this process of client telling and therapist learning, as Rorty suggests, something begins to happen spontaneously: The familiar begins to be talked about in unfamiliar or unusual ways, giving new meaning to the familiar to the usual.

Dialogue is a relational and collaborative activity. It is influenced, of course, by the multiple larger contexts, discourses, and histories in which it takes place. Of prime importance, however, is the relationship between the dialogical participants or the "conversational partners." As I mentioned in Chapter 1, Wittgenstein talked of relationship and conversation as going hand-in-hand: the kinds of conversations that we have with each other inform and form the kinds of relationships we have with each other and vice versa.[2] Dialogue invites and requires of its participants a sense of mutuality, including genuine respect and sincere interest regarding the other.

Dialogue, by its very nature, involves not-knowing and uncertainty. Sincere interest in another necessitates not-knowing the other, their situation, or their future ahead of time, whether the knowing is in the form of previous experience, theoretical knowledge, or familiarity. Believing that you know the other person, whether from acquaintance with them or as a type of person, can preclude being inquisitive and learning about their uniqueness. As well, dialogue requires a not-knowing attitude toward its outcome. Because perspectives change and dialogue is inherently transforming, it is impossible to predict, for instance, how a story will be told, the twists and turns its telling may take, or its seemingly final version. Combined, these characteristics distinguish dialogue as a dynamic generative joint activity and as different from other language activities such as discussion, debate, or chitchat. (I discuss not-knowing more fully later in this chapter and in Chapter 4.)

Listening, Hearing, and Speaking: Their Importance in Dialogue

Dialogue involves the intertwined reciprocal multifaceted processes of listening, hearing, and speaking. Each is critical to the other. Each member of a conversation constantly moves back and forth between these processes. They are part of the natural spontaneous way of conversations; they are neither discrete step-ordered methods nor techniques.

In my interviews with clients over the years about their experiences of therapy, they often commented on the therapist's listening and hearing: "She listened to me," "He heard exactly what I said," and "All I really wanted was for someone to hear me." The most common factor in unsuccessful therapy was not being listened to or not being heard. I remember talking with a man in Sweden that I met in a consultation interview. He had been given a diagnosis of paranoid schizophrenia and had been in treatment over five years with several different psychiatrists and psychologists. He told of those who asked questions to "gather details and facts" and those who asked questions to hear "the story I assume they already knew." He said none of them ever "heard me" or "knew me." And, with intense emotion, he said that it was "sad" and "painful." Assumingly, he felt they did not have a need to be interested in him and his story; perhaps they already knew him as a diagnostic category. The man felt that no one had been interested in listening to him and hearing what he had to say until he met the current therapy team who had invited me to meet with him. He felt that they listened and heard, and that if at times they did not understand, at least they sincerely tried.

The voices of fictional characters sometimes capture what I want to express better than I can. The words of Smila, the main character in the mystery *Smila's Sense of Snow*, beautifully illustrate the kind of listening that I am talking about:

> Very few people know how to listen. Their haste pulls them out of the conversation, or they try internally to improve the situation, or

they're preparing what their entrance will be when you shut up and it's their turn to step on stage. ... It's different with the man standing in front of me. When I talk, he listens without distraction to what I say, and only to what I say. (Høeg, 1993, pp. 44–45)

I define listening as attending, interacting, and responding with the other person. Listening is part of the process of trying to hear and grasp what the other person is saying from their perspective. It is a participatory activity that requires responding to try to understand—being genuinely curious, asking questions to learn more about what is said and not what you think should be said. It requires checking with the other to learn if what you think you heard is what the other person hoped you would hear. Checking necessitates using comparable terms or different words from those that the other is using, providing opportunity for the therapist to compare and contrast meanings, and providing opportunity for the client to clarify, correct, or confirm the therapist's missed or different understanding. That is, if you simply use the same words as the speaker, neither of you can confirm nor disconfirm understanding. I make a distinction between responses such as questions to participate in the storytelling that in turn help, for instance, clarify and expand, and responses such as questions that seek details and facts to determine things like diagnoses and interventions or aim to guide the conversation in a particular direction.

It is important to keep in mind what kinds of responses are facilitative and what kinds hinder dialogue. What signals, for instance, if what the other said is respected and valued versus dismissed or discounted? What signals that the listener thinks the speaker has said enough or that it is okay to continue talking? A listener can respond with or without words. A body movement like a glance, a shrug, or a sigh is a response. As Andersen suggests in Chapter 6, spoken words are accompanied by body movements. It is also important to keep in mind that a lack of response is a response—it is a communication that the receiver interprets just as they would any other kind of response. In my interviews, clients reported that a therapist's no-response sometimes made them feel unimportant, discredited, doubtful, and so forth. Clients also reported wondering if the therapist had a private silent response that they did not share. In this latter case, clients often thought the response must have been too judgmental or otherwise to share. I am reminded of overhearing a colleague talk about a discussion that she had had where she did not agree with or value what the other person had said. Earnestly and a bit proudly, she said, "I was a 'good' listener, I didn't say anything. I just listened and waited patiently until he finished." I do not know how the other person in this situation received the listener's response. I give this example to emphasize the importance of a response and that a seemingly no-response *is* a response. The "difficulty of difference" is part of the dialogic process. Instead of rejecting what is disagreed with, whether through silence or rebuke, advantage can be taken of the opportunity for dialogue by, for instance, trying to make sense from the other's perspective and be curious about the different view. A good listener responds, as John Shotter (1995) suggests, "into" the conversation; we act responsively "into" a situation, doing what 'it' calls for" (p. 62). I have heard Tom Andersen (2003) speak of how responding is "critical to inviting and encouraging in both relationship and dialogue." I have also heard Jaakko Seikkula (2003) say, "Nothing is more terrible than a lack of response."

This perspective of listening differs from listening as it is historically discussed in the psychotherapy literature, where its primary role has been to gain clinical information. Mostly, such listening has been a passive task. The active part has been the silent sorting out and making sense of what is heard through the therapist's interpretive ear.

In my experience, you learn more about the other person and their situation when you listen to them as if you are listening to a story. When you listen to a story, you primarily attend to the whole of the story; when you are engrossed as such, you do not necessarily note the details and facts. Interestingly, surprisingly, and perhaps paradoxically, when you let go of focusing on the details and facts, you develop a better memory for them as well. Likewise, I think it is difficult to give full attention to a story when you are occupied with writing notes while the other is telling their story. Also, in my experience, when you imagine the other person as talking about their story, and a new one at that, you become engaged in the story and with the storyteller. Picture how you would listen to a story if you truly believed that you had not heard it before and were hearing it for the first time. The unfamiliarity of it invites curiosity and anticipation.

I am reminded of the time that I heard the Pulitzer Prize winner Jhumpa Lahira read from her novel, *The Namesake*. I was captivated as she read the chapter about the name of the little boy who was the protagonist, Gogol. I eagerly hung on every word, picturing the characters and their actions. The chapter was a collection of scenarios of the influence that his name had on his relationships and his identity. When she finished the reading, I was anxious to hear the rest of the story; I did not know it. I still remember many things about Gogol and the events and people in his life: words and phrases as well as facts and details, remained vividly with me even though I was not collecting them while she was reading.

The storytelling process in therapy is far more complex than one person telling a story and another person simply listening to it. The listener has to be actively involved, hearing and speaking as well. This hearing Susan

Levin (1992) defines as "a process involving a negotiating of understand-ings" (p. 48), "an interactive struggle for shared meaning that occurs when two people (or more) attempt to come to a mutual understanding of something" (p. 50). Listening and hearing go hand-in-hand and cannot be separated.

In my experience, negotiation of understanding in and through dia-logue is done in a distinct way that includes special therapist attitudes and actions that I call—influenced by Shotter's notion of responsive lis-tening—responsive-active listening-hearing. Responsive-active listening-hearing invites clients to tell us what it is like for them, what are their inner concerns. To help a story be sharable, a therapist must plunge into a client's world and show an interest in that client's view of the problem, its cause, its location, and its solution. Equally important, a therapist should learn a client's expectations of therapy and therapist.

As I have said elsewhere,

> This kind of listening, hearing, and responding requires that a thera-pist enter the therapy domain with a genuine posture and manner characterized by an openness to the other person's ideological base—his or her reality, beliefs, and experiences. This listening posture and manner involve showing respect for, having humility toward, and believing that what a client has to say is worth hearing. It involves attending considerately, showing that we value a client's knowledge about his or her pain, misery, or dilemma. And, it entails indicat-ing that we want to know more about what a client has just said or may not yet have said. This is best accomplished by actively interact-ing with and responding to what a client says by asking questions, making comments, extending ideas, wondering, and sharing private thoughts aloud. Being interested in this way helps a therapist to clar-ity and prevent misunderstanding of the *said* and learn more about [and participate in the creation of] the *unsaid* …
>
> Such comments and questions that seek not to misunderstand must be offered in a tentative, curious manner that conveys genuine interest in getting it right.
>
> Responsive-active listening-hearing does not mean just sitting back and doing nothing. It does not mean that a therapist cannot offer an idea or express an opinion. Nor does it mean that it is just a technique. Responsive-active listening-hearing is a natural therapist manner and attitude that communicates and demonstrates sincere interest, respect, and curiosity. The therapist gives as much room and time for a client's story as necessary, and, yes, at times, without inter-rupting. That is, it does not bother me nor do I draw an inference if a client chooses to talk for a long time. (Anderson, 1997, pp. 153–154)

Inner Dialogue

I should say explicitly that dialogue refers to both outer and inner dialogue. Inner dialogue is the conversation that we have with ourselfs or an imagined other. The therapist's inner dialogue is the first step toward dialogue and is critical to fostering it. I often say to my students that the most important conversations in the therapy room or the classroom are the silent inner ones that the client and the student have as the therapist or teacher speaks. The expression of silent thought is itself generative; that is, the expression of thought, whether through articulation or gesture into the relational space, is an interpretive and meaning-generating process. The process of expression further forms and gives shape to the yet-unspoken thought.

Articulating inner dialogue, for instance, can help the therapist gain an awareness and clarity of his or her thoughts. As Harry Goolishian used to say, "I never know what I mean until I say it." This articulation can take place in the therapy room or in an after-therapy conversation with colleagues or oneself. My preference is always to keep the client in these inner dialogical loops. Private conversations, aloud or on paper, such as reviewing videotapes of sessions without the client present, can risk therapist monologue. A therapist's private interpretations also risk, though sometimes unwittingly, assuming a position of knowing and authority. In supervising student clinical therapy teams, I find that students want to talk seemingly without end about the client after the session. I propose that such talk lacks relevance because the person most important to the conversation is not part of it. I suggest that they save their comments and questions and pose them to the client in the next session. Share their private thoughts *with*, and talk with, the client not *about* them. Usually, however, when the next session rolls around, the things the students were so occupied with at the time do not hold the same importance.

Listening, hearing, and speaking are all equally important. As I mention above, the therapist listens to the client but must ask to determine if the spoken words are heard in the way that the client wants the therapist to hear them. How can the therapist ask to find out if he or she has understood well, has partly understood, or has misunderstood without expressing and articulating his or her inner thoughts? Again, if the listener simply repeats back the speaker's words, the speaker can only confirm having spoken those words. Neither speaker nor listener will have a clue whether or not the listener understands the meanings of those words for the speaker. Accomplishing understanding and promoting dialogue are both part of an active process in which the listener interacts with the words and thus the speaker (Anderson, 1997). The risk lies in the pervasive potential for misunderstanding in dialogue (a misunderstanding is simply an understanding that differs from the speaker's intentions). (I talk more about inner dialogue in the therapist as "Being Public" section of Chapter 4.)

Enhancing the Possibility for Dialogue

Dialogue is an interactive process of interpretations of interpretations. One interpretation invites another. Interpreting is the process of understanding. In the process of trying to understand, new meanings are produced. In this sense, interpretation is not a silent, inactive process. It involves the active, interactive, and responsive process of listening, hearing, and speaking as discussed above. The listener responds (e.g., with an utterance, a gesture, a look) to the speaker; the speaker responds to the listener. Each is both a speaker and a listener. What is said acquires its meaning in this going back and forth with each other.

Listening, hearing, and speaking are expressions of a way of being—a way of being that invites a space that becomes a gathering place for the relational process of dialogue. But how can you assume a way of being that invites dialogue? How can you invite another person to talk *with* you? Based on my interviews with clients, therapists, and students, I believe that it involves authentically living what most of us desire for ourselves: to be believed and trusted as a worthwhile human being, no matter what our life circumstances; to be accepted, no matter how nonsensical our words and actions may seem; and to have a safe place and ample opportunity for full expression. Below are some ideas to keep in mind when the intent is to invite and participate in dialogue (along with the philosophical stance discussed in Chapters 1 and 4).

Listen, hear, and speak, respectively. Respect is a relational activity; it is not an individual internal characteristic. Respect is having and showing regard and consideration for the worthiness of the other. It is communicated by attitude, tone, posture, gestures, eye movements, words, and surroundings.

Listen, hear, and speak as a learner. Be genuinely curious about the other. You must sincerely believe that you can learn something from them. Listen and respond with expressed interest in what the other person is talking about—their experiences, their words, their feelings, and so forth.

Listen, hear, and speak to understand. Do not understand too quickly. Keep in mind that understanding is never-ending. Be tentative with what you think you might know. Knowing interferes with dialogue: it can preclude learning about the other, being inspired by them, and the spontaneity intrinsic to genuine dialogue. Knowing also risks maintaining or increasing power differences.

Listen, hear, and speak with care. Pauses are important. Take time before you speak: give the other person time to finish and give yourself a moment to think about what you want to say and how you want to say it.

Listen, hear, and speak naturally. Listening, hearing, and speaking are relational activities and processes; they are not techniques. When we minimize the complexity of a dialogue by reducing it to techniques we risk loosing or interfering with our natural social and conversational abilities.

Dialogue operates along a continuum. Sometimes we are less in a dialogical process and sometimes we are more so. I do not want to suggest that dialogues are always harmonious or easy. We do not always resonate with each other. When dissonance occurs, I find it helpful to think about the dialogical-monological distinction. (I discuss this in Chapter 4.) This is when I also find it helpful for therapists to pause and reflect on their inner dialogue: might the therapist's inner conversation (monologue) be contributing to the difficulty and if so, how? I do not, however, look for or think, for instance, in punctuations in a conversation such as dialogical or monological moments. The whole or overall of the conversation and the relationship is what counts.

To paraphrase Wittgenstein, dialogue allows us to find ways to go on from here. So, perhaps this is what is helpful in dialogue: We find ways to go on. Or, at the very least, we have a sense or a hope that it is possible that we will be able to go on.

Endnotes

1. This chapter was originally written as a presentation for the Eighth Annual Open Dialogue Conference: What is Helpful in Treatment Dialogue, Tornio, Finland, on August 29, 2003, and was revised for this book.
2. My colleague Glenn Boyd also discusses this in *The Art of Agape-Listening*.

References

Andersen, T. (August 2003). Reflecting teams. In *What is helpful in treatment dialogue*. Symposium conducted at the Eighth Annual Open Dialogue Congress, Torino, Finland.

Anderson, H. (1997). *Conversation, language and possibilities: A postmodern approach to therapy*. New York: Basic Books.

Boyd, G. (1996). *The art of agape-listening*. Sugarland, TX: The Agape Press.

Høeg, P. (1993). *Smilla's sense of snow*. (T. Nunnally, Trans.) New York: Dell.

Levin, S.B. (1992). *Hearing the unheard: Stories of women who have been battered. Dissertation Abstracts International*. T.U.I. Doctoral Dissertation, Cincinnati, OH: University Microfilms.

Rorty, R. (1979). *Philosophy and the mirror of nature*. Princeton, NJ: Princeton University Press.

Seikkula, J. (2003, August). Open dialogue. In *What is helpful in treatment dialogue*. Symposium conducted at the Eighth Annual Open Dialogue Conference, Torino, Finland.

Seikkula, J. & Olsen, M. (2003). The open dialogue approach to acute psychosis: Its poetics and micropolitics. *Family Process, 42*, 403–418.

Shotter, J. (1995). In conversation: Joint action, shared intentionality and ethics. *Theory and Psychology, 5*, 49–73.

Wittgenstein, L. (1953). *Philosophical investigations*. (G.E.M. Anscombe, Trans.) New York: Macmillan.

CHAPTER 4

The Heart and Spirit of Collaborative Therapy: The Philosophical Stance—"A Way of Being" in Relationship and Conversation

HARLENE ANDERSON

The postmodern conceptualization of knowledge and language inform the heart and spirit of collaborative therapy: the "philosophical stance" (Anderson, 1997, 2003). The philosophical stance refers to a "way of being" in relationship and conversation: a way of thinking with, experiencing with, relating with, acting with, and responding with the people we meet in therapy. I distinguish my work as a "philosophy of life" in action, as an approach and not as a theory or model of therapy. Theory, as Shotter (2005) suggests, provides a map that instructs practice. Theory, as hermeneutics proposes, can become a myopic preunderstanding that assures seeing what is sought, obscuring the uniqueness of the person, the word, etc. This distinction is similar to Shotter's (2005) bias toward Wittgenstein that, "Theories are aimed, ultimately, at justifying or legitimating a proposed course of action by providing it with an already agreed grounding or basis" (p. 6). The focus of theory is retrospective—after-the-fact. Philosophy, on the other hand, focuses on questions about ordinary everyday human life such as self, identity, relationships, mind, and knowledge. Philosophy involves ongoing analysis, inquiry, and reflection with self and others. It is not about finding truths, scientific or otherwise, nor is it about objects or things: it is about people.

Consistent with this view, the philosophical stance becomes a philosophy of life that informs and forms both a professional and personal way of being in the world: the two cannot be separated.[1] This means that there is congruence in the way that I think about and relate with the people in my life, whether I encounter them in my personal relationships or in my work relationships in various arenas such as therapy, education, and research, and in the world of organizations and businesses. In talking with students who are studying collaborative therapy, they often remark on the surprising influence that the perspective has in their private lives. In particular, they note that they become more attentive and thoughtful about how they relate to others and how this consideration affects the quality of their relationships and their lives.

Characteristics of the Philosophical Stance

The philosophical stance is an authentic and natural way of being that flows from the postmodern perspective of knowledge and language. The stance embodies a belief that communicates to the other through attitude, tone, body gesture, word choice, and timing, among other expressions, the special importance that they hold for you. It conveys to the other that they are valued as a unique human and not as a category of people; that they have something worthy of saying and hearing; that you meet them without prior judgment of past, present, or future; and that you do not hold a secret agenda such as investigative, tactic, directional, or otherwise. When a therapist holds this belief, it forms and shapes the essential nature of their position as they connect, collaborate, and construct with the other in relationship and conversation. The significant word here is *with*, a "withness" process that is intrinsically more participatory and mutual and less hierarchical and dualistic.

The distinctive feature of the philosophical stance is its "interconnected" characteristics that influence the therapist's expertise and participation: creating and fostering a metaphorical "space" for a dialogical conversation and a collaborative relationship. Though each characteristic is identifiable and can be elaborated, not any one of them stand alone. This notion of their interrelatedness is key to collaborative therapy. Importantly, the characteristics are not rules or techniques. Equally important, though the stance may have common identifiable expressions, it is unique to each therapist and human system and to the circumstances and desires of each: collaborative therapy is nonformulaic. Following, I identify and discuss the interconnected characteristics of the philosophical stance that form the heart and spirit of collaborative therapy.

Client and Therapist as Conversational Partners

The participants become *conversational partners* who engage in *collaborative relationships* and in *dialogical conversations* with each other. The notion of *with* cannot be overemphasized as it describes human beings encountering and responding with each other as they reciprocally engage in the social activity and community we call *therapy*. Shotter similarly talks of *"withness (dialogic)-thinking,"* "a form of reflective interaction that involves coming into living contact with an other's living being, with their utterances, their bodily expressions, their words, their 'works'"(2004, p. 150).[2] According to Shotter, *withness* is dynamic: "people's meanings and understandings are *in* their responsive expressions (p. 157). People are responsive with each other; they touch and are touched. Shotter contrasts *withness* with *"aboutness (monologic)-thinking.*[3] Quoting Bakhtin, Shotter iterates: "[in its extreme pure form] another person remains wholly and merely an object of consciousness, and not another consciousness. ... Monologue is finalized and deaf to the other's response, does not expect it and does not acknowledge in it any *decisive* force" (Bakhtin, 1984, p. 293). Tom Andersen (1996), similarly to "withness thinking," speaks of "being touched" by the other's words, being in close contact with their words. Wittgenstein talked of relationship and conversation as going hand-in-hand: the kinds of conversations that we have with each other inform and form the kinds of relationships that we have with each other and vice versa.

The participatory nature of the conversational partnership is of prime significance. To invite the client to participate into a partnership and to foster it requires: (a) meeting and greeting a client in a manner that communicates they are welcomed and respected, (b) showing that you are interested in engaging with them and learning about them as they choose to present themselves, and (c) entering the relationship as a learner who listens and responds by trying to understand the client from their perspective and in their language. The client, along with their agenda and story, take center stage. For instance, what do they want you to know about them, what do they want to talk about, and what story do they want to tell and how.

I find it helpful to use a host–guest metaphor: it is as if the therapist is a host who meets and greets the client as a guest while simultaneously the therapist is a guest in the client's life. I ask my students to think about how they like to be received as a guest. What does the host do that makes them feel welcomed or not, at ease or not, and special or not? What did the quality of the meeting and greeting feel like? These are not rhetorical questions. I do not expect specific answers. Instead, I want the students to think about the sense of their experience in the relationship and conversation and what it communicated to them. I sometimes show students

"The Greeting" by video artist Bill Viola. The viewer sees two women talking and the arrival of a third. The forty-five second video is presented in slow motion (extended to five minutes), allowing the nuances of the greeting to be seen and highlighted. The students consider and reflect on their descriptions and interpretations of what they think they see and discuss the significance of the often unnoticed fleeting moments of meetings and greetings.[4]

It is important to keep in mind, however, that even though we each have what may be thought of as our style, we must be able to spontaneously adapt to each new and continuing relationship and conversation (e.g., conversational partnership) and the circumstance of the occurrence. Each relationship is unique; it forms and evolves, and it mutually readapts and periodically redefines itself over time.

Client as Expert and Therapist as Expert

In collaborative therapy, client knowledge has a prominent position. The client is considered *the* expert on his or her life and is the therapist's teacher. The therapist respects, honors, privileges, and takes the client's reality (e.g., words, beliefs, and story) seriously. This includes what story, or parts of it, clients choose to tell and the way they prefer to tell it—how they choose to express their knowledge. The therapist, for instance, does not have expectations that a story should unfold in a certain order or at a certain pace. The therapist does not expect certain kinds of answers and information and does not make judgments about the same (e.g., that an answer is direct or indirect, or right or wrong and that certain information is important while other is not). Nor does the therapist think in terms of, or look for, theory-suggested linguistic cues that inform problem definitions and solutions. The therapist trusts that clients know themselves best and will talk about what is important to them—as well as when and how. This prominence of client knowledge contrasts with other therapy approaches in which professional knowledge brought in from the outside externally defines problems, solutions, outcomes, and success—creating expert–nonexpert dichotomies.

If you think about it, the therapist is only in relationship and conversation with the client for a split second in the client's life. It is impossible to become fully acquainted with a client in that time period. The therapist is often faced with the temptation and associated risk of filling in the gaps or creating missing parts of a story with their own knowledge. Though some therapists are of the persuasion that they have this expertise, the collaborative therapist relies on the client's expertise. This does not mean that therapist knowledge is not valued; it simply means that the therapist is not considered the expert on the client's life: the client is. Instead of being an expert on the client (including their problem, resources, preferred solutions, etc.) the therapist's competence or expertise is in establishing and fostering an environment and condition that naturally invites collaborative relationships and generative conversational processes. It is in creating a culture in which participants mutually explore and share expertise or knowledge as they strive to understand each other and achieve desired futures. In and through this activity, newness in meanings, understandings, and agency— newness in expertise and knowledge—that has local relevancy and usefulness are collectively created. (Therapist knowing and not-knowing will be discussed more fully below.)

Sometimes a therapist works with more than one member of the client's personal or professional helper network. The therapist multi-partially and simultaneously appreciates, respects, and values each voice, each reality, and each expertise. Differences—the multiple distinct voices and descriptions— that are often viewed as "in need of resolution," are instead viewed as an inherent and infinite source of richness and possibility. In other words, differences are seen as worth exploring and learning about. Through this learning process (the generative process of mutual inquiry as discussed further on) differences are not resolved but instead something comes from them.

Client and Therapist Join in a Mutual Inquiry

The therapist's stance invites the client into a mutual or shared inquiry about the issues or tasks at hand. This inquiry is initiated by the therapist's entering the relationship as a learner (as mentioned above) and the client as the therapist's teacher. The therapist wants to learn and understand the client from the client's perspective and preferences. The therapist wants to learn the client's lived experience and the meanings and understandings associated with it.

I have found it helpful to think of it as if the client begins to hand me a "story ball." As they put the ball toward me, and while their hands are still on it, I gently place my hands on it but I do not take it from them. I begin to participate with them in the storytelling, as I slowly look at/listen to the aspect that they are showing me. I try to learn about and understand their story by responding to them: I am curious, I pose questions, I make comments, and I gesture. In my experience, I find that this therapist learning position acts to spontaneously engage the client as a colearner; it is as if the therapist's curiosity is contagious. In other words, what begins as one-way learning becomes mutual learning as client and therapist coexplore the familiar and codevelop the new, shifting to a mutual inquiry of examining, questioning, wondering, and reflecting with each other.

This begins the more noticeable dynamic dialogical process: a two-way process that involves a back-and-forth, give-and-take, in-there-together connection and activity in which people talk with, not to, each other. In this kind of conversation and relationship all members develop a sense of belonging. And, in my experience, a sense of belonging invites *participation*, which in turn invites *ownership*. Ownership, in turn, invites *shared responsibility*.

I say the "more noticeable process of dialogue" because I think the dialogue between the client and therapist may begin well before they meet face-to-face and engage in relationship and conversation with each other. Each may have a silent inner conversation, expectations, and assumptions about the imagined other and the encounter. These inner conversations may be present when they meet. What might a therapist's greeting communicate to the client? How might the client interpret the greeting? What might the atmosphere of the therapist's physical space communicate? As mentioned above, the nuances and subtleties of meetings and greetings are important; they give a beginning shape to the tone and quality of the relationship and conversations. (I elaborate on the form and process of dialogue in Chapter 3.)

I want to emphasize the connection between the client as the expert, the mutual inquiry, and the not-knowing that is discussed below. I am reminded of the similarity to the Brazilian educator Paulo Freire who favored informal education, education that was based in dialogue and in the lived experience of his "students." He talked about "generative words," "naïve knowledge," and the "power of language" to create. In helping his students learn how to teach the oppressed and the peasants to read, he asked the students to pay attention to the words that the people often used. The students then asked the people about the meanings of the words and engaged them in discussions about the words. Freire called them *generative words*. In the interactive, partnership process of learning and discussing the meanings of the words, where the teacher was both the teacher and the student, new learning developed. Of course, a distinction is that for Freire the educational process and the new learning supported his dedication to social and political change.

Therapist Not-Knowing Approach to Knowledge

Not-knowing refers to the the therapist's view regarding knowledge—for instance, truth, reality, wisdom, and expertise—and a positioning of knowledge. A collaborative therapist takes a skeptical and tentative approach to knowledge, including its substance, its use, its certainty, its risks, and its implications. Following, I identify and discuss four aspects of not-knowing that are critical to the philosophical stance and hence to inviting and fostering collaborative relationships and dialogical conversations.

The idea of preknowing vs. knowing with. Therapists do not believe that they can know another person or their circumstances beforehand. Nor do they believe that they can know the outcome or product ahead of time.

Assuming knowledge of the other in advance has several risks. There is the risk of knowing them as a category or a kind of person, the risk of knowing them as a character in a theoretical script, and the risk of seeking verification of the imagined knowing. Such knowing can inhibit being interested in and learning about the uniqueness of that person as well as preclude becoming familiar with the novelty of their life as they want you to understand it. I strongly believe that to understand the other as fully as possible as a unique person with unique life circumstances requires letting go of knowing in the modernist sense. You must learn about the person from the person.

The way the therapist thinks about knowledge. The knowledge that each participant brings to a relationship and conversation is equally valued. Valued does not imply agreement. It means respecting, learning more, and trying to understand. In genuine dialogue, what each person brings to a conversation will be influenced and changed in some way. The risk of influence and change applies to all participants including the therapist. Therapists, therefore, remain ever willing and able to have their knowledge (including professional and personal values and biases) ignored, questioned, and changed.

The intent with which the therapist uses knowledge. The therapist introduces knowledge as a way of participating in and fostering a conversation. In line with the earlier discussed belief that knowledge cannot be sent (or received) to one person from another, therapists do not have an investment in privileging their knowledge over another's or persuading them of it. Knowledge, what ever its form—questions, comments, opinions, or suggestions—is offered as food for thought and dialogue, as a way of participating in the conversation. It is not offered with the intent of being authoritative, objective, or instructive.

The manner in which the therapist offers knowledge. Therapists honor, make room for, and give authority to the client's voice and do not overshadow, divert, or subjugate it with their own knowing. Knowledge is introduced in a tentative and provisional manner. As well, the therapist pays attention to the timing, manner, and intonation with which knowledge is introduced. The introduction must be in sync with the client and the conversation at the moment.

Not-knowing is sometimes understood as diminishing the therapist's full participation in dialogue. This is not the case. The therapist does not withhold or deny his or her voice, but just the opposite; the therapist can offer anything into the conversation. There is no intention or need to holdback, but what is offered must be considered in light of the aspects mentioned above. Not-knowing is also sometimes understood as a therapist's becoming a blank slate, pretending ignorance, or forgetting what has been learned from books or experience. Likewise, this is not the case. Our knowing, our history, and our biases are always with us and part of our sphere of influence.

Maintaining a not-knowing position and living with the uncertainty that accompanies it is vital for the freedom of expression and for the natural unplanned paths of dialogues. Not-knowing is equally critical to the maintenance of inner- or self-dialogue and to not slipping into monologue. (I discuss monologue later.)

A word of caution is warranted here. I do not suggest that all of a sudden a therapist decides to introduce his or her knowledge or is always aware of its being introduced. All of a conversation and its participants exist in and flow from already existing knowledge. Therapists always participate with their knowledge, and like client knowledge, it is continually being introduced in the course of the give-and-take of conversation. (*See* Anderson, 2005 for a fuller discussion of not-knowing.)

Being Public

Therapists often learn to operate from invisible private inner thoughts—professionally, personally, theoretically, or experientially informed inner talk—understandings such as diagnoses, judgments, or hypotheses. These thoughts can influence how the therapist listens and hears, and can guide the therapist's questions and responses. From a collaborative stance, therapists are open and make their invisible thoughts visible. The therapist may share any idea—for instance, an opinion, question, or suggestion—with the client. The intent of the sharing or being public with one's inner thoughts is to offer them as food for thought and dialogue. It is not a matter of what therapists can or cannot say, comment on, or ask about; rather, what is important in fostering dialogue is the manner, attitude, tone, and timing in which they do so.

Making private thoughts public invites what Bakhtin (1981) refers to as responsive understanding. He suggests that, "A passive understanding of linguistic meaning is not understanding at all" (p. 281). Shotter, influenced by Wittgenstein, suggests a relational-responsive kind of understanding. In other words, understanding cannot take place unless both the speaker–listener and the listener–speaker are responsive to each other. An unresponsive inner conversation is in danger of leading to missed-understanding or understanding that does not fit with that of the speaker or their intent (e.g., the client's).

Putting private inner talk or thoughts into spoken words produces something other than the thought or understanding itself. The expression of the thought organizes and reforms it; therefore, it is altered in the process of articulation. The presence of the client and the context, along with other factors, affects the words chosen and the manner in which they are presented.

As well, the client then has the opportunity to respond to the therapist's inner thought. The client's response—in the many forms that it may take, such as expressing interest, confirming, questioning, or disregarding—will, in turn, affect the therapist's inner thoughts.

When a therapist does not put their inner thoughts into spoken words, it is possible that therapists' inner talk, as well as their speaking, will become monological and risk contributing to the potential, creation, or maintenance of therapist–client monologue. Keeping therapists' inner talk public minimizes the risk of the therapist being ensnared in monological inner and outer talk. By monologic, I refer to the same thought continuing, like having a tune in one's head that plays over and over again. I have elsewhere talked about dueling monologues or realities: when one or both parties put energy into further defending or persuading the other of their view (Anderson, 1987, 1997; Anderson & Goolishian, 1988). The monologic voices become like skyscrapers side-by-side without windows, doors, or bridges—each closed to the other. In such instances, the conversation reaches a standstill; there is no longer the criss-crossing or cross-fertilization of either the therapist's or the client's perspective that is present when people are in the process of trying to understand one another. Put differently, dialogue or "withness thinking" can easily collapse into monologue or "aboutness thinking."

I do not want to suggest that all private thoughts must be spoken in a session. This would be impossible. The important thing is to beware of the risk of monologue, how what is heard and spoken is filtered through it, and how to shift back to inner dialogue. I suggest to my students that if they have difficulty putting their monologic thoughts into spoken words that they might speak them to or from the voice of an imaginary person in the therapy room; take a break during a session; or do something nontherapy-related between sessions such as reading a book, going to a movie, or talking with a colleague. I do not offer these suggestions with the expectation that they will follow them but to help them begin to access their own creativity regarding what might help them shift an inner monologue to dialogue. Each therapist will have their unique way of dealing with monologic inner talk, and how they do so will vary from client to client and situation to situation as well.

A note of clarification: I use monologue to make a distinction. I think that everything is dialogical to some extent, but at times it may not seem so.

Client and Therapist Transforming Together

In the space and process of a collaborative relationship and a dialogical conversation, therapist and client become mutual participants who try to understand and respond to each other from within the conversation and the relationship. When the therapist is involved in this kind of common and dynamic activity, the therapist like the client is shaped and reshaped—formed and transformed. I find Shotter's (1993, p. 9) words capture the meaning that I want to convey: "For to talk in new ways, is to 'construct' new forms of social relation, and to construct new forms of social relation (of self–other relationships) is to construct new ways of being (of person–world relations) for ourselves." Shotter (2005, pp. 23–24), in referring to Wittgenstein's style of writing, further speaks to this idea:

> And it is in our own active responding to his expressions in this way that we can find ourselves unexpectedly confronted with novel connections within our experiences that we had not previously noticed … that we come to see the relevant circumstances in a new light.

Therapist and client construct something new with each other. The something new is not an outcome or a product at the end of the encounter. It continually emerges throughout the duration of the encounter while at the same time informing it and continuing afterwards. That is, each conversation will be a springboard for future ones, inside and outside the therapy room, for client and therapist. When client and therapist meet again, each will have been influenced by the in-between inner and outer conversations and neither will be in the same place where they left off. (I address the generating and transforming process of dialogue more fully in Chapter 3.)

Trusting Uncertainty

Being a collaborative therapist who becomes a conversational partner, who values the other's expertise, who joins in a mutual inquiry, and who forgoes the security of preformed knowledge, invites and entails uncertainty. When a therapist accompanies clients on a journey and walks along side them, the newness (e.g., solutions, resolutions, outcomes, or futures) develops from within the local conversation. It is mutually created and is uniquely fitting to the person(s) involved. How that transformation occurs and what it looks like will vary from client to client, from therapist to therapist, and from situation to situation. Put simply, there is no way to know with sureness the direction in which a story will unfold or the outcome of therapy when involved in a dialogical conversation and collaborative relationship. Trusting uncertainty involves taking a risk and being open to unforeseen change.

Collaborative therapy, thus, may be thought of as improvisational or making it up as client and therapist go along together. It is not making it up in the sense that anything goes. The therapist is always responding to the client, to what the occasion calls for, and in the manner called for. This requires trust in the client and trust in oneself. Interesting, I might add, I was surprised when students, during an interview with a researcher who was studying their experiences of learning collaborative therapy, talked about the certainty of uncertainty. They had concluded through their experiences that "there is certainty in uncertainty," referring to the unexpected enhancement of their self-confidence, self-competency, and self-agency when they began to trust uncertainty and let go of the need to know and, for instance, the pressure to ask the right questions or have the best solution. They expressed a newfound sense of autonomy, flexibility, and creativity and a release from the constraints of certainty to the possibilities of uncertainty.

Perhaps a caveat is warranted. Client expertise, therapist not-knowing, and uncertainty do not suggest that a therapist acts or talks without confidence, withholds response to a client's request for answers, or ignores a client's need for certainty. Instead, what I want to emphasize is the manner in which therapists position themselves and respond that invites the client to join with them and that in turn invites and enhances the client's self-agency.

Therapy as Everyday, Ordinary Life

Therapy from a collaborative perspective places importance on everyday understandings that are embedded in history, culture, and linguistic practices. That is, therapists are more interested in the client's understandings and than in their own professional ones. Given this, therapy then more resembles everyday conversation and its ordinary speech, and the intimate connections that most people prefer. As such, collaborative therapy can be characterized as less formal than perhaps is usually so in the institution of therapy. It also challenges institutional traditions such as boundaries and self-disclosure as critical to proper and successful therapy. Instead, importance is placed on the client and therapist as human beings involved in human interaction, hopefully minimizing the risk of the therapist's contributing to social and power inequalities. This does not mean chit-chatting without aim or being casual friends. Therapy conversations and relationships, of course, occur within a particular context and with a particular agenda.

Simply put: a client wants help and a therapist wants to help. I do not think of what clients want help with as "problems" as this word carries so much inherited baggage such as problems are dysfunctions or deficits to be fixed or solved (Anderson, 1997). And, as mentioned earlier, there is also the risk of making across-the-board assumptions about problems and slipping into "aboutness thinking" and monologue. In this same vein, clients are not categorized as types or kinds or by degrees such as "easy" or "difficult." Each client is simply thought to present with an everyday, ordinary life situation (e.g., a difficulty, a misery, a dilemma, a challenge, a pain, or a decision) that any of us could similarly encounter. Each client, each situation is unique, and so I will always meet a stranger and the unfamiliar. And in this sense, the ordinary becomes extraordinary.

In summary, if a therapist assumes the philosophical stance that is the heart and spirit of collaborative therapy, they will naturally and spontaneously act and talk in ways that create a space for, invite, and foster conversations and relationships in which clients and therapists "connect, collaborate, and construct" with each other (Anderson, 1992, 1997). Because the philosophical stance becomes a natural and spontaneous way of being as a therapist, theory is not put into practice and there are no therapist techniques and rules, as we know them. Instead, the characteristics give emphasis to a set of values and their implications for action. The philosophical stance is the "tone" of collaborative relationships and dialogical conversations as suggested above: a particular way in which we orient ourselves to be, talk, and act with another person that invites the other into the shared engagement and joint action of mutual inquiry—the process of generative dialogue and transformation (Anderson, 1997, 2003). In other words, the person takes precedence over techniques and rules: human beings are in relationship and conversation with each other.

Competency and Possibilities

In my experience, and corroborated in conversations with therapists and students, practicing collaboratively can enrich one's professional and personal life. Of note, therapists and students report an enhanced sense of competency and expanded possibilities for their clients and themselves. Some report an untapped excitement and new initiative for learning. They become more wondering, questioning, and curious. Similar to clients' experiences, they report a newfound sense of freedom as a therapist and sense of hope for their clients (Anderson, 1997). Most significant and inspirational, they become members of an international life-long learning community that provides support and sustenance.

About Collaborative Therapy: Distinctive Features

Collaborative therapy has several distinctive features that, combined, make it more of an open-ended therapy and allow a more improvisational therapist style. Some of these features are:

It is evolving, dynamic, and nonformulaic. Collaborative therapy is based in a reflexive process in which its assumptions inform its practice, and its practice informs its assumptions (or a search for new ones and vice versa). Consistent with postmodern discourse, the approach is dynamic, inviting infinite variety and adaptation, having the potential to correspond with macro and micro societal changes and to fit with the emerging value placed on the voices of marginalized and oppressed persons. It is also distinctively nonformulaic, offering practitioners and their clients the opportunity to tailor the application of its assumptions to their unique needs and circumstances, and to their institutional and cultural contexts.

The focus is shifted from the individual or the family to person(s)-in-relationship. The approach is based in an ideological shift that has applicability across people, situations, and contexts. Its usefulness is not determined by the social system (individual or family), the person's role in the system, the problem, or the goal. Its usefulness is determined by the therapist's value of its central assumptions and their ability to live the philosophical stance that flow from them.

Application extends beyond the therapy room. The approach has utility in systems and contexts other than therapy. Therapists take the assumptions of collaborative therapy and the philosophical stance to other systems that they often work in such as education (e.g., teaching and supervising) and organizations (e.g., consulting and team building) and extend their collaborative practices to include activities like life coaching and mentoring. Other professionals, such those in medicine, law, and community organization, report that the approach has proven useful in their practices.

(E)valuation becomes part of everyday practice. The practitioner and client (e)valuate their work together as they go along with each other. What they learn is used to inform their work, appreciating and building on what is useful and reconsidering what is not (Anderson, 1997). This is part of the assurance that the therapy and other collaborative practices are appropriately tailored and have continuous utility for the client.

Therapist burnout is reduced. Therapists report renewed appreciation and respect for their clients and renewed enthusiasm and energy for their work. They report a discovery of untapped or unknown creativity. They also report that they are more open and sharing of their work with colleagues and find support in doing so. Combined, these experiences influence reduction in burnout.

Clients and therapist have a sense of freedom and hope. Clients have a sense of belonging to, participating in, and owning their therapy. This, in turn, invites shared responsibility for the process and the outcome. The outcome—whether it is something tangible and doable, or whether it is simply a sense of something like, a sense of freedom or hope—strikingly becomes a feeling that I, that we, can go on from here.

Relationships with colleagues are enhanced. Therapists report that as they live the philosophical stance with their colleagues, as they do with their clients, they are better able to appreciate, be curious about, and be open to differences (*See* St. George and Wulff, Chapter 24 this volume). Supported by the belief that there is no one or right way to view or do any thing, potential or once awkward and tense relationships become less troublesome, more compatible, and sometimes even enjoyable ones.

Effectiveness

The history of collaborative therapy attests to its effectiveness. Early on, the approach evolved as a therapy of last resort in practice settings in which "challenged" therapists worked with "challenging" clients. These included chronic treatment failures, patients in outpatient and inpatient psychiatric contexts, and the often-mandated clients of public agencies such as children's protective services, women's shelters, and adult and juvenile probation (Anderson, 1991; Anderson & Goolishian, 1986, 1991; Anderson & Levin, 1997, 1998; Levin, Reese, Raser, and Niles, 1986).

Early evidence of the effectiveness of collaborative therapy is mostly focused on the therapy experiences of clients, therapists, and students, and it is mostly anecdotal and based in qualitative research.[5] The usefulness of the approach is illustrated in articles on child abuse and other types of domestic violence, eating disorders, substance abuse, and supervision (Anderson, 1997; Anderson & Levin, 1997, 1998; Anderson, Burney, & Levin, 1999; Bava, 2001; Chang, 1999; Levin, 1992; London, Ruiz, Gargollo, and MC, 1998; Roberts, 1990; St. George and Wulff, 1999; Swim, Helms, Plotkin, and Bettye, 1998).

In departure from the usual practice of therapist-voiced therapy success, collaborative therapists and researchers have invited client accounts of therapy (London, Ruiz, Gargollo & MC, 1998; Swim, Helms, Plotkin, and Bettye, 1998; Weisenburger, 2003). Qualitative research studies have looked at the effectiveness of collaborative therapy and an analysis of whether therapists' behaviors and attitudes were consistent with their therapy philosophy (Gehart-Brooks & Lyle, 1999; Swint, 1995). Some have studied the application of the ideas in supervision and education (Anderson, 1984; Bava, 2001; St. George, 1994; Tinez, 2002) and in community work (Weisenburger, 2003). Finnish psychologist Jaakko Seikkula and his colleagues have aptly demonstrated the effectiveness of an open-dialogue approach through a quantitative/qualitative research project with a five-year follow-up with psychotic patients and their families (Seikkula, 1993; Seikkula, Aaltonen, Alakare, Haarakangas, Keranen, and Sutela, 1995; also see Haarakangas, Seikkula, Alakare, and Aaltonen Chapter 14 of this volume).

What I find most exciting is the growing number of students around the world who have chosen collaborative therapy (or a collaborative language system approach) as the subject matter of their masters' theses and doctoral dissertations and collaborative inquiry as their methodology. Specifically, topics have focused on the usefulness of collaborative therapy with a variety of clinical populations (e.g., children with somatic illnesses, young women with eating disorders, and grief) and with work in communities. Some have concentrated on therapist's descriptions of the influence of a collaborative perspective on their professional and personal lives and some on their own experience of learning a collaborative approach.

Where Are We Going?

I am often asked, "Where are you going from here?" and "What's after postmodern?" I respond, "I don't know for sure, but I have some ideas." Postmodern is still in its infancy in regards to its usefulness in our broader intellectual and social cultures. Unlimited, yet-to-be-tapped challenges, possibilities, and opportunities will undoubtedly deepen and broaden the postmodern perspective and its applicability in psychotherapy and beyond. I am currently interested in increasing my exploration of its value in the domains of education, research, organizational systems, and leadership development, and in larger institutional and social structures (Anderson, 2000, 1998; Anderson & Burney, 1997; Anderson & Swim, 1994). I have expanded my long-time interest in the voices of therapy clients to include the voices of learners in educational systems and people in businesses and organizations. In the business arena, for instance, I am interviewing women who are executive assistants to CEOs to learn from them about their roles, relationships, and experiences in their organizations, what advice they have to help others in this same career track to succeed, and what advice they have to help bosses better utilize the talents of their assistants. I am also interviewing women who are successful business owners to learn what they believe has contributed to their success and what wisdom they can share with other women business owners. I am interested in what collaborative therapists have to offer other professionals who are interested in collaborative practices such as physicians, lawyers, and the clergy. Inspired by my colleagues at Grupo Campos Elíseos in Mexico City, I am interested in the relevance and use of art and literature in all my practices. And finally, I am interested in the ways in which through collaboration and withness, we can develop less violent and more peaceful ways to live and go on with each other.[6] All in response to, in one way or another, my ever-present question: *How can professionals create the kinds of relationships and conversations with their clients that allow all parties to access their creativities and develop possibilities where none seemed to exist before?*

Endnotes

1. *See* St. George and Wulff in this volume.
2. Lynn Hoffman talks about "the art of withness" in Chapter 5.
3. Over the years I have found *dialogue* and *monologue* as having useful distinctions. (*See* Anderson & Goolishian, 1988 and Anderson, 1997.)
4. *See* www.billviola.com

5. Readers engaged in research on the effectiveness of collaborative therapy, or who know of others who are, are invited to contact the editors and we will place the information on a website.

6. I am particularly inspired by the work that my generous colleague Tom Andersen is doing around the world toward this aim and by the community work, with its social justice emphasis, of colleagues in South Africa and in the South American countries of Argentina, Brazil, and Peru.

References

Anderson, H. (1984). *The new epistemology in family therapy: Implications for training family therapists.* Doctoral dissertation. Union Institute: University Microfilms.

Anderson, H. (1987). Therapeutic impasses: A break-down in conversation. Adapted from paper presented at Grand Rounds, Department of Psychiatry, Massachusetts General Hospital, Boston, MA, April, 1986 and at the Society for Family Therapy Research, Boston, MA, October 1986.

Anderson, H. (1991a). Opening the door for change through continuing conversations. In T. Todd & M. Selekman (Eds.), *Family therapy approaches with adolescent substance abusers* (pp. 176–189). Needham, MA: Allyn and Bacon.

Anderson, H. (1991b, October). "Not-knowing": An essential element of therapeutic conversation. Paper presented at the American Association of Marriage and Family Therapy Annual Conference Plenary, Creating a Language of Change, Dallas, TX.

Anderson, H. (1997). *Conversation, language and possibilities: A postmodern approach to therapy.* New York: Basic Books.

Anderson, H. (1998). Collaborative learning communities. In S. McNamee & J.K. Gergen (Eds.), *Relational responsibility.* Newbury Park, CA: Sage Publications.

Anderson, H. (2000). Supervision as a collaborative learning community. *American Association for Marriage and Family Therapy Supervision Bulletin* (Fall), 7–10.

Anderson, H. (2003). Social construction therapies. In G. Weeks, T.L. Sexton, M. Robbins (Eds.), *Handbook of family therapy.* New York: Brunner-Routledge.

Anderson, H. (2005). The myth of not-knowing. *Family Process, 44*(4), 497–504.

Anderson, H. & Burney, P. (1997). Collaborative inquiry: A postmodern approach to organizational consultation. *Human Systems: The Journal of Systemic Consultation and Management, 7*(2–3), 177–188.

Anderson, H., Burney, P., & Levin, S.B. (1999). A postmodern collaborative approach to therapy. In D. Lawson (Ed.), *Casebook in family therapy.* Pacific Grove, CA: Brooks/Cole.

Anderson, H. & Goolishian, H. (1986). Systems consultation to agencies dealing with domestic violence. In L. Wynne, S. McDaniel, & T. Weber (Eds.), *The Family therapist as systems consultant.* New York: Guilford Press.

Anderson, H. & Goolishian, H. (1988). Human systems as linguistic systems: Evolving ideas about the implications for theory and practice. *Family Process, 27,* 371–393.

Anderson, H. & Goolishian, H. (1991). Supervision as collaborative conversation: Questions and reflections. In H. Brandau (Ed.), *Von der supervision zur systemischen vision.* Salzburg: Otto Muller Verlag.

Anderson, H. & Levin, S.B. (1997). Collaborative conversations with children: Country clothes and city clothes. In C. Smith & D. Nylund (Eds.), *Narrative therapies with children.* New York: Guildford Press.

Anderson, H. & Levin, S.B. (1998). Generative conversations: A postmodern approach to conceptualizing and working with human systems. In M. Hoyt (Ed.), *The handbook of constructive therapies: Innovative approaches from leading practitioners.* San Francisco, CA: Jossey-Bass.

Anderson, H. & Swim, S. (1994). Supervision as collaborative conversation: Combining the supervisor and the supervisee voices. *Journal of Systemic Therapies, 14*(2), 1–13.

Andersen, T. (1996). *Language is not innocent.* In F.W. Kaslow (Ed.), *The handbook of relational diagnosis and dysfunctional family patterns.* Oxford, England: John Wiley & Sons.

Bakhtin, M. (1981). *The dialogic imagination: Four essays.* (M. Holquist, Ed., and C. Emerson & M. Holquist, Trans.) Austin: University of Texas Press.

Bakhtin, M.M. (1984). *Problems of Dostoevsky's Poetics. Edited and trans. by Caryl Emerson.* Minneapolis: University of Minneapolis Press.

Bava, S. (2001). *Transforming performances: An inter-researcher's hypertextual journey in a postmodern community.* Doctoral dissertation, Virginia Polytechnic Institue and State University, Blacksburg, VA. Available http://scholar.lib.vt.edu/theses/available/etd=01062002-234843.

Chang, J. (1999). Collaborative therapies with young children. *Journal of Systemic Therapies,* *18*(2), 44–64.

Gehart-Brooks, D.R. & Lyle, R.R. (1999). Client and therapist perspectives of change in collaborative language systems: An interpretive ethnography. *Journal of Systemic Therapies,* *18*(4), 58–77.

Levin, S.B. (1992). Hearing the unheard: Stories of women who have been battered. *Dissertation Abstracts International.* T.U.I. (Doctoral dissertation, Union Institute, 1992.) *53*, 123.

Levin, S., Raser, J., Niles, C., & Reese, A. (1986). Beyond families: The clinical implications of working in and with problem-determined systems. *Journal of Strategic and Systemic Therapies,* *5*(4), 62–69.

London, S., Ruiz, G., Gargollo, M., & MC. (1998). Clients' voices: A collection of clients' accounts. *Journal of Systemic Therapies,* *17*(4), 61–71.

Seikkula, J. (1993). The aim of therapy is to benerarate dialogue: Bakhtin and Vygotsky in family session. *Human Systems: The Journal of Systemic Consultation & Management,* *4,* 33–48.

Seikkula, J., Aaltonen, J., Alakare, B., Haarakangas, K., Keranen, J., & Sutela, M. (1995). Treating psychosis by means of open dialogue. In S. Friedman (Ed.), *The reflecting team in action: Collaborative practice in family therapy* (pp. 62–81). New York: Guilford.

Shotter, J. 1993a. *Conversational realities: Constructing life through language.* London: Sage.

Shotter, J. (2004). *On the edge of social constructionism: "Withness"-thinking versus "aboutness"-thinking.* London: KCC Foundation.

Shotter, J. (2005). *Wittgenstein in practice: His philosophy of beginnings, and beginnings, and beginnings.* London: KCC Foundation.

St. George, S.A. (1994). Multiple formats in the collaborative application of the "as if" technique in the process of family therapy supervision. *Dissertation Abstracts International.* (Doctoral dissertation, Univ. of Iowa, 1994.) *55*, 3006.

St. George, S. (1994). Using "as if" process in family therapy supervision. *The Family Journal: Counseling and Therapy for Couples and Families,* *4*(4), 357–365.

St. George, S. & Wulff, D. (1999). Integrating the client's voice within case reports. *Journal of Systemic Therapies,* *18*(2), 3–13.

Swim, S., Helms, S., Plotkin, S., & Bettye (1998). Multiple voices: Stories of rebirth, heroines, new opportunities and identities. *Journal of Systemic Therapies,* *17*(4), 61–71.

Swint, J.A. (1995). Clients' experience of therapeutic change: A qualitative study. Doctoral dissertation, Texas Women's University, *Dissertation Abstracts International,* *56*, 1123.

Roberts, H. (1990). *The experiences of black families who are involuntarily involved in family therapy treatment.* Unpublished doctoral dissertation, Union Institute, Cincinnati, OH.

Tinez, D. (2002). *Relational transformation in family therapy supervision: An emerging inquiry in a postmodern collaborative learning community.* Unpublished doctoral dissertation, Iowa State University.

Weisenburger, G.A. (2003) *Dialogical conversations in community transformation.* Thesis, Universidad de las Americas, A.C., Mexico City, Mexico.

Other Voices: Netting and Expressing

CHAPTER 5

The Art of "Withness": A New Bright Edge

LYNN HOFFMAN

> Living utterance becomes an active participant in social dialogue.
> If we imagine such a word in the form of light, then the living and
> unrepeatable play of colors and light on the facets of the image that
> it constructs can be explained as the spectral dispersion of the ray
> word, in an atmosphere filled with the alien words, value judgments,
> and accents through which the ray passes on its way to the object; the
> social atmosphere of the word, that atmosphere that surrounds the
> object, makes the facets of the image sparkle. (Bakhtin, 1981, p. 277)

The idea that propelled this title was given to me by Tom Andersen who
kept telling me that I must come to the north of Norway in the "Darktime."
So he invited me for the first day of spring, just as the sun was going to
appear. The occasion was a meeting of Andersen's "Northern Network,"
composed of teams handling acute breakdowns from hospitals in countries all across Europe's northern rim. Andersen took me to his top floor
office at the University of Tromsø the morning of the conference, and out
the window, I saw the first rays. They appeared in the cleft of two snow-
covered mountains and then faded away, followed by colors of pink, mauve,
and gold which lit up the edges of landscape and sky.

From time to time as I have passed through the history of this field,
I have been given the chance to see such first rays. And I have in some
way known or guessed which newcomer approaches would establish
themselves and persist. One is taking shape now, like a ship hull-up on

the horizon. It has already been referred to as the "conversational" or "dialogical" therapies, terms used by Roger Lowe (2005) in a recent article. Lowe distinguishes between approaches that use "structured questions" like Narrative and Solution-focused work, as aids to practice, and what he calls, following John Shotter (Shotter & Katz, 1998), a "striking moments" approach, which do not. I am interested in establishing a train of forebears for this last effort, which is now branching off into the future in interesting ways but includes some distinguished ancestors.

The work of these forebears was foreshadowed by Gregory Bateson (1972) who, at the end of his life, emphasized the preverbal communication styles of what he called the "Creatura," or the world of the living. Putting these ideas to work, Harlene Anderson and Harry Goolishian (1986) took a sharp turn away from purposeful interventions in their "not knowing" stance. Then Tom Andersen (1991) introduced the "reflecting team," which inspired those of us like Peggy Penn and myself who were trying to work in a less instrumental way.

More recently, we have been introduced to a cornucopia of philosophical treasures based on the writings of Ludwig Wittgenstein and Mikhail Bakhtin. We have a new "in-house philosopher" in social thinker John Shotter (1993), who has described how these writers can help us understand what Bakhtin (1990) calls "dialogicality." We are beginning to have new terms for what we do, like Tom Andersen's idea of "withness practices." We also have some unusual examples of these ideas embedded in the work of innovators such as Jaakko Seikkula and his colleagues in Finland, who have been developing an approach called "Open Dialogue," joined by Mary Olson (Seikkula & Olson, 2003), who is teaching dialogic network therapy at the Smith School of Social Work. Finally, let me mention Chris Kinman in Vancouver, who has been experimenting with a "language of gifts" that is producing entire system change in local areas. But let me go back in time, and talk about the early genius who started it all: Gregory Bateson.

Bateson and Syllogisms in Metaphor

There were several philosophical pioneers in the last century who made it their life's work to study how the forms of Western discourse entangle us. The two most important ones, in my view, were Ludwig Wittgenstein and Gregory Bateson. In Wittgenstein's (1953) famous book of arguments with himself, *Philosophical Investigations*, he explores ways to get out of the invisible linguistic trap he called the "fly bottle." His work has generated an industry of explainers. Bateson's writings have not yet called forth such an industry, but he took on a similar charge in describing a style of prelinguistic communication that animals use and that is common to religion, humor, some forms of madness, playfulness, and art.

This type of communication, Bateson held, applied specifically to what Jung called the "Creatura," the world of the living, as opposed to the "Pleroma," meaning Newton's world of force and mass. The Pleroma has no mental process, no names, no classes. The Creatura, on the other hand, is founded on pattern and communicates through "as if" language, using similitude and metaphor in a variety of embedded and embodied ways. Bateson's daughter Catherine (Bateson & Bateson, 1987) tells us that, at the end of his life, her father was fascinated with what he was calling "syllogisms of metaphor." This idea, she explained, was tied in with the central concern of his research, which was "the beginning of a Creatural grammar" (Bateson & Bateson, 1987, p. 192).

So what might that mean? In contrasting the truths of logic with the truths of metaphor, Bateson explains that classical logic describes causal word structures called *syllogisms* that are built on classification and which follow the form "If this is true, then that is true." If Socrates is a man, and if all men die, then Socrates will die. But there is another word structure that Bateson describes that is built on likeness, the example for which is "Grass dies, men die, [therefore] men are grass." Logicians disapprove of this kind of syllogism because it does not make sense (they call it "affirming the consequent"), but Bateson believed that this formula indicated the way the natural world communicated. He fires off this ringing salvo:

> The whole of animal behavior, the whole of repetitive anatomy, and the whole of biological evolution—each of these vast realms is within itself linked together by syllogisms in grass—whether the logicians like it or not. . . . And it became evident that metaphor was not just pretty poetry, it was not either good or bad logic, but was in fact the logic on which the biological world had been built, the main characteristic and organizing glue of this world of mental process that I have been trying to sketch for you. . . ." (Bateson & Bateson, 1987, pp. 26–30)

This statement thrilled me. It felt accurate, and it justified the enormous importance my community placed on sensory pathways and emotional gesturing in the work we did. It also justified the efforts of philosophers like Wittgenstein, mentioned above, in not only searching out an alternative logic but finding that it could be strikingly different from the classical logic that Western thinkers had come to see as the norm. The nonverbal, analogical vision of Bateson seemed especially pertinent to the project of psychotherapy, because it indicated that advice and expertise were not enough; you had to reach for connection at levels that lay beyond the scope of words.

I felt that Bateson was saying that there is a hidden language known to animals and mad people and artists. Current researchers in neurology

(Damasio, 1994) have pointed to a specific area of the brain—the amygdala (also called the "emotional brain")—saying that this is the brain's "smoke alarm," because this is where the intense memories are stored that warn us away from bad things and toward good ones. It makes sense to believe that messages directed toward this area have to use this ancient grammar of nature or they will not be recognized. Of course, when Bateson talked about syllogisms in metaphor, he didn't mean that we should literally use figures of speech, but rather that sensory and feeling-level channels must be used to carry messages of life importance, as the channels of reason and logic are untrustworthy.

As an example of the still-unfolding nature of this tradition, let me refer to a recent article by Peter Rober (2005) who suggests that "not knowing" has two aspects: the receptive one of listening and the reflective one of responding. He offers the Bakhtinian notion of the "dialogical self" in order to include those voices that are elements of a therapist's inner and outer thoughts. In taking up the term "generous listening" from Lois Shawver (Hoffman, 2002), it struck me that there is a parallel operation that includes what you might call "connected speaking": ideas and reactions that come up from what I call the "deep well," and when shared often turn out to be evidence of increased psychic attunement.

I also want to say that such messages can break through private walls. Why is this emphasis on the wider web so important for a therapist? Because it turns us away from looking at individuals and their inner life, which is what modernist psychology trains us to look at, and points instead to the threads that link everybody to the social web. If you stay with modernist psychology, you will forever be trying to see your job as a matter of building logging roads, putting up bridges, and various other engineering projects. If you move to a postmodern psychology, you have to jump, like Alice, into the pool of tears with the other creatures. This situation is a great equalizer and carries some dangers, but it is the only source of information with the power to transform.

My Three Pillars of Wisdom

But let me move to what I call my Three Pillars of Wisdom, the three major anchors of the kind of work my community and I do. These are the practices that have signaled the shift from a modernist view that sees emotional problems as within-person phenomena like medical complaints, and the postmodern view that they are relational and dialogic in nature. The first pillar is the idea of "not knowing" brought into the field by Harry Goolishian and Harlene Anderson. I once asked Harlene if they took it from the writings of the French philosopher Gaston Bachelard (1964), who speaks of "non-knowing" and defines it "not as a form of ignorance but a difficult transcendence of knowledge." However, I was wrong. Harlene told me that they began to use the phrase because their students would ask them their thoughts or hypotheses about clients: Why did the client do this or that? Didn't they think the client should do x, y, or z? They would always say they "didn't know" and would suggest that the best person to talk with about their curiosities was the client. Finally, they made a principle out of "not knowing," to the scorn and derision of many in the field. But this simple concept made a difference in basic stance that was extremely powerful.

A related warning against "knowing" comes to us from French philosopher Jean Francois Lyotard. In a short book called *Driftworks* (1984) he asks:

> Where do you criticize from? Don't you see that criticizing is still knowing, knowing better? That the critical relation still falls within the sphere of knowledge, of "realization" and thus of the assumption of power? Critique must be drifted out of. Better still: Drifting is in itself the end of all critique. (p. 13)

My second pillar is the practice called initially the "reflecting team," contributed by Tom Andersen (1987) and his colleagues in Tromsø. This format challenged the methods favored by early family therapists, undermining the one-way screen and other devices that walled the family off from the professionals dealing with them. Asking a family to comment on the reflections of the professionals was even more unheard of. It was Harlene Anderson who suggested to Tom Andersen that he broaden the term to "reflecting process," feeling that to link this format to a specific method was limiting.

The third pillar is "witnessing," a concept that partially came out of the reflecting team and which I call, following Harlene Anderson, "witnessing process." There is some internal history of the field to report here. Soon after Tom Andersen went public with his reflecting format, narrative therapist Michael White adopted it, too. In line with his preference for anthropological rather than psychological language, White (1995) used anthropologist Barbara Meyerhoff's term "definitional ceremony" to describe it. He saw that having an appreciative audience for any therapeutic interview strongly reinforced the creation of a more inspiring identity. His experiments with this form led him to create what he called an "outsider witness registry," where persons who had already worked with him could be invited back to help others in similar situations.

As soon as I began to use reflecting teams, I, too, was struck by the layering power of the many voices and groupings it put into play. It was a prismatic endeavor, where one moment's witnesser became another moment's receiver. But White's version threatened to muddy the waters.

As with the reflecting team, we needed a term that did not belong to any one person or school. "Witnessing process" was a suitably large tent under which many of us could fit, regardless of our therapeutic allegiances.

And here I would like to thank philosopher/clinician Lois Shawver (2005) for a new insight. She has spent years studying Wittgenstein's ideas and applying them to her views of postmodern therapy. Recently, during a conversation on her "Postmodern Therapies List Serve Discussion Group," she made a distinction between "theories" and "language games" (which is Wittgenstein's [1953] invention), saying that the latter is more useful to those of us trying to describe therapy approaches because it chooses such a specific set of descriptors: words, phrases, or practices. To invoke large abstract categories like postmodernism in defining a specific therapy approach puts the discourse on the wrong level and confuses the matter. In regard to White's use of reflecting and witnessing, it feels better to me to say that his ideas come out of a different language game than Andersen's do, rather than saying that White is a deconstructionist and Andersen a social constructionist, for example. But this is a digression—let me go on to some of the novel ideas which are asking for our attention.

The Contributions of John Shotter

A primary source of this new bright edge I am talking about comes from John Shotter (1993), a postmodern social thinker whose writings on the nature of dialogical communication have become increasingly relevant to the relational therapies. He has been creating a little intellectual whirlpool around the ideas of two philosophers in particular—Mikhail Bakhtin and Ludwig Wittgenstein, and applying them to clinical practice. In addition, he and Tom Andersen have been giving workshops together, and this has been a happy development.

For my part, I felt that Shotter was our in-house philosopher. He was leading us away from the belief that we could change social reality by purely linguistic means. In its place was a picture of communication as a more bustling, jostling enterprise. Shotter (2005a) speaks of "embodied knowing" vs. "language-based knowing" and describes it as "the sense that addresses itself to feelings of 'standing,' of 'insiderness or outsiderness' in any social group." He says it's not a skill or a theoretical knowing, but has to do with the anticipations we bring to a conversation, and the influence these impressions have on us and others.

This development seems to have led Shotter (2005b) to move away from social constructionism, which was the theory I had given most credence to. He feels it is lacking in any description of the constraints inherent in social exchange. In his view, communication is like a social weather. It fills our sails, becalms, or sometimes wrecks us. Sensing what is called for in a particular context, responding correctly to gestures like an extended hand, feeling a black cloud settling over a discussion, are all examples of a weather system that can impact us in concrete and material ways. The truth is that the famous "linguistic turn" of postmodernism gives us almost too much flexibility in regard to what is or is allowed. This is the reason many people have accused it of being "relativistic," if not morally delinquent. And there are particular reasons why therapists can feel liberated by giving it up. A move to a sublingual vocabulary, like pills that melt under the tongue, often brings us closer to the matters therapy tries to address.

In fact, Shotter points out that people with emotional problems do a lot of gesture talk and often the problem itself is gesture talk. For this reason, he is very keen on Wittgenstein's (1953) appreciation of this more hidden realm. He quotes Wittgenstein as saying, "The origin and primitive form of the language game is a reaction; only from this can more complicated forms develop." Wittgenstein goes on to say that "this sort of behavior is 'prelinguistic': that a language game is based on it, that it is the prototype of a way of thinking and not the result of thought." In this respect, Wittgenstein's and Bateson's views were very similar.

Shotter feels that the move toward embodied knowing also takes us away from Descartes and the Western tradition. The Enlightenment valued the objective eye of the observer. In contrast, dialogical reality is based on the shared subjectivity of the participants. Instead of a "representational" understanding, Shotter offers a "relational" one. Instead of seeking to be a master and possessor of nature, as Descartes favored, Shotter wants us to respect its "shaped and vectored" qualities. He further observes that in matters that concern the world of the living, many important things occur in "meetings." All the more reason that we should study the kind of talking that goes on in them. Not all meetings make the kind of difference psychotherapists are looking for, and it behooves us to examine what is the special nature of those that do.

One of Shotter's biggest contributions from this point of view has been to translate the lofty abstractions that Bakhtin and his colleagues have given us into terms that are more ordinary. I like particularly his turning the concepts of "dialogical" thinking vs. "monological" thinking into "withness" vs. "aboutness thinking." According to Shotter (2005b): "'Withness thinking' is a dynamic form of reflective interaction that involves coming into contact with another's living being, with their utterances, with their bodily expressions, with their words, their works." In describing "aboutness thinking," he says that it turns the other person into an object, that has no consciousness of its own.

The beauty of the notion of "dialogicality" or "withness" is that it addresses the criss-cross of merging and overlapping voices, and their silences too, in normal, ordinary exchange. Instead of the "expert" individual being assigned the most influence in this activity, as usually happens in psychotherapy, a "withness" conversation allows voices to emerge that have often been stifled or withheld. Attempts to manage meaning may be the norm in our societies, and many psychotherapy models have been built on such attempts, but in these circumstances "withness" does not automatically occur. In fact, there are some who say it is more apt *not* to occur. In thinking back on an interview, the best outcome is that people would feel the conversation itself was the author of what was said.

The "Withness" Practices of Tom Andersen

These ideas fed into my own belief that our theory had to take the mysterious world of the senses more into account. I was using the idea of "underground rivers" to depict the sensory channels that flow between people when they seem to be connecting. I also looked back at my own journey, from an emphasis on sight in "An Art of Lenses," (1990) to an emphasis on hearing in *Exchanging Voices*, (1993) to the current emphasis on touch and feeling. Andersen, of course, had always been persuaded of this emphasis. Influenced by the late Aadel Bülow Hansen and Gudrun Øvreberg, two well-known physiotherapists in Norway, Andersen has always placed the body at the center of his work. As a result, he is attentive to breathing; to posture; to tone of voice, as well as to his own inner and outer voices, and what is going on in his own body. He says:

> The listener (the therapist) who follows the talker (the client) not only hearing the words but also seeing how the words are uttered, will notice that every word is part of the moving of the body. Spoken words and bodily activity come together in a unity and cannot be separated ... the listener who sees as much as he or she hears will notice that the various spoken words "touch" the speaker differently.... Some words touch the speaker in such a way that the listener can see him or her moved. (1996, p. 121)

In another article, Andersen follows the action of an interview he did in Finland step by step. He first describes his talk with the host team, who tell him about a mother with two daughters, one of whom, age 19, was "hearing voices." The team said they were worried because so many other persons in that family had been hospitalized for psychosis. Andersen said he could always meet with the team alone, if that was what they wanted to consult him about, but asked if it would not be better to find out from the mother and daughter directly what their own concerns might be. The team agreed.

After asking the translator what her preferred method of working might be, Andersen went on to describe the body language of the mother and daughter as they came into the room. The mother seemed very preoccupied, the daughter withdrawn. After hearing about various concerns - the daughter's refusal to go to school, the history of family members' hospitalizations, the mother's divorce from the father ten years before, Andersen asked the mother if she had any other children. She said yes, from a former husband, whose parents raised this daughter and kept her from her mother. The daughter had become a street person, taking drugs, but now she had written to her mother, asking to come live with her. Andersen asked the mother if she thought the daughter had missed her, and was told yes. Did she in turn miss her? Yes. The sister nodded yes too.

Andersen then said, "It sounds like your daughter is lonely." When the mother confirmed this, he asked her if she too were lonely. At this point she said, "I have so much pain." Andersen asked where in her body was the pain. "In the heart and in the thoughts." "If the pain found a voice what would it say?" "It would scream." With words or without words?" The mother only looked at him. Andersen asked "Who would you like to receive your scream? She said, "God." "How should God respond to your scream?" She said she hoped God could take care of her three daughters. A long pause followed, and a long silence. The audience seemed very moved, as was Andersen himself.

In the next part of the interview, Andersen found out that this mother had no adults in her life that she could talk to; she had no one else but her daughters. She had been close to her father's parents, but they were both dead. If they had been here, might they have helped her? Might she have been able to scream to them instead of God? She began to weep, saying yes. Andersen asked "If your grandmother had been here, what would she have said?" The mother answered: "Little girl, you have been so good to your daughters." Andersen: "What would you say back?" "Grandmother, I love you so much." And what would Grandmother then do? "She would put her arms around me and I could smell her. She smells so good." Many people in the audience were now openly weeping. Andersen asked the daughter what her thoughts were. She said she knew her mother was in pain, but did not know much about her grandparents. She said that she would rather hear about the pain than not hear anything.

Andersen closed the interview with a suggestion that the mother take her two daughters to the grandparents' grave and talk to the girls about them. Andersen then asked the team and the audience to share their thoughts with him, while the mother and daughter listened. The team said they had been very moved by the mother's feelings for her daughters. Andersen asked if there was a grandmother's voice in the audience, and found one; then he asked for a grandfather's voice. These persons said that they had also been moved, and the grandmother said how important it was for a granddaughter to have a grandmother and for a mother to have a mother. Mother and daughter left the meeting "with firm handshakes and firm looks," and Andersen was told by a team member three months later that the daughter had no more fears or voices and was going to school in the fall.

Andersen (Chapter 6 this volume) describes his work as a communal enterprise rather than an individual-oriented one, and makes this very interesting point about language:

> "Language is here defined as all expressions, which are of great significance in the above-mentioned communal perspective. There are of many kinds of expressions, for instance, to talk, write, paint, dance, sing, point, cry, laugh, scream, hit, and so on–and, all are bodily activities. When these expressions, which are bodily, take place in the presence of others, language becomes a social activity. Our expressions are social offerings for participating in the bonds of others." (p. 82)

I like that idea, as it underscores the "networks talking to networks" idea that we will be seeing in the work of Jaakko Seikkula which I will be describing next. But first, I want to comment on Andersen's ability to connect on a mind-and-body level. The late (and much-missed) Gianfranco Cecchin used to mock me for my interest in the idea of "empathy." "Why do you need empathy?" he used to ask. "What is so important about this empathy?" I tried to tell him that this is a word that I call "tempathy," for "traveling empathy," to make it interactive.

My insight was backed up when I recently read about cells within the brain that researchers like Anthony Damasio (2003) call "mirror neurons." For example, scientists at the University of Groningen (The Economist, May 14, 2005) have found an action-sensitive type of cell that fires not only when a rhesus monkey reaches out for food, but in a different rhesus monkey who sees the first one reaching out. Descriptive experiments with humans are finding the same thing. In other words, when I see someone who is moved and shows a reaction, some small piece inside my own brain also moves. It is these action-sensitive cells that are moving. It is interesting to note that researchers who study autism say that autistic children strikingly lack these cells. So there is beginning to be some backing for the idea that empathy is more than a trait in the individual but is central in the formation and reinforcement of the social net.

The Open Dialogue Approach

Let me move on now and talk about Open Dialogue. This term refers to the work of a group from Keropudas Hospital in the North of Finland that includes family therapy pioneers Jukka Altonen, Yrj Alanen, and Jaakko Seikkula (1995), among others. Over the past decades, these teams have come up with a new approach to persons with first time acute psychosis in which the treatment meeting itself undergoes radical change, becoming an open and shared endeavor between the social network of the afflicted person and the team from the hospital.

One such team, headed by Jaakko Seikkula at Keropudas Hospital, recently concluded a five-year outcome study on Open Dialogue in which the Keropudas subjects were compared with those of persons receiving "treatment as usual" from a hospital in Sweden. By "treatment as usual," was meant the use of hospitalization-plus-neuroleptic medication, which had become the accepted method for handling acute breakdowns in many hospitals across Europe, to say nothing of the U.S. This group was interested in Russian philologist Mikhail Bakhtin's concept of "dialogicality" because it fit with their emphasis on creating a common language rather than curing a disease.

This study excited enormous interest. Five years after it began, 80 percent of the Open Dialogue patients were working, studying, or training for a job and only 20 percent were on neuroleptic medication. In the comparison group, by contrast, 80 percent were on neuroleptics and 80 percent were on disability. By design, hospitalization played a much smaller part in the Open Dialogue group than in treatment as usual, and often was avoided altogether. Repeat hospitalizations were also much lower. I had to ask myself: what is the secret of this approach, and how does it work?

It was then that I heard that Mary Olson, a colleague of mine who was teaching at Smith School of Social Work, had been asked to apply for a Fulbright at Yvaskyla University in Finland. Tom Andersen had invited me to come to another of his conferences in Norway, and I asked if Olson could come with me. Since she was a good writer, as well as a good teacher and therapist, I wanted her to meet the Norwegian and Finnish researchers whose work I had been following for so many years. So I was able to introduce her to Andersen's "acute" team at Tromsø Hospital, and on getting the Fulbright, she did indeed go to Yvaskyla University and met Seikkula too. One result of their meeting was an article they co-wrote describing the Open Dialogue approach (Seikkula & Olson, 2003). They have now applied for a grant to set up a pilot program using the Open Dialogue method with children admitted to the Emergency Room at the Community Services Program at UMass Worcester Medical School. As with the Keropudas Hospital study, it will compare the outcomes of the children's research group with those of children who are admitted and treated in the ordinary way.

Networks talking with Networks

Seikkula puts great importance on the meshing between the treatment team from the parent hospital and persons from the social network of the afflicted person. The hospital team, usually three or four people, meets as soon as possible, preferably on the client's own home ground. Since all staff in Keropudas are required to take a three year course in family therapy, regardless of discipline, it is possible to pull out at short notice an ad hoc team that is on the same page. Hospitalization is often avoided, and so are the heavier drugs, although of course they are available. The network meets daily, as often as needed, until the disturbance has died down. Later, individual or family therapy might be offered, but the hospital team continues to monitor the situation.

Another important feature is an aspiration that the conversation be "without rank." This is a concept offered by Bakhtin who, in his description of dialogism, talks about "the development of familiar and intimate forms of address . . . more or less outside the framework of the social hierarchy and social conventions, 'without rank,' as it were." (1986, p. 97) What makes Open Dialogue of interest to communications researchers is the stated hope to create a common language. This means never challenging the strange words of the patient, no matter how irrational, but continuing to turn them over in the belief that a more mutual way of wording the situation will evolve. This forestalls the traditional effect of family therapy meetings, which is often to highlight the gap between the "sick" and "well" members of the family, or the similar gap between the patient and the professional. The end of such disparities would be a key characteristic of speaking together "without rank."

Seikkula says that in its early days, their team followed structured methodologies like the Milan Systemic approach, but found that they failed to generate the hoped-for engagement between the team and the family. Then they heard that family therapist Yrj Alanen in Turku had started to organize open treatment meetings which included the patient in every conversation about his or her problem, as well as inviting the family and other interested parties in as well. Seikkula's group found that the ideas about dialogical conversations proposed by the Russian philologists Miklhail Bakhtin, Lev Vygotsky and Valentin Voloshinov allowed them to create a new description of the open treatment process they had started to use. Seikkula (Seikkula & Olson, 2002) puts the matter pungently:

> "Coming into engaged meetings or dialogical meetings (as we started to call them), means giving up the idea of primarily having control over things and, instead, jumping into the same river or rapids with our clients and trying to survive by taking each others hands." (p. 403–418)

In their article, Seikkula and Olson (2003) make an important contribution by tying the Open Dialogue format to Bakhtin's concept of "polyphony." Bakhtin lays out the difference between a writer like Tolstoy, who wrote from a God's Eye View, with Dostoievsky's ability to become one with his characters and speak with their voices. Bakhtin goes on to talk about the presence in social life of "a universe of innumerable consciousnesses, each with its separate world." A conversation within which these different possible worlds could express themselves, Bakhtin (1981) called "polyphonic." This seems like an important value if one is hoping for common understandings to emerge that all have participated in making.

The Meaning of Chronification

The most startling impression I got from the articles that members of the Keropudas team (Seikkula et al., 1995) have written about their work was that the aim of the treatment group seemed to be not so much to alleviate symptoms as to prevent chronicity. I proposed to myself, "What if we all decided that the purpose of therapy of any kind was to prevent chronification?" It then occurred to me that the term "calcification" might be a more general metaphor. How often we have used the word "stuckness" to describe a family's difficulties? How often have the problems people come in with developed a thick, isolating carapace that hardens with time, often trapping other family members within it? This effect seemed to be one of the most striking discoveries of the family therapy movement, even though most treatment models have not been specifically set up to combat it.

Perhaps we are getting closer to doing that. The dialogic process I have been describing seems to target this carapace. Goolishian and Anderson (1988) used to describe the calcifying process as a "problem-determined system," and talked about not solving the problem but "dissolving" it. Andersen's deeply gestural work is one example of countering calcification, as is Harlene Anderson's collaborative style and the dialogic network practice of Jaakko Seikkula and his colleagues. The main idea here is that one type of social discourse can counteract another. Perhaps the clearest example of this is the way Open Dialogue deliberately sets out to create a common language that knits people together, pushing against the isolation and apartness that often is the result of a frightening eoisode.

The Rhizome Connection

Let me move now to the story of my connection with Rock the Boat, an unusual helping business run by Chris Kinman, a family and community therapist and former minister, together with his partner, criminologist Peter Finck.

For 12 years, I have been crossing the continent to Vancouver almost on a yearly basis to see what Kinman and Finck are up to. Like the work I have been talking about above, this process also involved "networks talking with networks." I'll share a few of my experiences with them that illustrate this point.

Chris brought me into contact with the powerful traditions of the First Nations people, particularly the art and culture of the Haida Gwai from the Queen Charlotte Islands. Chris was working with First Nations youth and families and had been fascinated by the ancient ritual of the potlatch, where the idea is "to give" rather than to get. It was not surprising to me when he told me that he wanted to work from the idea of "bounty" rather than lacks and disabilities.

Chris also showed me examples of a "Local Wisdom" series he had put together based on sayings from the persons he was working with. Some of the titles were "Local Wisdom of the Mothers" or "Local Wisdom of the Kids." He would transcribe what people said to him and put it into a kind of chapbook. Sometimes he would intersperse their comments with passages he wrote or quotes from writers he admired. I felt it gave the people he worked with a special dignity to be set down in print like that.

Another innovation Kinman (2001) came up with was what he called a "Collaborative Action Plan." This document was an alternative to the usual problem-oriented intake record, widely used by services in that area. What was special was that it was organized around the "language of gifts." The first page asked, "What are the gifts and potentials this person can give to the community?" The second asked, "What are the gifts and potentials the community can give to the person?" The third page read, "What are the roadblocks to these gifts and potentials?" This was the gist of it, although it varied over time. Kinman told me that just the use of this document altered his relationships with the people he worked with in a very positive way.

The Fairy Godfathers

On one occasion, I had sat in on a weekly conference attended by a group of men who were in charge of homes for troubled youth. They were all bikers and had vivid tattoos winding up their forearms. Not having been introduced, I felt like a foreign object, but I sat and listened with interest. A large dog under the circular table kept going from one set of feet to another, finally settling on mine. At this point, the leader of the group, still without introducing me, asked me for my opinions. I said that what had most impressed me was their tenderness.

Then I ventured something outrageous: I said "To me, you are just a bunch of Fairy Godfathers." A moment of appalled silence, and then the group burst into a huge roar, looking especially hard at the leader, the one who had the most impressive tattoos and who, luckily, was laughing, too. This man and a colleague came to our community meeting the next day and commented powerfully on their past experience of class prejudice from persons in social service agencies. But what most caught my eye was a small tag pasted on the shirt of the leader, saying "Fairy Godfather."

The conference finished with all of us listening to the Mood Clinic. This was an informal club that played an advocacy role between patients and medical doctors on issues to do with medication and treatment. Their stories enlisted both our sympathies and a feeling of hopefulness. The event, as a whole, had given me a depth knowledge of the helpers and workers who toiled, you might say, in the shadows of desperately troubled clients, but kept their optimism intact.

The Conversational Therapies

The secret of talk that moves through underground channels is that it operates on a felt-sense level rather than following codified rules for change. In Lowe's article, mentioned above, he compares what he calls the "structured question" approaches a new style of working which he calls *dialogical* or *conversational*. I like the term *conversational*. It suggests a quality of open-endedness together with an emphasis on spontaneity, more like the way a creative artist operates than a trained professional. As Andersen says in an unpublished paper, "My wish is at this moment that we stop talking about therapy and rather talk of it as human art; the art to participate in the bonds with others."

Whatever we call this new big tent, it seems obvious to me that we have gone beyond social constructionism's "linguistic system" idea with its emphasis on the malleability of meaning. Instead, we are looking for "withness practices." These entail a special kind of exchange. Being "without rank," they bypass the hierarchy implicit in most social interaction. They do not lead to some predetermined goal or depend on a prearranged technology. If a sense of having "got there" occurs, it must come spontaneously, much as Wittgenstein suggests when he says that the aim of philosophy is to help us know "how to go on." Above all, they operate on a feeling level, which is the field where goods are struggled for and contests go on, and where a sense of justice is a constant living thing.

The Gee's Bend Quilts

Let me end with the story of the Gee's Bend Quilts, made from scraps of old clothes by four generations of African-American countrywomen living in isolated community called Gee's Bend, Alabama. Their work is and hailed as triumphant examples of unexpected folk art.[1] The family therapy field is also made of scraps and patches. Just as the Gee Bend quilters used worn-out pieces of material, with their accumulations of history, to create bed quilts, so our movement is made up of pieces of practice from many stages: structural, strategic, interactional, solution-focused, possibility-oriented, systemic, narrative, reflecting, collaborative, to name just a few. Now comes a new term, *dialogical*, or as I prefer, *conversational*. This title suggests an elusive quality called "withness" and is represented by those special kinds of conversation or "language games" that give us our bearings in the matter of social bonds. There is no end point toward which this movement of ours is trending. It is only a folk quilt, and its only purpose is to keep us warm at night. However, much of this warmth is due to the fact that it is made of various patches of family therapy's history, memories, and lore.

Endnote

1. See '*Talk of the Nation*', National Public Radio, February 4, 2003.

References

Anderson, H. & Goolishian, H. (1988). Human systems as linguistic systems: Evolving ideas about the implications for theory and practice. *Family process, 27*, 371–393.

Andersen, T. (1987). The reflecting team: Dialogues and meta-dialogues in clinical work. *Family Process, 26*, 415–428.

Andersen, T. (1991). *The reflecting team: Dialogues and dialogues about the dialogues.* New York: W.W. Norton.

Andersen, T. (1996). *Language is not innocent.* In F.W. Kaslow (Ed.), *The handbook of relational diagnosis and dysfunctional family patterns* (pp. 119–125). Oxford, England: John Wiley & Sons.

Anderson, H. & Goolishian, H. (1986). Human systems as linguistic systems. *Family Process, 27*, 371–393.

Anderson, H., Goolishian, H., & Winderman, L. (1986). Problem-determined systems: Towards transformation in family therapy. *Journal of Strategic and Systemic Therapies, 5*, 1–13.

Bachelard, G. (1964). *The poetics of space.* Boston: Beacon Press.

Bateson, G. (1972). *Steps to an ecology of mind.* New York: Ballantine.

Bateson, G. & Bateson, M.C. (1987). *Angels fear.* New York: Macmillan.

Bakhtin, M.M. (1981). *The dialogic imagination.* (M. Holquist, Ed., and C. Emerson & M. Holquist, Trans.) Austin, TX: University of Texas Press.

Damasio, A. (1994). *Descartes' error.* New York: Putnam.

Damasio, A. (2003). *Looking for Spinoza.* New york: Harcourt.

Hoffman, L. (1990). Constructing realities: An art of lenses. *Family Process. 29*, 1–12.

Hoffman, L. (1993). *Exchanging Voices: A Collaborative Approach to Family Therapy.* London: Karnac Books.

Hoffman, L. (2002). *Family therapy.* New york: w.w. Narton.

Kinman, C. (2001). *The Language of gifts.* Vancouver, B.C.: Rock the Boat Publications.

Lowe, R. (2005). Structured methods and striking moments. *Family Process, 44*, 65–75.

Lyotard, J.F. (1984). *Driftworks.* Cambridge, MA: Semiotexte.

Rober, P. (2005). The therapist's self in dialogical family therapy. *Family Process 44*, 479–497.

Seikkula, J., Aaltonen, J., Alakare, B., Haarakangas, K., Keranen, J., & Satela, M. (1995). Treating psychosis by means of open dialogue. In S. Friedman (Ed.), *The Reflecting team in action* (pp. 61–80). New York: Guilford Press.

Seikkula, J., Alakare, B., and Altonen, J. (2001). Open dialogue in psychosis. *Journal of Constructivist Psychology, 14*, 267–284.

Seikkula, J. & Olson, M. (2003). The open dialogue approach to acute psychosis. *Family Process, 42*, 403–418.

Shawver, L. (2005). *Nostalgic postmodernism*. Oakland, CA: Paralogic Press.

Shotter, J. (2004). *On the edge of social constructionism: "Withness-thinking" versus "aboutness-thinking."* London: KCC Foundation Publications.

Shotter, J. (2005, May). Wittgenstein, Bakhtin, and Vygotsky: Introducing dialogically-structured reflective practices into our everyday life. Presentation at Special Education Conference, Copenhagen, Denmark.

Shotter, J. & Katz, A. (1998). "Living moments" in dialogical exchanges. *Human Systems, 9*, 81–93.

Shotter, J. & Katz, A. (2005, July). Poetics and "Presence" in Practice. Presentation for Kensington Consultation Center Summer School, Kensington, England.

Shotter, J. (2005). *Wittgenstein, in practice: His philosophy of beginnings, and beginnings, and beginnings*. London: KCC Foundation.

White, M. (1995). *Re-authoring lives: Interviews and essays*. Adelaide, Australia: Dulwich Centre Publications.

Wittgenstein, L. (1953). *Philosophical investigations*. Oxford: Blackwell.

CHAPTER **6**

Human Participating: Human "Being" Is the Step for Human "Becoming" in the Next Step

TOM ANDERSEN

Sensing Reality

To see, to hear, to smell, to taste, to feel a stroke on the skin or a blow to the body—this is what this chapter is based on: what we can experience "on our bodies," which means that we can sense in our sense organs all that are on the surface of the body. We can think of and say, "Sure, I can see it." This "sensing" "on our bodies" has been seen by some people under certain circumstances, for instance, by Lev Vygotsky in his study of children and my Norwegian physiotherapist colleagues during their physiotherapeutic activities.

Two remarks from Wittgenstein's *Philosophical Investigations* (1953) can serve as good reminders:

Consider for example the proceedings that we call "games." What is common for them all? Don't say: "There <u>must</u> be something common, or they would not be called 'games' " but <u>look and see</u> whether there is anything common to all. For if you look at them you will not see something that is common to <u>all</u>, but similarities, relationships, and a whole series of them at that. To repeat: don't think but look! (p. 66)

81

The aspects of things that are most important for us are hidden because of their simplicity and familiarity. (One is unable to notice something because it is always before one's eyes.) The real foundations of his enquiry do not strike a person at all. Unless that fact has at some time struck him.—And this means: we fail to be struck by what, once seen, is most striking and most powerful. (p. 129).

Background for This Chapter

An Absence of Theories and Methods

Theories and methods will not be mentioned, and I have some comments regarding not doing so, the most lengthy dealing with theories. Theory stems from the Greek verb *theoreïn* which means "to look" and the Greek noun *theors* which means "envoys sent to bring back accounts of spectacles seen in foreign countries." Theory is strongly related to "seeing," and to see is to see the visible. Two of three parts of reality are visible, one of which is nonmoving and the other is moving. An example of the first is a mountain and the second, a man who walks, for instance, on the mountain. The third part of reality is invisible; for instance, the loneliness of the man who walks on the mountain. We cannot see his loneliness, but we can feel in our bodies how his look and movement of loneliness impacts us. We can have assumptions of what loneliness is, not theories. In this chapter, *assumption* is a bigger word than theory; assumption actually includes theory as one rational part, but has an additional feeling part. Therefore, assumptions will be preferred instead of theories.

Neither will methods be mentioned. The problems with methods are that they are preplanned in another context and at another point in time than where the practice happens.

Assumptions about Reality

Reality comprises three parts: (1) the visible but nonmoving, for instance, a bone in a hand; (2) the visible and moving—for instance, the hand that in one moment opens and lets go, and in the next moment closes and holds on; and (3) the invisible but moving—for instance, the handshake.

We can explain what the bone "is," but we can only explain what the hand "might be." Regarding the handshake, we don't know what it is, but this is not so important as long as we know how to relate to it. Some will say, "I know what a handshake is; it is a meeting between two hands!" But "where" does the meeting take place? In the skin? In the touches against the bones? In the looks that follow the handshake?

The first two realities can be described so that thought can grasp them, whereas the third can only be experienced by the body. The visible, nonmoving part of reality will be described best by using numbers and nouns, whereas descriptions of the moving part of reality will benefit from using verbs. In our attempts to describe invisible, moving reality, we will be most helped by using metaphors that help us feel what we are in touch with.

Jessica and Her Parents

A Swedish journalist, June Carlsson, has made a film consisting of fifteen phases of children's lives from birth through the teens. A Swedish female voice follows and comments as the film emerges. The first glimpse is of Jessica, just born, held up by someone's hands. As she screams, she is placed in warm water and the screaming stops. She moves in the water with slow movements. As she is taken out the water and then wrapped in a towel, the photographer zooms his camera in on the scene. We see her face closely, and the voice says, "When Jessica turns her look at us, our love is generated." Then she is lifted up and laid on the mother's chest. We can now see Jessica, her mother, and her father together. The mother, who is holding her hands close to the baby ready to assist but letting her move freely, smiles towards Jessica. The father is in the background: we see him at the side of his wife with his one hand touching his cheeks, looking intensively at Jessica with wide-open eyes. He cannot let his eyes go from her. With small, slow movements, the fingertips of his right hand touch his wife's right shoulder gently. The miracle begins. Only a few minutes after Jessica is delivered, she starts to crawl on her mother's chest and, in a short while, finds one of her mother's breasts and then finds the nipple and starts to suck. In her effort to find the breast, we can hear the mother with an encouraging, laughing voice first saying: "You went a bit too far." But the mother lets the baby find her way without assisting, and Jessica finds it.

> Philosophy simply puts everything before us, and neither explains nor deduces anything. Since everything lies open to view there is nothing to explain. For what is hidden, for example, is of no interest to us. (Wittgenstein, 1953, #126)

What do we view? Sometimes we see what we are used to looking at, other times what we are drawn to see, and other times what we are told to see, and so on. We might see different parts of this event according to the perspective we belong to. Some are drawn to the father in the background. His looking at his daughter is so intense with so much warmth, and we could wonder, "If his eyes could speak what would the words be?" Not unlikely, they would say, "Thank you Jessica for coming! You have made me so happy! You are a big gift to us! I am already looking forward to all we are to do together!" And what would his hand that touches his wife's right shoulder say? Maybe, "Dear wife, I am so thankful to you! You are the most fantastic woman in the world! Be sure, I will protect the relationship between you and Jessica!"

Bonds of Exchanges

I see that the look of the father is part of a relational bond with Jessica, as Jessica's presence is part of the same bond. His touching hand is part of a bond to his wife, and her encouraging words to Jessica, that he also hears, is part of that bond. The same words of the mother are also part of her bond with Jessica, as Jessica's crawling body, which the mother feels in her body, is part of the same bond. Jessica's scream creates a bond that others contribute to by putting her in warm water to comfort her. Jessica's scream is her expression of feeling "the cold reality," and the answer of the others is their response of putting her in warm water. Actually, Jessica's expression is both an answer and an expectation to be helped. This is the crucial circle of life being played out right in front of us!

In front of us, we see that Jessica is born into bonds, as we all have been, and we remain in bonds the rest of our lives. There are many kinds of bonds in life: handshakes, talks, embraces, being silent side-by-side, writing letters, and so on. We participate in bonds all the time. We express ourselves into the bonds with others, as the others receive our expressions and become touched and moved by them. That is what happens with others when they are touched and moved by experiencing Jessica; they return to Jessica and others with their expressions. The expressions contribute to connect them all. And I think that this circle—where expressions are given and become received and affect the receiver who returns that affect—is the basic circle in life.

Breathing

When Jessica screams, she is on exhalation. Before the first exhalation, there is an inhalation. That is what we do first in life—we inhale. In Norwegian, we have two words for breathing: the more daily "to breathe" (*puste*) and the "more sacred" (*ånde*), which in English would mean "to spirit or to admit the spirit".

The first act we do in life is to "spirit in," or let the spirit come, and the last act we do in life is to spirit out, or let the spirit go. Those movements in the body that take part in breathing are extensions of those movements the child has performed already more than four months in the mother's womb. The breathing movements of a person have a pattern that is as personal as the person's fingerprints; the breathing movements can be projected as a curve on paper, and that curve of a person's breathing is very personal, different from other persons' curves. Jessica's smelling that draws her to the breast is accompanied by inhaling, as sucking is the same.

Even swallowing follows breathing, and one can swallow both on inhalation and on exhalation. But much more happens in the body if we swallow on exhaling. Just try! Inspire deeply and start exhaling, take a sip of water and swallow! When you do so, all the air in your chest is emptied. After that comes a big inhalation, and thereafter a sigh follows. With that sigh, some of the tension in the body is released, "everything lies open to view, there is nothing to explain!" We also can see that, just in front of us all, our emotions go with exhaling. We weep on exhaling; shout in anger on exhaling; laugh in joy on exhaling; whisper in fear on exhaling; and so on. Every time we express emotions on exhaling, some of the tension in us disappears. Sobbing is the best; laughing is also good—for the body.

The cycle of breathing through inhalation and exhalation goes on constantly. Physiotherapists can see two pauses that must be mentioned: one shorter pause just between the end of inhalation and the start of exhalation, and one longer pause after the exhalation before the inhalation starts. Occasionally, some people are so eager "to be inspired," wanting to take in impressions, that the pauses are impinged upon. Other times they can even be so eager to take in that they cannot let go of air before new air is taken in. The person has become "over-inspired."

Social Voices

Babies are not much more than four weeks of age before they make a sound that the parents can then receive and return. This sound is a strong connection by voice, and this voice is the beginning of the child's social voice, or better, social voices as we have many social voices. In the seed of a human being is an activity of imitation that unfolds very early. The child plays with and imitates the sounds that are exchanged with others, and through that play, the baby broadens its repertoire of sounds. One day there is a word, and more words come soon. Vygotsky reminds us to think that those early words are imitated sounds, and I think that it might be difficult for the baby to distinguish between the sound (the word), what the sound stands for, and the baby itself.

Language as a Gift

Vygotsky—who said that words are given to children through the parents or others who, in their time, received words from others—saw language as a gift to the child from culture or society. He perceived language as coming from outside, which is opposite of what Jean Piaget was thinking, as he believed that language grew from inside as a seed unfolds to a flower.

Egocentric and Inner Talk

When the child has many words and can talk in sentences, Vygotsky makes us aware of the time when the child is alone, playing and talking to itself.

Vygotsky and Piaget both called that *egocentric talk*. Vygotsky said that this is a play of necessity, not always a play of joy. Through such play, the child implements living rules in its life. One example from my hometown, Tromsø, may illustrate this. A young mother came to a shop with her four-year-old daughter. The shop owner had put piles of chocolate at the register, and when the girl saw them, she said, "Mom, may I have chocolate?" And the mother said, "No, you can not!" The girl said, "But mom, I want a chocolate!" And the firm and calm mother said, "You can not!" The little girl started to cry and all in the shop looked at the two as she said, "I must have a chocolate!" The mother said, "You have to wait until Saturday. Then, you will have a chocolate when you watch the children's TV program!" And they left the shop with the girl crying. When they came home, the little girl played with her doll and talked loudly. Suddenly, she had one of her dolls say, "Mom, may I have a chocolate?" "No," the girl replied, "you can not." She pretended the doll was crying and raising its voice, saying: "Mom, I will have a chocolate!" The little girl answered in a firm and calm way, "You have to wait to Saturday, and you will have chocolate when you watch the children's program on TV!"

Approximately at the time a child reaches school age, play with egocentric talk disappears, and Vygotsky says that the child has developed a third kind of talk, inner talk. In that inner talk, there are many inner voices, and Vygotsky says, "We are the inner voices that have inhabited us." The inner life of a person is, according to Vygotsky's assumptions, composed of moving inner voices, whereas the inner life according to Freud's assumptions were more permanent structured "things." Peggy Penn (1994, 2001) is one who has paid much attention to inner voices. She has noticed that we have many of them, and they might oppose each other as they speak. Difficulties easily arise when one of them becomes dominant over and marginalizes the others.

Collaboration with Physiotherapists

Collaboration with physiotherapists over the years, especially with Aadel Bülow-Hansen and Gudrun Øvreberg, both Norwegian therapists, has had a major influence on the development of the descriptions in this chapter (Øvreberg, 1986; Ianssen, 1997). The meeting with these two women had a significant impact on my way to see, first, that muscles have two functions, to make movements and to stop movements and, second, that all movements are related to the movements of breathing which are the most important movements in the body. If we tense up somewhere in the body—for instance, pressing the tongue against the backside of the teeth—we will notice that the breathing movements in the abdomen stop. If we let the press of the tongue go, the abdominal breathing becomes immediately free again.

We have muscles that have bending functions—for instance, those on the back of the knee and those on the front side of the hip—and those with stretching functions, like those on the front side of the knee and the back side of the hip. When all these muscles, which have opposite functions, are in activity at the same time, the body is in balance; for instance, we can stand in balance. In certain life situations, as when we become afraid, we tend to "pull ourselves together," the bending muscles dominate over the stretching ones and the whole body tends to "creep" together. Simultaneously breathing is constrained.

Aadel Bülow-Hansen died in 2001, but Gudrun Øvreberg is in full activity. When they are described here, I chose the present tense of verbs because even though Bülow-Hansen has passed away, it feels like she is still present.

Tense muscles become both stiff and painful, and Aadel and Gudrun make a massage grip of the muscle ... that produces a pain ... which influences a stretching ... that stimulates inhalation ... that stimulates stretching... which stimulates more inhalation ... and so on, until the chest is filled with air. When the air goes, some of the tension in the body disappears.

The breathing movements, and not the massaging hand, exhale away the muscle tension. When this happens, the two physiotherapists encourage the person "to let air come." It is like hearing, "Let life come." They follow carefully how the breathing movements respond to the massaging hand. If they see that the breathing exertions increase and that the air goes, they are satisfied. If their hands are too careful, there will be no breathing response. But if the hands are too abrupt or too strong or hold too long, a big inhalation can be seen, but it is not followed by any exhalation; the breathing stops. If this happens, they let their hands immediately go. These observations were formulated in principles that I took directly to my way of doing psychotherapy. If our contributions in psychotherapy are too close to how our clients talk, little happens. If, however, they are "appropriately" unusual, life comes to the conversation. If our contributions are too unusual—for instance, if they make people fearful or create pain—the flow of the conversation stops. We must, therefore, carefully watch the ways our clients participate in the conversation to see if it is of value or not, which means how they respond to what we say.

Gudrun and I wrote a book about Aadel's work. We first filmed her in action and then transcribed all that happened during her time with the patients (Øvreberg, 1986, in Norwegian). We sent the manuscript to her, and she read it carefully, often expressing surprise, "It is so interesting to read because I have not been able to describe what I have been doing." Her words reminded us of Wittgenstein (1953): "Don't think but look!" (p. 66).

Aadel's eyes and hands worked well together, and they seemed to suffice without her thoughts' help. She had such great sensitivities for connections—for instance how the person's body she worked on responded to her hands. Another Wittgenstein (1953) remark seems to fit well with what she was doing, "And we must not advance any kind of theory. There must not be anything hypothetical in our considerations. We must do away with all <u>explanation</u>, and description alone must take its place" (p. 109).

Aadel and the famous Norwegian psychiatrist Trygve Braatøy had six rich years of collaboration prior to his death in 1953. They were both interested in breathing functions, and sometimes he asked her to investigate this or that on this or that person, saying, "Come back and tell me what happened!" Other times he said, "I will lie down and I want you to do this or that on my body, and I will tell you what happens." It was a fascinating research design, and I believe Wittgenstein (1953) would have praised them: "One is unable to notice something because it is always before one's eyes" (p. 129).

About Language

Ten Assumptions about Language and Meaning

What I write here is very condensed compared to the sources I refer: Ludwig Wittgenstein (Wittgenstein, 1953, 1980; von Wright, 1990, 1994; Grayling, 1988; Gergen, 1994; Shotter, 1996, 2004, 2005), Lev Vygotsky (Vygotsky, 1988; Morson, 1986; Shotter; 1993, 1996), Jacques Derrida (Sampson, 1989), Michael Bakhtin (Bakhtin, 1993; Morson, 1986; Shotter; 1993, 1996, 2004, 2005), and Harold (Harry) Goolishian (Anderson, 1995). The sources also include my own experiences of putting these assumptions into praxis. Participating in a number of reflecting processes in very different circumstances has been significant in formulating these ideas. These processes are open conversations during which questions and answers come from all perspectives that are present (Andersen, 1995).

1. *Language is defined here as all expressions,* which are of great significance in the aforementioned communal perspective. There are many kinds of expressions—for instance, to talk, to write, to paint, to dance, to sing, to point, to cry, to laugh, to scream, to hit, and so on—and all are bodily activities. When these bodily expressions take place in the presence of others, language becomes a social activity. Our expressions are social offerings for participating in the bonds with others.
2. *We create meaning through expression.* If one kind of expression—for example, talking—is not available, another kind of expression—for instance, painting—could make the creation of meaning possible.

3. *Expression comes first, and only then is meaning created.* Harry Goolishian used to say, "We don't know what we think before we have said it."

4. *Meaning is in the expression, not under or behind it.* Meanings in expressions—for instance, in words—are very personal, and some of the words will, when we hear them, bring us back to and help us reexperience something we have experienced before.

5. *Expressions are informative.* They tell something about us to others and to ourselves. At the moment, I think that a person who speaks out loud first of all speaks to herself. The pause that comes after talking, when she thinks over what she just said to herself, is an extremely important pause that we must not disturb. As the words I express are so strongly connected to my understanding, I may by listening carefully to what I say, investigate my own understanding. The expressions are also formative; we become those we become when we express ourselves as we do it. It would be more appropriate to say, "Grandfather always did something kindly, so he became kind all the time," instead of saying "Grandfather was kind" or "Grandfather had so much kindness." By using the verbs "to be" and "to have" without including time and context, we can easily be bewitched by our own talking to believe that the described is static: "Grandfather 'is' kind," "He 'has' that character," or, "Grandfather 'has' much kindness," "He 'has' a kind personality." When we talk such to ourselves, we can easily be supplied with the ideas that a human being can "have" character and personality.

6. *Expressions, both in the inner and personal talks and those in the outer and social talks, are accompanied by movements.* Those movements that follow inner talks are smaller and nuanced; those that follow the outer talks are bigger, like waving hands. Sometimes both therapists and researchers misunderstand when they say that the spoken does not "match the body language." For instance, when somebody says with a sad look on the face, "I am so happy," I see that the words "I am so happy" are a social offer to bond with the other, as the sad look on the face belongs to an inner, likely sad, talk, which the person most probably is not interested in telling the other. Therefore, as long as the person does not wish to talk from his inner talk, I see it as ordinary politeness "not to see" how the inner talk is presented in bodily expressions. Accordingly, it should be a continuous challenge for the therapist and researcher to evaluate which expressions are offered to a person's participation in social bonds and which are not. Laurence Singh, a psychotherapist and

participant at a workshop I held in Johannesburg, March 2001, offered me the phrase "a social offering" to describe those expressions that contribute to a social bond as opposed to those that are personal and not meant for a social bond.

7. *Movements are personal.* The movements that accompany expression, not least the breathing movements that form and bring forth the inner and outer voices, are personal. The breathing movements are as personal as fingerprints. Vygotsky said, "We are the voices that have inhabited us" (Morson, 1986, p. 8). Maybe one could nuance that to, "We are the movements that form and bring forth the voices that have inhabited us."

8. *Everything is in change.* In his time, Heraclites said: "Everything is in change, but the change happens according to an unchangeable law (logos), and this law comprises a mutual interplay between opposites, but however such that the interplay between the different forces makes a harmony, in total" (Skirbekk, 1980, p. 29). Maybe one could dare to make some small changes: "A person is in movements, but the movements happen … " or even: "A person is movements, but … " When we stand, and stand in balance, those muscles that bend in the knees and the hips are active "at the same time" as those muscles that stretch the knees and the hips.

9. *When one speaks aloud, one tells something to both others and oneself.* At the moment, I think that the most important person I speak to is myself. As mentioned above, expressions are formative and form our understanding. Wittgenstein and Georg Henrik von Wright wrote that our own speaking bewitches our understanding. We cannot "not" be bewitched by our own speaking. When we belong to a community, for instance a professional community, we certainly have to talk the language of that community. One has to be willing to let oneself be occupied by that language if one wants to stay there. If this language uses the verbs "to be" and "to have" without simultaneously indicating context and time, one may, as said before, easily come to understand that human beings are static. Different kinds of language—for example, the language of competition, the language of strategic management, the language of pathology, and so on—all have their consequences, both for those who are described and for those who describe.

10. *Meanings are created problems.* In 1985, Harry Goolishian launched the concept "the problem-created system." He said that a problematic situation quickly attracts many persons' attention. The attracted persons usually make meaning of "How can I understand

this?" and "What shall I do?" If two or more persons have the same meanings, a talk among them will easily make them repeat and confirm their meanings, and very little new is developed. If two or more people have somewhat different meanings and are able to listen to each other, a talk among them will easily create new and useful meanings. If two or more persons have very different meanings, they might find it difficult to listen to each other and may even interrupt and correct each other. When that happens, often the talks break down, and if that happens, a really big problem is created.

A Sketch of a Conversation

In Figure 1 the person to the left is talking and the person to the right is listening. The listener does not only listen to every word, but also *sees* how the talker receives her own words. The listener will notice that some of the talker's spoken words are not only received and heard but they also

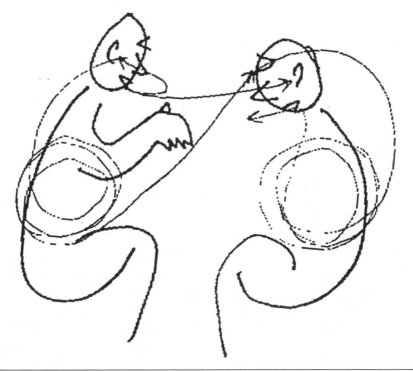

Figure 6.1 Two Talking Persons.

move the talker. (This is illustrated in the diagram by the arrow from the talker's ear to the heart.) These movements of the talker can be seen and/or heard. Sometimes a shade crosses the talker's face, the hands are closed or opened, there comes a cough, a tear can appear, or the person pauses, and so on. The listener understands that the spoken words carry a meaning that makes the talker re-experience something she has experienced before without understanding what that is. Often the listener is carried away and moved by noticing that the talker is moved. (This is noted by the arrow to the heart.) Those moments when both are moved are good for launching a question or a comment, which, in turn, keeps the speaker's movement and the common movement going. A change or an expansion of expressions that moves can make a new understanding of a difficult situation, or a new idea of how one shall take the next step, from this, maybe problematic moment to the next, hopefully, less difficult moment. (See Figure 1)

Three Kinds of Pauses

We are to be aware of three kind of pauses: (a) the one that comes after exhaling before the next inspiration starts (if we as therapists go slow and not rush the client to find answers, we might contribute to the next inspiration that starts spontaneously, not by will or force), (b) the one that comes after the person has spoken and thinks to herself of what she just said, and (c) the pause that comes when a reflecting talk occurs, when what was said becomes talked of once more and thereby thought of once more, maybe even in a new way.

With the help of these words, this chapter comes to a pause.

References

Andersen, T. (1995). Acts of forming and informing. In S. Friedman (Ed.), *The reflecting team in action* (pp. 11–37). New York: Guildford Press.

Anderson, H. (1995). *Från påverkan till medverkan.* Stockholm: Mareld forlag.

Bakhtin, M. (1993). *Toward a philosophy of the act.* (M. Holquist, Ed., and V. Lianpov, Trans.) Austin, TX: University of Texas Press.

Gergen, K.J. (1994). *Toward transformation in social knowledge* (2nd ed.). London: Sage.

Grayling, A.C. (1988). *Wittgenstein.* New York: Oxford University Press.

Ianssen, B. (1997). *Bevegelse, liv og forandring.* Oslo: Cappelen Akademiske forlag.

Kolstad, A. (1995). *I sporet av det uendelige. En debattbok om Emmanuel Levinas.* Oslo: H. Aschehougs forlag.

Morson, A.C. (1986). *Bakhtin: Essays and dialogues on his work.* Chicago, IL: The University of Chicago Press.

Norsk utg (1997). *Filosofiske undersøkelser.* Oslo: Pax forlag.

Øvreberg, G. (1986). *Aadel Bülow-Hansen's fysioterapi.* Tromsø, Oslo: I kommisjon med Norli forlag.

Penn, P. (1994). Creating a participant text: Writing, multiple voices, narrative multiplicity. *Family Process, 33,* 217–232.

Penn, P. (2001). Chronic illness: Trauma, language and writing: Breaking the silence. *Family Process, 40,* 33–52.

Sampson, E.E. (1989). The deconstruction of the self. In J. Shotter (Ed.), *Texts of identity* (pp. 11–19). London: Sage.

Seikkula, J. (1995). Treating psychosis by means of open dialogue. In S. Friedman (Ed.), *The reflecting team in action* (pp. 62–80). New York: Guildford Press.

Seikkula, J., Alakare, B., and Aaltonen, J. (2001a). Open dialogue in psychosis I: An introduction and case illustration. *Journal of Constructivist Psychology, 14*, 247–266.

Seikkula, J., Alakare, B., and Aaltonen, J. (2001b). Open dialogue in psychosis II: A comparison of good and poor outcome. *Journal of Constructivist Psychology, 14*, 267–284.

Seikkula, J., Alakare, B., and Aaltonen, J. (2001c). El enfoque del dialogo abierto. Principios y resultados de investigacion sobre un primer episodio psicotico. [Foundations of open dialogue: Main principles and research results with first episode psychosis]. *Sistemas Familiares, 17*, 75–87.

Seikkula, J., Alakare, B., and Haarakangas, K. (2001). When clients are diagnosed "Schizophrenic." In B. Duncan and J. Sparks (Eds.), *Heroic clients, heroic agencies: Partnership for change*. Ft. Lauderdale, FL: Nova Southern University Press.

Shotter, J. (1993). *Conversational realities*. New York: Sage.

Shotter, J. (1996, June). *Some useful quotations from Wittgenstein, Vygotsky, Bakhtin, and Volosinov.* Paper presented at the Sulitjelma Conference in North Norway.

Shotter, J. (2004). *On the edge of social constructionism: "Withness" thinking versus "aboutness" Thinking*. London, England: KCC Foundation.

Shotter, J. (2005). *Wittgenstein in practice: His philosophy of beginnings, and beginnings, and beginnings*. London, England: KCC Foundation.

Skirbekk, G. (1980). *Filosofihistorie I*. Oslo: Universitetsforlaget.

Von Wright, G.H. (1990). Wittgenstein and the twentieth century. In L. Haaparanta et al. (Eds.), *Language, knowledge and intentionality* (pp. 83–102). Helsingfors: Acta Philosophica Fennica.

Von Wright, G.H. (1994). *Myten om fremskrittet*. Oslo: Cappelen's forlag.

Vygotsky, L. (1988). *Thought and language*. Cambridge, MA: MIT Press.

Wittgenstein, L. (1953). *Philosophical investigations*. Oxford: Blackwell.

Wittgenstein, L. (1980). *Culture and value*. Oxford: Blackwell.

PART **2**

The Therapy Room

Collaborative Therapy: Relationships and Conversations That Make a Difference is based in a host–guest metaphor. I (Harlene Anderson) invited the contributing authors, all of whom I am personally familiar with, to bring their innovative works to the editors' table. I suggested aspects of each author's practice that I thought would be appealing to readers and that would create a volume with continuity. The choice of what to write about, however, was theirs. As well, Diane and I did not create a template for the chapters nor demand a certain writing style. To the contrary, we asked each author to tell their story in their way, feeling this was in keeping with our approach, more fitting with the variety of therapist styles that the authors represent, and that people write more passionately and creatively when the writing is "theirs." A similarity among the chapters is the storytelling, conversational style which is reflective of the approach.

The contributing authors are experienced psychologists, family therapists, social workers, and psychiatrists, who are internationally known theoreticians, clinicians, researchers, and teachers from university, postgraduate training institutes and practice settings, and those from the next generation. The presentation and discussion of practices in various countries demonstrate usefulness across cultures and languages and invite intercultural dialogue. The majority of the chapters are co- or multiauthored, characteristic of the collaborative nature of the practices. The book itself is a collage of practices influenced by collaboration and an illustration of the communal construction of knowledge.

Parts Two and Three provide numerous examples of the diverse practice possibilities of collaborative therapy and the creative ways that the authors put its assumptions into action in their daily work. The chapters serve as a practical guide for practicing therapists, therapists-in-training, and those who educate and supervise therapists. As well, most of the chapters have usefulness for professionals in other disciplines such as medicine, law, and community organization. By practical guide, the intent is not to provide examples of practices that can be duplicated as this is antithetical to the assumptions of collaborative therapy. Instead, it is hoped that the reader will interact with the authors' voices and will be inspired to reflect on their own everyday practice and to create fresh knowledge that is unique to each of them.

Part Two focuses on applications and innovations in the therapy room. Though the therapy in each chapter focuses on work with an individual, family, or group with varied clinical dilemmas, the authors do not necessarily think in terms of the "unit" to be treated or "category-based" populations. Most chapters include the voices and perspectives of clients and their reflections on their therapy."

Peggy Penn, who has long considered and written about the importance of client voices, leads off with a touching story of her work with a boy and his family. Her story serves as a background as she draws our attention to the value of the therapist's listening "inner voice" and listening with compassion and empathy. In the next chapter, Sue Levin talks about what she learned from her "interviews" with women who defined themselves as having been battered. She shares the process of her study in which her starting point of "not-knowing" allowed her to hear the "unheard," providing generative conversations for the clients and herself as well as the effects of categorizing people. Elena Fernández, Alejandra Cortés, and Margarita Tarragona follow with a story about their work with young women with eating disorders. They display carefulness and flexibility as they respond to each client's defined needs and unexpectedly find unique ways of working. Next, comes Jennifer Andrews' tale of how she and her students discovered the world of elders, and through it questioned what "therapy" is. They detail how by being responsive to the elders' leads and by doing what the occasion called for, the lives of elders' as well as their own were enriched.

Two chapters, one by Marsha McDonough and Patricia Koch and another by Diane Gehart, showcase work with children and their families. As one of my students, Kristen Mauro, who read the McDonough and Koch chapter noted, "It reflects how a collaborative practice can initiate change by doing very little 'changing.'" This student's reflection also captures the subtleness of the authors' work, including what may appear to the reader as simply standard procedure when working with children and their families. Indeed, it is not. Gehart follows and calls our attention to the importance of therapists keeping in mind that children's constructions of the meanings of their worlds and their realities are different from adults. The points that she makes throughout her chapter serve as helpful hints for therapists who practice collaboratively as well as for those who practice from other perspectives.

CHAPTER 7

Listening Voices

PEGGY PENN

Ben is a dreamy boy, with red apple cheeks that make him appear younger than his thirteenth year. His hand is eager to hold onto any member of his family who offers. He walks in my door with his family, slumps on the couch and eventually slides further and further down until he lies stretched out on the floor of my office with his eyes closed. It is the way you feel when you've had a bad fall; even breathing is painful and important: he complained that a headache roared behind his eyes. It was a lot of pain. I thought he was in the grip of something sinister he didn't understand.

It was the end of June, and he was starting summer school to make up several courses. He was under instructions from his school that he had to do well this summer to continue to the next grade. He had seen several neurologists about his headaches and presently saw a good individual therapist, but the family called me to be sure there wasn't something else that they could do for him. He described the headaches as "storming out of nowhere and flattening him"; it was hard to feel they could be attached to something as earthbound as a cause. "Tell me what has happened to you," I said, "and don't leave anything out."

I had seen the parents briefly in marital therapy and really enjoyed them. It happened to be at the time when the father's father was dying. Over the seven years, I often thought about this family, and hoped all was well. When we first met, they had an older daughter, Nicole, who was about ten and looked very much like her mother, Gloria, a beauty. All Gloria's emotions were out front and expressed like Nicole's and she cared about her brother Ben. The family seemed to physically sag as they told what they knew of the story. I felt myself slipping into what I call my worry pit.

About a month ago, a woman who was a close friend of the family and had worked with Ben's mother died of cancer very quickly. Gloria's office was in the house and her friend was there every day, especially at the time Ben came home from school. Gloria's friend, Sylvia, and Ben managed to spend a daily hour together; he was a particular favorite of hers. Inexplicably, without a word to anyone after her funeral he came home alone, locked himself in the garage, and turned on the car engine.

Ben reminded me of his father, David, who is tender, very intelligent, quiet, and readily available to his family. Ben said he had locked himself in the garage after the funeral, and he didn't know why; even though he loved Sylvia, the family's friend, it really made no sense to him. He didn't feel he had a "reason." It scares him because the upsetting feelings aren't gone yet. He said his grades had slipped, and he hopes they're getting better, but he still feels bad. "Show me where in your body these upsetting feelings are?" Ben points to his head. First, I ask if he had a bad headache and upset feelings after the funeral when he was in the garage. "Yeah, I guess so." I ask, "What would these feelings say if they had decided to talk … to speak right out?" He looked at me strangely for a moment and said very softly, " … they would cry."

There is a long pause here as Ben and I find a new place together. "Do you cry?" I ask him. He turns to look at me. "Sometimes. Mostly I am in pain." "Would it make sense to think about your pain as a kind of crying?" "Hmmm, yeah, I guess so," he allowed.

His mother, outspoken but also tender, reached down for his hand, and he partially sits up. "We have so many, too many, doctors in our lives and wish you could help us organize this." I asked if perhaps Ben's individual therapist spoke to them given their many needs right now. I was concluding they came to see me to find a path they could travel together, staying in each other's good company and sharing information. I said I would be happy to help them all collaborate—that made sense to me, too. I remembered David's father; his death was an unbelievable emotional loss for David, and I guessed if I asked him, he would still want to talk about it. So Ben comes from a line of deep-feeling men. I remembered how moved I was by David and his love for his father. His mother also loved his father similarly. Ben, it seemed, was suffering from more feelings than he could handle or knew what to do with.

One by one, I listened carefully to each voice in the family. There are questions I always ask myself as I listen to a family, aroused by them. I wonder first if there are any voices from the past that could have something important to say here—and I remind myself to check the available internal voices in the present; I include my own voice among these.

I asked if Ben had a sentence that repeated itself in his head. He looked like I had read his mind. "Yes—I kept thinking there is nothing I can do—or, could have done." I asked if he felt anyone else could have done anything for Sylvia. "Maybe the doctors … maybe not," he answered.

This next question flashed across my mind. "Have you ever thought if you had been a doctor, you could possibly have saved her because of your love for her and your expertise?" Ben fully opened his eyes and sat up. I knew from his shift that this voice of "wishing to help" her was important, though, up until now, it had remained an unspoken wish of Ben's. Now, perhaps, it included being a doctor! There was a long silence in the room and Ben spoke, "Recently, I wanted to volunteer in the ER at Bellevue. My father thinks he could help get me a volunteer job, but my mother doesn't want me to—she's afraid of my seeing blood."

In this small exchange lay a solution Ben had found for himself that might help him deal with these overwhelming, painful feelings. He could help others also experiencing difficult feelings. I asked what he knew about Bellevue. He said that it was a place where you could volunteer safely—he looked at his mom—and he wanted to be helpful. I have heard many definitions of Bellevue but never exactly that one. I asked each person individually what he or she thought of Ben's wish to see what it might be like to be a doctor through this volunteer experience. Everyone was startled that Ben might be thinking about medicine—no one had guessed.

I asked if there was a way to respect his mother's wishes and find out how much blood young volunteers typically saw—and his father said he would investigate. Then I asked a kind of testimonial question—would each of them describe the qualities they thought Ben would have as a doctor. He smiled as he listened. They offered careful, descriptions: he would be warm and helpful, he'd have to do a math brush-up, he would really listen to people, be interested in them, be trustworthy, humorous, and so on. I said to Ben, "Would you agree that your family likes this image of you as a doctor?"

Part of listening for me is listening to my own inner voice, which is relaying my feelings as it speaks to me. I actively ask myself questions as I listen. This is a balance I try to strike between emotionally following clients and assessing my feelings—what is happening to me—and listening to my own questions at the same time. I wondered if I was to Ben something like a doctor. As no one in his family is in the healing profession, I decided to lend myself as a short-term volunteer to answer any questions he might have about the profession if I could.

He said he would think about it. I asked him if I could tell a story of the time I volunteered at Bellevue for a summer. He said he would like to hear that. When I was twenty-one, I went once a week and was put into one of the back wards where there were unhappy adolescents divided by gender. Basically, I accompanied them to different places in the hospital or out to the playground to the basketball court. I was supposed to talk only to girls; but since the girls talked only to boys, I talked to the boys as well.

My big interest was in talking to the aides—that was where I thought something needed to change. The aides mocked the kids and made fun of them. They were trying to rise above them. It upset me that the kids were locked up and had almost no freedom of movement—being adolescent. The aides on the wards taunted the kids and called them "crazy." Ben and I agreed that was unfair, and he felt if someone had really "talked" to the kids or listened to them they could have found out more about their problems and maybe the kids would have been able to talk them over. I said we had the same idea. He felt the teasing worked against any therapy they might be getting—making fun of someone is no help and works against solving problems. He asked me what I said to the aides and though I edited some of it, I said I asked them how they had solved problems, what had worked for them? Did they talk to anyone about it? Who? Then he asked how long I had to wait to really help someone, did my interest last, and were there times when it was easy. I answered each question.

Ben was engaged with me now. I had an idea: I asked the family if they would be willing to try some writing, and they all agreed. I asked who should begin, and Nicole volunteered. Dad and Ben kept a list that week about he differences between his headaches each day and contrasted that with his worries. They read the list in our second session, and it ranged from Ben being carefree and upright, to his being stretched out alone with his eyes shut. Ben and Dad had the same count of headaches, but somehow they, both noticed that Ben was upright a good deal of the time this week, and he was going to school.

Nicole read aloud her letter to her brother saying she really was available and would love to have a letter back from Ben. In this session, we talked about the worries Gloria had about Ben's seeing blood and as well as her concern that he might be further depressed by the ER. I asked if Gloria was afraid of blood, and she said she was not. How did she accomplish that? "Was there ever a time where you were afraid, and perhaps it changed?" "Yes," she said, "There was a time." "Did anyone help you?" I added that perhaps Ben would like to hear that story, as it might come in handy. Everyone helped think of ways Gloria could find out what Ben's experience would amount to if he went to the ER. He had his first interview set up for the following week.

During that second session, I asked Gloria if she would write a letter to her friend who died—perhaps her friend didn't know how much this family missed her and how prominent she remains in their thoughts. She agreed, even saying she looked forward to writing her. I was aware what an important voice David's father had in this family so I asked him if he thought his father would have any advice to offer right now. He said, "I knew you would ask me that. I will write, it will feel good to talk to him." "Would you talk to him about Ben, and see if he ever went through anything like this with you? He might have something of value to say to us."

This happened to be a Thursday. I knew the TV show *ER* (for "emergency room") was on at ten p.m. that night and asked Ben if he watched it. "Yes," he said enthusiastically, "It's my favorite show!" "Mine, too!" I said. He and I were the only people in the room who particularly liked or watched this show. I asked if he was worried about the lead doctor who was struggling with a brain tumor. "Not really," he said. "They can't lose him, so he'll pull through somehow." We discussed how we felt the producers managed the show—personal stories vs. medical emergency material. Did he flinch? Sometimes I admitted I did. Both of us agreed we would each watch the show that night and discuss it the following week.

On our third visit, we spoke about the show, which dealt with the removal of a brain tumor. As they cut into the brain, they tested the man during the procedure and immediately afterwards to assess his language skills. Ben commented on how different it was with his friend; she had had a pancreatic tumor and only one surgery from which she did not recover. I thought this might be a good time to hear his mother's letter.

Gloria unfolded the letter saying how hard it was to write, and there were tears in her eyes. However, the beginning of the letter was witty. She said, "First, I want to know if you're still blond?" Slowly the letter unfolded into a compassionate picture of how everyone missed her and what she had meant in this family. The family's response was to listen with their heads slightly bowed.

I felt they were absorbing—even needing—the words of the letter. Some had tears, others sat quite still. She explained to their friend how Ben had reacted in his mourning and that it had concerned them. He shook his head no on hearing that. The other family members thought the letter was moving and an accurate portrayal of their feelings about her. I asked everybody what part of the letter Sylvia might have responded to if she really had heard it. Of course they said—the part about Ben. "What might she have said to him if she had written back to Gloria?" I asked. Gloria thought she might tell him what a wonderful young man he was and how he had to stay with his convictions that had always persuaded her. She would say she missed this family, too, and maybe Ben, in particular. I could feel their love for her, but I hardly spoke—the family had much to say to each other.

Ben managed to get a summer job volunteering in the emergency room at Bellevue and did so well and made so many friends that he asked to continue in the fall. As his grades were up, his parents agreed. Once he told his mom to tell me he'd learned a lot. I had the feeling he would.

When September 11 came, he insisted on going directly to the emergency room to volunteer; his mother thought he should wait, but he said he'd come home early if they didn't need him so she drove him to the hospital. When he walked in the door, his coworkers said, "Thank God you're here, man the phones, they're driving us crazy. Here's the information to give them." He slipped into place and began giving out information to every one calling relating to this emergency. Though everyone hoped to come to the hospitals in New York—and all the doctors were on call—the hospital remained remarkably empty; so many people had been killed.

Listening as Our Most Profound Source of Healing

Lately, I have been looking at my cases in order to think about how listening is perhaps the most profound source of healing we have to offer—to listen attentively and responsively to the family's voices, their tone as well as their content. And to listen to your own inner voices and be able to surrender them when following the voices of the family. I think we all do this quite creatively and individually, and it helps people heal. One important ingredient is keeping our imaginations open so when our inner voices are needed, we have them ready. In listening, we remain open to the experience of others. And when we are tuned with their language, we begin to open significant words, as Tom Andersen (1996) suggests, in order to find other words in their words. Just as when we reflect, we choose our words quite carefully. In doing these things, we are communicating our presence to the family and/or its various members, palpably. From there we may decide together what to do and sometimes write.

Looking at this family when they first came in, their pain by anyone's standards would be seen as dire. I felt their suffering to be serious, that it was urgent that it take a different turn. I had a double feeling, too; though personally moved when I heard their story and looked at this young boy lying on my floor, I was immediately reminded of one of my own children who, at age eight, contracted a terrible case of measles with a 106-degrees temperature for two days. My four-year-old daughter was alone with me, and we slept on the floor of his room several nights in a row, while I monitored that fever, constantly bathing him down and speaking back to him as his thoughts wandered.

For me, listening consists of several ideas: First, I am always alert to whether I am feeling empathy or compassion for the family or within the family, among its members. Next, I listen to their important words, so we can open them up, volunteering a particularly chosen word of my own as I would in a reflection and making sure the family feels morally validated.

Our "listening voices" are our primary form of care, and they both participate and witness. They are there to appreciate the whole story of the suffering "as many times as it must be told." Riikonen and Smith (1997) have written that when we listen deeply, the speaking person feels understood. Being understood is a way of feeling you are "morally worthwhile." This listening act depends on your finding similar values that you share with your clients; it is a form of ethical listening because you are choosing to have them feel valuable. I use my version of what Kaethe Weingarten (1995) calls "radical listening"—listening also to what is absent and unspoken. I ask how that absent utterance proves constraining to the family. How could it be introduced? Using the idea of radical listening creates the conditions for new voices to be heard there in the room and releases the constraints that have kept them silent.

My next consideration is more complex because it details the act of compassion that we feel as we listen. It is our compassion that brings our "presence" forward and makes us available to our client. With Ben, it was the pause we shared when I asked if he ever thought of being a doctor. As families, we feel clearly responsible for our children. But as I listened to the family "stall" around ideas of responsibility and judgment, I heard the "why" question growling behind their fear. Was this his fault? Why did he do it? I realized that in fact it was Ben who really felt that Sylvia's death and her suffering were undeserved. I asked him what meaning her suffering had for him. It's a hard question but he tried, and as he spoke the family became more organized around his love for her and not around the "fault" they felt to be within themselves or in Ben. The growling stopped. We know that reunion fantasies are common after a significant death and though he did not say this, perhaps he felt if he were with her, that she would at least not be alone, or perhaps for that hour he felt he could not be without her. As we continued to talk, I hoped the family would see this as a misguided act of love and not an act that was anyone's fault.

The compassion Ben felt for Sylvia could now be shared in our conversation and belong in his family for they, too, suffered her absence. Here was my job: to listen for any sign of compassion from Ben "for" his family. If Ben can have compassion for others, recognize another's suffering, perhaps he'll understand that the things we value are not always safely under our control. Disease occurs, people die, wars take place, defeats come, we fail and are in pain—but we love each other. There is no predicting or controlling the events that may fall on your life. And still we praise it. And still we hope. When I saw him lying on the floor, these were my feelings and thoughts. So I set out to listen for compassion, particularly in Ben, "but also always in me."

My questions focused on the family's similar possibilities as people. Could they stand in each other's shoes—particularly, in Ben's shoes. What would be the focus of their collaboration over time? Perhaps I would ask them how we should do this and proceed following their advice. Ben's voice is getting stronger. Whose shoes could he stand in? Does Ben know when his dad is thinking about his own father? Does he believe everyone can expect to suffer these things? I asked Ben if he thought I could suffer pain. "Yes," he said, "I think you would suffer losing a good friend." I agreed and said I had on three occasions. At one point in our discussion of our similar possibilities, he asked if I had ever had real pain. I said I had. He nodded without further inquiry. "Does that help you understand people?" "Yes," I said, "that is its greatest value." In that small exchange we agreed that knowledge of one's own weakness or frailties might be an important ingredient of how we feel for others. I ask if locking himself in the garage with the car running could maybe be seen that way. Did that experience enable him to think about others who were also suffering as he had? Perhaps that would come in handy in the emergency room. Did he think he could stand beside the people he would meet, similar to the way we are trying to stand beside him? Now he smiled.

Empathy and Compassion

Martha Nussbaum (2001), a philosopher of ethics and law, has written a book called *Upheavals of Thought*, where she defines empathy as our ability to imagine ourselves in the sufferer's position, enduring his or her torments. But empathy is combined with the recognition that one is not, in fact, suffering. We never lose the perspective of our separate lives. It is like being a skilled Method actor; we strive to feel like another, as separate from ourselves, and that enables and increases our understanding, but we don't think we are them. Our question is how does empathy relate and differ from the act of compassion and how is that expressed in the act of collaboration?

The conditions of empathy are not sufficient for the feeling of compassion. We can easily empathize with joyful states but compassion requires the recognition that the sufferer is in a bad state, maybe even tragic, like the survivors of the September 11 tragedy. Nussbaum makes the point that empathy is the "understanding of someone's suffering," but it differs from compassion where you "feel" the person's suffering. A person's suffering may be serious without necessarily being a serious tragic event. For instance, even a torturer may feel empathy—understand the feelings the victim has but, at the same time, enjoy the victim's suffering. A juror may understand through empathy a person's plight but without necessarily experiencing compassion for them. Nussbaum feels that what defines compassion is that it is an "emotion" in the make-up of the witness.

When we feel compassion, it means we look carefully at our own beliefs that are present in the act of suffering. First, we view the suffering of the other as serious and not trivial—that is a belief we hold. Suffering is not trivial. Second, we feel that this person does not deserve the suffering that has been visited upon him or her; this is an accident of fate, and there are no personal reasons attached. Third, we assess our own possibilities in life and see that they are similar to those of the sufferer. This is what I consider real collaboration. Ben's family moved slowly toward each other through a series of subtle moves in treatment. Thus, their collaboration with one another increased.

References

Andersen, T. (1996). Language is not innocent. In F.W. Kaslow (Ed.), *The handbook of relational diagnosis and dysfunctional family patterns* (pp. 119–125). Oxford, England: John Wiley & Sons.

Nussbaum, M.C. (2001). *Upheavals of thought: The intelligence of emotions.* Chicago, IL: University of Chicago Press.

Riikonen, E. & Smith, G.M. (1997). *Re-imagining therapy: Living conversations and relational knowing.* London: Sage Publications.

Weingarten, K. (1995). Radical listening: Challenging cultural beliefs for and about mothers. In K. Weingarten (Ed.), *Cultural resistance: challenging beliefs about men, women, and therapy* (pp. 7–22). New York: The Haworth Press.

CHAPTER 8

Hearing the Unheard: Advice to Professionals from Women Who Have Been Battered

SUSAN B. LEVIN

Women who have been battered by men in intimate relationships have been the focus of research in various disciplines within the social sciences for almost four decades. Despite this attention, there is little consensus among theorists and clinicians about what is sufficient, ethical, and appropriate theory and practice in this area. The majority of the research has been empirical, scientific research methodologies. A limitation of this research is that its focus stays on proving or disproving the researcher's hypotheses; information that is outside the researcher's area of interest is discarded as extraneous.

The traditional research relationship is essentially hierarchical, wherein the researcher is the "knower" whose ideas are the ones that are valued or "heard." There is, however, a growing interest in studying social and clinical problems from other research perspectives. I designed a research project in which I invited a collaborative research relationship, based on social constructionist and language systems theory. I created an in-depth, collaborative inquiry that allowed the researcher and participant to work together to explore each woman's experience out of which emerged her unique and untold story. I will discuss the design and process of the research and include excerpts from the interviews to illustrate the uniqueness and richness of the stories I heard.

Performing Research

One of the most important differences between empirical, scientific research and collaborative, social constructionist research is the researcher's stance. Much social research occurs in a context that replicates the scientific laboratory setting. Researchers collect "data," reducing the "subject" to a container of information, which then must be extracted. The scientific experiment is encased in a "reductionist" paradigm, based on the notion that entities or wholes can be best understood if broken into their smallest individual components (Bateson, 1990).

This language of the scientist studying a "subject," "collecting data," and "analyzing the results," illustrates the inherent view that research is a discovery process. The scientist discovers new and better understandings of his[1] subject, through the careful and disciplined development and enactment of an experiment. The discovery position of the hard sciences and its applicability for the social sciences and family therapy, in particular, was critiqued. An alternative theory evolved into constructivism (Gleick, 1987; Maturana & Varela, 1987; von Glasersfeld, 1984).

Constructivism is based on the notion that reality is a product of one's own creation. Our view of reality results from our unique and individual interaction with "what is out there" and the ways in which we are capable of giving meaning to those experiences (Watzlawick, 1977). From this perspective, it is impossible to use research to generate truths and universals. Each individual (researcher) sees and interprets the world and her experiences through her own meaning and belief systems; truth and similarity are only in the eye of the beholder. Scientific objectivity, therefore, is nothing more than a socially constructed myth (Gergen, 1991). Social constructionism shares some of these assumptions.

Social constructionists consider that we, as humans, construct what we know. This occurs in a shared, social exchange in language (Anderson & Goolishian, 1988; Anderson & Goolishian, 1992; Gergen, 1982; Gergen, 1985; Hoffman, 1990). Individuals, from this viewpoint, operate in an intersubjective and "shared" meaning system. That is, in order to interact in a particular community (whether a family, a work place, a conversational dyad, etc.), it is necessary to have mutual understandings about what we mean when we talk to each other. Difficulties arise when we fail to recognize that we are using a meaning for a word that others in conversation do not share. When this becomes clear, however, we are then able to renegotiate with each other. We can redefine mutually agreeable usages or stop that particular conversation. This way of thinking about the negotiation of meaning in language and conversation has many implications for research.

Hearing the Unheard

A social constructionist and collaborative interview approach created a context in which I could pursue understanding with each woman. Though each woman's story reflected unique and complex experiences, feelings, and descriptions, there appeared to be a strong commonality of feeling unheard by professionals, family, and peers alike. The women reported that there were important consequences for feeling unheard. Current interest in hearing and voice has many roots. Hearing, and particularly hearing women's "voices," developed as a goal of feminists in the social sciences (Gergen, 1991). Gilligan (1982) was one of the first to encourage this pursuit. She describes the field of psychology as biased toward men and against women as many theories have been based solely on data collected from white, upper-middle-class male college students. She called for new theories, and research focused on women that would honor "their" voices. Miller (1976, 1991) has contributed to this work, proposing an alternative understanding of women's psychological processes, based on what she learned from hearing and valuing women's experiences. Tannen (1990), from a slightly different perspective, looks at how gender influences communication. Despite gender differences, she reports, "We all want, above all, to be heard — but not merely to be heard. We want to be understood — heard for what we think we are saying, for what we know we meant" (p. 48).

Hearing is more than listening: "It is a process involving a negotiation of understandings." This process can involve one's own voices (internal dialogues) or multiple people. Hearing is not a unidirectional or receptive-only activity. Anderson and Goolishian contributed to my ideas about hearing through my close work with them and the development of their innovative language systems theory (1988, 1992). They describe the interactive process of understanding as mutually collaborative and dialogical in nature. Anderson and Goolishian's early ideas about the nonlinear process of understanding were influenced, in part, by the work of Humberto Maturana, a Chilean biologist who greatly impacted the field of family therapy.

Information and meaning, according to Maturana, are not independent, discrete, and objective representations of reality that are carried in language from one person to another. Instead, they are evolving socially constructed interchanges, which are influenced by one's own prejudices, biases, and experiences, as well as the setting in which conversation takes place. There are multiple interacting influences that affect the exchange of words. Therefore, "one does not simply" hear what another person is saying but is actively interpreting what she thinks is being said.

Hearing sometimes sounds like a simple concept—an everyday experience in which we all participate. People are always talking to us, and we are always responding. But do we spend much time attending to whether the person we are talking to feels heard? Often, we respond based on our ideas of the meaning of the words that we hear. Unfortunately, our tendency to act as if we know and understand is often generalized to all situations, which often proves not to be useful. Therapy and psychological research are activities in which this tendency may be unhelpful.

In my interviews I tried to hear what the women thought was important about their experiences of having been battered. This happened in a conversational interchange between each participant and me. It began in different ways with each person, but was organized around a general invitation for them to tell me what they considered important for me to know about their experiences.

Hearing and Research

As discussed above, the premise for this inquiry was that people are not heard in research projects when they are the subject of a search for similar behaviors, characteristics, or typologies. Their experiences and stories are reduced to coded bits of data (Bateson, 1990). Nobody likes to be considered exactly the same as anyone else (Tannen, 1990) nor could it possibly be accurate to consider them so. My project was created to value the uniqueness of people and allowed them to explain what they considered important.

Without a narrative or story format for women who have been battered to be heard, they would simply be reduced, by statistics, to labels and categories of language. These can keep us distanced from the people that are pained, hurt, and jeopardized by the battering. Not hearing and not connecting with the human suffering through the personal reports of women who have been battered can keep us detached. It is much easier to believe that it won't happen to me, if I am staying at a distance. It is not until facing each woman and hearing her story that we can face our own vulnerabilities (Levin, 1992, p. 51).

As a researcher, I wanted to hear what the participant thought was relevant to share regarding her experience. I attempted not to be the one to define what battering was, or whether someone was battered. I took the position that as long as each woman considered that she had been battered, she could be included in my study. I did this to maintain my goal of not limiting or predetermining the stories I would hear. I did not want to define what battering meant in any way that would rule out women from participating or that would reinterpret an experience for someone who did not already characterize it that way.

Researcher Inner- and After-Thoughts

A constructionist perspective does not restrict (or free) me from having biases, values, theories, and positions. Some people disagree, believing that if all ideas are socially and linguistically situated, then none are better than others; one should not privilege some ideas over others. This is often labeled a relativistic perspective. I disagree. I believe that this perspective recognizes and respects that people are always taking positions and privileging ideas and that these have important implications that should be explored. I make an effort to recognize and clarify values, biases, and my perceptions of the social, political, and linguistic contexts as well as the narratives that have influenced me to privilege certain ideas and positions at any point in time. I discuss my view of the implications of these ideas and conclusions as they are relevant to the research.

I attempted to be open to what might "come to me" in this research—to explore the possibilities that would be present. However, I realized in reading *Naming the Violence* (Lobel, 1986) that I had excluded and failed to be open to "hearing" lesbian women who had been battered. Although careful to avoid using limiting and labeling language in my recruitment announcements, I inadvertently stated that I was interested in hearing from women who had been battered by men. Therefore, I participated in reinforcing the assumption that battering is gender-related, that men batter women. I was more deliberate in choosing not to include men who had been battered in my study.

Although interested in being as inclusive as possible with women who had been battered, I found that I only ended up interviewing Caucasian women. Despite the large culturally diverse population of people in the Houston area, I did not have a diverse group of women to interview. In retrospect, I recognized that I targeted groups for recruitment without considering or specifying a goal of racial and cultural balance. This was inadvertent and another reminder of how difficult it is to be as open and inclusive as one wants to be.

The use of the word *battering* to describe the violent nature experienced by the women I wanted to interview was also a choice that carried certain implications and limitations. A number of words and terms are available to label this experience. They each carry different meanings and are used differently by different people. I use the term *battering* because I consider it to be specific to violence between intimate partners, while *beating* and *abuse* are terms that are also used to describe parent–child and stranger violence.

When describing my own positions and views, I do not use the phrase "battered women" but rather talk of "women who have been battered." In carefully making this distinction, I try to emphasize that "these women are not the battering, nor do I think they should be grouped together." I contend they are not the same, not cut from the same mold, nor exhibiting all of the same characteristics; neither as the result nor as the precipitant of the battering episode. These women are more than "battered women." And I believe it is important to remember this.

Although I do not find it useful to use the label "battered women" in my work, I understand that there are other contexts in which this label is very important. For example, conducting descriptive research to assess needs of women is critical for people to be able to be identified as "battered." The counting and reporting of incidences of battering and population statistics are necessary for public policy and funding decisions. The need for shelters, police, legal protection, etc., can only be established by the identification and reporting of statistics. Inevitably, this reduces people to categories and numbers; however, there are times when this is necessary. If our society and culture are going to recognize this problem, accept that it occurs, and develop ways to begin addressing this problem, bringing statistical information to the public is required. This information, however, is not all there is to know about women who have been battered.

Interviewing and Collaborative Constructed Knowledge

What is the intention of interviewing if one accepts that language does not transmit fixed, objective meaning from one to another? One may never "really" know what someone else means. A not-knowing position is described by Goolishian (1990) and Anderson and Goolishian (1992). As Goolishian (1990) reports in his discussion of the not-knowing position:

> This process of emerging new understanding is, in large measure, stimulated by [therapeutic] questions that are the result of the event and that are not predetermined by a theoretical understanding. It is as if the newness of the [client(s)] demands the question as opposed to the question being driven by the theory or methodology [of the therapist] (p. 1).

The researcher, therefore, is mutually responsible for the creation of meaning through questioning and responding to the newness of each client or research participant. Each interviewee is different as is the interviewer's responses to them.

The not-knowing position in therapeutic conversation (Anderson & Goolishian, 1992) can be applied to research conversation. This position is described as:

> ... the [researcher's] actions and attitudes express a need to know more about what has been said, rather that convey preconceived opinions and expectations ... The [researcher] therefore, positions him or her self in such a way as to always be in the state of "being informed" by the [participant]. This "being informed" position is critical to the assumption in hermeneutic theory that the dialogical creation of meaning is always an intersubjective and always a continuing process. (p. 5)

The researcher, from this position, is participating in an exploration, using her own ideas and curiosities, which are being triggered in conversation with the participant. One of the most likely contexts for this type of research is the interview.

A not-knowing approach challenges traditional positivist research (Morgan, 1983). Oakley (1981) describes the interviewer in traditional research as someone who must balance ". . . between the warmth required to generate "rapport" and the detachment necessary to see the interviewee as an object under surveillance . . . ." (p. 33). This traditional position does not fit with a not-knowing approach as it maintains the idea that the researcher knows what to accomplish. It also utilizes a notion of boundaries that can be maintained or crossed, providing rapport or objectivity.

The constructionist view that understanding emerges through collaboration sharply contrasts with traditional interviewing methods. To collaborate is defined as "to work jointly with others or together especially in an intellectual endeavor" (Internet, 12/08/05, http://www.m-w.com/dictionary/collaboration). As this definition implies, the researcher and participant are working together to develop new ideas. The women I interviewed became collaborative partners in the research process.

I created an interview format that allowed the participant and me to negotiate the conversation based on our mutual interests. I worked at fitting our interests together, with my main goal being to follow where each woman led. However, it must be acknowledged that I used my interpretations and understandings about what we were talking about to ask further questions. Having predetermined questions, categories, or hypotheses would have led to confirming or disconfirming my own ideas instead of the ideas of the women I talked with.

Each interview involved the development of a unique research relationship that involved a connection established for the purpose of the interview. My goal in the development of this relationship was to establish myself as a learner—a not-knower—making the woman who had been battered the expert and "knower." My responsibility was for how I responded, questioned, commented, and tracked her story. However, most participants expected me to be "in charge" of the interview, often anticipating a series of structured questions. The research relationship developed based on how we negotiated these expectations.

The position of wanting to hear and understand each woman's story was important and kept me from "redirecting" her back to my question if she had not answered it (or if I was "unsatisfied" with the answer). Dissatisfaction with participants' responses is common in traditional research. Interview methodology is often described as requiring the ability to "follow-up" questions to get the participants to be more specific, or, in other words, to get them to talk in definable, quantifiable terms. The interviewer may also return to previous questions to test the reliability of the participant, to compare answers, and to evaluate coherency. Instead, my approach was to follow the women in the telling of their story.

Sharing Their Stories

I interviewed eight research partners; all were women who had been battered. This small group was quite diverse. Of the eight women, two were separated, one was maintaining a marital relationship, and five had ended the relationships that they had come to talk about. Some of them had remarried; some of the remarriages had also involved battering, and some had not. All had been to therapy at some point in their lives. Half of them reported experiences of violence as children; half of their partners drank alcohol regularly.

The degree of battering described and experienced by these women was varied. Three reported incidents of pushing and emotional and verbal abuse with infrequent hitting incidents. One reported that there was seldom physical violence, but she was always strictly controlled by her husband. Another described detailed accounts of assaults, which left her with shattered facial bones, a skull fracture, black eyes, and other injuries. Two women reported their conviction that continuation of their battering relationships would have resulted in their deaths, and one of them related having blurred vision and epileptic seizures as the result of repeated head injury from battering. Another woman referred little to the physical aspects of the battering marriages she endured, but rather she discussed the emotional effects as well as the abuse she suffered as a child in a dysfunctional family.

I did not have any women participate who were currently shelter residents. One of the women interviewed reported having been to a shelter during her marriage. Another described volunteering at a shelter while she was in her second marriage, during which she was battered. One woman reported that she was unaware that shelters existed, and they probably did not in the small, north Louisiana town where she lived in the 1970s. Several women reported finding other places to get refuge. One woman went to live with friends, while another went to a psychiatric hospital to get out of the relationship. One woman, in an attempt to leave her husband, described moving to Texas from Louisiana, and another woman had her husband move out after the police were called. All of the women interviewed requested assistance from a professional helper at least once. They had all participated in therapy at least once. I was surprised to learn how much they felt (and feared being) blamed, misunderstood, coerced, and invalidated. I was surprised to learn how much they felt unheard.

The Research Conversations

The following excerpts from the women I interviewed illustrate the general experience they all seemed to have regarding helpers: the police, counselors, and therapists. It also gives a sense of the collaborative research style that I developed.

Claudia:[2] And I wouldn't have come to see you, except that [Diane, her previous therapist] asked me to. That's the only reason I guess, is that she asked me to. 'Cause I really like her a lot and felt like she deserves a lot of credit for me being able to get control of my life. And, you know, now I have a happy, wonderful relationship. But she was the first person I ever met that I felt like, and I don't know why, but I felt like that I could tell anything in the world to and she didn't judge me or think oh, you're some horrible, awful, terrible, very bad person that's just the most awful person I've ever met for just thinking such a thing, you know.

Sue: I'm sure you were really sensitive to that.

Claudia: Oh, yes. Very much so.

Sue: And particularly from someone who's supposed to be a therapist.

Claudia: Yeah. And she never made me feel that way.

≈

Jean: When I went to court in November of last year, for the divorce, my husband went before the judge and that's when he said that I was throwing twenty-eight years of a good marriage down the drain. And the court recommended counseling.

Sue: For you?

Jean: For both of us. They didn't grant the divorce, they recommended counseling.

                                          ∽

Sue: I'm curious about your experience with police ... with your parents' marriage as well as in your marriage.

Carol: Well, my mother never called them. I don't know what her motivation was, why. I just know that we never had the police out to our house. I think, knowing my mother, it had to do with pretenses and having the perfect family, and you just don't have the police out in front of your house. Furthermore, if she was being a good wife, then you wouldn't have to have the police out front.

Sue: So, it's your fault, so you can't call the police if you're responsible.

Carol: That's right. It looks bad on you if the police are in front of your house.

Sue: They'll blame you, too.

Carol: And you know what, they would have. Because society as a whole—let me put it that way—in the sixties and early seventies .... But you know what, I was becoming of age, shall we say, thirteen, fourteen, during the revolution, early seventies, and we had these commie pigs, you know. And we began to realize the police weren't all they were cracked up to be. We began to, you know, the riots, and the police were beating .... They had a warped sense of control, too. So my mother wasn't quite off track to know that they wouldn't do her any good anyway; she had to fight for herself. So, anyway, my point was, there was an evolution in thinking, so we began to demand that the police do more, that the police help us. So, I called the police a couple of times, and learned for myself that it didn't do me any good because, quote unquote, "It was a domestic squabble." And I mean, I'm here with blood running down, out of my nose, and my mouth is huge, and my face is huge, and my eye is swollen shut, and I have bruises. And that's a domestic squabble. I wouldn't call it a squabble. But that's what they called it. As a matter of fact, they wouldn't even come to the house but maybe on two occasions. The more you called them the less they came. Because it was, the way of thinking was, "Well, you know, we came out before and by the time we got there everything was calmed down. So, by the time we get there this time, it's going be calmed down." I tried to have him arrested one time, and the policeman was going to arrest him. And his real mother begged me not to have him arrested. I had some affections towards her so I changed my mind. And after that, that policeman wouldn't help me anymore.

৶৻

Sheila: I really found there are very few people that come to a place in their life that [they] can just accept other people without a lot of strings attached, and I guess, basically, what I'm saying to you that all of our staff [at the women's shelter where she works] is not right there, and so I had to find out that fateful truth, too. And there are a lot of neat things that I've learned, and I just had to learn how to live. I never knew how, basically, and know what was healthier.

Sue: How come you think people in the helping profession— whether it is people at the shelter or the psychologists, therapists, you tried to find, people who organize support groups—how come you think they haven't been more helpful? How do you understand that?

Sheila: Lack of knowledge about the issues, because just in the last few years people have been—and you may correct me because you probably know more about this than I do— how many colleges, how many institutes say that, "Hey, this is family violence" or "This is threatening or manipulative behavior"? Or just ways to identify things that are going on in our society. Everybody just accepts [battering] as normal, and I've had people tell me lately over the last few years … several that stuck in my mind: one lady who was working on a master's degree at the University of Houston, and she came and sat in on one of the groups I ran, and she said, "I will have a piece of paper one day but I will never have what you have because I have not walked where you walked and lived through it." It is surviving, I guess.

৶৻

Sue: You mentioned having reached out to a number of people: family, friends, previous therapists, church. Did you ever feel like that anybody understood?

Nan:	Never really did.
Sue:	Never did.
Nan:	Never ran into another person who had been through it. Therapists were the worst because I would, um, each time we would select a new one, I would get hopeful. And we would go in there, and things would get worse, usually. Things would usually get much worse because my husband was not capable of dealing with issues. He just couldn't— I mean the man was very sick. So, we would go to therapists who would be working on some kind of model. You know, where you're supposed to take whatever it is that caused the fight, and work it out. And the fact is the fight was there before whatever caused it was there. The fact is — that I understand now — is that when the tension started building up in him, then he started looking for whatever it was that he would select as the reason for the fight. And the dynamics, um, didn't come out of causes you could write on paper or work out in a therapy room.
Sue:	And yet, that's the way the therapists would choose to talk about it with you, and with him. And you talked about them not paying attention at all to the violence. How would the two of you talk about it at that time?
Nan:	It was not directly addressed. It may [have been with] the first or second therapist [when] we actually mentioned that our fights became physical. I think the one that was most discouraging for me was a Presbyterian minister in Florida who came with really good credentials. I mean, he had a degree in social work in addition to his theology work, and I remember one time, we'd been seeing him for some time, maybe five months, and I had just had sixty-nine stitches in my arm as a result of going through a picture window. And we were sitting there and my arm was all taped up and my eyes were both black, I mean this was not invisible what I was going through. And Bud brought up something like forgetting the oranges for fresh-squeezed orange juice or something, and I said, "What about me? This, what we're going through, is costing me too much." And Bud became furious and got up and left. And the minister looked at me and said, "Why do you egg him on like that? You know he has a short fuse. Why don't you just work around it?"
Sue:	Mmm. So really blaming you.

Nan: That was what I got. Most of our therapists were men, and most of them blamed me. And, by that time I came across as incredibly inept. It was hard for me to accomplish anything.

Making Sense: What Did It Mean?

After completing the interviews, I reviewed the transcripts multiple times, wanting to absorb and identify both familiar and unfamiliar themes (stories, issues, and theories). Research often identifies familiar and common themes; themes often associated with and considered relevant to women classified as having been battered. Those that I heard include: "Why she couldn't leave"; "I shouldn't have provoked him"; "Christians have good marriages"; and "Maybe I didn't really want to leave."

It is interesting to consider whether the appearance of these issues and stories validate social and scientific perceptions, or whether they are products of the current social–scientific milieu. Other common stories about battering were also mentioned including: the cycle of violence (Walker, 1979), the increase in degree of frequency and intensity (Sonkin, Martin, & Walker, 1985), a concern over their partner's use of alcohol (Walker, 1987a), and the use of creative arts.

Much of what I heard in the interview–conversations was on unfamiliar themes; they have not been discussed in the research literature. The uniqueness of each story could not be communicated or appreciated in the context of mainstream research. Nor, unfortunately, does mainstream therapy provide a place for people to be heard in the completeness and uniqueness of the situations in which they live and struggle.

Implications for Therapy

People want to be known for who they are, what they believe, and what their struggles are. Therapy is a place where people expect this to happen. Most people coming to therapy say, in one way or another, that they have not been heard or respected by others, which is often a component of the current problem situation. Therapists fail to hear their clients when they try to understand them and their problems too concretely (as factual, statistical, or diagnostic representations), too enthusiastically, too expertly, or too quickly.

As I mentioned earlier in the chapter and illustrated in the excerpt with Nan above, people in therapy may even experience being unheard by their therapist. Women who have been battered may tend to fall into this group. When they have asked for help, many of the women I interviewed did not feel heard by therapists. Furthermore, they did not find support or respect from others in the community. Their churches told them that they should be better wives. Their parents told them that all couples fight. They were told by their friends that it could not be that bad. They learned from society that they had few options. Finding jobs, education, childcare, economic aid, and protection from retaliation were difficult.

Obviously, women who have been battered have not been heard or respected by their battering partners. To that, adding their families, friends, churches, therapists, and community resources to this void can contribute to and exacerbate the appearance to women that they are helpless and ineffective. When therapists do not hear, we become part of the problem rather than the solution. We limit our options for relating and understanding and add to our clients' problems. Therapists must learn to hear their clients: their suffering, their dreams, their stories, and their lives.

Others who make up client populations have had similar struggles. People who have had psychotic experiences, including those labeled schizophrenic, find few people who are willing to hear about their voices, visions, and powers. They are not heard, so they withdraw and do not trust. They do not interact appropriately and end up not knowing how to talk to people. The things that are important to them with which they can connect with others are not acceptable for others to hear.

Many people have the experience of not being heard at some time or another or in one relationship or another. Based on what I have learned from my clients, I suspect that if this happens frequently and repeatedly, particularly in meaningful situations, it can result in psychological distress, symptomatology, and an inability to pursue effective action. This may be why women who have been battered do not leave their partners. They have been so unheard, so disrespected, that they become disillusioned and disconnected from their own abilities to act.

Couples Therapy

In therapeutic work with battering, one of commonly accepted rules and procedures includes not seeing couples together (Almeida & Durkin, 1999; Kaufman, 1992). The concern about conjoint therapy when there is battering involved is legitimate, in my view. The concern centers on risk: that one or both partners will minimize or ignore discussing the violence and that battering may result from sessions that inflame or escalate the person who batters.

There are risks to using conjoint therapy when there is battering; however, risks also exist when couples "are not able to be seen" (Goldner, Penn, Sheinberg, & Walker, 1990; Stith, Locke, Rosen, & McCollum, 2001; Stith, Rosen and McCollum, 2003). Couples who contact therapists and are told they cannot be seen together often decide not to do individual therapy. Therapists who take this position risk turning people toward dangerous situations and away from therapy altogether when they are not willing to conform to the therapist's idea of how they should be seen.

Couples seeking help when battering exists are already involved in interactions where they are not being heard by each other, by their family, friends, and their community. Having therapists not hear them may add to their isolation and feelings of being hopeless, misunderstood, blamed, and shamed. I believe that approaching therapy with couples when there is battering is similar to starting work with any client(s): therapists should respect the couple's perspective and start where the couple wants to start. I believe it is quite hopeful that a couple is bringing this issue to therapy. I take the position that at least one of them wants to work on this (and/or other) issues.

I believe that "hearing" clients' stories, which involves curiosity, respect, a learning position, and therapist flexibility, is critical to provide a context for change (Anderson, 1997). When people do not feel heard, they can end up retelling their stories, defending their positions or giving up the quest for understanding. When people come to therapy to talk about battering or any other concern, the therapist's responsibility is to create a way for people to tell their stories.

Each person has his or her own ideas about what they need in terms of relationship and safety to talk about what brings them to therapy. Some clients might take quite a while to express their most private concerns or innermost thoughts, while others seem to explode with their intimate story within the first thirty minutes. Some clients are totally unconcerned about having a team or a reflecting team participate, and others may never be willing to have more than one therapist in the room. Despite having occasional preferences myself, I always start with asking clients about their preferences, how important these are, and what meanings they attach to them.

When a partner in a couple calls to request conjoint therapy, the discussion before the first session includes what the goals are, whose idea therapy is, whose idea it is for them to come together, how much agreement they have about these items, what if the therapist ended up wanting to see them separately, and so forth. When battering is mentioned in this phone call, I will usually ask whether it is something that they both agree we can talk about in therapy. Additional questions are generated by each answer to the above.

Learning the answers to the above questions creates a beginning conversation, usually with only one of the partners, about what we will talk about and how. If battering is mentioned but seems not to be something that we could talk about together, I begin a conversation about that. For example, "What do you think will happen if we start therapy but don't talk about the battering?"

Generative Conversations about Battering

I do not believe that there is a script or a recipe that would help therapists work with couples when there is battering. Instead, the emphasis of therapy should be to create a space and relationship for generative conversations in which all parties take part in choices and decisions in the beginning and throughout therapy and regarding how those choices and decisions may influence the stories that are told. When couples state that they want to talk about battering in therapy, they have already both acknowledged the problem and are in the process of change.

One way I contribute to generativity with such couples is by sharing ideas that I have from my research, clinical experiences, and other current influences. I intend this as a way of continuing to learn more about their meanings and finding ways to talk about the familiar in new ways, thus broadening the conversation. I do not, however, have an investment in what the conversation broadens to regarding its content. I might tell a couple, "Many therapists will not work with couples when there is battering because current research shows that disclosure may lead to more battering. Have you thought about that?" We talk about how they would talk about current and future battering—if it happened. "How would you want me to learn about an incident if you ended up beating your partner during our work together?" "Would it be okay for me to ask about it regularly or would you want to bring it up if it happened?" I might ask what they would do if there were issues that they would prefer to discuss in separate sessions. Could they say this to me or would it be too challenging for their partner to hear? I might also mention typical therapists' assumptions; for example, that drinking is connected to violence, that abuse will escalate, that women have a hard time leaving, and so on. I bring in these ideas as things that are talked about in the field, not necessarily my beliefs. This approach allows me to introduce provocative and challenging possibilities without "owning" the ideas so they can be rejected. If asked directly about my view of these assumptions, I will share my beliefs, which are that research does tend to show the above, but that research findings are based on a "majority" of cases rather than not all people. I share that I try not to generalize about my experiences with clients and that what one family can accomplish does not predict what another can or cannot do.

Continuing a Learner's Journey

The opportunity to learn from the women I interviewed and intensely study the literature in this area is a privilege that not many people have. However, my perspective and values do not permit me to become an expert on women who have been battered. What I have learned from this study will never assure me that I "know" the people who are sitting in my therapy office, what they want for themselves, and what it will take for them to make accomplishments. In fact, I have learned that it is more important to start from a "not-knowing" perspective. I have learned I must be able to "hear the unheard" and to be free to have hope, energy, and connection with each of my clients. I have learned that clients must be free from the labels and limits they expect to get in therapy that may already use on themselves.

Learning from theory, from practice, and from research involves asking questions of the choir of voices who influence you (i.e., your profession, your clients, and your "self"). Hearing requires one to go beyond what is being said to learn what is not said and not known. Hearing the unheard is a generative and endless learning process that connects people in meaningful and valuable therapeutic ways.

Endnotes

1. The masculine is used here to remind readers that historically the field of science, including human research, was constructed and dominated by men.
2. Pseudonyms have been used to protect the anonymity of research participants.

References

Almeida, R.V. & Durkin, T. (1999). The cultural context model: Therapy for couples with domestic violence. *Journal of Marital and Family Therapy, 25*(3), 313–324.

Anderson, H. (1990). Then and now: A journey from "knowing" to "not knowing." *Contemporary Family Therapy, 12*, 193–197.

Anderson, H. (1995). Collaborative language systems: Toward a post-modern therapy. In R. Mikesell, D.D. Lusterman, & S. McDaniel (Eds.), *Integrating family therapy: Family psychology and systems theory* (pp. 27–44). Washington, DC: American Psychological Association.

Anderson, H. (1997). *Conversation, language, and possibilities: A postmodern approach to therapy.* New York: HarperCollins.

Anderson, H. (2000). Becoming a postmodern collaborative therapist: A clinical and theoretical journey. Part I. *Journal of the Texas Association for Marriage and Family Therapy, 3*, 5–12.

Anderson, H. & Goolishian, H. (1988). Human systems as linguistic systems: Evolving ideas about the implications for theory and practice. *Family Process, 27*, 371–393.

Anderson, H. & Goolishian, H. (1992). The client is the expert: A not-knowing approach to therapy. In S. McNamee & K. Gergen (Eds.), *Therapy as social construction* (pp. 25–39). Newbury Park, CA: Sage.

Anderson, H., Goolishian, H., Pulliam, G., & Winderman, L. (1986). The Galveston Family Institute: Some personal and historical perspectives. In D. Efron (Ed.), *Journeys: Expansions of the strategic and systemic therapies* (pp. 97–124). New York: Brunner/Mazel.

Atkinson, B., Heath, A., & Chenail, R. (1991). Qualitative research and the legitimization of knowledge. *Journal of Marital and Family Therapy, 17*, 175–180.

Bateson, M.C. (1990). *Composing a life.* New York: Penguin Books.

Bograd, M. (1984). Family systems approaches to wife battering: A feminist critique. *American Journal of Orthopsychiatry, 54*, 558–568.

Dell, P.F. (1983). From pathology to ethics. *Family Therapy Networker, 7,* 29–31, 64.

Fee, E. (1981). Is feminism a threat to scientific objectivity? *International Journal of Women's Studies, 4,* 378–392.

Fisch, R., Weakland, J., & Segal, L. (1982). *Tactics of change: Doing therapy briefly.* San Francisco, CA: Jossey-Bass.

Flax, J. (1987). Postmodernism and gender relations in feminist theory. *Signs, 12,* 621–643.

Gergen, K. (1991). Emerging challenges for theory and psychology. *Theory and Psychology. 1,* 13–35.

Gergen, K. J. (1982). *Toward transformation in social knowledge.* New York: Springer-Verlag.

Gergen, K.J. (1985) The social constructionist movement in modern psychology. *American Psychologist, 40,* 255–393.

Gilligan, C. (1982). *In a different voice: Psychological theory and women's development.* Cambridge, MA: Harvard University Press.

Gleick, J. (1987). *Chaos.* New York: Viking.

Goldner, V. (1985). Feminism and family therapy. *Family Process, 24,* 31–47.

Goldner, V., Penn, P., Sheinberg, M., & Walker, G. (1990). Love and violence: Gender paradoxes in volatile attachments. *Family Process, 29,* 343–364.

Goodrich, T.J., Rampage, C., Ellman, B., & Halstead, K. (1988). *Feminist family therapy: A casebook.* New York: Norton.

Goolishian, H. (1990). *The position of "not knowing."* Unpublished manuscript.

Hare-Mustin, R. (1978). A feminist approach to family therapy. *Family Process, 1,* 181–194.

Hoffman, L. (1985). Beyond power and control: Toward a "second-order" family systems therapy. *Family Systems Medicine, 3,* 381–396.

Hoffman, L. (1990). Constructing realities: An art of lenses. *Family Process, 29,* 1–12.

Kaufman, G. (1992). The mysterious disappearance of battered women in family therapists' offices: Male privilege colluding with male violence. *Journal of Marital and Family Therapy, 18,* 233–242.

Keeney, B. (1983). *Aesthetics of change.* New York: Guilford Press.

Keeney, B.P. & Bobele, M. (1989). A brief note on family violence. *Australian and New Zealand Journal of Family Therapy, 10,* 93–95.

Kitzinger, C. (1987). *The social construction of lesbianism.* Newbury Park, CA: Sage.

Levin, S.B. (1992). Hearing the unheard: Stories of women who have been battered. (Doctoral dissertation, The Union Institute, 1992). *Dissertation abstracts international. 57*(3).

Levin, S.B. (2002). *Relationships and conversations: Collaborating with a client considered a chronic treatment failure.* Unpublished manuscript.

Lipchik, E. (2002). *Beyond technique in solution-focused therapy: Working with emotions and the therapeutic relationship.* New York: The Guilford Press.

Lobel, K. (Ed.). (1986). *Naming the violence: Speaking out about lesbian battering.* Seattle, WA: The Seal Press.

MacGregor, R., Ritchie, A.M., Serrano, A.C., Schuster, F.P., McDonald, E.C., & Goolishian, H.A. (1964). *Multiple impact therapy with families.* New York: McGraw-Hill.

MacKinnon, L.K. & Miller, D. (1987). The new epistemology and the Milan approach: Feminist and sociopolitical considerations. *Journal of Marital and Family Therapy, 13,* 139–156.

Maturana, H.R. & Varela, F.J. (1987). *The tree of knowledge: The biological roots of human understanding.* Boston, MA: Shambala.

Miller, J.B. (1991). The development of women's sense of self. In J.V. Jordan, A.G. Kaplan, J.B. Miller, I.P. Stiver, & J.L. Surrey (Eds.), *Women's growth in connection: Writings from the stone center* (pp. 11–26). New York: The Guilford Press.

Morgan, G. (1983). Exploring choice: Reframing the process of evaluation. In G. Morgan (Ed.), *Beyond Method: Strategies for Social Research.* Beverly Hills: Sage Publications.

Oakley, A. (1981). Interviewing women: A contradiction in terms. In H. Roberts (Ed.), *Doing feminist research* (pp. 30–61). London: Routledge and Kegan Paul.

Selvini-Palazzoli, M., Boscolo, L., Cecchin, G., & Prata, G. (1978). *Paradox and counterparadox.* New York: Jason Aronson.

Selvini-Palazzoli, M., Boscolo, L., Cecchin, G., & Prata, G. (1980). Hypothesizing—circularity—neutrality: Three guidelines for the conductor of the session. *Family Process, 19,* 3–12.

Sonkin, D.J., Martin, D., & Walker, L. (1985). *The male batterer.* New York: Springer.

Stith, S., Locke, L., Rosen, K., & McCollum, E. (2001). Domestic violence focused couples treatment. *Family Therapy News, 32*, 10–12.

Stith, S. & Rosen, K. (2003). Effectiveness of couples treatment for spouse abuse. *Journal of Marital and Family Therapy, 29*, 407–426.

Taggart, M. (1985). The feminist critique in epistemological perspective: Questions of context in family therapy. *Journal of Marital and Family Therapy, 11*, 113–126.

Tannen, D. (1990). *You just don't understand: Women and men in conversation.* New York: William Morrow and Co.

Von Glaserfeld, E. (1984). An introduction to radical constructivism. In P. Watzlawick (Ed.), *The invented reality: Contributions to constructivism* (pp. 17–40). New York: Norton.

Walker, L. (1979). *The battered woman.* New York: Harper and Row.

Watzlawick, P. (1977). *How real is real?* New York: Vintage Books.

Watzlawick, P. (Ed.). (1984). *The invented reality.* New York: W.W. Norton and Company.

Watzlawick, P., Weakland, J., & Fisch, L. (1974). *Change: The principles of problem formation and problem resolution.* New York: Norton.

Weedon, C. (1987). *Feminist practice and poststructuralist theory.* Oxford: Basil Blackwell.

CHAPTER **9**
You Make the Path as You Walk: Working Collaboratively with People with Eating Disorders

ELENA FERNÁNDEZ, ALEJANDRA CORTÉS,
AND MARGARITA TARRAGONA

Traveler, there is no path
You make the path as you walk
(Caminante, no hay camino
se hace camino al andar)

Antonio Machado

"Making the path as we walked" describes our learning journey as we began to work collaboratively with people who struggle with eating disorders. In Mexico, as in other countries, many women and some men live with eating disorders. At Grupo Campos Elíseos (GCE) in Mexico City, we implemented a two-year clinical research and training project with the goal of exploring the usefulness of a postmodern collaborative perspective in working with people who suffered from bulimia, anorexia, or excess weight. Our approach centered on dialogical conversations using a reflecting team format that we called "consultation interviews". We viewed eating disorders with a wide-angle lens, focusing on the clients' personal stories and broadening out to the biological and social processes that impact the development and recovery from eating disorders. Our collaborative approach included ideas from biology, medicine, psychology, and sociology, which were incorporated in the therapy conversations. When our clients gave us feedback about their therapy experiences, they described the importance of being listened to, exploring new ideas about the social implications of their situation, and the biological aspects of being undernourished. In this chapter, we present the experiences of therapists and clients during this collaborative process.

How the Project Began

Elena and Alejandra began collaborating when Elena requested consultation and support for her work with a client who was struggling with bulimia. Alejandra, a physician also trained as a therapist who specializes in eating disorders joined Elena as a cotherapist. They soon began seeing other clients together as they realized that they each had special knowledge and experience, which, when combined with what their client brought in, resulted in a true collaborative process: Alejandra was able to "take off her white coat" and become more comfortable in her role as a psychotherapist, exploring the nonmedical aspects of the client's experiences, whereas Elena benefited from Alejandra's medical knowledge incorporating the biomedical aspect of eating disorders into her therapeutic work. This collaboration created new options for helping clients.

The collaboration grew when, in the same year, 1999, the founder of the Mexican Association of Eating Disorders (AMTA) who had heard of Elena and Alejandra's collaboration, asked them to help the association train therapists to work with eating disorders. This presented the perfect opportunity to start a clinical research/training program to explore the possibilities of working collaboratively with people with eating disorders.

The training/research project began initially as a one-year project and, at the end of the year, expanded into a two-year project. The training group met once a week to discuss theoretical issues around eating disorders and to see clients working with a reflecting team. Participants could enroll in the training for the full year or elect to enroll in a three-month section. The members of the group were graduate and postgraduate level professionals. On the average, the team was comprised of nine members who were present during conversations with clients. The majority of the members of the team were psychologists, along with two physicians, a nutritionist, and an artist who did art therapy. Over the two-year period, we met with approximately 100 clients. All of the clients who came to a session with the team either had an individual therapist or began to see one of the members of the team in therapy after an initial interview with the group. Most clients were seen with the team for one or two consultations while they continued meeting with their therapists.

How We Worked

We approached this project from a curious stance, attempting to open dialogical conversation with all members of the group and with clients in the style influenced by Harlene Anderson's teachings. We divided each team meeting into two parts: an hour-long theoretical discussion and a "live consultation" with a client that included a reflecting team, which usually lasted an hour and a half. In the theoretical part, we worked as a seminar format and reviewed writings on collaborative therapy (Anderson, 1997) and the use of reflecting processes in therapy (Andersen, 1991, 1995). These ideas provided the guidelines and defined our stance for the clinical work. We also read medical literature on eating disorders. Working from a collaborative postmodern approach, we saw the medical information as a valuable resource that we could have "alongside" us in our conversations with clients and that we might include if it became relevant. We remained aware, however, that the most important knowledge about what life with eating disorders is like would come from our clients.

The clinical part of our meetings consisted of a consultation with a client. Both the group leaders and the therapists in the group invited their clients to a session with the team. We worked exclusively with clients who were already in a therapeutic relationship with one of the members of the team or began to see one of the team members after an initial session with the team; therefore, the team was never a client's only therapeutic connection. Most of the clients who came to the group had severe long-term eating disorders. Many had previously been in therapy (often multiple therapies), and some of them had been hospitalized. The therapists conducted the session with the team members present in the same room. The therapist and client could pause at any time during the session and request reflections. After the client left, we discussed the interview briefly. Early in our work, one of the team members asked: "What if the client is listening to us behind the door after she leaves?" Elena proposed that it might be good to always talk about the client as if she were present and so we adopted this approach for subsequent discussions. Eventually, we decided to invite the clients to stay and join the group's discussion of the interview and to share their experience of the session if they wanted to. For the "after discussions," the therapists and the client joined the reflecting team members around a large table. Because the team members and the clients were in this kind of intimate and informal setting and relationship, the clients found it easy to join in the discussions.

Initially, we worked as a reflecting team in which one of the therapists[1] had a conversation with a client for approximately thirty minutes. If the client was interested, we conducted a traditional Andersen reflecting team for ten to twenty minutes. We did not use a one-way mirror, but a clear separation (about four meters) between the "interview system" (therapist and client) and the team was maintained. Soon, however, our own style of conversation and reflection process evolved which we called "sitting at the square table." This is how it came to be: One day, Elena talked about something that had happened in a different group, where clients had asked if they could sit down at the table with the therapists. The clients felt that it was "natural" to sit around a table where the therapists already were. The group felt it would be "rude" to discourage them from sitting there, so the interview was held around the table. We shifted the reflecting team format in order to satisfy the clients' needs.

As the eating disorders team usually worked around a large square table that seats twelve people, they decided to experiment with this new format, inviting clients to sit around the table with them if they wished. These conversations around the table were somewhat different from the consultation interviews with reflecting teams. Although the therapist that brought the client was in charge of initiating the interaction, the whole team was involved in the conversation. We made comments, asked questions, and had reflecting exchanges or "mini-reflections" among two or three members of the group interwoven with the ongoing interview.

Eventually, at the start of each interview, we gave clients the choice of working around the table or with a reflecting team. Some preferred one style, some the other. We adapted to what the client preferred, even shifting within a session. Clients told us that they enjoyed "feeling as a part of a working team" but also said that having the physical distance and a listening position were very helpful. It is possible that some clients might feel overwhelmed in a conversation with so many participants, but this was not our experience. We always try to make clients feel comfortable and let them know that if a format is not working for them, it can be modified.

Characteristics of Our Work

As is often the case with collaborative, conversational therapy, it is hard to convey "how we worked" because by definition in this approach there are no steps to follow, no specific "techniques" or interventions. Our goal was to create a dialogical space (Anderson, 1997) and to have meaningful, generative conversations and collaborative relationships with our clients and team members. Anderson (1997, 2004) has stressed that certain kinds of relationships permit certain kinds of conversations and vice versa: having a particular conversation can build or transform a relationship. Anderson (n.d.) has said:

Dialogical conversation and collaborative relationship refer to a two-way process: a back-and-forth, give-and-take, in-there together activity and connection where people talk "with" each other rather than "to" each other. Inviting this kind of partnership requires that the client's story take center stage. It requires that the therapist constantly learn—listening and trying to understand the client from their perspective and in the client's language.

This is the kind of partnerships that we strived to create in the group.

Generative Interaction

Our work was very interactive, meaning there was a constant exchange of curiosities and different ideas among us and with our clients. New knowledge was generated as we discussed our readings and talked with clients and group members. For example, some therapists in the group believed the generalized idea that eating disorders are frequently linked to sexual abuse. When we talked with our clients, we began to question this assumption, because most of them had not experienced sexual abuse. Some therapists had a "radical" antidiagnostic stance and the conversations with the clients made us broaden this view. Some clients did not seem to mind having a diagnosis; some of them talked about how having a diagnosis made them feel less alone and that they were, as they said, "not crazy."

Evolving Processes

We adapted our way of working as we moved along with each other and with our clients. We elicited feedback at the end of the sessions from the clients about the therapy and their experiences of the therapists and the reflecting team. We used what we learned in these informal evaluations to modify our work, giving our therapy consultations and reflecting processes many forms that were unique to each client instead of fitting the clients into ours. It truly felt like a shared inquiry and this brought new ways of working and thinking about us as therapists and about each of our clients.

Not-Knowing

Even though team members had seen many people with eating disorders before they joined the project, we approached each client and each conversation from a "not-knowing position" (Anderson, 1997, 2005). There was no predetermined way of working; we allowed the clients to show us the way they wanted to participate in a conversation with "us." We did this by inquiring about their expectations for the session, asking them what they wanted to talk about, and giving them choices about the format of the interviews, the group's participation, and who they would like to include in the sessions. We did not hold private hypotheses or offer interpretations to our clients about their narratives or their descriptions of their lives and their "problems." Instead, we tried to learn about their realities, their narratives, and the premises on which they based their descriptions of themselves and their situation.

Flexibility and Uncertainty

As we saw each client and each session as unique, we had a lot of flexibility in our work. There were no standardized questions or interview protocols, and we invited clients to be a part of the decision-making process of the therapy. For example, sometimes they would choose to bring family members or friends to a session and at times some clients wanted to open up the therapy conversation to include all of the participants in the room. Flexibility also entails being able to work with uncertainty. Harlene Anderson (n.d.) has said, "When a therapist accompanies a client on a journey and walks along side them, the newness (e.g., solutions, resolutions, and outcomes) develops from within the local conversation, is mutually created, and is uniquely tailored to the person or persons involved. Put simply, there is no way to know for sure the direction in which the story will unfold or the outcome when involved in a dialogical conversation and collaborative relationship."

Clients as Experts

From the onset of the group, we knew that we wanted to treat our clients as experts in their own lives. We realized that keeping this intention was not easy when we were faced with extreme health situations. One of the most challenging aspects of the project was working with people who were in a precarious physical state, sometimes at risk of dying. Despite our vigilant concern regarding their physical well-being, we did not force our clients to talk about things that therapists and physicians usually find imperative to discuss such as food, weight, diets, and health. Instead, we followed the clients' lead on their readiness to talk about these things. In some cases, if the clients did not broach the issue of their health or weight, but one or several members of the team were worried about the physical state of the client, they might talk about this in their reflections. We did not try to monitor such reflections nor use the reflection to manipulate a discussion. We assumed, or knew, that others in the clients' lives had expressed similar worries. We simply asked the client their thoughts about the team members' comments. We offered our ideas in an exploratory manner and were ready to accept that the client may not agree.

Medical Risks

When faced with a grave physical concern, we would talk about and suggest nutritional supplements[2] that were easy to take and would slowly bring the client back from starvation. Nutritional "interventions" were, however, never imposed or required in therapy because these clients had already experienced many impositions from people trying to help them, often from therapists, too. We explained to them what goes on in the brain, why there is a difficulty with attention and it becomes hard to concentrate, and why there is memory loss. These were issues that many of our clients were experiencing and about which they were not concerned. When they realized that their grades were slipping or that they could not hold a conversation with their friends or were unable to muster the energy to get someplace, they worried about what was happening to them and oftentimes asked if that could change if they ate something. Our approach was that although they decided whether to eat or not, it was important for them to protect their brain, their heart, and their vital organs. So they were asked to decide what was the minimum amount of food they could eat to preserve these. They proposed what they thought they could eat that would not make them fat but would offer some nutrition to their system. Many of them chose egg whites or ice cream, but each one made her own decision. This was proposed as an experiment or exploration—telling them to try eating what they had chosen and seeing how they felt, how it suited them, and to see what happened just for a few days. The suggestion came from the conversation. It was not strategic because we really saw it as an experiment. The client could try it, reject it, or maybe try something else. Their decision to eat a little bit of food came from the explanation of what was happening to them right then. These young women were frequently warned by family, friends, and doctors about the dangers they could face in the future, but in our group, we focused on what they were actually experiencing in the present. When they could not go to a party because they did not have enough energy, did not pass an exam because their memory failed them, or complained about being very distracted lately, they realized that something worrisome was happening in their bodies. They often saw that eating a little helped them a lot and a "virtuous" circle began, in which food became their ally instead of their enemy.

We would like to emphasize that these conversations about health, nutrition, and "experiments" with food took place in the context of a strong relationship between the young woman and her therapist. Alejandra would sometimes invite a client to have lunch or dinner at her house, or she would go to their homes to have a meal with them[3]. While they were at the table, Alejandra would reassure them that a certain food would not make them get fat and that it would help them rebuild a muscle. She explained that it was possible that they might weigh more because muscles weigh more, but they would not get fat. They talked about what the client saw as "ally foods" and "enemy foods." Protein was seen by many girls as the strongest ally, especially when they were experiencing cognitive difficulties.

The atmosphere of the group was also important. Clients told us they felt listened to, that it was not like they came to hear the expert on anorexia telling them what they had to do. The therapists in the team listened to what was going on in the young women's lives and what each of them said she wanted. The clients often expressed surprise because they did not feel scolded or attacked with information. It was not like attending a biology lecture; the information that was introduced was just what seemed relevant in that specific situation.

When Alejandra started to speak about medical issues, Elena would ask many questions (because she really did not know about these things), and so would the group members. In a way, it was like having an additional reflecting team during a session. This process illustrates for us the creation of a "local knowledge" that included the client's ideas and experiences, medical information, and ideas that came from the team members.

As a physician, Alejandra sometimes prescribed medications to help with some of the effects that stem from eating disorders like gastritis, colitis, headaches, anxiety, and depression. If a client was in a critical health situation, Alejandra would suggest hospitalization. Her suggestion usually came from the client's own story. When a young woman would say, "I am going crazy," "I just can't take it anymore," or when she was fainting and asking, "What do I do?" this might be the time to talk about going into a hospital. Alejandra also attended to her own experience and would speak of hospitalization when she felt that she was looking after a client constantly, if she saw that a client's cognitive functioning was noticeably deteriorated, or when a client was very afraid of food. For some clients, it was helpful to feel that they could relinquish control to something outside themselves for a while.

The conversation about a possible hospitalization was different for each client. Again, these conversations did not follow any steps or a script. The hospital was seen as one resource and never as a punishment. Hospitalization was often discussed in several conversations, with different people. Sometimes Alejandra would say, "You are not being able to do this alone" or "There is something I can't avoid seeing: you are dying and I can't let you. What would you do in my place? What would you think of me if I let you go on like this?" As most clients were minors, Alejandra would speak to their parents if she was worried about a girl's life. The parents had to make the decision to hospitalize their daughters, and Alejandra would tell the client that her parents could force her to go into the hospital, or they could discuss it together and she could be part of the discussion. The conversation about hospitalization was an evolving decision-making process: the team members, the doctor, and the parents were involved, and the client's opinion was taken into account.

It is important to note that only three clients were hospitalized in the two years that we worked as a team. When clients were hospitalized, Alejandra and some of the team members would continue to meet with them in the hospital, which would keep the space for dialogue open.

Emerging Themes

As we mentioned above, we sought to enter each conversation with clients from a "not-knowing position" (Anderson, 1997). We tried to avoid reliance on theoretical explanations about eating disorders or our previous personal and professional experiences when we talked with our clients. We wanted to learn from them, starting with their unique experience and their personal understanding of their situation. We also wanted to learn about their experiences with previous therapy and how it had or had not worked. In our theoretical discussions and conversations with clients, we found that a "local culture" began to emerge in the group. Three sets of ideas about working with eating disorders seemed particularly interesting and useful to us: (1) the social-cultural aspect of eating disorders, (2) the biomedical consequences of undernourishment, and (2) the usefulness of a collaborative and conversational approach to therapy with these clients.

Sociocultural Aspects of Eating Disorders

Through our readings and discussions, we became aware that, from a sociocultural perspective, ideas around eating and body image had changed dramatically over the past thirty years. We read many articles that looked at eating disorders from gender-sensitive and feminist perspectives. For example, Mary Pipher (1995) says that, "the popular media—movies, television, advertising, and magazines—are the major promoters of 'lookism' in women. Females are generally . . . young, slim, handicap-free, and white" (p. 19). This definition of beauty changes over time, and, with it, our identity, the way we perceive others, and the subtle aspects of what is acceptable change as well. Pipher (1995) also comments that "research has shown that men tend to evaluate their bodies realistically and their self-appraisals match up with the appraisals of others. Women behave differently. As a group, women consistently see themselves as fatter and less attractive than others see them. Many women come with laundry lists of complaints about their bodies" (p. 16).

Hesse-Biber (1996) says that human beings learn to see themselves as others see them, as social standards dictate the ways of perceiving. Kenneth Gergen (1994) maintains that, "the degree to which a given account of world or self is sustained across time is not dependent on the objective validity of the account but on the vicissitudes of social process" (p. 51).

Many clinical and epidemiological studies have found that eating disorders are "over represented in women" (Weeda-Mannak, 1994). In the feminist literature, there are also numerous studies that show the connection between the media and eating disorders. In Esther Rothblum's (1994), chapter "I'll Die for the Revolution, But Don't Ask Me Not to Diet," she asks the question, "Why haven't feminists focused on hatred of fat in our society?" (p. 53). She contends that women's body weight must be included in the feminist agenda, that we must understand that "women's attractiveness has important consequences for their social and interpersonal success and even for the success of the men in whose company they are seen" (p. 71). She concludes, "In this regard, the media perpetuate stereotypes about physical appearance and set norms for attractiveness" (p. 71). Waller and Shaw (1995) similarly maintain,

> … through the ideological promotion of selected issues, the media inform girls and women what their major preoccupations should be. In particular, this "culture of femininity" focuses on representations of an ideal female body: For many women, such media images produce strong emotional responses, including dissatisfaction with their own bodies and the desire to attain the ultimate ideal. Such emotional responses might be among the factors that initiate the cycle of dietary restraint and binge eating which is often identified as a precursor to the development of an eating disorder. (p. 45)

In addition to our theoretical readings, team members would sometimes bring in newspaper ads and magazine clips that exemplified the messages that women constantly receive about weight and beauty. The "ideal" women depicted in the media were extremely thin and apparently had been getting progressively thinner. Advertising seemed to send the message that "thin is good and fat is evil."

Many clients spontaneously expressed that the influence of culture and the media had a tremendous impact on the way they perceived their bodies. They told us things such as, "only thin girls are popular" in school and with boys. For example, our client Rebecca[4] told us that both her parents were always dieting, saying, "Ever since I can remember, they have always been very aware of what to eat and not to eat." Cynthia, a young married woman, said that the wives of her husband's friends were all very thin, and she felt great pressure to be like them.

Our reading materials helped us reflect on the messages women are receiving and, if deemed relevant in a conversation with a client, we would introduce the information we were gathering. Talking about gender and culture often took our conversations with clients in unpredictable directions. Some of the clients were quite enthusiastic talking about media and social messages, agreeing completely with the idea that cultural context was a determining factor for eating disorders and offering examples of how they had personally experienced the detrimental effect of this cultural pressure for thinness. Patty, a client, expressed it this way:

I need my eyes back; sometimes I can only see myself with the eyes of the magazines I read, the TV programs I watch, and I see myself and I look fat. When I see myself through the eyes of my family and friends, I see myself as too thin. Whose eyes are saying the truth? I need my own eyes back. Could you lend me your eyes so I can see myself like you see me?

We had a group conversation with Patty about how she might get her eyes back. Ideas that emerged included taking photographs of herself and writing her perceptions down in order to differentiate herself from others.

Some clients remembered the times when they were overweight and the criticism that accompanied that experience. They shared stories about the delight many people expressed when they lost some of the weight. Alicia shared her dismay at how unfair and paradoxical it was that the same people that had applauded her initial efforts to lose weight were now upset that she had reached "her" goal of being thin. She was perplexed.

Other clients, however, did not agree with the idea that sociocultural forces had had an effect on their life and did not see the relevance of a "media explanation" for their situation. Lorena and Malinali who had become friends in Alejandra's waiting room illustrate their differing perspectives around this issue. We had seen each of them separately in the group, until they requested a one-time conjoint session. They told us they shared much in common: both of their mothers were accountants, both of their fathers were economists, and they both were studying architecture but had to leave the university because of the impact of bulimia. When they came to a session together, they talked about these coincidences and how being friends and sharing their experiences had helped them cope. But they explained that although they had so many things in common, the "origin" of their "affliction" was quite different. For Lorena it was clearly a societal and cultural problem: seeing her favorite actresses on TV and in magazines had triggered a need to be as thin as possible, to try to be as attractive as they were. For Malinali, it was biopsychosocial: she thought that the stress of a bad relationship between her parents had made her "release tension through binging and vomiting."

Biomedical Aspects of Eating Disorders

One of the unique aspects of our work was that Alejandra introduced biomedical perspectives into conversations with clients. One of the features that characterize her work is that she often includes medical information in her sessions. She does this in a collaborative way. She brings medical knowledge into the conversation only when she thinks it is relevant to what the client is discussing. The information is seen as an offering following a client's lead. The therapist introduces information in a tone and manner that conveys that the client may choose what to do with it. The information is, as Harlene Anderson likes to say, "food for thought," something else to be considered and discussed and not the only explanation or the last word.

This is Alejandra's account of how she started telling clients about the physiological aspects of malnutrition:

> A client of mine, Claudia, came to see me in a state of starvation. She had told me several times that she didn't know why she was coming and that she didn't understand what was happening to her. She felt confused, depressed, angry, and sometimes she felt that she was going crazy. She had lost the inner light in her eyes. I felt she was trying to communicate something from deep inside, but she could only tell me that she wanted to feel at peace with herself and that she needed someone to listen to her confusion. I don't know why but I decided to open one of my medical books and I showed her the diagram of a cell. I explained to her that the cell is the unit of vital functioning in our body and that if the cell was affected every organ in the body would become affected as well. I explained to Claudia about the cell membrane and how it is formed out of protein and fat. I told her that through this membrane vital functions are processed. When there isn't enough protein and fat, the cell loses its consistency and those processes fail. This in turn will produce changes in the chemistry of the body.
>
> I told Claudia that when this happens in the central nervous system it is especially problematic. Alterations in the spinal fluid can impact the lateral ventricles and the third ventricle of the brain. When there is malnourishment, there are changes in the electrolyte balance inside the brain (Lask & Bryant-Waugh, 1993; Szmukler, Dare, & Treasure, 1995). This produces compression on the brain mass, which can cause lack of attention and concentration, insomnia, motor hyperactivity, alteration of emotional states, et cetera.
>
> Claudia was especially interested when we talked about body image and wanted to know more. I showed her in my books how when starvation produced changes in the brain, a distortion in the perception of body image occurs. Women with anorexia or bulimia see themselves as fat, and the people from the outside see them as extremely

thin. I told her that I believed both things were true. Claudia asked me about her feelings and her unstable emotional state. I told her that when you are starved there are not enough nutrients in the body to form neurotransmitters in the brain; you can feel depressed and anxious. The good news is that once you start eating, anxiety diminishes and you feel better emotionally. I also told Claudia that when the brain is under such stress you can present what could be interpreted as personality disorders or mental illness, like profound depression, psychosis, etc. I again reassured her by saying that in my experience, and as others have reported (Szmukler, Dare, & Treasure, 1995), these symptoms disappear when people renourish themselves.

When we finished talking her face changed. She told me she was feeling like she was going crazy before our conversation and that now she understood what was happening to her. In future sessions, we continued to talk about how the human body works, and she told me that this information was very useful to her.

When clients like Claudia come to an understanding of the disorder and begin ingesting food again, another set of problems arises. The digestive system, with little food intake over a long period of time, changes, and clients may present with gastritis and a delayed gastric emptying (Szmukler, Dare, & Treasure, 1995). So, Alejandra had to explain to Claudia this biological process and how, when this happens, a person can feel full (satiated) with very little food. Therapists, family members, and even clients often confuse this hunger with an "eating compulsion," as people recovering from eating disorders often feel full and hungry at the same time.

Another disadvantage of this delayed gastric emptying is that it produces bloating of the intestines, making Claudia and other clients feel that they are getting fat. Also, family members are often disbelieving and scoff at them when they say they are full after eating so little. Claudia and I talked about all these issues and she asked for a special session for her parents to explain to them the physiological part of her problem.

An important observation in Alejandra's experience is that people often have lab tests done to assess their condition and, for the most part, results are negative.[5] For example, blood counts, liver functioning, and glucose levels often appear to be within normal ranges. Parents and clients are frequently perplexed by these reports. Sometimes the clients use this information to tell the therapist or the physician, "I told you: nothing is wrong with me."

When this happens, Alejandra opens a discussion and asks the clients if they feel tired, if they can follow the conversation, if their attention at school or work is okay, and if there is any dizziness. She also asks about

hormonal problems. Many clients answer at least one of the questions affir-
matively, although early on they say this has nothing to do with starvation.
Alejandra tells them that they are the experts in the way they feel and asks
them to contrast how they felt when they were eating regular meals and
how they feel now. They often report and discuss feeling differently.

Clients reported that they found Alejandra's biomedical perspective
very helpful; she subsequently included more of it in her conversations with
clients. It was also seen as therapeutic by the team of therapists at Grupo
Campos Elíseos, so we began to include it in our conversations as well. Many
of our clients told us that understanding what was happening to them from
a physiological perspective was extremely useful and made a significant
difference in their experience of themselves and the eating disorders with
which they were struggling. We would like to stress, again, that this offering
of information was done in the context of a close relationship with clients.
Alejandra describes her main goal as a physician/therapist as "to be present"
with her clients throughout their process and to share this information. She
looked for the grammatical root of the word "cure" and found that it comes
from the German *sorge*, which means "to take care, to be with" (Acevedo,
1985). For Alejandra, what she and the team did in those two years of learning was to "be with" the clients while they regained their inner peace.

Collaboration

Collaboration was the most important aspect of our work. As Anderson
(1997) points out, a collaborative approach can be described as a philosophy of therapy, as a stance or way of being in relationship and in conversation with other people, more than a model or set of techniques.

Listening to clients' stories allowed us to continue being curious about
their lives and their understandings of their problems. Sharing our readings with them gave us new opportunities to talk and to include them in
this "learning state of mind."

While we were in conversation with our clients, we were also learners.
We not only learned from their stories, we shared knowledge about the
complexities of life for women in our time, the sociocultural dimension
of eating disorders, the mechanisms of our biology, and the interaction
between physiology and psyche.

Approaching our clients from a collaborative stance helped us create a
space for possibilities and transformation. Our clients told us that this way
of working was particularly helpful because there was room to learn and to
be listened to. Many of them had been long-term clients in other therapies,
trying in vain for years to find relief from eating disorders. They described
this collaborative way of working as a new and useful option. When the
conversations and reflections were successful, therapists and clients alike

developed new ideas that expanded their understanding of the present and of what might come in the future.

Clients' Voices

We would like to conclude with two of our clients' voices. Since we were exploring and learning as we worked, we understood our project as a form of "action research." Our work fitted with Anderson's (2000) conceptualization of research as part of everyday practice: we continually got feedback from our clients and used it to modify our work. Additionally, some of the clients were also interviewed about their therapeutic experiences with the team. These interviews were conducted in a different context and by a colleague who was not a member of the team[6] in order to understand the clients' experiences in more detail. In the following paragraphs, we present some of what they had to say about their experiences in therapy and with the group.

Brigitte

Brigitte was a young woman who presented with excess weight and bulimic behaviors like the use of laxatives and amphetamines, and binging and vomiting episodes. Her therapist invited her to two sessions with the group and a reflecting team in each session. A few weeks later Brigitte was interviewed about her experiences in therapy and during these two visits. Here are some of her comments.

- I have not lost all the weight that I originally wanted to lose when I got here. It is a slower and more complex process, but there have been many changes: I haven't vomited in four months, I haven't used laxatives for a long time, and now I go to the gym. I can see that I am more than a fat woman.[7]
- This is different from other therapies that I have had that were more traditional. In this therapy, I feel closer to the therapists. There are less hierarchical differences. We use the same chairs; there is no special chair for the therapist. Here I feel more comfortable, we laugh. I can curse if I want to. It is a more normal relationship.
- I visited the reflecting team twice. I have taken with me a wealth of information that I've been churning around. . . . Listening to the team is hard, and it is enriching. It is hard because you come here to talk about yourself. You think that you come here to talk about diets and you talk about more important things.
- The team has many ideas, but they do not give advice. When people tell me what to do, I do not take that into account, and I do whatever I want.

- Those two sessions have made me write a lot in my diary ... one of the things I would highlight is that when I only saw a fat woman, the team saw in me another person. They asked me about other areas of my life and this led me to think and question why do I only see a fat woman when I can be much more? They saw other aspects of me.
- I didn't know that I was a secure woman. Here I discovered that I was self-confident. The team commented about this, and I proved it when I went abroad to present a paper at an international conference. I did it with great ease and self-assurance. I remembered the team and I thought they were right, that I am confident.
- My two visits with the team were very meaningful. Listening to how they saw me made me think that I only had a negative view of myself. It reminded me of a scene in *The Dead Poets' Society*, when Robin Williams stands on a table and makes the boys turn and say "Why look only in one direction? There are many ways to see things!" The team was like that; they had many ways to see things.

Natalia

Natalia was a young woman who presented with a relapse of bulimia, including vomiting and anxiety toward food. She was in therapy with Alejandra and Elena, who worked together, and she had gone to two consultations with the group. Here is part of what she shared with us about her therapy process.

- In therapy, it was helpful to be able to "decompress." I was able to bring out things, fears, and emotions. We talked about food, but not only about food. I had never talked about so many different topics.
- There were several things that helped me. My mother helped me a lot. We talked like friends; she was in my team, not in front of me. My mother, like the therapists, did not challenge me; they supported me.
- After coming to therapy and the team, one day I decided I was not going to vomit anymore. I made a commitment with a friend via e-mail. We each had a calendar and we crossed off the days that I didn't throw up.
- In the team, you see different ways of facing a situation. What helps me the most is that they talk to me in a simple way, they are straightforward. This is a treatment for a "grown-up," not a therapy where they control you from the outside. Here I depend on myself. I feel free to take or leave what they say; they were very respectful with my decisions.

- They treat you like an equal, like a person who is going through a difficult time and not like a sick person. It's a difficult time that you have to overcome. Through words, you can either discuss "pathology" or a "situation." Here, we spoke about a situation, and this helped me understand that it is not the end of the world. The pressure that I felt was lifted, and it was easier to make the right decisions.
- I didn't feel like I was with a group of psychologists. For me it was like a chat, like a talk with a group of women who you know are professionals but who do not use such a complicated language. It is not a space where you are the patient and, therefore, there is something wrong with you, and the psychologists analyze you and define what is happening to you. Being analyzed generates a big distance, and the fact that they didn't do that here helped me open up.
- One of the most important things that happened was that they gave me information about the physiological part, not just of bulimia and anorexia, but also of the changes that go on once you start to recover. That calmed me a lot. Understanding the physiological process helped me continue down the road. This is something that had not been given to me in any other treatment, and it made all the difference.
- In the beginning, I said, "I have to" and now I say, "I want to." It is the difference between an obligation and a decision. Now I give myself permission to think what I want and what I feel and then act on it. This is what they taught me when they would ask me questions, and thus I learned to think about myself.
- I have been feeling a great growth as a person. I do not feel like a sick person.
- In my experience, the members of the team are open, and they feel that they learn from me as I learn from them. In other therapies, the therapist had the last word. Here there is feedback, and we all learn.

We agree with Natalia. During those two years, we learned alongside our clients. We learned about their problems and how they coped with and were able to overcome them. We read, shared our ideas with clients, and solicited their feedback. Their reactions and thoughts interacted consistently with our own and those of the authors we were discussing. We learned that there is no one right way to work with anorexia, bulimia, and overeating. We found that working from a collaborative stance helped us and our clients contemplate new understandings and new actions.

We believe that together we developed a learning community that changed the way therapists viewed women with eating disorders, and helped clients focus and broaden their views of themselves. Many of these women were able to make much-wanted shifts in their lives.

One of the members of the group was recently invited to create an eating disorders clinic in one of the largest hospitals in Mexico City. Three other members of the team will be on the staff. Alejandra continues to work with many people who struggle with eating disorders and has started a clinic of her own, where she now also integrates art, drama, and dance in her work with clients. Elena and Margarita continue to be in touch with members of the team in supervision and "clinical conversations" groups. We feel that we are making paths as we walk together.

Endnotes

1. It could be the client's therapist or another member of the team.
2. These were generally commercially available protein drinks, but sometimes whatever the client was willing to eat, like a little bit of ice cream, Jell-O, or cooked egg whites.
3. Alejandra practiced in a house that served as an informal gathering and conversational space for her clients.
4. All of the clients' names have been changed to preserve their anonymity.
5. In her practice through the years, Alejandra has noticed that many physicians ask people with eating disorders to get lab tests, like a standard blood work, and the results of these appear to be normal. She believes that the tests that are most frequently used are not sensitive to the changes that take place in the body of a person who has an eating disorder. Influenced by the work of Lask, and Bryant-Waugh (1993) she has designed a specific protocol of laboratory tests that in her experience is more useful to assess a client's health, especially when there is serious malnourishment. This protocol may include, for example, an assessment of cholesterol levels, bone density, an electrocardiogram, or an EEG.
6. The interviewer was Margarita Tarragona.
7. The authors translated of the clients' words from Spanish to English.

References

Acevedo, G. (1985). *El modo humano de enfermar*. Buenos Aires: Fundación Argentina de Logoterapia Victor Frankl.

Andersen, T. (1987). The reflecting team: Dialogue and metadialogue in clinical work. *Family Process, 26*, 415–428.

Andersen, T. (1990). *The reflecting team*. New York: Norton Books.

Andersen, T. (1991, May). *Relationship, language, and pre-understanding in the reflecting process*. Paper Presented at the Houston Galveston Narrative and Psychotherapy Conference, New Directions in Psychotherapy. Houston, TX.

Anderson, H. (n.d.). *A postmodern collaborative approach to therapy: Broadening the possibilities of clients and therapists*. Retrieved August 21, 2005, from http://www.harleneanderson. org/writings/postmoderncollaborativeapproach.htm.

Anderson, H. (2000, October). Postmodern therapists as researchers: Research as part of everyday practice. Presentation at the American Association for Marriage and Family Therapy Annual Conference. Denver, CO.

Anderson, H. (1997). *Conversation, language and possibilities: A postmodern approach to therapy*. New York: Basic Books.

Anderson, H. (2003). A postmodern collaborative approach to theraphy: Broadening the possibilities of clients and therapists. In *Ethically challenged professions: Enabling innovation and diversity in psychotherapy and counseling*. In Y. Bates & R. House (Eds.). PCCS Books: Herefordshisre, UK.

Anderson, H. (2005). The myth of not-knowing. *Family Process, 44*(4), 497–504.

Gergen, K. (1994). *Realities and relationships: Soundings in social construction*. Harvard: Harvard University Press.

Hesse-Biber, S. (1996). *Am I thin enough yet? The cult of thinness and the commercialization of identity*. Oxford: Oxford University Press.

Lask, B. & Bryant-Waugh, R. (1993). *Childhood onset of anorexia nervosa and related eating disorders*. U.K.: Lawrence Erlbaum.

Pipher, M. (1995). *Hunger pains: The modern woman's quest for thinness*. New York: Ballantine.

Rothblum, E.D. (1994). I'll die for the revolution, but don't ask me not to diet: Feminism and the continuing stigmatization of obesity. In P. Fallon, M. Katzman, & S. Wooley (Eds.), *Feminist perspectives on eating disorders* (pp. 53–56). New York: Guilford Press.

Szmukler, G., Dare, C., & Treasure, J. (1995). *Handbook of eating disorders: Theory, treatment and research*. New York: John Wiley and Sons.

Waller, G. & Shaw, J. (1995). The media influence on eating problems. In B. Dolan & I. Gitzinger (Eds.), *Why women? Gender issues and eating disorders* (2nd ed., pp. 44–56). London: Athlone Press.

Weeda-Mannak, W. (1994). Female sex-role conflicts and eating disorders. In B. Dolan & I. Gitzinger (Eds.), *Why women? Gender issues and eating disorders* (2nd ed., pp. 15–20). London: Athlone Press.

CHAPTER **10**

Honoring Elders through Conversations about Their Lives

JENNIFER ANDREWS

> Childhood years,
> Sweet childhood years
> Always awake in my memory
> When I recall you
> I am filled with pain
> Oh, how quickly I've grown old
>
> *Childhood Years* (**Translated from the
> Jewish folksong "Kinder Yahren"**)

Sarah, a retired executive with a doctoral degree, had worked for an agency that delivered services to the elderly. She had participated in inventing "Meals on Wheels" for her agency, many years ago. Celia, a recently retired social worker in her nineties told us that had she cofounded the first Family Therapy Center in New York, with Nathan Ackerman in 1959. Lillian, ninety years old, had assisted her husband in running a small recording studio. They had helped performers who could not afford expensive studio time. Working with elders has humbled and fascinated me, and I have continued to be in reciprocal relationships with elders who look forward to our conversation groups as much as I do.

Six years ago, I founded The Elder Project, a program that arranged for marriage and family therapy students to visit elders in the community and

local retirement homes. In efforts aimed at combining definitional ceremony (Myerhoff, 1976, 1978, 1992), collaborative conversation (Anderson &
Goolishian, 1988; Goolishian & Anderson, 1987, 1990, 1996), and reflecting
processes (Andersen, 1991, 1995), my students began their work.

The project's initial goals were to offer conversations with elders as
an avenue toward collecting client hours; to provide my students with
greater exposure to postmodern therapy ideas; and to empower elders
through nonpathologizing and nonhierarchical conversations. Instead
of identifying deficits in their lives or requesting psychotherapy, the
elders welcomed the contact with the students. Unexpectedly, the students also felt enriched through these connections. Unlike respected
colleagues who would typically diagnose elders immediately, we started
from the premise that they were functioning normally (Frederickson
& Handlon, 2003). As the project came to life, we found that we were
increasingly looking for the strengths and resources in the lives of the
elders (Andrews & Clark, 2003).

In sharing stories about the vital and productive times, two things happened. First, the elders became infused with energy as they retold stories.
Second, we developed a great respect for their enthusiastic participation
in the program discussed here. This chapter describes how this process
evolved in various settings and used different conversational forms. The
stories of five elders are described in depth to illustrate the effects of this
process. Similar stories are published elsewhere (Andrews, 2001).

Influences

While serving on a dissertation committee in the late 1980s, the late Harry
Goolishian had introduced me to ideas that he and Harlene Anderson were
developing. They and their colleagues at the Houston Galveston Institute
had been interested in how language shaped reality. Drawing upon the
ideas of Gregory Bateson, Humberto Maturana, and Francisco Varela,
and combining them with their interest in hermeneutics and the emerging social constructionist writings of social psychologists Kenneth Gergen
(1991) and John Shotter (1993), Goolishian and Anderson had formulated
a new theoretical premise. In developing their conversational approach,
soon to be recognized as Collaborative Language Systems (Goolishian
& Anderson, 1988), their view of clients had shifted from pathologizing
descriptions to an appreciation of clients' strengths and resources. Their
theory suggested that people have potential for creating the lives that they
would prefer to live. The focus of "therapy talk" shifted from rehashing
and gathering data about problems to listening carefully to client narratives using a therapeutic stance that interactively responded to what clients

were saying. Through a dialogical process, the client is placed at center-stage, creating an egalitarian atmosphere based on sincere curiosity and interest and on respect for their voice and reality.

In addition to the work of Goolishian and Anderson, the work of anthropologist Barbara Myerhoff (1976, 1992) provided an important foundation to our project by offering a description of a community-based reflecting process. Myerhoff studied the practices of an aging Jewish community in Venice, CA, listening to and collecting stories from them and reflecting comments and questions in return. She called this process a "definitional ceremony" and suggested that, in our society, as people age they tend to become isolated and "dis-membered" from their community. Myerhoff suggested that they can rejoin or "re-member" themselves into the meanings of their life and life itself through a process of telling their stories to people they respect, who in turn, reflect on what they say. Her conversations were immortalized in the documentary film *Number Our Days* that won the 1976 Academy Award for best short documentary. As part of the film's script, Myerhoff, a young woman, discussed her own future as an aging Jew. However, she did not survive to experience her own old age, dying prematurely of cancer, which made her references to death throughout the film particularly poignant. The more recent developments of reflecting processes by Tom Andersen (1991, 1995) were also incorporated into our work. We also drew from Erikson's (1959) developmental stage of "despair versus integrity". Most people have viewed the elderly as people who experience their lives with diminishing returns. Many elders have felt resigned to this, and depression has been commonly reported. Activity schedules that are offered at retirement hotels have typically depended upon available funds; many offer little more than weekly games of bingo and "sing-alongs." Therefore, this project provided a unique possibility for a real qualitative enhancement in the lives of elders.

From Humble Beginnings

Our students learned standard counseling methods and were exposed to postmodern practices only in the optional courses that I taught. Up until that time, I had not found community-based training opportunities for students to practice a collaborative conversational approach. When the requirement for clinical contact hours was increased, I was pressed to find new clinical opportunities and, knowing of Myerhoff's work, I decided to create The Elder Project.

The project began with eight students who were studying the collaborative approach (Anderson, 1997) and reflecting team practices (Anderson, 1991). There were many retirement communities in Southern California;

we therefore had access to an unlimited number of clients and were heart-edly welcomed at each facility. We were not in the usual therapist position, wherein a client (or referring person) initiated the contract because they wanted or needed something. Instead, the students were the ones who initiated a relationship because they needed the clinical practice. We held many conversations about the ethical concerns pertaining to this unique situation. And in the end, we believed that the conversations would have meaning and therapeutic value for the elders.

Sometimes, the conversations that we initiated with the elders did not seem to go anywhere; no matter what wonderful conversational or generative questions we asked, no matter how we tried to be responsive to their stories, and no matter how interested in them we remained, they were ultimately more curious about us. For these people, we became the bearers of news from the outside world and a source of stimulation, friendship, and caring. For others, we became an audience to their stories. They wanted to talk with us uninterruptedly. If we attempted to ask questions or make comments of any sort, they politely waited for us to finish and then continued telling their story without responding to our inquiry.

The reflecting process ran into unexpected challenges. Even though we explained the process of taking turns, with the team listening at first to the therapist–client conversation and then having a conversation about it while the therapist and client listened, the process did not make sense to many elders. They politely allowed the team to start and then began to converse with them, interrupting when they felt the need to contribute. Without the boundary of the traditional mirror, we did not conduct our usual reflecting process. As we were all in the same room, the elders wanted to talk with the reflecting team members directly. Although we may have wanted to practice the typical reflecting process, which we referred to as "opening space," the elders did not share our agenda. We learned a great deal regarding what it meant to really be listening to the client, quickly placing our goals on the back burner. Out of necessity we became flexible, shifting our goals from reflecting to maintaining a coherent conversation with the elders.

Soon after the project began, we conducted our discussions about what therapy represented and what constituted a therapeutic endeavor? How were our experiences with the elders relevant to our efforts in learning to be a therapist? Miriam Polster (1967) has defined therapy as a coming together where two people meet for the benefit of one. Given this definition, it seemed reasonable to ask the elders if our meetings were benefiting them. We consulted our clients about their experiences with us. Students surveyed the elders about what they received from our visits. Were we helpful to them? Did they want us to continue to meet with them? Based on their enthusiastic responses and reports, using our words about how their qualities of life were changing because of our presence, we concluded that they were experiencing a therapeutic benefit. Our interest was genuine and the connections were satisfying to them as well as to us. The project continued and grew.

The Elder Project: Contexts and Modalities

The elders we worked with entered their retirement communities for different reasons. Most were placed into the retirement hotels by concerned relatives. These residents sometimes felt that they had been "kidnapped" or "placed" against their will but, for the sake of peace, consented to their relative's wishes. A few had chosen this lifestyle as they began to realize their limits due to growing fragility. There were major attitudinal differences between the voluntary populations and the mandated ones. Statistically, it has been atypical for aging adults to live in retirement or assisted living facilities, since most seniors still live in their own homes or with relatives. Today, quality rather than quantity of life has become the greater issue.

Over the years, The Elder Project has worked with elders in different contexts using different modalities, including (1) groups in retirement communities, (2) individual sessions at the university, (3) individual sessions in retirement communities, and (4) independent elders from the larger community.

Working with Groups in the Retirement Hotel Community

The way I work with a group has evolved from the context of the work and the interests and needs of the group's membership. Frequently, the physical environment and surroundings of the facility has been a major determinant. For example, the present group has a form that was based on function. We met in a corner of a large room with couches against both walls; a circle was created by adding additional chairs. There were many additional couches and chairs scattered around the room that served as an outer circle. Given that most of the residents were hard of hearing and the large size of the room, a microphone was typically necessary. Management had placed the residents on a master calendar and every week posted flyers in the elevators and on bulletin boards. Our group activity was one of approximately nine activities that could occur on this particular day, and attendance was always voluntary. Presence in the room qualified someone as a member. The inner circle sat between 20 and 25 people. The people who sat in the larger circle generally did not expect to use the microphone and participated primarily as listeners. Membership between circles was fluid, although those present in the room changed little from week to week.

Many in the larger circle were caregivers for disabled participants. Several men regarded the inner circle as a space reserved for women but occasionally would jump in with a comment. We started by passing the microphone around the inner circle, and each was invited to speak freely. Some members chose to share about how they were doing, a concern they had, or an agenda item to be discussed later in the meeting. Nothing was preset for the meeting; each meeting evolved according to the wishes of the group.

If there were new people in the room, the group delighted in having them introduce themselves, including where they had came from, what had brought them there, and what they had done in their younger years. People in the room would call out if they or someone they knew came from the same place. Sometimes members discovered that the new people were relatives whom they had never met. The social aspect of the meeting was very special for the members because there was no other activity where residents could speak about themselves so publicly.

When the microphone traveled, I participated and, within appropriate boundaries, self-disclosed. For example, one time I had mentioned that my husband had died. In their response, the group became advisors to me, offering support and information from the experiences that they had lived. They also were supportive of each other. The microphone time was magical, and the hour could go by quickly with interactions between group members building as the microphone was passed around. When someone wanted to be listened to, I usually asked questions that were designed to expand their view or add voices to the ones they already had.

The women seemed to have unlimited possibilities for conversation topics: family, career, where they had come from, politics, movies, or a recent conversation. If a man had served in the military, experience had taught me that he would want to speak about that. When I spoke with a man for the first time that had served in the military, he most always initiated a conversation about that time in his life. For them, being in the military was the most unusual and profound experience of their lives. They remembered themselves in their youth, away from home, and facing unknown and often horrible situations. Many recounted fighting in battles during the Second World War, and although they had not suffered from post-traumatic stress syndrome (PTSD), they were still shocked by what they had seen. Something happened there that they would remember forever and that probably could never be fully understood by others in their lives.

Sometimes, I brought with me a new issue of Ken and Mary Gergen's online newsletter, "Positive Aging" (www.healthandage.com) and read a topic aloud to the group hoping to stimulate discussion. Other times I offered a book to stimulate discussion, sometimes taken, other times rejected. On one occasion, we read from the book Aging Well (Valliant, 2001), that discussed how our attitudes could influence our abilities to age well; the discussion that ensued lasted for several weeks.

Miriam's Story. We have had challenging experiences with the group. Since some residents struggled with memory problems, it was not surprising to us when someone repeated something that they had said before or said something irrelevant to the conversations in the room. One morning two years ago, when my student Phil and I were meeting with the group, a woman, Miriam, created a great deal of anxiety among the other members as she responded to an outer circle member who was cognitively challenged. Rose, 92 years old, said, apropos of nothing, "I've been married three times and I expect to marry again." This brought murmured comments from first-timers who did not know Rose: "Do you have someone?" "Are you engaged?" "Are you serious?" To all of this she replied, "Of course. But I can't tell you who yet."

Miriam, who knew Rose, and was also 92, blind, nearly deaf, and hardly able to walk, was sitting next to me. She asked for the microphone and announced, "Girls, if you are interested in meeting a man, I would like to give you advice. Look for a window washer!" The room became momentarily silent because nearly everyone seemed dumbfounded. I assumed that Miriam was attempting to rescue Rose. Perhaps Miriam was doing standup comedy, or showing signs of dementia? Not sure, no one responded and Miriam continued:

> I tell you that window washers are a good population of men because they are so fit. And, they all belong to a union so you know their jobs are secure. If you want to meet a window washer, wait till a convention of window washers comes to town. Don't be cheap about the cost of the convention because it is worth it since you will have a large choice of window washers to pick from. But, act quickly as they have a short life span. Now if you want a window washer, you have to remember that they are in very good shape. Very fit, and you should be exercising, too, to keep up with him. Do you know about exercise? The heart isn't the only organ in the body. Now that is one exercise I recommend that is very important.

At this point she leaned forward and started demonstrating abdominal crunches and accompanied them with a loud noise—"OOOF, OOOF, OOOF"—that sounded like someone had just hit her repeatedly in the stomach. Or it could have been construed as something entirely different—my mind wandered to the restaurant scene in the movie *When Harry Met Sally* when Meg Ryan showed Billy Crystal that she could fake an orgasm.

I wondered if I should try to regain control of the group, so I took the microphone from her and said, "Thank you." Half of the group was doubled-over laughing and the other half look horrified. Phil had tears running down his face, and I was trying hard not to laugh and maintain my professional demeanor, but the situation captured us and grew. She grabbed the microphone back from me and said,

> I am 92 years old and I've seen everything. I am deaf, I'm blind, I can't walk, and my hips and rotator cuffs are gone. I've had everything happen to me that can happen to a person. Can anyone think of anything else that can happen?

Again, I fumbled the microphone away from her grip and said, "Thank you." Instantly retaking the microphone, she announced, "Wait, I thought of something else that could happen to you" and then very slowly and distinctly she spoke the words "club feet, hammertoes, and bunions." "Thank you," I said and reached for the microphone again. By this time I thought that this was a comedy routine, and I imagined Elaine Boosler or Paula Poundstone performing, although it was funnier watching a really little, really old lady doing it. I laughed because I could not help it. She wanted the microphone again. Public acclaim awarded it to her. Miriam took a deep breath and started speaking slowly,

> You know, I was born in Odessa, Russia, and came here when I was four. I have pictures of my family at that time. In the pictures, I look exactly like my mother. My mother used to tell funny stories. We lived near a park. There was always a crowd of people waiting for my mother to come and tell her stories, and they would laugh and laugh.

However, our group time was up, so I took a deep breath and again said, "Thank you. I hope that you all have a wonderful week and a good Thanksgiving and I'll see you next Friday." When everyone left, my students and I discussed the session and laughed until we cried. We were reminded of how a sense of humor could be such a precious asset—both in the giving and in the receiving.

In addition to group conversations, we often developed activities to engage residents. For example, when one team of students discussed possibilities for using group time, the residents decided to document their life stories. The students brought a digital camera and a laptop computer to document the stories of each and assembled the photos and stories into albums. Everyone received copies of "Our Family Album." As some of the residents had passed away after the albums had been completed, the album served to preserve their stories and images and was regarded as a treasure.

I was reasonably sure that we had helped these elders, and I knew that they had certainly helped us. Over the years of meeting with this population,

I have realized how they, as a group, were generous with my students and with me. Their participation in helping to foster young people was very appealing to us all. The elders felt useful and were motivated to "sponsor" the students and their needs. The elders took pride in the fact that they had participated in creating solid futures for our students.

Sessions with Individuals Held at the University

Every Friday morning, we held group meetings in a university classroom that contained a mirrored observation room. We had real-time supervision with the elders who could meet with us. The typical reflecting processes included a clinical conversation in the therapy room while the reflectors observed from behind a one-way mirror. Toward the end of the session, the therapy room members and the reflectors switched places, and the reflectors discussed their conversation while the therapy room members observed. Then the two groups switched again, continuing the session. The stories presented by John and Anna, both in their eighties, exemplified the team's work.

Harmonica John's Story. After describing The Elder Project in one of my regular classes, a young woman from the class asked if her 80-year-old grandfather could participate in the project. At our next supervised group meeting, the student arrived with her mother, Linda, who was pushing her grandfather in a wheelchair who was wearing a cap embroidered with the words "Harmonica John" across its brim. As we began to talk, it was obvious that he had been overtaken by a serious depression. John told us that his life had been stimulating until 6 months ago, when he had underwent a coronary artery bypass surgery. During the surgery, he had a stroke that had caused serious damage to his mind and body. Subsequently, the previously independent and vibrant man was now wheelchair-bound and suffered significant memory loss. Furthermore, John had been an avid reader but now found that he no longer had the attention span to read or retain information. He was now "confined" to a skilled nursing facility. In addition to these personal losses, two months after his stroke, his companion of 19 years had died suddenly of a heart attack. In just a few months, John's life had changed radically. Finally, when we met, John was a sad man engulfed by tremendous loss with little hope for the future.

He told us about his earlier life. We learned that John's mother had died during the Great Depression when he had been 8 years old. His grieving father, unable to find work, had moved to Venezuela to work in the oil industry, leaving John to shift between relatives. That same year he went to a Salvation Army camp, and the leader of his group gave each little boy a harmonica as a gift. This event began a life-long relationship with music and the harmonica, and ultimately earned him his nickname, "Harmonica John." John always had a harmonica and an empty coffee can with him.

He would play familiar songs for us, using the coffee can as "a poor man's amplifier." Watching John enjoy himself as he played his harmonica would frequently move us to tears.

John talked about his life's adventures, including his time as a volunteer in the U.S. Navy when he was 17. He had rejoined the Navy later during the Second World War and served in the Pacific. When he told his familiar life stories, he came alive, and our witnessing and responding to his life stories allowed him to become the vibrant person that he once was. In spite of his recent tragedies in life, he appeared resilient. When we asked about this, he claimed that it was something he was born with—"the Man" just gave it to him. "It was luck," he said.

We saw John for an hour every other week for 5 months, and he frequently mentioned how much he valued our visits. Our conversations about his life and travels cheered him, and he appreciated our interest in him and in his life stories. The audience of the reflecting team was a social event for John, which he looked forward to during our visits. Early in our relationship, we had to modify our reflection process for John. When we realized that the time spent changing rooms was too long for John to remember what had been said, we had the reflectors sit in the therapy room. Consequently, he responded immediately to the reflectors reflections; his responses became spontaneous and appropriate. Remarkably, as time passed, John improved. His ability to read returned, and his depression significantly lessened. Although there was never a declared goal for therapy, it was clear that our meetings were benefiting John. He said so, and his daughter Linda agreed, as did his granddaughter.

We were impressed with John's improvement and wanted him to appreciate his progress. We videotaped and edited one session and viewed it with him and his daughter during one of our meetings to experience their reaction to this wonderful interview. John openly wept while viewing the video and asked if he could take it to show it to the other residents at his facility. We gave him the video, and he proudly took it with him. On his next visit he smiled as he told us that we had made him a celebrity. He had been elected as the representative of the "inmates," as they called themselves. When a nurse asked him if he was going to appoint a cabinet, he showed his sense of humor, "Yes, and I'll make you the Secretary of Depends." The residents at the facility became very curious about us and asked if we could come and talk with them; one team member arranged to visit one day a week. After the university's public relations person had publicized our project to local newspapers, a reporter and photographer interviewed John and the team. An article with John's picture appeared in the local paper. Delighted John said, "First you made me a celebrity and now you're going to make me famous."

Anna's Story. The second person that the supervision group saw was referred by one of the students enrolled in the Project. Anna, 88 years old, was recovering from a second cataract surgery, lived in her own town-house, and was fiercely independent. She had been widowed for 10 years, after her husband died after a prolonged deteriorating illness. She and her husband had shared successful acting careers until his memory became affected by small strokes, and he could no longer act. He had become bed-ridden and eventually developed dementia. The loss of her husband had been the loss of her dream, and she was still very much in love with him.

Anna had joined a bereavement group eight years before, finding some solace and companionship but never could fully recover her life's passion. Age was also taking its toll. She had had hearing loss, had been in physical therapy for torn rotator cuffs, had lost her driver's license because of poor vision, and had a host of other physical ailments that simply came with aging. However, by far, her greatest loss had been the feeling of companionship that she had received from her relationship with her husband. She spoke of an intense romantic and sexual relationship with her husband. As she described her relationship with him, we each ached for that quality of connection in our own lives—a relationship so perfect that whenever they entered a room, a hush fell onto everyone present.

In spite of the fragility of her body, she was still a strikingly beautiful woman. Our conversations with her revealed her intelligence and a won-derful sense of humor. She had acted on the stage, in movies and televi-sion, and had written stories, plays, and lyrics. She feared however, that she had forever lost her connection with creativity. We listened to her life stories and were curious about her talents and accomplishments. At times, I was the therapist, and sometimes the students stepped into the therapist position. Anna referred to us as her team.

On Anna's third visit, she announced, "My muse has returned." For me, this statement required some explanation as I had never lost a muse or had met anyone else who had. She told us about how on a recent evening walk, she had noticed the crescent moon in the sky and immediately felt recon-nected to life. This had inspired her to write a poem as she walked, and as the poem came together, she realized that she had become in touch with her muse again. When she read it to us, we realized that she had a great tal-ent for writing. Our team served as an appreciative audience to her stories, and became a fan club for her muse and her poetry. Anna's "re-member-ing" and a reconnection to her creativity revitalized a part of her that she had lost many years ago.

Our conversations continued every other week, and Anna continued to write her poems. As their numbers increased, she gained the courage to submit them for publication. Among the letters of regret, she also received letters of acceptance and was a published as a poet in a number of journals and magazines. Several members of the supervision group who continued to meet with Anna, not surprisingly, became inspired to write poetry or as some students reported, "to think more descriptively and feel poetic." It is difficult to discern who gained the most from therapy within this reciprocal relationship.

Anna's memories of travel, when she and her husband had been on location for a movie being filmed in Rome, inspired the following poem:

In the Pantheon

One early misty Autumn morn I sought refuge from a threat'ning storm
within the awesome Pantheon, my favored shrine in all of Rome,
I stood beneath the Open Dome that graced this massive round of stone—
A pool of raindrops from the night sat silent on this sacred sight.
The tear-stained sky was clean and chaste, as drizzle gently kissed my face
there was no breath except my own, no single sound, no single tone—
I was alone, Encircled by the hallowed stone.
Then suddenly the silence broke—from somewhere high an organ spoke—
familiar chords rained down on me—'twas major Bach in minor key!—
Arpeggios swirled around and 'round, enveloped me with gloried sound
then surged and soared out through the Dome, merged with the mist, and all of Rome.
My naked heart began to cry "My love come share this or I'll die!
It's more than I can bear alone, The Pantheon and Bach
In misty ancient Autumn Rome."

Anna has kept in touch with us. She is now 95 years old and has moved into a retirement facility with some assisted living arrangements. She still writes poetry.

Working with Individuals in Retirement Hotels

Ruth's Story. An activities director at a facility where we were seeing residents in groups asked if I would speak with a particularly needy resident. Ruth was in her seventies and had suffered a severe stroke the previous year that had left her cognitively impaired. Although I explained that our work was most helpful to people without cognitive deficits, I wanted to be cooperative and obliged my helpfulness.

A student and I went stepped into Ruth's room to talk with her. She was indeed disoriented, did not know where she was, how she got there, or where she has been before she came to the hotel. We tried using objects scattered throughout her room as stimuli for creating connection and conversation. Noticing a framed photo of a child, I asked if it was her grandchild.

"Oh, no" she replied, "I never married." "Ruth," I asked, "do you remember your mother and your father?" She replied that she did and I asked their names. When she remembered their names, my student quickly got pencil and paper and started to draw a family map. She also remembered that she had had an older brother and a younger sister, although their names escaped her for the moment. We spent the next half hour trying to build more bridges. I asked her if she had a card in her wallet that said, "In case of emergency call ... " She did and showed us the card that she had placed in a small address book. With her agreement, we browsed through the address book and were able to reconstruct her family. She had never married but had been close to her brother and sister on the East Coast. After they had died and following Ruth's major stroke, a nephew who had taken responsibility for her had her transported to Los Angeles and eventually placed her in the retirement facility. She was quite anxious about not knowing what had brought her there and fearful that she could be put out on the street at any moment. We promised to return to visit and left her with a family map with the names of all of her family members that we had identified. As we left, I noticed an envelope on her nightstand. "Whom do you correspond with?" I asked. She didn't know but invited me to look at the letter:

Dear Ruth,

This was to confirm our telephone conversation. I told you I would also write you with the news that our mutual friend, John Smith, died of a heart attack last week. Ruth, I want you to remember that you are a renowned reflexologist and that you have helped hundreds of people in your work here at the Cancer Foundation.

Your Friend,
Jane

I was startled at this note and became even more surprised as two enclosed pieces of paper fluttered down to the floor. On each piece of paper was a map of the palm, one for each hand, with all of the acupressure points labeled. As I picked them up I commented to Ruth that a note said that she had been a well-known reflexologist. She in turn asked me if I knew what a reflexologist was. I replied that I did and that I wondered if she could use these maps to stimulate some points on her own hand. She asked for my hand and her hands flew into life as she ran over the major pressure points of my palm. Her hands seemed to be moving on pure "muscle memory" and unrelated to any logic in our conversation.

As the weeks progressed, she demonstrated her "work" on the hands of all of my students. Things would occur to her as she did this. She might say, "I need to wash my hands between treatments," or "I need to shake the energy out of my hands." Through the activity of using her hands as she once had, facts and memories for her past flourished into conversation. As word spread around the facility that Ruth had rediscovered and "re-membered" her once talented skill, she gained a kind of popularity status in the community, and she became more cooperative and less of a problem. In this unusual way, she "re-membered" herself into her own life. When I moved to a new faculty position, I left Ruth in conversation with two of the students. She told them that she regarded them like close family. They kept in touch with me concerning Ruth. She suffered a series of additional strokes, and my student continued to made hospital visits to her. She did not survive a final major stroke.

Minna's Story. Curiously and somewhat selfishly, I have asked elders, "How do you explain how you have aged so successfully?" I have listened carefully to their answers and hoped to gather some secret wisdom to store away for myself. One of these special women, who managed to age incredibly well, was Minna whom I met at a retirement hotel near my home. I have continued to offer a conversation group there even though my teaching situation has changed. I have felt a strong connection to this group as I have been meeting with them for nearly six years. Minna celebrated her 101st birthday two years ago, with all of her wits about her. A geometry teacher who retired in 1959, she reached "great old age," the category that now defines people who are older than 85.

One day Minna told the group that she felt like she was failing, and although the doctor could not identify a problem, she felt that was experiencing some negative changes. When anyone expressed a desire to talk more than group time allowed, a student or I would make an appointment to see them individually. I decided to spend time videotaping some additional conversations with Minna and hoped to preserve some of her incredible history and spirit. Minna recalled the day that women had got the right to vote, the First World War, the 1929 stock market crash, and the evolution of industrial inventions—such as the motor car, indoor plumbing, electric lights, and the telephone—and other changes in our world that we take for granted. She also had been a political activist, continuing even now at the age of 101. She chastised me for not becoming more politically involved and wanted me to join the League of Women Voters, where she was still an active member.

One of the stories that she shared in the group was falling in love at first sight when she met her husband. Wanting to hear more, I asked her to tell me more about her husband. "Which one?" she asked. I was surprised because she had never spoken about a second husband in the group. She explained that after 20 years, her first husband that she loved so much died suddenly, devastating her and her 17-year-old daughter. "But human beings are what we are and after another 12 years I remarried." "What was that marriage like?" I asked. "It wasn't a good marriage. He was mean-spirited and critical. We argued and I couldn't express myself, and it was difficult."

I asked her how long she had stayed in this "uncomfortable" situation, using my own chosen words. "Forty-three years" was her simple reply and without skipping a beat, she continued to speak about her second husband, "He died two years ago, and I left Florida and came to Los Angeles to be near my family." I was stunned and asked what kept her in the marriage. "I was afraid to be alone," she said, but before she continued, I briefly wondered how she had managed to sustain herself for all that time. She continued, "I wrote poetry. Poetry has kept me sane. I think that everyone must have a creative outlet to be healthy, and people need to keep growing. They need to learn new things to stay alive." As I was thanking her for the time we spent together that afternoon, she surprised me by saying, "I am so glad that you do this. You inspire me."

Although she was legally blind, she continued to read using talking books from the Braille Institute. She exemplified her advice and kept her selection of books growing. One was about Joan Sutherland becoming a "diva"; another was about the creation of the universe. Minna continued to write poetry. Like Anna, she brought her poems to the weekly group meeting.

Minna became confined to her room when she developed a painful case of shingles. She continued to require increasing levels of assistance and was finally transferred to a convalescent home where she died shortly thereafter. Given her vitality, it had not occurred to me that Minna could die. She left me her written history and a self-published volume of her poetry including this one:

Stages

Life has seven stages, So the Bard did say,
But now they fill new pages, To see us another way.
Senior Citizen, the Golden Years. It drives me up a tree.
The latest way was fractions, Divide your life by three.
Makes me want to know, What year, what month
The question's not absurd, Exactly when to launch
Upon my Third Third. But hark! And prithee list
My statement I'll amend. If the beginning I did not know
Who wants to know the end?

Working with Independent Elders from the Larger Community

People who have lived independently have not usually felt displaced or disowned. They knew their turf, their neighbors, the paperboy, and the mail carrier. They have had maintained conversations with grocery checkers, they maintain pets, and they attend church or related activities during the week. Generally, even though they may no longer drive, they have enjoyed a sense of independence and have sustained their continuity of identity.

Many of my students have identified other contexts in which elders might benefit from the student's volunteering efforts. One student described our project to his church congregation and offered to visit with elder church members in their homes. He soon found that the 15 weekly hours with which he devoted was insufficient in allowing enough time to visit all of the elders who wanted to participate. He also quickly found himself over-whelmed with the stories that they told him. The adventures and cour-age that these elders had in meeting the challenges of their earlier lives amazed him. When he offered to author a newsletter to share their stories, they enthusiastically collaborated with him in a monthly "history" news-letter for the church. As members of the congregation became interested in the stories, the elders had once more become a vital part of the church community.

Dealing with Loss

Working with elders has required from us the abilities to connect, to be genuine, and to be caring and curious, and, in the end, a willingness to "let go" when called for. When Lillian, who had helped her husband oper-ate their recording studio, had a major stroke while visiting relatives in Northern California, The Elder Project group in her hotel all signed and mailed a card to her. She responded with a letter addressed to, "My Good Friends in Jennifer's Friday Morning Conversation Group," and explained that she had decided to move closer to her family. A particularly caring and social person, Lillian's absence was devastating to the group at first. But as I listened to the group speak about loss, I saw how they accepted the passing of people who had been important to them. There was a sense that the group felt enriched by the "re-membering" conversations. With a roster of between 250 and 300 residents, there have been multiple and frequent experiences of the natural circle of life. Out of necessity, each of us and all that were involved in the group have had to developed ways to cope with inevitable loss.

Students' Reflections on Their Experiences

In their class evaluations, students stated that participation in the project was a life changing experience for them. They now looked at people who were aging through a very different lens, realizing that they all have vibrant life histories—histories that should be shared with others to the benefit of all. They were surprised at the differences that they now experienced in their ability and desire to listen with intense intention whenever someone spoke. Many students commented about changes in their relationships with their grandparents and had begun to tape or document their stories.

The training aspect of this class involved reflecting teams and activities to promote listening from a curious stance. There was a turning point where students began to listen for the strengths of the elders rather than pathologize their deficits; this shift in their approach changed who they were at a personal level. The group meetings supported the student's development, enabled them to feel connected to the ideas that grounded the work, and allowed them to address questions and critiques from others. Importantly, we concluded that while students could learn this method, we could not necessarily teach it. Finding our practices and approach too difficult to incorporate, some students continued to be committed to more traditional therapy models. Nevertheless, for many students who could comfortably follow our lead, they wrote that this was the most important semester in their education.

Closing Reflections

Although identifying myself as a postmodern therapist, I have found that working with elders has created a relationship very similar to my former humanistic-experiential therapy days. Even within the paradigm of making contact and being authentic, I have at times questioned if I am delivering therapy when (a) there has been no request for a therapy meeting and (b) there has been no "formal" identification of a problem, a therapeutic goal, or a client. As a postmodern therapist, I have found it refreshing to operate in the absence of an identifiable problem, causality, or pathology. I have noticed that even the humanistic-experiential therapies focus on the assessment and treatment strategies of problems (Woldt & Stein, 1997). Through our observations of the many calamities that can arise within the context of aging, some have simply represented natural stages of development. In the midst of one's physical decline, a person who has successfully negotiated these stages of development has consequentially integrated the making of their own meaning and has achieved a sense of integrity rather than mere despair (Erikson, 1959).

The elders we have worked with have shown us how to develop a sense of integrity and hope. Re-capturing and utilizing their creativity assisted Anna and Minna to feel whole and alive. John and Miriam rediscovered that laughter is healing, especially when shared. Ruth's will to connect using skills she has "re-membered" enabled her to become part of her community again. It has been a privilege to meet and accompany them on the re-visiting of their life journeys. The roads they chose may have paralleled old roads, but they also took a turn toward something new.

By example, they taught me something important that I have come to appreciate through my own writing: that you are always young enough to continue in growth and become part of a community, even at 101 years old. If your mind is working, you are never too old to learn new ideas, and it is important to do this. Being generous makes you feel rich. Being connected to other people—listening and being heard—allows us to remember who we were, who we are, and who we are becoming.

References

Andersen, T. (1991). The reflecting team: Part I and Part II. In T. Andersen (Ed.), *The reflecting team: Dialogues and dialogues about the dialogues* (pp. 3–97). New York: W. W. Norton.

Andersen, T. (1995). Reflecting processes: Acts of forming and informing. In S. Friedman (Ed.), *The reflecting team in action* (pp. 11–37). New York: Guilford.

Andersen, T. (1999). Reflecting elder stories: An interview with Tom Andersen [Videotape]. Andrews & Clark Explorations, Inc. Los Angeles, CA.

Anderson, H. (1996). *Conversation, language and possibilities: A postmodern approach to therapy.* New York: Basic Books.

Anderson, H. (1997). *Conversation, language, and possibility: A postmodern approach to therapy.* New York: Basic Books.

Anderson, H. & Goolishian, H.A. (1988). Human systems as linguistic systems: Preliminary and evolving ideas about the implications for clinical theory. *Family Process, 27,* 371–393.

Andrews, J. (2001). Witnessing lives. In D. Denborough (Ed.), *Working with the stories of women's lives* (pp. 253–267). Adelaide, Australia: Dulwich Centre.

Andrews, J. (2003). A social constructionist's perspective. In G. Corey (Ed.), *A case approach to counseling and psychotherapy* (6th ed., pp. 369–383). Belmont, CA: Thompson, Brooks/Cole.

Andrews, J. & Clark, D.J. (2003). Response to the later years. *Gestalt Review, 7,* 103–108.

Erikson, E.H. (1959). *Identity and the life cycle.* New York: W.W. Norton.

Frederickson, I. & Handlon, J.H. (2003). The later years from a gestalt systems/field perspective: Therapeutic considerations. *Gestalt Review, 7,* 92–102.

Gergen, K. (1991). *The saturated self: Dilemmas of identity in contemporary life.* New York: Basic Books.

Gergen, K. & Gergen, M (2002). *The positive aging newsletter.* Retrieved from http://www.healthandage.com.

Goolishian, H. & Anderson, H. (1987). Language systems and therapy: An evolving idea. *Journal of Psychotherapy, 24,* 529–538.

Goolishian, H. & Anderson, H. (1990). Understanding the therapeutic system: From individuals and families to systems in languages. In F. Kaslow (Ed.), *Voices in family psychology* (pp. 91–113). Newberry Park, CA: Sage.

Goolishian, H. & Anderson, H. (1996) Narrative e self: Alguns dilemmas pos-modernos da psicoterpia, por. In D. Schnitzman (Ed.), *Novas paradigmas, cultura e subjetividade* (pp. 191–200).

Myerhoff, B. (1976). *Number Our Days* [Documentary film]. Los Angeles: Channel 5.

Myerhoff, B. (1978). A symbol perfected in death: Continuity and ritual in the life and death of an elderly Jew. In B. Myerhoff & A. Simic (Eds.), *Life's career aging: Cultural variation on growing old* (pp. 163–206). Newbury Park, CA: Sage.

Myerhoff, B. (1992). Life history among the elderly: Performance, visibility and remembering. In *Remembered lives* (pp. 231–247). Ann Arbor, MI: University of Michigan.

Polster, M. (1967). Personal Communication.

Shotter, J. (1993). *Conversational realities: Constructing life through language.* London: Sage Publications.

Vailliant, G.E. (2001). *Aging well.* Boston, MA: Little Brown.

Woldt, A.A. & Stein, S.A. (1997). Gestalt therapy with the elderly: On the "coming of age" and "completing gestalts." *Gestalt Review, 2,* 163–184.

CHAPTER 11

Collaborating with Parents and Children in Private Practice: Shifting and Overlapping Conversations

MARSHA MCDONOUGH AND PATRICIA KOCH

Learning is not linear but a spiral progression;
Learning happens by doing and revisiting ideas.

**The Hundred Languages of
Children Exhibit, 2000**

When we converse, connect, and collaborate with children, their families, and their communities, ideas flourish and problems dissolve. In this chapter, we show how possibilities are burgeoning for one family as we invite vital voices into our conversations about their dilemmas. Throughout the chapter, we pause to reflect on the postmodern and social constructionist ideas about therapy put forth by Harlene Anderson (1997). We illustrate Collaborative Language Systems (CLS) therapy, an approach that has guided us since graduate school in Austin, a city located near the Houston Galveston Institute. We have also been influenced by the writings of Harry Goolishian, Tom Andersen, Lynn Hoffman, and Peggy Penn. Over the years, each of us has developed a professional identity as a collaborative therapist, supervisor, and teacher.

Introduction to the Premises of Collaborative Therapy

Collaborative therapy embraces the following premises: the therapist facilitates therapy from a nonhierarchical, not-knowing position; she invites multiple perspectives into conversations to promote a shared inquiry into clients' dilemmas; and she creates space for rich dialogue and conversation, both in and out of the consultation room. The therapist is a conversational partner who fosters mutual relationships and who values conversations that are multivoiced and multistoried. The collaborative therapist is less concerned with diagnosis or pathology and more interested in communicating respect for clients through heartfelt curiosity about their stories. To guide reflections on and contributions to therapeutic conversations, the collaborative therapist listens carefully to her own inner dialogue created in response to the dialogue among all conversational partners. To sustain and enliven therapy, a collaborative therapist joins with clients and others to reflect on their work, sometimes through coresearch. This shared inquiry promotes belonging as well as diversity, leading to changes in language and relationships. Transformation in language, narrative, and relationships allows creativity, self-agency, and new meaning to emerge (Anderson, 1997).

In this chapter, we illustrate therapy as a dialogical process composed of "shifting and overlapping" conversations (Anderson, 1997) among individuals who coalesced around one family's problems. We describe how one small conversation expanded to include family, friends, and many others. We show how we facilitated both therapy and coresearch with our clients, emphasizing our preference to include a chorus of voices. We demonstrate therapy as shared inquiry among a variety of conversational partners wherein space is made for multiple points of view and multiple conversations. We reflect on turning points for therapists and clients along the way. We show how through awareness and practice of collaborative principles, we facilitate therapy as "polyphony" (Anderson, 1998) in which all voices play an important part as they flow in and out of continuous conversation.

Introduction to Our Collaborative Story

Our story begins with Paul, an eleven-year-old, and Heidi, his mother. As their therapists, we have remained open and spontaneous, following assorted conversational and relational strands in the coconstruction of a new narrative of their lives. The process reminds us of circuitously weaving diverse threads into colorful cloth. Paul shared a different metaphor during a coresearch project. He excitedly urged us, "Think of a sandwich! It's like we put all our ideas together . . . . put all the meat and stuff in there together, choose the kinds of meat, whether or not you are going to have cheese . . . " He noticed how, together, we talk about various parts of the story and those parts are put together in different ways. Paul's mother agreed that the possibilities seem immeasurable.

A Conversation Takes Shape

Heidi phoned me (Marsha) immediately after checking herself out of the psychiatric hospital. The hospital staff had convinced Heidi to look elsewhere for assistance. Heidi insisted she was "out-of-control"; she had to speak with someone before something terrible happened to her and her family. She felt unable to care for her three boys. Since my schedule was full, I asked Heidi to stay on the phone while I checked with Pat. Fortunately, as I peered across the hall, Pat's door was open for me, and, soon thereafter, for Heidi.

Reflection

Initial telephone conversations present potentials for dialogue, relationship, and the generation of shared meaning. Our first responsibility is to take the client seriously by listening for how she wishes to be in dialogue and relationship with us. We suspend assumptions about pathology and listen with budding respect for and curiosity about the person and their dilemma. Harlene Anderson (1997) says that the smallest conversation can be moving, meaningful, and important.

A "rolling conversation" (Hoffman, 2003) began when Marsha connected with Heidi on the phone in a way that the conversation continued and led to a meeting between Pat and Heidi. From this beginning encounter, a series of "shifting and overlapping" conversations ensued (Anderson, 2004). As the relationship between Pat and Heidi grew, Marsha later rejoined them and many others in an expanding collaborative and dialogical partnership.

Pat and Heidi Talk: A Green Life Vine Grows

During our brief phone conversation, Heidi and I (Pat) arranged to meet as soon as possible. On the phone, Heidi spoke of being flooded by memories of severe sexual abuse. She wanted to find a way to live through this. When Heidi came for her appointment, she settled into the soft carpet on my office floor. I sat across from Heidi and listened attentively as she described a life filled with sexual abuse by family and friends. As the story of her horrendous past and current struggles unfolded, I wondered how one person could endure so much and find the will to live.

During this first conversation, I was struck by the determination to thrive that shone in Heidi's eyes and reverberated in her voice. She firmly stated, "I have a sixth sense and I know when things are not right. I am committed to working and changing things." Heidi wanted to take care of herself, her second husband, Ken, and her boys: Paul, age eleven, son of her first marriage; Ben, age seven, and Sam, age three. Heidi said that a "being a family" was something she missed when she was growing up. She wanted to do whatever it took to live differently.

When Heidi was late for our next appointment, I immediately called her. She answered the phone saying her medication had put her to sleep. Heidi stated that she felt "manic" and was frightened that she might harm herself. Yet, despite these concerns, her resolve to live remained apparent. Rather than giving in to her depression, Heidi reported that she had a tattoo drawn on her left hand to remind her of her reasons to live. After this intriguing update, Heidi made another appointment.

At our next visit, I marveled at Heidi's tattoo. A beautiful symbol, the tattoo consisted of a green vine cascading gently over her wrist, stopping at her wedding band. Three leaves represented each of her sons. One final leaf, closest to her ring, represented her husband, Ken. The tattoo was to become, as Heidi had planned, a constant reminder to her of the importance of creating the family of her dreams. Heidi invited Ken to our next meeting because she wanted him to better understand her crisis. As Heidi, Ken, and I talked, it was clear that Ken loved Heidi and was willing to "step into her shoes" to learn how the past abuse haunted her. I wondered in what ways the other "leaves" on Heidi's life vine would join in our conversations.

Reflection

Pat arranged to meet with Heidi as soon as possible because Heidi wanted to talk immediately. When Heidi felt most comfortable sitting on the floor, Pat followed her lead and sat across from her. Sitting in this position allowed Pat to look into Heidi's eyes and to become curious about what Heidi wanted to share. Anderson (1997) addresses these seemingly small "practicalities" as tools that reflect a collaborative philosophical stance.

A conversational partnership began when Heidi and Pat engaged in Heidi's account of relevant life events and experiences (Anderson, 1997). What emerged from this conversation was shaped by emotional connection and dialogue, rather than by an external theory or professional discourse about sexual abuse or survivorship. Anderson (1997) believes that the therapist and client are equal partners in the conversation and in the relationship. The therapist does not listen or speak as an expert on the client's life or dilemmas. Rather, she speaks and listens in ways that demonstrate her desire to maintain a close working relationship and to contribute to their partnership through language that is useful and generative.

Pat maintained a "nonexpert" position when Heidi missed their next appointment as well as phoned with genuine interest in how Heidi was feeling.

Pat's interest stemmed from a "not-knowing" stance (Anderson, 1997), meaning that any assumptions Pat may have had about Heidi's absence were held in abeyance until talking with Heidi.

When Heidi arrived for their next visit, Pat was again touched by Heidi's tattoo and its symbolism. Pat made a mental note that each leaf represented a distinctive voice in the system that was presenting itself for therapy. Anderson (1997) states that each family member has a "distinctive language that reflects the differences in the members' experiences, explanations of, and meanings attributed to the same event" (p. 61). Pat did not know, nor did she plan, who might become future participants in the therapy conversations that she and Heidi initiated.

Shaping the Family of Heidi's Dreams

Among varied conversational topics, Heidi and I (Pat) most frequently talked about Heidi's desire to be a good mother. Heidi was especially concerned about Paul's complex medical, emotional, and educational needs. Our therapeutic relationship lent itself to puzzling together over questions such as: "How can I be a good parent to Paul, Ben, and Sam when I didn't have good role models?" "Do I have appropriate professionals in place for Paul, considering his special needs?" "Why do my boys fight with each other?" "Am I teaching my boys to be respectful?" We talked about seemingly simple things, such as housework and cooking, as well as complex problems like Heidi's tendency to "freeze" in overwhelming situations.

When pondering Heidi's questions and concerns, we often made distinctions between her life as an abused child and her current life. From these distinctions, Heidi posed more questions, generated ideas, and took action. When I was moved by Heidi's choices, I expressed my admiration for her determination. Increasingly, she became driven by a powerful realization: "I have choices."

Two particularly stirring stories about "choice" involved Heidi's grandmother and her mother. Arriving for an overnight visit at her grandmother's house, Heidi's grandmother greeted her with the proclamation: "Your mother should have aborted you." Heidi chose not to stay with her grandmother and, instead, stayed with her aunt and uncle, who were "positive role models." Another time, Heidi asked her mother to be a positive role model for herself and the boys by honoring certain house rules: no cursing, no racist remarks, and no belittling. Heidi made it clear that her mother must abide by these rules during her visits.

Heidi began to talk more with family members and friends about her concerns, and we had conversations about these conversations. Heidi would "chew" things over with people and discover that these conversations shed light on her many questions. As she "bounced ideas off" trusted others, Heidi gained momentum in her quest to have the family of her dreams.

Reflection

"Self-agency" (Anderson, 1997) emerges from the telling, retelling, and the doing and undoing of the client's story. The process takes place, over time, through dialogue, in and out of the therapy room, as the client, therapist, and others participate in multiple conversations and relationships. Heidi described it like this: "I find that when I am faced with a challenge and I come to therapy, I chew it up and spit it out again and I chew it up and spit it out again, and it does not seem as big as it was before." Heidi developed new language, meaning, and relationships as she accessed her knowledge: "I have choices." Anderson (1997) states, "Having self-agency, or a sense of it, means having the ability to behave, feel, think, and choose in a way that is liberating, that opens up new possibilities or simply allows us to see that new possibilities exist" (p. 231). As Heidi experienced herself making preferred choices, she began to experience herself as the mother, the wife, and the woman she wanted to be.

Team Spirit

Heidi and I (Pat) referred to her network of family, friends, and professionals as a "team." This reference derived from several sources: (a) Heidi's desire to have herself, her children, and her husband work together to build a solid family; (b) Heidi's movement to join in conversations with others outside of her immediate family; (c) our talks about the needs of Paul, her eleven-year-old son, who was under the care of a team of medical and educational professionals; and (d) my preference to collaborate with others as part of a team with many points of view.

Heidi actively customized her team and Paul's. She wanted a new psychiatrist to evaluate her medication. She also sought a neuropsychologist to assess Paul's learning abilities, social skills, and emotional functioning. When she asked my advice, I provided her with the names of a psychiatrist and a neuropsychologist with whom I knew would collaborate with our team.

Several months into our talks, Heidi's team grew to include local community college personnel when she enrolled in college as a result of seeking her own neuropsychological evaluation. Paul's assessment piqued her curiosity about her own learning abilities. When Heidi received the results of her testing, she called me and exclaimed, "I'm smart!" Today, at the age of thirty-one, she continues into her second semester, proudly maintaining a 4.0 grade point average.

After Paul's evaluation, Heidi further adjusted Paul's team. She was dissatisfied with the child psychologist who had served as Paul's play therapist for years. I offered to have Paul join in our meetings, but Heidi felt that she and Paul should have separate therapists. Upon Heidi's request, I phoned Paul's play therapist, but he did not return my phone calls. This situation, coupled with a crisis, led to a change in Paul's team and to an expansion of our conversational partnership. Heidi remembered her earlier conversation with my collaborative colleague, Marsha. She called Marsha to ask her to become Paul's new child psychologist.

Reflection

To collaborate is to invite multiple perspectives into the conversational partnership and into the process of coconstructing new knowledge. Collaborative colleagues may not view dilemmas exactly the same, but they are interested in keeping conversations and relationships alive. We find working as a team to be inherently complex, generative, and effective. Working as a team allows for what Anderson (1997) describes as "multiple authors of yet-to-be-told-shifting and emerging-narratives" (p. 95). Collaborative therapists work with others without pressure to strive for consensus or agreement. Rather, a collaborative therapist values diversity because of the creativity that accompanies a chorus of varying viewpoints.

We have working relationships with psychiatrists, nurse practitioners, school counselors, and others who enjoy the challenge of working collaboratively in a private practice setting. These professionals are valued because they return phone calls and attend conjoint meetings. In order to cultivate relationships with collaborative colleagues, in 1996 we established a permanent supervision and training group within our private practice setting. Guided by postmodern ideas, this group of students, supervisees, and health professionals act as consultants to one another and to their clients. Professional members of this team gain experience in collaborative practices in exchange for a fee.

A Jumble of Concerns about Paul and the Family

Even though it had been six months since I (Marsha) first spoke with Heidi, I recognized her determined voice when she called to make an appointment for Paul. She told me she had concerns about Paul's progress with his current psychologist. Additionally, the family was in a crisis due to Paul's fighting at school, which left him with a "goose-egg-size knot on his head."

Engrossed in this crisis, Heidi justifiably had little patience for the administrative details I introduced as we set up the first appointment. I requested school reports, insurance information, medical information, parent questionnaires, and checklists to be completed by involved adults. Keeping in mind the crisis, I was not offended when Heidi answered my queries in a clipped tone. She sounded especially terse when she informed me that Paul's biological father was currently not a part of the picture, and that Paul's stepfather, Ken, acted as Paul's father. I extended an invitation to Ken to join us for the first appointment.

Our first talk meandered around serious concerns including a brief introduction to Paul's congenital medical problems as well as divorce, remarriage, blending families, special education, and a report to Child Protective Services (CPS) about a bruise behind Paul's ear after a recent visit with his biological father. There were issues of parenting, fighting in the family, cursing, and noncompliance. My mind whirled as I listened to each person. I offered Heidi and Ken options to determine whether Paul should join in some or all of our conversation. They chose to have Paul with us most of the time but occasionally asked him to step into the waiting room.

Paul impressed me as energetic, loving, forgiving, and eager to please. He helped us find focus when I asked him to draw a picture of his worries. Each stick figure had a distinctive feature: Paul's hands were giant fists; his brother, Ben, had a wide-open mouth and his arms wrapped around him in protection; Heidi's mouth was a squiggled line. Paul provided words for each figure, saying he was "angry/mad," Ben was "scared," and Mom was "worried." When asked to draw a picture of his wishes, Paul drew himself and Ben jumping on a bed, with smiling faces, arms flying in the air, and hands outstretched. He added dialogue bubbles that respectively proclaimed, "Hooray, I'm having fun" and "I am too." At the close of our first meeting, we all agreed that Paul and I would talk alone sometimes. We agreed to determine as we went along who else should be talking with whom about what.

Reflection

Pat neither suggested nor insisted that Heidi replace Paul's child psychologist. As a consequence of her collaboration with Pat, Heidi decided to call Marsha. This serves as one example of what Anderson (1997) proposes: that change is the natural consequence of a generative dialogue and collaborative relationship.

On the phone, Marsha positioned herself for dialogue and relationship with Heidi, at the same time making "public" her administrative preferences. According to Anderson (1997), a collaborative therapist is "public" when she expresses preferences while conjointly determining the nature of a therapeutic relationship. By asking parents and others whom the parents deem relevant to complete a few assessment tools and to obtain copies of salient professional reports, Marsha sets a tone for wider collaboration. Marsha does not aim to interpret or diagnose, but to expand partnership and language by including all persons who have coalesced around the family's dilemmas. Diagnosis can be introduced into initial conversations for mutual consideration, if necessary.

Typically, a swirl of concerns arises when first meeting with a child and family. The therapist "listens in order to speak and speaks in order to listen" (Anderson, personal communication, April 23, 1999)[1]. She is guided by the postmodern idea that she is engaging in shared inquiry—a crisscrossing of unique, and often competing, ideas. This process calls for the expertise of all persons participating in the conversation, including the child. In Paul's case, he poignantly drew a picture of his concerns and all agreed to talk more about them. Together, Marsha and the family members determined who should be present during their talks.

Many Voices, Near and Far, in and out of the Consulting Room

As I (Marsha) perused the formal reports that accompanied Paul's first visit, I became curious about potential collaborators. Paul was under the care of a neurologist for serious medical conditions: seizures, hydrocephalous, and intraventricular hemorrhage along with sequential shunt failures. His existing shunt worked well. Paul saw the same psychiatrist as his mother and was on a new medication. A neuropsychological evaluation spoke to Paul's unique learning style; school reports addressed his educational plan. An insurance card revealed coverage through Paul's biological father, who lived in another state. The insurance card was attention-grabbing because Heidi reported that Paul and his biological father had minimal contact. I made a mental note to ask Heidi about whether or not I should talk with some or all of the people involved in Paul's care, and if so, whom.

Reflection

Marsha views reports from others as doors to increased dialogue rather than conversational dead ends. A therapy system is contextually based and a product of social communication rather than social role (Anderson, 1997). For example, by speaking with a CPS caseworker, Marsha learned that the abuse report filed on Paul's biological father had been dismissed. When meeting obligations, such as these, set forth by codes of ethics and law, Marsha considers the codes as distinctive voices to be included in the mix of perspectives.

Marsha interacts with doctors, teachers, and school counselors. She is creative in finding ways to talk and to meet with involved others, making collaboration financially feasible in a private practice setting. For example, Marsha facilitates teleconferences, shares videotapes of consultations, and uses e-mail for efficiency and effectiveness. Intentional collaboration with others results in conversations that overlap and shift. Talk becomes more lively, interesting, and generative, leading to self-agency, change, and problem dissolution.

Room for All Parts

After the initial meeting with Heidi, Ken, and Paul, the combination of family members who most often met with me (Marsha) was: Paul, his mother and two brothers, Ben and Sam. Our meetings resembled a lively form of "musical chairs" with family members rotating in and out of my office, expressing their points of view. We often compiled Paul's ideas, as well as the ideas of his brothers and mother, into lists, sculpting, drawings, and dramas to share with each other, significant family, friends, and professionals. The boys were excited about sharing and often responsive to the reactions of others. As a result, the family members used new strategies for getting along. Heidi reported life at home was more stable and, for the first time in her life, she devised a schedule for the boys to follow at home for the upcoming school year.

Despite a work schedule that disallowed Ken from joining us, he influenced our conversations "as if" he were with us. To invite his point of view, I often asked what Ken might say if he was with us. When one of us pretended to speak from Ken's perspective, our speculation magically brought his voice and ideas into the mix. In order to involve Paul's biological father, Heidi thought it might be helpful if I contacted him. Paul had not seen his biological father for several months since the report alleging physical abuse during his visitation. I e-mailed Paul's father offering to talk about Paul. Paul's biological father did not respond; however, he remained welcomed by our team.

Reflection

Collaborative therapists understand that all ideas, including children's ideas about their lives, are vital to therapeutic conversations. A collaborative therapist values children's language because the child's point-of-view equally shapes the definition of problems and of possible solutions (Anderson & Levin, 1997). Through her curiosity about the children's ideas and through the use of art, play, and drama, Marsha found ways to invite the children into conversation with each other, with Heidi, and with other important persons in their lives. The free flow of ideas among many persons, whether or not they were actually present in Marsha's consulting room, led to a turning point for Heidi. She realized that she could actively join forces with others as a part of Paul's therapy. This demonstrates the power of maintaining what Anderson (1997) calls a multiperspectival philosophical stance. Anderson refers to the practice of speculating about an absent partner's perspective as speaking from the "as if" position. Ken's perspective was kept alive in the partnership this way. Marsha's openness to further dialogue with Paul's biological father also demonstrates this philosophy.

On videotape, made for a coresearch project, Heidi remarked:

> The atmosphere in the office is something I noticed right a way. . . . it's relaxing. One of the things that I feel like is definitely different. . . . is coming together as family and working together. . . , bringing [all] the children in, even though you are specifically hired to work with Paul; being able to say, okay, this is an issue with all of us; and being able to get some resolution out of that, helps to make things better.

School: An Essential Ingredient

When Paul started the fifth grade, we all agreed to exchange ideas with Paul's teacher. I called and asked his teacher to share her goals for Paul. She invited me to attend an admission, review, and dismissal (ARD) meeting at school and to meet Paul's teacher, his speech therapist, his occupational therapist, and his principal. Parents and professionals make important educational decisions at the ARD meeting. Prior to the meeting, I visited Paul's classroom and discovered new conversational threads.

Reflection

Collaborative therapists view school meetings as a setting for "open dialogue" (Seikkula, 2002). Open dialogue at school is when a client's extended formal support system joins into the conversation with clients and others about problems. Similar to Seikkula's discoveries about the effectiveness of open dialogue in a psychiatric setting, Marsha has found that therapy progresses when she connects face-to-face with all relevant parties at a child's school. It seemed miraculous to Heidi that Paul's current fifth grade year had been so different from previous years. In coresearch videotape, Heidi said:

> Since working with you, I hear you tell Paul that a lot of these ideas came from him, but there seems to be some kind of difference in that the things that you discuss here, he takes and uses! I'm not sure what you are doing differently. Yet, there is definitely something there. Our life has improved 50 to 75% over just the course of the last few months that we have seen you. He is very popular in school. We walk through the hallways and he is constantly being told: "Hey, Paul, how are you doing?" Last year it was not like that. . . I'm getting reports back from the teachers that they notice more confidence. There's more partnership in working with others. Whereas he used to just get maybe 50% of his work done, he's actually getting all of it

done now. There's, there's just so many things. . . . With you, the fact that you did go up there and did make your presence known, it made a difference, it did. His teachers are not afraid to say something to me if they have a question about something. I feel like there is more communication that has been set up.

Brothers Build Agreements

Heidi confided in Pat that she wanted to address an especially worrisome concern about sexual immodesty among the boys. I (Marsha), in response to this, spoke briefly with Heidi and learned that she and the boys had previously spoken with the pediatrician. He reassured her not to worry about this. Yet, Heidi continued to feel uneasy and to wonder: "Does something more need to be done?" Since Paul and I were already talking about "personal space" vis-à-vis his teacher's goal for him, I asked Heidi if she, Paul, Ben, Sam, and I might all talk about "touching." Heidi approved, although, when the time came to talk, she opted to stay in the waiting room.

As a conversation starter, I provided each boy with an outline of a child's body. The boys circled parts of the body where touches felt safe or comfortable. Using a second set of the outlines, we similarly discussed unwelcome touches. As our frank conversation continued, Heidi joined us at Sam's request. Although Heidi urged us to continue, she felt uneasy and fell silent during our talk. The boys were honest that their "privates" were not remaining private. They felt safe with the adults in their lives, but they felt unsafe about appropriate touching with each other.

The three boys eagerly worked toward finding ways to be safe. With Heidi observing quietly, the brothers made a set of agreements to which they have been faithful. These agreements, entirely from the boys, were:

1. Don't barge in the bathroom.
2. Tell Mom and Dad about uncomfortable touches and uncomfortable actions.
3. Close a bathroom door that is open when you see it open.
4. Knock before entering a room.
5. Don't lock a door unless everyone agrees and feels safe for it to be locked.

"Safety" became a powerful word in our common vocabulary. Often, according to Heidi, the boys have announced to her on the drive to my office, "I'm going to tell Marsha that I feel safe today."

Reflection

Whether in our offices or out, from the beginning, all the conversations within this therapeutic story have been sensitive, emotional, and filled with strong competing beliefs about serious concerns. Pat and Marsha, without being hierarchical, strive to be experts on keeping these complex conversations going in generative directions. They are willing to "not-know" and to be "uncertain" (Anderson, 1997). Collaborative therapists do not discount their professional knowledge. To be "uncertain" is to be careful about allowing one perspective to totalize one's understanding. The collaborative therapist attempts to stay in a state of "being informed" so that when she listens and speaks, there is room for change.

Prior to the "touching" conversation, there had been other conversations about touches among Heidi, the boys, and others. The "never-ending" nature of therapeutic conversations (Anderson et al., 2004) contributed to the success of the touching conversation in Marsha's office and to the success of the brothers' agreements. Anderson refers to these as "rolling conversations" or conversations leading to other conversations. Two important talks came on the heels of the touching talk—one in Pat's office and another at Heidi's home. These conversations anchored the brothers' agreements and changed the way family members talked.

Two Pivotal Dialogues

Concerned that she fell silent during the touching conversation, Heidi approached Pat with the suggestion that I (Marsha) provide a written narrative of the "touching" talk for them to review. As Heidi and Pat talked about the narrative, Heidi felt relaxed and confident that she could keep a "safety" dialogue going with her boys. She told Pat that she was afraid to share her worries about the boys' immodesty with Ken because of her fear that he might blame Paul and "leave their marriage."

Heidi was eager to tell me about the other pivotal conversation. At Paul's next appointment, she came bounding up the stairs, her three boys in tow. Smiling, Heidi insisted on talking with me alone. She scolded me for failing to include one of the inappropriate behaviors in my written narrative. I cringed, becoming aware of my accidental oversight. Yet, I could sense playfulness as she spoke openly. Heidi said that shortly after the brothers made their agreements, Ben brought up the unmentioned incident. The family was sitting at the dinner table and Heidi froze. However, Ken kept eating, looked the boys in the eye, and simply said: "That's not appropriate and it's really dumb. Don't do that again." Heidi was amazed and relieved by how calmly Ken provided the exact guidance that was needed—neither leaving their marriage nor blaming Paul.

Reflection

Our intention, every step of the way, was to provide abundant dialogical space and to foster the kinds of interrelated, simultaneous, overlapping, and sequential dialogue put forth by Anderson (1997). According to Anderson (1997):

> One conversation leads to another. Internal and external dialogues within the therapy room allow people to talk with themselves and others differently outside the therapy room as well. This is part of the transformational capacity of dialogue and narrative. It is not static, contained by walls or by time: rather, it is a fluid ongoing process in which each conversation becomes and is influenced by other conversations. (p. 128)

Coresearch: Conversations Influencing Conversations

When we conducted a research project, we asked Heidi and Paul to join us, along with other families, as coresearchers (McDonough & Koch, 2004). Using videotaped interviews, we asked them about their experience of collaborative therapy. With permission, we presented our coresearchers' ideas at a professional meeting. For Heidi and Paul, the project and presentation, offered another turning point.

At the presentation, we reflected with our colleagues on our feelings of gratitude to the families who helped us learn. This led to a spontaneous suggestion to write brief thank-you notes to the families. Twelve colleagues wrote notes to Paul and Heidi. The notes touched Heidi and Paul, expanding their story of self-agency. Some comments from the audience were:

- From my brief moment of watching you on video I saw your creativity and excited willingness to create a different life.
- Paul, you are awesome! I enjoyed learning how many strategies you have developed for helping manage strong feelings.
- Thank you for letting us hear your voices and your story. We therapists learn so much from our families.
- Both of you were such a wonderful inspiration. Hearing your story and seeing the positive and happy attitude about the therapy sessions and how it has helped was wonderful.

Heidi's comment upon reading the notes:

- I will save these letters and I will pull them out and read them and I will be thinking: these people don't even know me and in some small way I touched their lives. It is an honor. . . . Being called an inspiration, it is not something I would look to be in this situation. Hearing my story and being a positive influence is wonderful . . . it is encouraging to me to keep going.

Reflection

Heidi and Paul's story illustrates the effectiveness of a CLS approach. One small conversation, over two years, evolved into multiple conversations among many conversational partners. Currently, Heidi's story of abuse is transforming into a story of choice, hope, and self-competence. Paul, now thirteen, is no longer a victim at school but an honored student and friend to others. Heidi's dream of the family she wanted, symbolized by her vibrant tattoo, continues to become a reality. We are curious about how the story of Paul and Heidi may have touched you. As readers, you are now participants in our conversational partnership. With Heidi and Paul's permission, we invite you to contact us with any thoughts you might want to share with us or with Heidi and Paul. We know that you join us in thanking them for teaching us how to be better therapists.

References

Andersen, T. (1990). *The reflecting team: Dialogues and dialogues about dialogues*. Broadstairs, Kent, U.K.: Gorgmann.

Anderson, H. (1997). *Conversation, language, and possibilities: A postmodern approach to therapy*. New York: Basic.

Anderson, H. (1998, January 25–27). Polyphonic music: A metaphor for connecting, collaborating, and constructing in dialogue. In *Food for thought and dialogue*. Houston Galveston Institute, Galveston VII Symposium, 20th Anniversary Celebration. Garrett Creek Ranch, Paradise, TX.

Anderson, H. Personal communication, April 23, 1999.

Anderson, H. & Levin, S. (1997). Collaborative conversations with children: Country clothes and city clothes. In C. Smith & D. Nylund (Eds.), *Narrative therapies with children and adolescents* (pp. 255–281). New York: Guilford.

Anderson, H., London, S., & Rodriquez, I. (2004). Never ending stories: Children and reflecting teams. Presented at the 31st Annual Conference of Texas Association for Marriage and Family Therapy, January 14–17, Houston, TX.

Hoffman, L. (2003). *Family therapy: An intimate history*. New York: W.W. Norton.

McDonough, M.L. & Koch, P.K. (2004). Playful and poignant: Children's voices in family therapy. Presented at the 31st Annual Conference of Texas Association for Marriage and Family Therapy, January 14–17, Houston, TX.

Seikkula, J. (2002). Open dialogues with good and poor outcomes for psychotic crises: Examples from families with violence. *Journal of Martial and Family Therapy, 28*, 263–274.

CHAPTER 12

Creating Space for Children's Voices: A Collaborative and Playful Approach to Working with Children and Families[1]

DIANE GEHART

Without a word being spoken, I knew it had been a "bad" week the moment I entered the waiting room. There they sat: Maria motionless, her eyes fixed on the carpet below her feet; her adoptive parents' faces tight and tense. The inertia had set in again. For a few weeks the family was hopeful and satisfied with their progress; then things became worse. Despite my attempts to invite each to share his or her views of the situation, the parents only saw hopelessness, leaving Maria, generally a vivacious eight-year-old, increasingly silent and withdrawn. I wondered how I could make our conversation this week different. How could I create a space that allowed the parents to share their concerns while providing Maria a safe place for her voice and thoughts?

After a long walk down a short hallway to our room, I suggested that we try an entirely new way of talking. The parents interrupted, insisting that they had to tell me about Maria's mischief and poor attitude during the week. Again, I asked if we could try something different. Though I was uncomfortable with not allowing the parents to talk in the way they chose, especially since they described their parenting style as consistent with their traditional Mexican upbringing, I knew I had to find a way of talking that made room for their daughter's voice. I decided to suggest we assign questions to each of the three colors of *Jenga*, a "tumbling tower" game in which the players remove blocks until the tower collapses. We decided to ask about "What has gotten better since coming to therapy?" "What is one thing you would like to see improve?" and "What is one of your favorite family memories?" I hoped that the structured nature of the game, requiring each person to have a turn, would provide space for Maria's voice to be heard while simultaneously providing the parents with a new way to explore the frustrations they were eager to share with me.

The game began slowly. Each would role the die to determine the required color, then they would work together to find the most strategic block; Maria was particularly enthusiastic about advising her parents on how best to proceed. It was difficult for each person to share at first, and we waited quietly as each thought about the answers. Much to my amazement, all three had noticed many improvements of which I was unaware: Maria no longer lied, did her homework, and completed her chores. The parents' concerns for the week also came up: defiance, rule breaking, and disrespect. Each turn brought new emotions: tears, laughter, frustration, and silliness. Maria emotionally "checked in" for a time and then "checked out" when it became too much. We talked about her rhythm and ways to honor it along with the rhythm of her parents in session and at home. Although much of the content and emotion was not "news" to the family, the process or way they spoke and listened was different. Something shifted for the mother and daughter during this session as they heard each other in a new way. This later resulted in a transformation that—like dominos—led to other transformations in the family. This session and game marked the "beginning of the end" of the family's need to see me.

Creating Space for Children's Voices

Working with children and families has challenged me to find new ways to be in conversation. Children construct meaning differently than most adults. They rely less on words and shades of meaning and instead must *do*, touch, grab, feel, and experience the world to make sense of it. To make matters more confusing, the meanings that adults commonly assign to events are quite different than a child's interpretation of the same event. As I have explored ways to create dialogical space that includes children's voices, I have been challenged to think about my collaborative approach through the eyes of a child. In this chapter, I will share how I have expanded the ways I think about social constructionist, collaborative approaches to inform my work with children (Andersen, 1991; Anderson & Goolishian, 1992; Anderson, 1997; Hoffman, 2002; Penn, 2001). I will also share some of the specific ways that my clients, students, and I have applied these ideas. This approach is certainly not the only way to work with children using postmodern ideas, but I share them as one way that has worked in a practice setting that serves culturally and linguistically diverse families and foster children.

A Child's Approach to Constructing Meaning

Social constructionists describe the construction of meaning as heavily reliant on words and verbal language (Gergen, 1999; Shotter, 1993). However, children are less reliant on words to construct their meanings, yet they construct meaning nonetheless. Two concepts in social constructionist literature are particularly helpful in conceptualizing how children construct meaning: (a) joint (Shotter, 1993) or coordinated (Gergen, 1999) action, and (b) common sense knowledge.

"Meaning is an *emergent property of coordinated action*" (Gergen, 1999, p. 145, emphasis in original). For adults, "coordination action" most always involves verbal language. However, children rely more on action than words to coordinate meaning. Before they are even able to speak, children learn what their culture and family take to be "okay" or "not okay" through their actions and the responses of others to their actions (Bruner, 1990). In these interactions, they learn how to navigate the social world: "We can see that in the ordinary two way flow of activity between them, people create, without a conscious realization of the fact, a changing sea of moral enablements and constraints, of privileges and entitlements, and obligations and sanctions—in short, an ethos" (Shotter, 1993, p. 39). This ethos, or communal sense of how to get along and continue on with one another is learned through childhood, first through action and later with words. In contrast to the therapists and parents who want to help them, children who enter therapy are often more comfortable and familiar with meaning-making through action rather than words. Therefore, when working with children, therapists need to reconnect with making meaning in ways that are less language dependent.

Furthermore, because children are less adept with words and language, they are still in the process of developing "common sense" (Shotter, 1993) and familiarizing themselves with dominant cultural discourses. This is often a source of stress for adults who complain that "my child just doesn't understand." However, this lack of "common sense" can also be used as a resource to explore meanings and possibilities that the well-educated adult mind cannot see because of the habitual ways we view, describe, and story our experiences. Thus, working with children sometimes requires an abandonment of "common sense," and instead one must embrace the wonder and mystery of seeing the world through the eyes of a child.

Revisiting Collaborative Therapy from a Child's Perspective

When I served as the director of a district-wide school family counseling program and a court-appointed therapist for foster children, I revisited the postmodern and social constructionist concepts that inform my practice and reconsidered how these ideas translate when relating with children and their families. I revisited these ideas with the natural language of children in mind: play. In particular, I found it helpful to reconsider the following practices:

- Creating a dialogical space
- Assuming a not-knowing stance
- Taking a position of curiosity and nonexpertise
- Offering "appropriately unusual" comments
- Generating multiple perspectives
- Entertaining alternatives to the spoken word

Creating a Dialogical Space with Children

One of the most significant shifts when working with children was to expand my definition and expectations of "dialogue." Anderson and Goolishian (1992) describe therapeutic dialogue as a two-way exchange in which each person's voice is heard. "Dialogues" with children often look different than dialogues with adults. Most notably, dialogues with children may not involve words; instead meaning may be created through play, movement, art, and other activities. Dialogues with children also rely more heavily on nonverbal aspects of communication, such as tone, emotion, and facial expressions, rather than the literal content of spoken messages. However, dialogues with children still involve a two-way exchange and cocreation of meaning.

When creating a dialogical space for children, I found that creating a child friendly physical environment is important. For children to feel invited into a conversation, it often helped for the physical environment to reflect an understanding of the world from a child's perspective. Having child friendly chairs, workspace, play media, and decor created an almost immediate sense of connection with young children and their families. The arrangement of the physical space communicates that the child's voice and worldview would be recognized in the room. For example, having interesting and engaging puppets and toys easily accessible invited children and adults to spontaneously engage their more playful sides.

A child-friendly physical context sets the stage for the child's voice to be invited into the therapeutic dialogue. Perhaps the greatest challenge for both therapists and parents is to take time to listen to what children have to say. Children often require more time to express themselves, and adults are quick to rush in and provide words for children. Once children do speak, adults sometimes dismiss what they have said as irrelevant or illogical from an adult perspective. However, my experience is everything a child says is significant and meaningful if the therapist takes the time to understand how the child fits seemingly unrelated pieces together to form a whole. For example, when asked a question about a specific incident, a child may start talking about a friend or fictional character, but usually there is a direct link to the child's situation if one slows down long enough to understand the connection.

Not-Knowing

A collaborative therapist takes a not-knowing stance with all clients, including children. The therapist's not-knowing stance invites the client to explore the situation in a curious fashion, encouraging a process of "mutual puzzling" (Anderson, 1997). The therapist does not try to understand too quickly but instead allows ideas to emerge through the dialogue, which may be a form of play. This stance implies that the therapist avoids certainties about the client's experience and instead remains open to new ideas and perspectives. Unfortunately, parents and therapists generally assume they know more about children and children's perspectives than they actually do. Adults are often blinded by their ideas about children and easily miss what is right in front of them. Therapists have an additional "handicap" in that they have many theories about development, families, and play that tell them what to notice and what to listen for. When these theories are followed without reflecting on their implications, a therapist can fail to see the person who is in the room. The challenge then becomes to suspend what one knows, at least temporarily, so that one can enter the child's world.

When working with children, I often find it is helpful to remember that a child entertains many possibilities that my adult mind fails to consider because they are not "real" in my adult world. I often find the child's world to be "magical" in the sense that it conjures up new connections, meanings, and possibilities that my adult mind could never have imagined. The "magic" and "wonder" I perceive is more a statement about my worldview than the child's. Therefore, it is important to remain humble and take a sincere stance of not-knowing when working with children. Sometimes what "really" happened remains a mystery.

One such mystery occurred when I was working with a young girl referred because she was unable to pay attention in class; the teacher believed she had attention deficit disorder. When I provided space for her to tell her story, she surprised me by sharing the "real" cause of her inattention, which was that she was not sleeping at night because a spirit would haunt her in her dreams as well as in other places; her mother verified the story. "Not-knowing" in this situation required that I suspend professional and dominant ideas about this type of phenomenon and instead explore this new realm from the family's perspective. I asked about the ways that the family and their culture have dealt with such matters and suggested the girl draw the spirit to illustrate the story. During the discussion, the girl stated that she believed that the spirit is trying to speak with her but she has been afraid to engage it. To explore these fears, I suggested she also draw the dreaded dialogue with the spirit. The next week she decided it was time to tell the spirit to leave, and she began to sleep better and focus more at school. What "really" happened is still a mystery to me. Entering a child's world often requires entering realities that can easily be dismissed and overlooked by the "well-trained" professional; yet these other realities often provide unparalleled resources for change. These situations can also leave the therapist with a healthy sense of mystery and a new and humbler appreciation for not-knowing.

Curiosity and the Nonexpert Position

In collaborative therapy, curiosity refers to the genuine desire on the part of the therapist to understand the client's worldview and perspective. The therapist must sincerely see the client, even a child, as an "expert" of his or her own story (Anderson & Goolishian, 1992). This may be difficult for some therapists to do when the client is a child because most children are not seen as an expert on anything, including their own experiences, thoughts, and feelings. If therapists approach children with a sincere sense of curiosity, they will find they have much to learn. Children generally do not construct the world in the same way that adults do. To access their world and their ways of making meaning, therapists need to be unusually curious about how children are making sense of their life experiences and the experiences within the family. Along with this, therapists need to be very careful to ensure that the words they and other adults use are understood by the child. For example, I have learned that young children generally understand the question "How was your week?" very differently from adults. Most children seem to refer back to the last 2 hours of the day and answer the question based on this recent history. Furthermore, what constitutes a "good" or "bad" week can differ even more markedly between adults and children. Therefore, I often find myself translating between the language of children and that of adults. This basic task of translating terms and meanings can significantly shift the perception of the problem and quickly open new possibilities for family interaction. For example, sometimes having parents and children clarify what each means by "being good" can pave the way to quickly alleviating family distress.

Appropriately Unusual

I find that Tom Andersen's idea of "appropriately unusual" comments is particularly useful in conceptualizing work with children and their families.

According to Andersen, a therapist's comments should be "appropriately unusual" to facilitate reflection and new understandings. If the comments are too usual or too unusual, clients will not be able to generate new meanings. When working with children, therapists must carefully attend to what is "usual" for the child to generate appropriately unusual comments and reflections that will be meaningful for the child and family. Therapists must also keep in mind that an appropriately unusual response may not be verbal when working with children. Rather than respond with words, sometimes I draw, write on a board, talk with a puppet, or use playful gestures to carry on a dialogue with a child.

For many children and teens, simply speaking in the therapy setting is too unusual. But as they develop a trusting relationship, they become open to the unusual conversational setting of the therapy room. However, until they are ready to hear anything different, children are usually quite clear and direct when the therapist is "too unusual." A hesitant shoulder shrug, the "I don't know" response, a persistent desire to play, and silent withdrawal are cues that the therapist is too far ahead of the child. In particular, I find teenagers suspicious of any comment on my part that is too different from their perspective and too similar to what most adults have already told them. When I get the cue that I am not in sync with their worldview, I slow down and try to move with their rhythm. Often "wondering" statements or questions that address being out of sync and how to get back in sync (e.g., I am wondering if we are talking about the right thing?) are helpful in this type of situation.

Multiple Voices and Perspectives

Collaborative therapists often find it helpful to use multiple perspectives to generate new meanings and understandings. The therapist facilitates this process by encouraging multiple, contradictory perspectives in conversation about a given problem (Anderson, 1997). When working with children, I find that there are many creative ways to generate alternative perspectives and that one does not necessarily need to use words to do so. The most literal way to generate multiple perspectives is to invite each member of the family to share his or her perspectives and to include the perspectives of support persons such as teachers, school counselors, friends, and extended or "unofficial" family members. For this process to be successful, the therapist must proceed carefully to ensure that the child's voice is not lost among the adult voices and that the child feels safe to freely express his or her viewpoint. If I sense that a child does not feel free to speak, I ask the child directly if this is a context in which he or she can honestly share his or her perspective. Sometimes it is helpful for adults to hear and know that they do not have the "full story." Other approaches to verbally introducing multiple voices includes inviting reflecting teams, sharing the therapist's perspectives, and allowing the child to give voice to different aspects of him or herself.

Perhaps the most exciting options for generating alternative perspectives with children and families are found in art, movement, and creative expression. By the very fact that they are nonverbal, artistic, and nonverbal forms of expression inherently provide an alternative to verbal description and meanings. A drawing or picture of an event always offers a perspective that words could not portray in the same way. Therefore, all forms of art and play provide an alternative description, and often it is these alternative descriptions that children find the most useful.

Moving Beyond Words

Perhaps the most unique aspect of working with children from a collaborative perspective is becoming comfortable with the idea that "therapeutic conversations" may not always involve words. Postmodern and social constructionist literature focuses on the construction of meaning using words, and therefore our descriptions of postmodern therapy have been language focused. However, when working with children one quickly learns that drawings, gestures, and play convey meaning and provide fertile ground for constructing new meanings. A drawing or sand tray can provide rich and colorful alternative descriptions and often capture a heart- or soul-felt sense that words could never convey. Similarly, moving in harmony with a child can take the form of a conversation that enters realms that words cannot.

For example, I once met with a young girl who was removed from her mother's care due to neglect, and her social worker and foster parent constantly complained that she lied and was manipulative. She refused to talk about any of the complaints from these outside parties and also refused to talk about any difficult feelings. Rather than insisting that she talk, I tried to find alternative ways to be with her. One day when I got the familiar shoulder shrug with hands tossed in the air in response to one of my questions, I decided to playfully mirror back her gestures. Then for several minutes we were silent as we experimented, played, and "conversed" with various gestures and movements. At times, it was a perfectly in sync dance, and it was difficult to determine who was leading and who was following. I rarely got the I-don't-know shoulder shrug after this, and she began to talk and write about things she previously could not express. I still am not sure of the precise meaning of our conversation that day, but I believe for a moment we were reconnected with the mystery and magic that only children know.

In addition to engaging in nonverbal conversations, I have also found that children sometimes process what Tom Andersen (1991) refers to as "inner talk" in unique ways. I have witnessed children engaged in play who enter a trance-like or meditative state. When working in a sand tray, painting a picture, or playing in a dollhouse, children can enter a very focused and intense form of play to which I am not usually invited. Sometimes this play appears to be an acting out or representational telling of their internal dialogue, and often they narrate it as such. For example, I have often seen abused children enter this state when they transform the familiar story of helplessness to one of proactively protecting themselves and others; they seem to simultaneously make new sense of the past trauma and open new possibilities for a safe and hopeful future. I witness in awe as the child tells or acts out a story that transforms meaning, interpretations, and experiences in ways that that shift their world from one of fear and pain to one of liberation and joy.

Ideas for Playfully Working with Children and Families

Putting collaborative ideas into practice with children and families can take many forms. I will share some of the ways that my students, our clients, and I have put these ideas into practice. However, I do so with hesitancy because I do not want this list of ideas to be interpreted as the "correct" way to do collaborative therapy with children and families. I believe each practice must be unique and developed spontaneously with each child and family to meaningfully "fit" into their lives. The ideas must emerge from the local dialogue rather than from a book such as this. So I offer these as food for thought to inspire you and your clients to find ways to address the concerns that clients bring.

Board Games with a Twist

Inspired by the creativity of my supervisees (Berger & Gehart, 2000), I have played with ways of incorporating traditional board games into child and family dialogues. We have explored the possibilities of adapting board games to facilitate communication, identify new possibilities, highlight strengths, and discuss concerns in new ways. Most often, we adapt a game by assigning questions or activities to be performed by each player on his or her turn. For example, the family may pair original questions that they develop to colors on a game board. As the players land on the designated colors, they answer the corresponding questions. I have found that this approach is most helpful when the family constructs the rules and develops the questions rather than having the therapist dictate the game structure. Their sense of ownership inspires active and thoughtful participation both in and outside the session.

I have found the collaborative use of board games to be helpful in several specific situations. First, board games are an excellent option for opening dialogue when families have difficulty allowing each other to speak or when there are certain family members who focus on a single point of view or perspective. Second, as illustrated in the situation with Maria above, games can provide a balance between parents' desire to talk about the problem and children's desire to play. Finally, we have had several families use games as a venue to practice new approaches to communicating and expand ways of relating based on prior discussions during therapy. The games become a playful and fun way to practice new ways of being with each other. The following are sample question for use with board games that can facilitate a dialogue

- What has gotten better since we started meeting?
- Share a favorite family memory.
- Name one thing you are willing to do to make things better at home.
- Share something that you appreciate about one/each person.
- Share one strategy that has worked for stated goal (communicating better at home, doing better in school, etc.).
- What is one idea for keeping things on track once we stop meeting?
- What helps the most regarding … ?
- What is the least helpful regarding … ?
- What is one way you show someone that you care (that he/she may not know about).
- What is your greatest concern regarding … ?
- What is your greatest hope regarding … ?

Puppet and Play Enactments

When children have difficulty verbally expressing their thoughts, the therapist can invite them to tell their stories with puppets, in a sandbox, or with art. Such enactments are particularly helpful in situations where adults in the family have difficulty listening to the child's story or pressure the child to tell the story in a certain way. Once the child has shared his or her story using play media, the child and/or family can be invited to play out alternative perspectives, endings or other variations that fit with the emerging dialogue. These alternative enactments provide children with a means of experiencing and practicing preferred ways to interact with others and new ways to respond to stressful situations. Often the "playfulness" of the first telling spontaneously inspires clients and therapists to play out alterative tellings.

Amy Tuttle, my former student and current colleague, used puppets with Sonia, a 6-year-old girl who was referred by the local school because she was unable to leave the house on any day that a cloud was in the sky. As her supervisor, she looked to me for guidance, yet I could not say that I had ever encountered a situation quite like this. Given her age we both agreed that puppets would be a helpful medium. In their play, Sonia assigned Amy and the mother to play the roles of her friends on the school yard who encouraged her to come out and play; Sonia's Ladybug, of course, refused to come out and play. Once Sonia told her story, they all decided to switch roles. In the second telling, the mother played the role of the Ladybug, and Sonia and the therapist were the friends asking her to play. Finally, all three switched again, allowing the therapist to play the role of cloud-fearing Ladybug. With each telling of the story, the Ladybug became braver and, with enough encouragement from Sonia's "friend" puppets, would come out to play. As they took on different roles, each person gained a slightly different perspective of the situation. Over the next few weeks Sonia was able increasingly to go to school and out to recess regardless of the weather, and the family then moved on to other concerns in therapy. The multiple tellings of the story enabled Sonia to explore her situation from different perspectives, which eventually allowed her to develop a new relationship with her fears.

Puppet Reflecting Teams

When I first introduced reflecting teams to families with young children, it did not take long to learn that children often have difficulty following the traditional conversational format. As the team talked, the children would either play with a toy, each other, or otherwise "check out." Introducing puppets, art, and other play media has allowed the children we work with to better follow and engage the reflecting team's conversation. We recommend that the team continue with the play themes and media that the child or family was using during the session rather than introduce material that does not fit with the family's current dialogue. Furthermore, solo therapists can create reflecting teams with puppets as another way to explore multiple views of the situation, making the reflecting process readily accessible without multiple therapists.

When the team is engaged in play, children often want to join in the activity. The therapist and team should consider this possibility beforehand and decide what might work best in each situation. Although research has shown that adults generally prefer the spatial distance between the team and themselves (Smith, Yoshioka, & Winton, 1993), children may not necessarily follow this general rule. Especially when all participants are interacting with puppets, children may find it natural to interject or interact with the team's characters

Possibilities for Using Reflecting Teams with Children

When Session Involves Puppets:

- Use puppets that have a thematic match (e.g., forest animals, sea creatures, medieval characters) and explore possibilities from the respective positions of each. For example, in the section above the child was a Ladybug concerned about clouds; the team could include other flight and land animals who discuss their unique relationship to clouds based on the habits of each animal.
- Interview a significant puppet in the family's play or the imagined parent, friend, or child of a significant character in the child's play.
- Have the team play out different perspectives or tellings from each puppet or person's perspective to highlight the different lived realities in a given situation.

When the Session Involves Conversation or Other Play Media:

- Continue with play media used by child or family if possible to offer multiple perspectives and tellings of the story.
- When family has been primarily in dialogue, a whiteboard or puppets can be used to reflect on the dialogue. If a certain family member's perspective was not clearly articulated in session, the team's reflections can wonder about what might not have been said.
- The team can use Play-doh and clay to illustrate their reflections. As alternative perspectives are discussed, the Play-doh can be reshaped and transformed to illustrate changes. Members can either pass around and reshape the same piece of Play-doh or clay or each can shape his or her own; the former is helpful to highlight transformations and the latter differences.
- If the family is struggling with allowing each person to speak, the team can play with options by using a play activity, such as throwing a ball or shooting baskets, to transfer talk their turns.

Artistic Reflections

Drawing, painting, whiteboards, and clay sculpting can be used to facilitate the telling of the child's story and to explore alternative perspectives. The artistic rendition or representation of a problem or situation provides alternative perspectives in and of itself. The expression "a picture is worth a thousand words" is particularly relevant when working with children. Many children, especially those who have been traumatized, find it easier to draw, write, or sculpt their experiences rather than speak aloud. Once they have expressed themselves on paper or in play media, children can then talk about something concrete and tangible. What was once beyond words becomes expressible and often transmutes and evolves through the "artistic telling."

I once worked with a foster child who was facing the difficult decision of whether to be adopted when he had been lead to believe he was going to be reunited with his mother. He also understood that he had two weeks to make a decision. When he came to my office and I asked him about his thoughts on the situation, he said, "I don't know and don't want to talk about it" but nodded his head when I asked if he wanted my help to make this decision. He was typically an extremely verbal 11-year-old, but I thought we might explore a more hands-on medium since words seemed to be difficult on this day. So I suggested we write down the "pro's and con's" of his options on the whiteboard. As he started writing, he added column for "confusions" between the two other columns. For the rest of the session, we were mostly silent as he filled up the columns on the board as I recorded on paper his well-formed and thoughtful descriptions of the positive, negative, and confused feelings he had toward his mother, prior foster parents, current foster parents, and life. Even though I had worked with him for over a year, I had never imagined he had reflected on the complexities of his situation as he demonstrated on the board and learned that despite his remarkable verbal abilities there was much he needed to express in other media.

Ideas for Getting Started with Artistic Expression

- Draw "current" and "alternative" (both better and worse) versions of the problem. Often the "worse" version creates a sense of hope and competence.
- Draw various aspects of the self/family identified in conversation.
- Sculpt in the problem in clay and reshaping the problem based on the different circumstances that the child/family describe or imagine.
- Draw the world and/or problem as the child sees it and modifying the drawing as the child identifies new ways to make sense of the problem.
- Use multiple layers of watercolors to paint out the various layers of the problem and/or various perspectives on the problem held by different members of the family.
- Illustrate the story as a child relates it on a whiteboard or on paper.
- Create joint drawings with the child in which the therapist and/or family and child create an artistic work together.

Concluding Thoughts

When working with children I keep one central thought in mind: create a safe space for the child's voice to be heard. The challenge then becomes remaining open and curious enough to assist each child in finding his or her unique way to express this voice. This process has taught me to be to comfortable dwelling in the infinite possibilities of silence and wordlessness. By remaining curious and open to the child's worldview, I find it possible to enter a wondrous and sometimes magical world with limitless promise.

Endnote

1. I want to thank Diana Pantaleo, M.S., my friend and colleague, for her feedback and comments that helped refine this chapter, and Lorraine Granger-Merkle for her skillful editing assistance.

References

Andersen, T. (1991). *The reflecting team: Dialogues and dialogues about the dialogues.* New York: Norton.

Anderson, H. (1997). *Conversation, language, and possibilities.* New York: Basic Books.

Anderson, H. & Goolishian, H. (1992). The client is the expert: A not-knowing approach to therapy. In S. McNamee & K. Gergen (Eds.), *Therapy as social construction* (pp. 25–39). Newbury Park, CA: Sage.

Berger, V. & Gehart, D. (2000). Feelings Jenga: Facilitating family communication through play. *Journal of Family Psychotherapy, 11,* 81–86.

Bruner, J. (1990). *Acts of meaning.* Cambridge, MA: Harvard University Press.

Gergen, K. (1999). *An invitation to social construction.* Thousand Oaks, CA: Sage.

Hoffman, L. (2002). *Family therapy: An intimate history.* New York: Norton.

Penn, P. (2001). Chronic illness: Trauma, language, and writing: Breaking the silence. *Family Process, 40,* 33–52.

Shotter, J. (1993). *Conversational realities: Constructing life through language.* Thousand Oaks, CA: Sage.

Smith, T.E., Yoshioka, M., & Winton, M. (1993). A qualitative understanding of reflecting teams: Client perspectives. *Journal of Systemic Therapies, 12,* 28–43.

Beyond the Therapy Room

Part 3 continues with authors' stories, specifically accounts of examples of how they translate postmodern collaborative and related assumptions in varied practices and contexts outside the therapy room. Part 3 has three sections. In the first section, *In Social and Institutional Settings,* the authors present alternative ways of working in social and institutional systems such as prisons, psychiatric hospitals, and schools and as collaborative colleagues. The chapters offer powerful and inspiring examples that document expanding resources, creating space for traditionally silent and marginalized voices, and finding hope and promise where often none seemed possible. The chapters also example the versatility and adaptability of the ideas and practices presented in this book across cultures.

The section begins with a compelling and hopeful story by Swedish therapist Judit Wagner, who illustrates how, when faced with serious and difficult social problems such as incarceration, her collaborative-reflecting dialogue practice with prisoners and warders offers rich potential. As Sheila McNamee pointed out when she read this chapter, the practice "embodies the ethic of collaborative work: that we are not too quick to impose our values, our understandings, or our judgments on others." Next Haarakangas and colleagues offer a provocative alternative—a network-language-based approach—to the institutional practices of psychiatry in Finland with first-episode and chronic psychosis. The efficacy of their approach, which is gaining widespread recognition around the world, is documented by their clients' voices, and it has been statistically documented through two-, five-, and 8-year follow-up studies. In the next two chapters by Sylvia London and Irma Rodríguez-Jazcilevich and by Sylvia London and Margarita Tarragona, the authors share how they faced the challenge of taking their collaborative therapy practices and training out of their familiar therapist-classroom settings in Mexico City and into a school and a psychiatric hospital, respectively. Most noticeable is the contrast of the challenge in each setting. In the school, it was a matter of the authors' being blinded by the "familiar" and how the associated "knowing" and "assuming" got them into trouble. In the psychiatric hospital it was a matter of "unfamiliar" territory as they lost and then regained their ability to live with uncertainty. In "Women at a Turning Point," Feinsliver, Murphy, and Anderson's story testifies to the power of an environment that invites and encourages collaborative relationships and generative conversations. Women once "categorized" as "substance abusers" and "victims of domestic violence" emerged and flourished as they realized "unidentified" strengths, "untapped" self-agency, and a newfound "sense of community." And, finally, Klaus G. Deissler from Germany talks about how a one-week visit to Cuba surprisingly turned into a training/consultation program that is now in its seventh year. He brings the voices of his Cuban colleagues to the pages to describe their experience of the program, the effect on their work, and its compatibility with their national ideology.

In the second section, *In Education, Supervision, and Research,* the chapters demonstrate the collaborative perspective in education, supervision, and research, and its influence on the person of the therapist. Sheila McNamee begins the section with an account of how she takes her collaborative-relational perspective to the university classroom. What I found most significant and hopeful in her "teaching" is how the students' learning extended beyond the classroom into their lives. And, in so doing, the striking ways in which they became "good citizens," involved in critical issues facing the broader university campus and the community and in related policy-making discussions. In the next chapter Sallyann Roth tackles the challenge of how to help therapists learn to be collaborative. She presents a detailed exercise that she has successfully used with therapy students, and with members of businesses, organizations, and community groups; she includes an example of how she used the exercise to invite a client to join her in a "relationship of collaborative inquiry." In "Curious George," Glen Gardner and Tony Neugebauer present a case study of a supervisor who has been a dear colleague of Harry and Harlene for over 25 years, a man characterized as generous and curious, and with an openness to transform himself. They bring in the voices of the supervisor and several therapists that he supervised over forty years to describe the man and his actions.

Many of the chapters in this book include a research component. This is not surprising as collaborative therapy places importance on the therapist and client as coresearchers who evaluate their work as they go along together. The chapter by Diane Gehart, Margarita Tarragona, and Saliha Bava, hence, provides a valuable discussion of how to conceptualize research as collaborative inquiry and illustrates ways the authors use research in their practice settings.

The chapters in the third section, *Never-ending Possibilities,* focus on the importance of keeping in mind that collaboration is useful in ways that we might not imagine, that it is not necessarily a continual process, and that it is not always easy. As well, the chapters expand the discussion begun by Roth in Chapter 20. Mary Gergen and Kenneth J. Gergen give a delightful and engaging account of the positive power of a process of "never ending" collegial collaboration and how it created something that neither of them nor their colleagues could have done singularly. They conclude with "lessons we draw from our work on the Newsletter to understanding the collaborative process, and to rendering it more effective." In the book's concluding chapter, Sally St. George and Dan Wulff's honesty and forthrightness is heart-warming as they share their personal experiences and struggles of "walking their talk": how they learned to relate and work with colleagues and students in more respectful, collaborative, and productive ways. In the end, they beautifully highlight what this book is about: collaboration as a philosophical stance and relationships and conversations that make a difference. We cannot think of a more appropriate place to pause this book.

In Social and Institutional Settings

Trialogues: A Means to Answerability and Dialogue in a Prison Setting

JUDIT WAGNER

My humanity is captured and un-dissolvably bound to yours.
We don't say: I am thinking, therefore I am existing . . . but rather;
I am human and for that I am belonging somewhere.
I am a part of something I share with others.

Desmond Tutu, 2000

I am writing this chapter in a place that conjures fairy-tale images of child-hood. It is a village called Kalmar, a well-preserved medieval town of 50,000 situated in southern Sweden by the Baltic Sea. The castle and other historic buildings date back to the 13th century, a time when Kalmar was a mer-cantile trading center and an important harbor. Please allow me to be your guide as we enter the site of our work, a small prison with high yellow walls and a barbed-wire fence housing 53 high-security inmates. It is here that we instituted a unique form of collaborative therapy, a system of therapy we call "shared talks" or "trialogues," which is an evolving work.

The stark contrast of the prison walls against the backdrop of the charming old castle is obvious to any visitor arriving in Kalmar by train. The walk from the train station to the prison leads us along a cobblestone path through the market square, passing a bridge and high water tower of old red brick that was once the Old City border. We arrive at a metal door, ring the bell and inform the guard that we have an appointment.

He opens the gate, and we enter a second door where the guard requests our identification cards and performs a security check. We are finally cleared, and we enter the prison.

I first walked through these metal doors in 1991 after being asked by the prison inspector to assist personnel and guards called *warders*[1] in talks with the inmates. Prior to that, I thought very little about this prison or its residents even though I passed it everyday as I biked to my office at the family counseling agency. I remember, however, feeling a sense of regret on the prisoners' behalf, when the long-awaited first days of spring finally arrived each year, and the city was in bloom. I felt the starkness of the prison building against nature's beauty and felt sadness for anyone who could not move freely amid the city's springtime splendor.

Those feelings resurfaced when I was asked to assist with the shared talks at Kalmar prison. Although I had sympathy for the prisoner's plight, I found myself reluctantly agreeing to the task, as I had no experience with the criminal justice system. Working with 53 inmates, 27 warders, and several inspectors behind these metal doors would be a new challenge and a major departure from my prior work with couples and families. The first step was to develop a plan.

Theoretical Foundations

In developing a plan, I first considered the project's goal: to assist the warders in organizing and optimizing their talks with the inmates. Searching for an appropriate theoretical framework, I revisited the concepts of psychodynamic therapy, the systemic models of Gregory Bateson and the Milan team (Boscolo, Cecchin, Hoffman, & Penn, 1987), Tom Andersen's (1987, 1991, 1992) reflecting team approach, and Harlene Anderson and Harry Goolishian's (1996, 1988, 1992) language system approach. I quickly eliminated the psychodynamic approach knowing that one-to-one therapy was not the administrator's intended plan. Family therapy as practiced within the Milan model would be difficult since the personnel did not have any experience with systems thinking or family therapy. In addition, the inmates are isolated, sentenced as individuals and cut-off from their families and outside world; one might think that the only company these men keep is with their criminal record. I decided the goal of facilitating personnel in their conversations with the inmates would be best served with reflecting talks as described in reflecting team and collaborative work.

After receiving permission for this innovative plan, I decided to ground the program with a solid connection to a well-founded theoretical model and university research. Andersen's model provided the epistemological foundation necessary for using an innovative approach in a not-so-innovative environment, where people were likely to question reflective and collaborative ways of talking. Tom Andersen, a psychiatrist and professor at the University of Tromsø, Norway, and an innovator in family therapy, assisted initially with practical support and later with the evaluation process. Also at the University of Tromsö, Georg Höyer, a doctor in community medicine who is deeply involved in criminal justice system work internationally, provided theoretical and practical support for the project (Wagner, Höyer, & Andersen, 2002). Both Andersen and Höyer visited Kalmar frequently for discussion, directly influencing the evolution of the process. I also connected with other colleagues including Peggy Penn, Lynn Hoffman, Harlene Anderson, and Marty Roberts (all from the United States); Gisela Schwartz (from Austria); and Torbjörn Andersson (from Stockholm). Four of us, Peggy Penn, Marty Roberts, Gisela Schwartz, and myself began to correspond frequently via e-mail in which we exchanged ideas and progressed toward a deeper understanding of the project.

The process of applying the theoretical concept of reflecting talks to actual work in the prison allows us to reevaluate the link between theory and practice. In these circular exchanges, neither practical nor theoretical knowledge is deemed superior; rather they exist side-by-side as in the Socratic tradition (Skirbekk & Gilje, 1987/1993). The collaborative approach creates a forum for exploring experiential and theoretical knowledge using a common language. This dialogical exchange allows each to inform the understanding of the other, assisting the creation of a common formation that deepens and widens our collective knowledge.

Invitation

In an effort to extend the collaborative process to you the reader, I invite you to imagine that you are taking part in the reflecting conversations or trialogues initiated at the prison. These conversations involve at least three participants who alternate their participation between conversing and listening. Were you to actually visit the prison, I would request permission from the inmates to allow you to participate in the conversation as a guest. You would be invited to observe the three of us—the inmate, the warder and I—in our reflecting talks and would probably notice that generally two of us speak as the third listens and that we alternate these roles to acquire different perspectives. As our conversation slows and then eventually comes to a close, we would ask you about your reflections on what you heard and witnessed. The inmate would then be invited to comment on your reflections and share what he had been thinking while he listened, perhaps responding to a particular comment that touched him, expounding on a point he thought you misunderstood, or asking for clarification on a specific point. As you read about our work in Kalmar, I invite you to imagine not only the castle and prison walls but also what these inmates might ask you, share with you, and teach you.

Trialogues

An inmate who participated in the project for one year describes his experience of the trialogue process:

> I have become aware of the weaknesses I have and understand that in the future, I should avoid being silent with my relatives. The major reason to be in conversation with them and with other people is that, as I now understand it, the conversations can help me avoid being carried away by my own thoughts and fantasies which can lead to new delusions and anxiety.[2]

Andersen (1994) says that "language is not innocent, language is powerful." Jaakko Seikkula (1990, 1993, 1995), a Finnish psychologist, asserts that psychosis is the "chaos of language." Reflecting on these assertions, I pondered the relation between language and crime and decided that crime might result from the breakdown of expression or language. If we accept that premise, it would follow that dialogic conversations, well-chosen words, and the performance of stories could be therapeutic for inmates.

I invite inmates to put their experiences into words by beginning with these questions: How did you come to find yourself in prison? Why are you here and not with your loved ones? Why are you here rather than studying in a university?[3] These questions invite their stories, which are their life histories. We avoid simplifying their stories to craft a neat yet one-sided version. Inherent to this prison context with jailer and jailed, there is contradiction; there are two sides to every story and the endings are often just the beginnings of new, more complex questions. Our aim is to listen to both sides with both ears, an ear to each, allowing for new paradigms and parables, more metaphors and more meanings to segue into new conversations.

Beginnings: Histories and Stories

The conversations are based on units of at least three participants: one inmate, one staff member, and myself as the therapist or facilitator. The talks can also be organized in groups: three to six inmates with two staff members. In-session supervision is organized in units of at least four: one inmate, two staff members, and myself. These talks typically involve one person or group who is listening while two or more converse.

The trialogue process generally begins with a conversation between the inmate and the therapist. The conversations make it possible to literally step into the inmate's story, listening attentively as he searches for words, expresses his thoughts and formulates meaning. We follow the inmate into his story, at times into his earlier life, at other times into his current worries. The path into another's story uncovers diverse, unique, and difficult life circumstances, often taking us to other countries and cultures. The facilitator introduces questions that conjure pictures and events that, as they are recounted, may be contradictory. The inmate invariably describes himself from the perspective of another time or life situation. Additionally, he provides hints of how family members might tell the story differently. Furthermore, stories from within the prison portray a person quite different when compared to stories from the "real" world. Preserving the discrepancies enables everyone to a better understanding of the complexity and richness of the inmate's story and personhood. If we encourage a single congruent description of the person, we risk excluding alternative understandings and sacrifice the richness of this person's character and potential. Our intention is to nurture the person's story until the details paint a picture, which are then filled in with meaning.

It is an arduous task to piece together a life history from discrepant details, but the work is worthwhile, as one sees the inmate struggle and then succeed in putting the pieces in place. The process helps them move from seeing themselves as criminals to seeing themselves as human beings with qualities ranging from good to bad with everything in between. Time and time again, we see that the work of assembling their own personal details into a whole helps them to better understand their history and supports the personnel's attempts to think more respectfully and compassionately about the inmate's situation. Therefore, the talks have a three-pronged purpose: (a) to communicate and be heard while constructing the story of one's history, (b) to come to an understanding of that story, and (c) to be influenced by it, to learn.

Questions

The introductory questions mentioned above are followed by the following: What occupies your mind? How do you spend your time? Describe your relationships with other inmates and with the personnel inside the prison? Describe your relationships outside, to your family and friends? Describe your relationships to outside society and its authorities?

In terms of physical space, the warders and inmates have common areas; the corridor, workshop, school, and dining room—areas not separated physically so conflicts between the two groups are common. We look at conflicts between individuals or groups, and we search for circumstances where the inmates interact well with one another and with the warders; this opens possibilities for seeing more than one side of the situation. Alternatively, the therapist could simply concur with the personnel's opinions concerning an inmate, but this would severely limit opportunities for resolving issues. On the other side, inmates can easily develop one set views of the warders. Therefore, we strive to honor the differing perspectives as a springboard for developing tolerance, negotiation, and compromise.

One inmate had recurring incidents that made the warders wary of him. We asked him to start a group for inmates to discuss cultural differences, hoping they would find new ways to express themselves related to this complex issue. Meanwhile, the chaplain and myself offered him individual reflecting talks. At one point during the talks while recounting years of struggling to attain a certain life style, he began to cry. He remembered what he was missing: his home, his family, and his children. His caring nature came through in the group—a potential for caring that had been buried while in prison but was once evident in his life. As we created space for him to express his losses, he was more open to rebuild relationships in the prison. We have continued to work regularly with him and believe he is motivated to learn to have patience with others, including the warders.

When we think the inmate is ready to talk about his crime, we approach him with the questions: Is this a good time to talk about the crime for which you have been sentenced? What are your thoughts about that particular event in your life? What kind of life were you living at the time of the crime? What was your highest priority at that time? What situation or event immediately preceded the crime? What was going on around you as a person? What kind of thoughts occupied your mind at that time?

Stories can be told in many different ways. Some of the inmates tell theirs using few carefully chosen words; some of the stories are short and told in rapid-fire fashion without pause. To our ears, these stories sometimes sound unusual, strange, and even violent. In each case, we enter into the scene of the crime; we reflect on what is offered and what is missing in the story. Often it seems the words fly about like feathers in the air, unconnected, without meaning, causing us to ask for more detail in order to lend the stories weight and help them land.

Some inmates tell of situations where they lost perspective because their lifestyle at the time was so frenetic, chaotic, and in most cases too busy for rest and reflection. The rapid pile-up of events without reflection in many cases led to a situation in which inmates found themselves isolated in their frenzy, with few people or no one at all with which to talk. No one else had time to listen and engage in conversation. If they did have someone to talk with, that person was often in the same situation and could not contribute another perspective, another lens through which to see things. This lack of a benevolent and engaged listener contributing an alternative perspective on a story is, in our experience, quite often the backdrop for the inmate's criminal history.

An inmate's story could include the tale of unmet expectations that precipitated his crime. One non-Swedish inmate spoke of his family's expectations for him to become a leading entrepreneur like his father and return to his country displaying his success by building a house there. However, this dream of success required several years of study and work that the inmate felt he was not gifted enough to complete quickly. To build the house, he needed money, which would have meant many years of work in Sweden; to expedite the process he found ways to make money other than through work. Such expectations can be so ingrained that the individual does not examine the potential costs: "What is the price I have to pay to provide the proof of my success? Are these my own personal goals in life? How would my beloved grandfather react to the means to which I have resorted in order to accomplish these inherited goals?"

Another inmate recounts a similar story:

> In growing up, it was very important for me and my family to be successful, especially to display it in the form of economic prosperity. As a young man, I became a clever sportsman and a clever broker. But I began to lose money in my stock market business and started to gamble to balance the losses. One thing led to another and I ended up committing a crime. Now I am here, and my life is shattered in pieces.

In the reflecting process, we try to consider each small detail including the words the inmate chooses to tell his story. We explore the words that we think have special significance to the inmate and ask him to clarify the meaning of the words for him personally. We find that the pronounced word is afforded more weight when it is verbalized in front of a person outside the immediate dialogue, which is the third person who witnesses in the trialogue process.

Our questions are grounded in the intention to follow the inmate's story and to form the next question based on what he has said. We strive to keep this goal pure in our minds as we follow the story and attend to our own prejudices. As one of the inmates declared: "A good conversation is one when she—the one I am talking to—is listening and asking me questions about what I have said and not about what she is thinking of me." This seemingly simple process can have profound effects:

> To be in conversation with three people was a bit confusing for me to begin with. However, after a while I found that these "trialogues" were not only interesting but fruitful. The best part for me was to

listen while the other two had their dialogue about me. I didn't have to defend or justify myself and therefore I could turn all my attention to listening to them and decide for myself which of the two was most right. I even discovered a kind of thoughtful thinking I had never experienced before. I'm now looking forward to these conversations. They have even stopped me from being carried away by thoughts of injustice. They have made room in my head for reflections and reviews. I have begun to use this new insight when I am together with and in conversation with people who are near me. It was unthinkable for me 10 years ago.

Listening

Up until this point in the chapter I have been talking about initial conversations with three participants—an inmate, one personnel, or a therapist conversing—and another observer listening. When we create these trialogues, we use reflective listening in order to hear the story while it unfolds and takes form. While listening, we struggle with and strive not to give in to our own prejudices and preconceptions. For example, a warder reflecting on an inmate's story about a conflict between them might be thinking the following: "Why is this man so occupied with focusing on my shortcomings. He is critical of everything I say when he should be grateful that I want to help him?" The inmate might be thinking, "How do I know if I can trust these two people talking with me? What do they want from me? Is there something they are driving at?" It may be the inmate's suspicious thoughts that lace his meanings with criticism, but it could also be that he cannot bear the reality that he is doing time for a serious crime, possibly his lifetime. It might mean that he is destined to wear the label "bad" or "evil." It is hard to live with being found guilty of hurting another or having committed behavior that is considered frightening to other people. Moreover, believing there is no future can destroy hope, making a person desperate.

In a final session, as an inmate was being released from prison after many years of sentencing, I asked him, "What was the most difficult aspect of your incarceration?" He replied:

> The most difficult feeling was when I totally lost faith in the future: when I felt that I could perish here, disappear, go crazy, die, and nobody would help me. Nobody would be able to pull me out of the deep feeling of desertion and loss. That was the worst. That feeling comes when everything is taken away from you, you have a feeling that no one counts on you, no one believes in you, no one takes you seriously, no one cares. The "others" do as they like, as they have agreed upon, as they have decided, regardless of what you think

about it. It is kind of total loss of your own will, integrity, autonomy, and determination.

It might be easier for the inmate to endure such feelings if he sees the "others" (warders) as having shortcomings. When the warders and I reflect on this perspective, we gain a better understanding of the inmates and formulate our responses with more respect. One warder who works with this process stated, "I have a sincere desire to understand my client and help him in here. As a contact man I take my task seriously and want to understand the inmate."

Answerability

Early on in our talks, we were preoccupied with the idea of "conscience" and wanted to explore the meaning of this word from the inmates' perspective. After receiving no real responses, we abandoned this exploration and focused on Russian philosopher Bakhtin's thoughts on relations and the concept of answerability. Bakhtin (1963/1991, 1993) uses the expression "answerability" to describe the process whereby one acts in order to take responsibility for his actions and consider them in the context of how they influence others. If we apply this concept in the prison setting, such questions about relationships might arise including: What kind of relationships does the inmate want to form? To whom must he answer and with what words? Have his words and actions been met with responses of respect from the others?

Regarding the concept of respect, here is an except from a story an inmate told about his understanding of the word *respect* before his crime and his new understanding as a result of our talks.

A young inmate relates the story of his relationships prior to committing his crime. He tells of relationships based on obedience: taking orders or being punished as a result of noncompliance. We ask about how he expects others to behave in relation to him. He replies that he would want to be shown "respect." In exploring his use of the word, however, we realize that for him "to respect" means "to obey." When we share this with him he seems surprised and becomes silent for a while obviously reflecting on what he has heard. He breaks the silence saying: "I don't think 'respect' is to obey. I think respect is tolerance toward another person and his opinions and meanings. I know now that I probably did not understand this fully, when I was on the outside.

Reflections as Relational Possibilities

Reflecting creates a moment of silence, a pause in which the inmate has the freedom to think through his own thoughts. The reflections create meaning in two directions: (a) in the direction of the professional helper and the warder and (b) in the direction of the inmate. The reflections are meant as a response to the content of the first conversation including the words chosen, the meaning of the sentences, and how these connect to the inmate's life. The reflections we create together should also bring something back to the first conversation.

In our reflecting process, I—as the therapist—and the warder can be personal, but we avoid being private. We incorporate common human experiences into the reflection, relating on a personal level while adhering to societal boundaries. Helping the inmates formulate an idea of one's "answerability," one's "answer" as responsibility to another human is a very important part of our job. Often the formulations are coconstructed as is evident in this contribution by an inmate who led us to adopt Bakhtin's concept of answerability and replace the more traditional concept of *conscience*.

> I have learned to listen to my inner voice, the self, or whatever I should call it. This is something much greater than a good or bad conscience. I was afraid of this thing before and I tried to hide it or to tell myself that it didn't exist. I can't explain it better than that at this point, but I think that this thing is present in every living human, in fact it could be the most important in life, something which is essential like breathing, eating ...

Within the context of the relationship, alternative or new thoughts such as this are introduced back into the conversation. The inmate may thereby be empowered to accommodate the new meanings and become motivated to pursue new ways of relating. A new story of who he is begins to emerge and, if nurtured, can crystallize into a new future, even inside the prison walls.

But how can one create a new future if one cannot imagine it? In these reflecting talks, we believe that we can introduce new imaginings that can lead to new stories and new alternatives in one's life.

Following the process of reflecting and adding to the inmate's story, the inmate is given ample time and space to comment on the reflections he has just heard. It is often very quiet leading up to the inmate's response, and he invariably takes time to choose his words carefully. When he speaks, his statements may expose a new perspective, a new starting point from which to formulate thoughts, understand, and ultimately act and relate differently than in the past.

Language Communion

Writing

I occasionally get requests from inmates asking me to formally assess their progress as part of their application for a temporary leave, or, in the case of those sentenced to life, for their "application for mercy" to the Minister of Justice. I, in turn, ask them to write their own statement, using their own words to describe their progress. Then, I agree to write my assessment together with the warder so that we, as a group, are able to collaborate and create a detailed picture of an individual. This representation in most cases must suffice to make the plea for the inmate.

Violent Acts and Imaginary Places

Sometimes it is hard on all of us to follow, or to be "in the story." Sometimes we are led into a violent scary place—a place where a serious crime was committed. Then we usually slow the story down in order to follow the events in detail. Sometimes we place the event on a stage that we create in our minds, and the three of us watch as it unfolds (Vygotsky, 1992; Penn & Frankfurt, 1994; Penn, 1998, 2000). We may decide to replace someone in the story, or bring an important person into the act. We can even stop the action, in effect stopping the crime from taking place and talking about what might have happened instead of what might have been. This theater of the mind can make the story bearable for all and allow the inmate to talk about this pivotal life moment. We also support him to reconcile with that part of himself that committed the violent act.

This part of the process is often very difficult for the inmate: to be confronted with the part of him that is rejected by society and counter to the values of humanity. We believe, however, that this internal reconciliation is necessary to healing and moving from despair into a hopeful future. This work requires patience; it cannot be forced. When we began this process, the warders were impatient and wanted the inmates to immediately admit their crimes and express remorse. Experiences like the case below taught us that this is an extremely difficult task, and we should approach it only when the time is right.

> When our conversation began, the inmate had no memory of the situation or any details surrounding the crime he committed: taking the life of another youth. Then, little by little he began to piece it together: he could name the victim, but was excusing the crime on the grounds that he was high on drugs and did not intend to kill his victim. We talked about drugs: how he began to use them and what they did to his life. The discussions turned to talks about how he makes decisions. Did he have the power to say "no" to the drug dealer the next time he was offered something inside the prison? We talked about personal decisions in his life, about what kind of relationships he was involved in and in what kind of relationships he felt free to talk? Who did he feel was willing to listen? If he made a decision, who respected it? Through this process he decided to make

new choices in his relationships with women and a particular male friend. As a result he stopped using drugs in prison. He was now free to talk about the crime in more detail. Using visualization, we went together to the scene of the crime. We saw ourselves as observers and watched what was happening, what he was doing, and what he wanted to do differently now as we stood there watching the situation together in the visualization. He wanted to stop the action and was able to say something to himself to make him stop. Although he was extremely uncomfortable in that moment, he was capable of staying there because he was not there alone.

Introducing the Ethical

It is perhaps inevitable that the conversations become political that take place in a building that stands as testimony to the dominant society outside its walls, with its norms, ethics, and values. I believe that regardless of which side of the fence you are on politically, we as human citizens have an obligation to examine our own values and the values of our society, and investigate whether or not they might be limited to the purpose of attaining and maintaining justice without the concomitant goal of understanding the motivation and random events that precipitated or accompanied the human behavior being punished.

These reflecting talks can accomplish much in societies that have a deep ethical connection to their failures—societies that seek to understand the roots of crime and the people who commit it. Such a path requires increasing societal tolerance of people with different lifestyles, beliefs, and values, and reaching out to those on the margins. Our perspective and the work we do is grounded in a paradigm of "humanity." To quote the inspector of the prison, "Each and every inmate who passes through the terminal should notice that this prison is a place where we talk to each other and that these talks influence all of us."

When we can create an open space where thoughts are allowed to develop and exist "out of ethics and aesthetics," then we are not only creating a response to our reflections but also answerability, meaning that we are responsible in a double sense. We are responsible for what we are saying to the other and for how he will respond (Levinas, 1993).

Participative System

The conversations described here are, by their very nature, circular. In addition, circularity is being realized on a broader plane. As soon as the warders participate, the closed system of a prison is opened to representatives of the normative "outside" society, and that society is thus represented in the shared conversations. The warder's participation literally throws open the doors to incorporate the culture, values, and law of a society that lives and breathes outside the metal doors.

A Meeting Place for Society

Another attempt to open the conversations to society was a project initiated by the prison staff that included participation of police, students, prison inmates, and prison personnel. These meetings were initially based on the American model of confrontation but were changed into a forum we call "mutual talks": one or two staff joining a few inmates who agreed to participate. The aim was not to use intimidation as deterrents to crime, but simply to converse about the experience of doing time in prison. In the conversation, the inmate's struggle is explored—thoughts about his crime and victims—as are the themes of loss and fear: the losses of freedom, future, and control coupled with the threat of continued violence inside prison. The warders also share their personal experiences, their daily routines, the searches, the taking of specimens, and the talks with inmates.

Effects on Participants

In evaluating the outcome, the inmates reported that they found them stimulating and useful. They acknowledged that the talks prompted them to consider thoughtfully their own dual identities, as an inmate and as a person with tenuous membership in a society that presses for justice and responsibility. When the doors are opened to society and the inmate no longer feels insulated by the security of those who share his fate, answerability becomes a real possibility. One of the great advantages to trialogues is that they provide for witnessed conversation, which inevitably seems to elicit more respect.

All who witness the story of a life and a crime look for answers to the question: "Where do we go from here?" In answering the question, the talks become participatory: we cannot "not" participate. We are involved and engaged in a conversation with others (Bakhtin, 1993). These participatory talks are the key characteristic of our work. The participatory nature of the talks helps the inmates stay connected to a society that many will eventually reenter. We are motivated by the idea that we are helping to foster that reentry process.

We find that these talks have become, in a sense, self-perpetuating. As we assess the logistics of space and scheduling, we find that the talks have become a priority and an integral part of what "time served" means. The attitudes of personnel regarding the talks have become inclusive and open as opposed to exclusive and closed.

The talks allow for diversity of perspective and opinion. The goal is not to find agreement on one overriding meaning of right and wrong but to facilitate new constructions that allow for a myriad of "takes" on a situation. This process breaks down the wall that formerly housed only partisan ideas coming from either "us" or "them." The overriding goal of the talks is to open up those doors and allow for new space in which both sides experience an increase in dignity and respect for one another.

One of the youth told us early on that he knows that he could not have acted differently the moment he committed his crime. He could not have turned his back on his people when they were in trouble and simply walk away. We talked at length about what would have been the ethical thing, the responsible thing to do, and our conclusions differed. Just recently, he told us that he had a discussion with fellow inmates about where the line for using violence could be drawn. He shared his newly formed opinion that one in fact could walk away, turn his back on trouble, in order not to harm another person. This is an example of how our reflecting talks allow for change and evolution. They seem to have ushered in a new kind of conversation between inmates that replaces other discussions that focused previously on crime as a way of life.

Effects on the Prison System

Open talks in various settings, whether in small groups, larger organizations or between two people, are always relational. In the relational context, we consider the elements of communication carefully; how we speak and what we say. We also consider what lies beneath the spoken interchange— the participant's personal attitudes and values, and his present patterns of communicating outside of the talks at hand. We are essentially combing the philosophical ground on which the talks are constructed, looking for clues to prejudices and assumptions that can weaken the project goals of increasing understanding and respect. In order to aid this process and ultimately strengthen the foundation of the talks, we arranged for the warders to take part in an educational program that provided a study in human behavior, psychology, systems, and language theory.

We also introduced the ethical responsibilities of confidentiality and informed consent. Inmates were made aware of the limits of confidentiality,[4] and personnel do not divulge information shared in the talks without permission. This was a major step in the transformation of the prison system and was a struggle to implement and maintain. Warders became curious about information inmates divulged in their talks. As more warders became involved in the talks and were therefore bound by confidentiality, the problem abated.

A new complication for the warders has accompanied the expansion of the talks. The warders now have dual and perhaps conflicting roles with inmates. On one hand, they guard inmates, restricting their freedom with cell searches and discipline; on the other, they listen reflectively, engaging them with respectful questions and concerns. This conflict became easier to manage after educating the warders in systemic thinking. Some warders chose not to confuse the roles and did not participate in conversations with inmates they searched; others discussed potential problems in advance to avoid conflicts whenever possible.

Evaluation and Follow-up

An important part of our collaboration with Tromsø University and Tom Andersen and Georg Höyer was outcome evaluation. We began this process with a request to the National Prison and Probation Administration to submit their questions about our work. They submitted numerous and complex questions which we have described elsewhere (Wagner, 1997; Wagner, 1998). The method for compiling the stories for evaluation was based on the Participatory Action Research (White, 1991) approach.

We then developed the follow-up project under the leadership of Andersen and Höyer which centers around the biannual meeting we call the "collaborative research meeting." The participants are divided into three groups: (a) former inmates, their families, and prison staff, (b) local social services, women shelters, probation authority, local education administration, and (c) local and national political leaders from the National Administration of Prison and Probation Service, its research arm, the National Ministry of Justice, and the Minister of Justice. Not everyone comes to every meeting, but most have participated in some. Andersen asserts that it is important not to mix the various groups.

He asks them to be seated with their own group and then starts by interviewing those "most remote" from the actual prison setting, the lawmakers, about their questions and concerns, for example: What would you like to know about the work with our talks in the prison? What questions would you like to ask of the former inmates or the prison personnel? He then proceeds to gather the questions and concerns of each group, keeping those directly affected until last. The former inmates and their relatives listen to this process and are told that they need not respond to all comments, just those that resonate with them in some meaningful way.

When they do answer, their responses tend to be inspiring stories about life and struggle. There are often stories about difficulties reentering society, about feeling like an outsider. These are balanced out by the positive stories of inmates who got a second chance for a new future—stories about rehabilitation, a new understanding, and a readiness for dealing with trouble in a different way. Those who ask the questions listen to their stories. Some experience a deep empathy and allow themselves to be moved and influenced by them.

Finally, when the groups have spoken and listened in turn, the talks are opened up to all participants; whoever wants to speak is welcome to do so. Unlike discussions in which discrete definitions of hard or soft probation policy are debated, these discussions are thoughtful and respectful of the continuum of hard to soft. We attribute this shift to the structure of the talks. When the process is organized so that one group talks and one listens, the listeners have time to process what has been said thereby gaining respect for the integrity of the speaker, their condition and their words. Thus, the responses are not automatic, but reflected.

Not to Forget

The bedrock of the prison system is punishment and loss of freedom. Therefore, an inmate does not have the expectation that he will be able to engage in equal and democratic dialogue once inside. In Kalmar prison, as in most, the rights of independence, self-management, and options to choose and move freely are taken away. Through this process, one loses a sense of integrity and the motivation to act on one's own behalf; initiative decreases as the inmate allows "the other" to think and act for them.

The inmate also learns with whom he can speak and how, if he is allowed to talk at all. These conditions breed frustration in humans as one inmate explains:

> When I was angry or disappointed with something or somebody I used to go to a place near the village in which I lived. The place had a deep ravine with a point. I used to stand on the edge of it and scream. Here, inside, it is impossible to go somewhere where nobody can hear me. I can't be alone for one moment.

The inmates are confined in close quarters. That lack of space, being in one another's face, contributes to frustration, causing them to be hypersensitive and reactive. This over-concern with what others are doing and thinking generates powerful emotions, which the environment forces them to repress in order to avoid conflict. The prison is fertile ground for hatred. Inmates expect professional helpers to be judgmental so they are quick to respond with suspicion and defensiveness.

Contrary to their expectations, we invite them to a space where inmates and warders meet one another as human beings. This experience defies the inmate's preconceived notions and short-circuits their defenses.

Prison time is the punishment meted out by society as a consequence stemming from committing unacceptable acts. By its very nature, it is a place of judgment with the purpose of correction and control. Confining its goals to these, the criminal justice system must content itself with minimal transformation. Having abolished the death penalty as inhumane in Western Europe, we must turn our attention to the other inhumanities inherent in today's justice system.

I want to close with the words of Bishop Desmond Tutu, a man who knows first-hand of what atrocities humans and their systems of "justice" are capable:

The most important purpose of healing the ruptured could be to reframe a balance in those broken relations, in order to try to rehabilitate both the victims and the perpetrator.

Endnotes

1. In this paper, I use the word "warder" to refer to prison guards and the word "personnel" to refer to other prison employees including nurses, priests, and inspectors.
2. All quotations were transcribed and translated by the author following the conversation.
3. This could appear to be an unusual or daring question. Not in our setting. Many of our inmates show great interest in education and are studying at the prison high school. They also have the opportunity to take distance and internet-based courses in association with a university or college. As one of them said, "Through studies I can leave the prison. The studies, the books I read give me a sense of freedom."
4. According to Swedish law, the rule of confidentiality is not valid if the information we hear is against the law and would lead to more than two years imprisonment; prison personnel and therapists (but not a chaplain) must report

References

Andersen, T. (1987). The reflecting team. *Family Process, 26,* 415–428.

Andersen, T. (1991). *The reflecting team: Dialogues and dialogues about dialogues.* New York: Norton.

Andersen, T. (1992). Relationship, language and preunderstanding in the reflecting process. *Australian and New Zealand Journal of Family Therapy, 13,* 97–91.

Andersen, T. (1994). If oppression is the opposite of freedom, what is psychotherapy? *Proceedings from the 6th Family Therapy World Conference,* Abstract 141. Budapest, Hungary.

Anderson, H. & Goolishian, H. (1988). Human systems as linguistic systems. *Family Process, 27,* 371–393.

Anderson, H. & Goolishian, H. (1992). *Från påverkan till medverkan* [From instructions to collaboration]. Stockholm, Sweden: Mareld.

Anderson, H., Goolishian, H., & Winderman L. (1986). Problem created system: Toward transformation in family therapy. *Journal of Strategic and Systemic Therapies, 5,* 1–11.

Bakhtin, M. (1963/1991). *Dostojevskijs poetic* [The poetic of Dostojevsky]. Sweden: Anthropos.

Bakhtin, M. (1993). *Toward the philosophy of the act.* Austin, TX: University of Texas Press.

Boscolo, L., Cecchin, G., Haffman, L., & Penn, P. (1987). *Milan systemic therapy.* New York: Basic Books.

Foucault, M. (1991). *Discipline and punish: The birth of the prison.* London: Penguin.

Levinas, E. (1993). *Ethiqe et Infini* [Ethics and infinity]. Stockholm: Syposion.

Penn, P. (1998). Rape flashbacks: Constructing a new narrative. *Family Process, 37,* 299–310.

Penn, P. (2000). Metaphors in region of unlikeness. *Human Systems: The Journal of Systemic Consultation and Management, 10,* 3–10.

Penn, P. & Frankfurt, M. (1994). Creating a participant text: Writing, multiple voices, narrative multiplicity. *Family Process, 33,* 217–232.

Seikkula, J., Aaltonen, J., Alakare, B., Haarakangas, K., Keranen, J., & Sutela, M. (1995). Treating psychosis by means of open dialogue. In S. Friedman (Ed.), *The reflecting taam in action: Collaborative practices in family therapy* (pp. 62–80). New York: Guilford.

Seikkula, J. (1993). The aim of therapy is generating dialogue: Bakhtin in family session. *Human Systems Journal, 4,* 33–48.

Seikkula, J. (1996). *Öppna samtal* [Open dialogues]. Stockholm, Sweden: Mareld.

Seikkula, J. & Sutela, M. (1990) Co-evolution of the family and the hospital: The system of boundary. *Journal of Strategic and Systemic Therapies, 9,* 34–42

Skirbekk, G. & Gilje, N. (1987/1993). *Filosofins historia* [The history of philosophy]. Sweden: Daidalos.

Tutu, D. (2000). *No future without forgiveness.* London: Mars Agency.

Vygotsky, L. (1992). *Thought and language.* Cambridge, MA: Massachusetts Institute of Technology.

Wagner, J. (1998). Are dialogical conversations possible behind the WALLS? *Human Systems: The Journal of Systemic Consultation and Management, 9,* 95–113.

Wagner, J. & Anderson, T. (1997). *Vad regionen vill veta om samtalsverksamheten på KVA Kalmar?*

Wagner, J., Höyer, G., & Andersen, T. (2002). Reflecting dialogs behind walls. Unpublished manuscript.

What the Region Wants to Know About the Conversation in Kalmar Prison? Kalmar, Sweden: Rapport KVM Kalmar.

White, W.F. (1991). *Participatory action research.* London: Sage.

CHAPTER 14

Open Dialogue: An Approach to Psychotherapeutic Treatment of Psychosis in Northern Finland

KAUKO HAARAKANGAS, JAAKKO SEIKKULA,
BIRGITTA ALAKARE, AND JUKKA AALTONEN

Open dialogue is a social constructionist approach to treating severe mental illness that was developed at Keropudas Hospital in Finland, where it continues to evolve and expand. It is more a way of thinking and working in psychiatric contexts than a defined method. In this chapter, we describe this approach to treatment, focusing on treatment meetings as the primary forum for generating dialogue. We first outline the project's history and identify seven guidelines for organizing treatment. We then detail the pragmatic and theoretical foundations for treatment meetings, which are the heart of the open dialogue approach.

Background

The treatment area of Länsi-Pohja, situated in Western Lapland and bordering Sweden to the west, serves a population of 68,500, which is linguistically, ethnically, and religiously homogenous. Located in Tornio, Keropudas Hospital houses the sole psychiatric treatment facility in the area and accommodates fifty-five patients, including thirty acute cases. Although the total land area of Länsi-Pohja is 7,000 square kilometers, 80% of the population is concentrated in two major cities: Tornio and Kemi.

The population distribution is problematic as reflected in Western Lapland's unemployment rate which is over 15% compared to 8% nationally. The rapid move away from an agrarian economy to a more centralized city-based service economy has significantly impacted the population in terms of mental health. The incidence of schizophrenia had been extremely high before the mid-1980s, with an annual average of thirty-five new schizophrenia patients per 100,000. The mid-1990s saw a rapid decline in that number to 7 per 100,000 owing to the development of the new family- and network-centered treatment systems, namely, the need-adapted and open dialogue approaches (Aaltonen et al., 1997).

From the Need-Adapted Approach to Open Dialogue. Psychiatric treatment of schizophrenia in Finland began to evolve in the early 1980s with the work of the Finnish National Schizophrenia Project and the introduction of the Need Adapted Approach (Alanen, Lehtinen, Räkköläinen, and Aaltonen, 1991). The Need Adapted Approach emphasized (a) rapid early intervention; (b) treatment planning to meet the changing and case-specific needs of each patient and family; (c) attention to the psychotherapeutic attitude in both assessment and treatment; (d) viewing treatment as a continuous process, thus integrating different therapeutic methods; and (f) consistent monitoring of treatment process and outcomes (Alanen, Lehtinen, Räkköläinen, & Aaltonen, 1991; Alanen, 1997).

The Need-Adapted Approach developed further in the 1980s into open dialogue by the psychiatric unit of Finnish Western Lapland (Länsi-Pohja). This model of intervention organizes psychotherapeutic treatment in treatment units consisting of mobile crisis teams, patients, and their social networks. By the mid-1990s, this kind of psychotherapeutic treatment was available for all patients within their particular social support systems. Currently, all five mental health outpatient clinics, together with the Keropudas Hospital, use case-specific mobile crisis intervention teams. All staff members (both inpatient and outpatient) can be required to participate in these teams; therefore, all are offered an opportunity to participate in either a 3-year family therapy or similar program. From 1989 to 2003, 94 professionals have participated in the family therapy program and have thus qualified to practice psychotherapy under Finnish law, increasing the number of psychotherapists per capita in this area to the highest in Finland.

In order to evaluate the effectiveness of the model and to develop it further, several research studies have been conducted (Seikkula, 1991; Keränen, 1992; Seikkula et al., 1995; Aaltonen et al., 1997; Haarakangas, 1997; Seikkula, Alakare, & Aaltonen, 2000, 2001a, 2001b). In a follow-up outcome study of first-episode psychosis, after 2 years of treatment,

83% had returned to their jobs or studies or were seeking employment, and 77% had no remaining psychotic symptoms. In some cases, problems reemerged with 21% having at least one relapse (Seikkula et al., 2000; Seikkula, 2002). Comparing these outcomes with more traditional treatment in Finland, there were more family meetings, fewer days of inpatient care, reduced use of neuroleptic medication, and a reduction in psychotic symptoms (Lehtinen et al., 2000). We have found that facilitating dialogic communication within the treatment systems is a highly effective approach.

Open Dialogue: The Working Model

Clinical experience and research studies with this model have identified seven key principles, both practically and contextually relevant, that can be applied in all psychiatric crises regardless of the specific diagnosis.

1. *Immediate intervention.* The first meeting is arranged within 24 hours of the first contact made by the patient, a relative, or a referral agency. This immediate intervention allows the treatment team to capitalize on the opportunities provided by the crisis, including mobilizing the patient's and family's social support networks. The crisis frees up formerly untapped resources and moves previously undiscussed issues out into the open, offering unique treatment potential. At this stage all possibilities are open.

2. *The social network and support systems.* Family members and others significant to the patient are invited to participate in the treatment meeting and follow-up treatment as agreed upon. Other support agency members such as social service workers, the patient's employer, health insurance workers, and other hospital employees or supervisors are also invited to take part in treatment.

3. *Flexibility and mobility.* The treatment is adapted to the specific and changing needs of the patient and family. We modify our working practices and integrate specialized therapies and interventions as needed. For example, in a crisis situation, we suggest meeting daily at the patient's home rather than adhering to traditionally prescribed protocols that rigidly define treatment frequency, form, and setting.

4. *Teamwork and responsibility.* The staff member initially contacted is responsible for organizing the first treatment meeting. A team is built according to the needs of the patient with the possibility of including both outpatient and inpatient staff. In the treatment of psychosis, for example, a three-member team is especially suitable: a psychiatrist from the crisis clinic, a psychologist from the

patient's local outpatient clinic, and a nurse from the ward of the hospital. All team members assume responsibility for the entire treatment process.

5. *Psychological continuity.* The team members remain consistent throughout the treatment process, regardless of whether the patient is at home or in the hospital, and irrespective of the length of treatment. For example, a first-episode crisis can be expected to last for two to three years (Jackson & Birchwood, 1996) requiring long-term commitment. Psychological continuity is also critical in the integration of different therapeutic modalities—an integration that can be accomplished through open conversation in treatment meetings.

6. *Tolerance of uncertainty.* In an acute crisis, the therapist keeps all avenues open and avoids hasty conclusions or treatment solutions, such as hospitalization and neuroleptic medication. The team must have faith and confidence in their own work in order to foster hope and trust in the family. Ample time is needed to create a safe working environment for the patient, family, and team members.

7. *Dialogue.* Our focus is primarily on generating dialogue in the treatment meeting among all participants. Dialogue creates new meanings and explanations that introduce possibilities and cooperation for all participants. It is critical that the treatment team create a safe environment so that everything that needs to be said can be openly discussed, which allows for the generation of a new collective understanding about the nature of the problem. Dialogue is seen as a forum in which the patient, family, and team members can create new meanings for the patient's behavior and symptoms (Anderson, 1997; Anderson & Goolishian, 1988; Haarakangas, 1997), helping the family and patient to acquire more agency in their own lives by discussing the problems (Holma & Aaltonen, 1997).

Treatment Meetings

The main forum for therapeutic interaction is the treatment meeting, which is attended by the patient and the immediate people associated with the problem. All management plans and decisions are made with everyone present. In the early 1980s, Alanen and his colleagues invited patients and family members to participate in the meeting. They called these meetings "therapy meetings" because they had documented therapeutic effects. According to Alanen (1997), the treatment meeting has three functions: (a) gathering information, (b) building a treatment plan based on the diagnosis made in the meeting, and (c) generating psychotherapeutic dialogue. In 1984, patients in Keropudas Hospital were invited to participate in the meeting in which their problems were discussed and the treatment plan was created. In all cases, family members were also invited in as soon as possible after the family member was hospitalized.

In 1987, the hospital created a crisis team that conducted treatment meetings prior to admission to decide whether hospitalization was the most appropriate option. Although these meetings were originally referred to as "admission meetings," alternatives to hospitalization, including home care visits were carefully considered. Research (Seikkula, 1991; Keränen, 1992) has since concluded that home visits are an effective alternative to hospitalization.

Dialogical Equality in Treatment Meetings

Psychiatric treatment has traditionally been very hierarchical. Psychiatrists have made critical treatment decisions that were then carried out by nurses. Psychiatrists have typically made decisions relying strictly on their medical experience, psychological tests, and/or opinions of other experts. Although there has been a certain level of collaboration among various professionals, the knowledgeable voices of the nursing staff in particular have not participated equally in treatment conversations. The psychiatrist has taken an authoritarian position that few nurses have dared to challenge.

Once family-centered treatment and treatment meetings developed, the participation of the patient and relatives became central to the treatment process. As family therapy earned a place alongside individual therapy, a new group of specialists—family therapists—appeared. Early on, many staff members viewed the methods and interventions of family therapists with apprehension and uncertainly, creating a sense of division and thus increasing the reluctance of nurses to take an active role in the meeting.

Given this context, all staff members who participated in treatment meetings at Keropudas Hospital were encouraged to express their observations and opinions concerning the treatment of a patient. Most notably, the family therapists began to ask nurses to describe their impressions of the situation, noting that there is not one single truth but rather many viewpoints which, when communicated, create a sense of shared expertise within a treatment team. Thus, the tacit knowledge of nurses was considered alongside the knowledge of psychiatrists and therapists, allowing their voices to be finally heard.

Although nurses in the Keropudas Hospital had attained some influence and the hospital sought an atmosphere of democracy, hierarchical attitudes seemed entrenched and difficult to change. An experienced mental health nurse commented on her difficult transition from the traditional nonexpert role to the role of contributing expert: "I wondered why he [the psychologist family therapist] asked me [for an opinion]. I don't know these kinds of things, do I?" To facilitate active participation in the open dialogue process, the head nurse consistently encouraged the nurses to communicate their individual opinions even though it was not traditionally their role. As a result, the nurses' occupational self-esteem improved, and their knowledge became a therapeutic resource.

Furthermore, the patient has long been viewed more as an object of treatment, rather than subject in treatment. Patients have not participated in conversations and decision-making concerning their treatments. After professionals had decided upon a treatment plan, patients were called to hear their decision. Family members were afforded an even more marginal role. Their participation might only have been as a name or note in a case record about near relatives or as an informant in an admission situation. Until the late 1980s, many hospitals did not accommodate family visits due to the stress that was placed on the staff. When the family and patient were finally invited to be a cooperating partner, treatment meetings became a forum for equal therapeutic conversation. The change toward a "polyphonic" treatment culture was not easy, where thoughts and opinions of different people could intermingle as independent, equal voices without one voice dominating or merely accompanying other voices (Bakhtin, 1984).

Multivoicedness in the Treatment Meeting

Multivoicedness is a natural part of family- and network-centered treatment. A "voice" in this context is a metaphor that represents the varying and specific viewpoints expressed within the context of the treatment meeting regarding the theme of conversation (Bakhtin, 1981; Haarakangas, 1997). For example, the viewpoints of workers in an outpatient clinic are different from the viewpoints of workers in a hospital ward. Occupational viewpoints, treatment ideology, and psychotherapeutic orientation vary with the level and type of education, training, and experience. Additionally, voices of the patient and family members usually represent the most intimate connection to the conversational themes in treatment meetings, given that family members are the best experts on their own life. Each person's voice reflects the multiple positions each person simultaneously holds in life. Considering that treatment workers are children of parents, parents themselves, and possibly grandparents, these varied and contradictory positions improve their chances of relating empathically to their clients.

Multivoiced conversation in the treatment meeting contributes to reaching meaningful understandings and therapeutic goals, because it allows for a more comprehensive, multifaceted therapeutic picture. For example, in the treatment of a psychotic patient, the experience and worry of the family and the team members must be considered from biomedical, psychological, and social perspectives. The patient's own voice including delusional thoughts and words must be seen as an important key to understanding the psychotic world the patient inhabits. Family members can greatly assist in bridging connections between the patient's life events and psychotic experiences. When necessary, various other psychotherapeutic or rehabilitative viewpoints can also be integrated into the treatment meetings. From the viewpoint of therapists, multivoicedness in treatment meetings is challenging. How do we create equality among the different voices? How do we create a safe atmosphere where difficult issues can be freely discussed?

Creating a Safe Atmosphere in Treatment Meetings

The first task in arranging a treatment meeting is appointing a time and place and identifying the participants. When these details are well attended to, clients have the feeling that their concerns are taken seriously, that they are listened to, and that they are cared for. In an acute crisis situation, the first treatment meeting has to be arranged within 24 hours from the first contact. A home visit is often an alternative that increases the sense of safety for family members because clients are on their own turf, and the treatment team members are the visitors. An advantage of home visits is the possibility to see and experience the context of the patient's life more directly than in a therapy room of the hospital or psychiatric clinic. In other cases, the structure and staff of the hospital or health center can provide physical and psychological security and necessary boundaries not available in the home situation. The presence of family members and familiar treatment professionals are especially important in the treatment meetings of a psychotic patient. The responsibility of treatment team members is to ensure that no one experiences physical or psychological threat.

Ample time is required for conversation in a treatment meeting. A suitable time frame has been shown to be an hour and a half, offering enough time to find understanding and create a "safe space" for everyone to participate in the conversation. At the beginning of the treatment meeting there is a phase of mutual coupling (Haarakangas, 1997) during which the participants make acquaintances and develop a connection that allows the conversation to unfold. The customary handshake and other social gestures are an important part of treatment meetings. In the first meeting and when new participants become involved, there is a need for a round of introductions, including participants' names and relationship to the patient, as well as an orientation to the treatment process. Following introductions, the therapist asks the patient and family to talk about their concerns. The therapist aligns his or her words to the patient's and family's, and respects the definitions and language voiced by each. The therapist can do this by using their words and expressions. The therapist may ask a person to "say more" about a general topic or story and may also ask more specific detail-oriented questions. At the very beginning, it is important to elucidate the onset of the concern, what exacerbated it, who noticed it, who is most worried about it, and what steps have been taken to relieve the worry. The therapist's task in the treatment meeting is to generate a psychologically safe atmosphere in which all members feel free to express what they want to say and to explore their individual worries, pains, and anxieties. And, there is no hurry. The therapist may share personal experiences or how other clients have done well despite the difficulties they face. These stories can give rise to trust and hope. What is needed is time and meaningful conversation with the family as a cooperative partner in the treatment process.

Maintaining conversation and generating dialogue in the treatment meeting is best accomplished in a therapy team of three; two therapists in dialogue while the third takes the reflective position. The team approach helps therapists face the distress and anxiety of a patient and family. High expectations and hopes about alleviating the patient's suffering are laid upon the team, and individual therapists often bear and endure uncertainty and occasional powerlessness as the treatment process progresses. As a team, therapists maintain hope and trust with their clients.

"Dialogicality" in the Treatment Meeting

Conversation in the treatment meeting is geared toward gaining an understanding of the patient's and family's situation. The participants search together for meaning, and through the mutual sharing of different experiences and perspectives, they find understanding. No one—not even the chief psychiatrist—needs to know, nor is it possible to know beforehand, what exactly the "right" solution might be for the patient's symptoms or the difficulties of the family. This position of "not-knowing," described by Anderson and Goolishian (1992), allows for knowledge and understanding to change and develop during conversations in the treatment process. The epistemological basis of this stance is social constructionism (Berger & Luckmann, 1966; Gergen, 1985; McNamee & Gergen, 1992).

Therapists strive to generate conversation in which the varied voices of the participants contribute different meanings; each from a unique but equal participatory place. According to Bakhtin's theory of the philosophy of language (Bakhtin, 1981; Voloshinov, 1996), the speaker's own word and the "other's" word (an "alien" word) meet, penetrate, and change each other. Listening to the other's speech, we are able to integrate their thoughts into our own thinking and consider matters from the other's viewpoint. Our next utterance will have incorporated new meaning from the speech of our interlocutor and from the meanings they have connected with the theme of the conversation. In this process, meanings change, matters may be considered in a new context, and new understandings can evolve.

Bakhtin (1986) says that "for the word (and, consequently for a human being), there is nothing more terrible than 'lack of response'" (p. 127). Every word and every human being desires understanding and response. In a treatment meeting, the responsibility of the therapist, as a member of the treatment team, is to ensure that everyone feels heard, responded to, and ultimately understood. Although it can be confusing and distressful for the listener, the delusional language of a psychotic patient also seeks to be heard, understood, and responded to. If the patient feels threatened, it is often important for therapists to assure a psychotic patient that they will be protected against the threat. With these words, therapists align themselves as co-partners against the threat. The patient's family members also have to be assured that they have the treatment team's support as well.

If a participant does not talk in a treatment meeting, they can be invited into the conversation by asking if they want to say something about the images that come to mind while listening to the conversation. Those who talk a lot might not be heard in spite of the volume of words or perhaps because of it. In this case, it may be advisable to agree that they can talk long enough to be heard while other participants listen. However, they should spend the same amount of time listening while others talk.

To attentively listen while another person talks and maintain interest in what the other is saying is a difficult but important skill. Do we hear and digest the other's words even though they might taste strange? While listening to the other's speech, we filter the words through our own system of meanings constructed by our personal history. Our personal filters edit for acceptability, comfort, or confrontation, and we seldom actually identify the preconceptions, thinking habits, and defenses we have erected to modify or reject what we have heard. Becoming conscious of one's own prejudices and predictable reactions allows one to reflect on and "suspend" the blocks to real listening. With this clarity comes a maturity as a person and as a therapist—as one who is capable of true empathy—capable of taking the position and the viewpoint of the other. This is a "suspensive" way to be in interaction with other people (Bohm, 1996; Ellinor & Gerard, 1998; Isaacs, 1999).

What we have thus far proposed is characteristic of a "dialogue" and "dialogic conversation." Yankelovich (1999) presents three distinctive features of dialogue that differentiate it from other forms of conversation. First, in dialogue, all participants must be treated as equals. In a treatment meeting, it is possible to generate cooperation among participants from a position of equality because all—even family members—are experts.

All are at the same level of "not-knowing," and their collective goal is to create understanding. The second feature is listening with empathy. Instead of defending one's own opinions, dialogue is characterized by understanding an interlocutor's viewpoint and feelings. The third feature is bringing underlying assumptions to light. The purpose here is to be aware of and inquire into both one's own and the other's assumptions and foundations of thinking and to move them into open dialogue. The attempt to prove one's own point or disprove that of another squarely misses the point. The goal of the open dialogue is to reach a shared understanding.

Dialogue is derived from the Greek word *dialegesthai*, which is the root of *dialogos* (Graumann, 1990). It refers to the fusion of talking and thinking, sharing of meanings "between" two or more partners. Graumann presents a metaphor of moving from two or more positions toward the same place, even if there is "agreement to disagree" as to what that place should be. Bohm's (1996) metaphor is that dialogue is like a "stream of meaning" flowing among, through, and between us. What is needed is space for the free flow of meanings. We have to provide space for people to talk and also to reflect on what they have heard. In the treatment meeting this means that we must not hurry thinking, because the thinking process is unique to the individual's own rhythm and readiness.

Reflective Activity of the Treatment Team

In the treatment meeting, therapists stand knee-deep in a stream of meanings. In dialogue, words emerge and vanish, then reappear and change. Some words carry special weight; they may be so emotionally charged that just saying them affects body language, and the speaker has difficulty keeping his or her passion in check. Sometimes, feelings surface for which words seem unavailable. When empathically listening, therapists are sensitive to both fully worded and wordless emotional messages.

A dialogical moment can pass without notice or can be captured by a therapist who identifies and reflects on a word that seems of great significance to the speaker. For example, when a patient names a fear using a particular word, a therapist explores what other words are contained within that word and what different feelings are connected with them. "Cancer is a serious and frightening word to many people. What words do you connect with it"? As evidenced by the question, this method is skillfully and sensitively applied by Professor Tom Andersen of Tromsø University who specializes in capturing fleeting dialogical moments and moving those defining words of a client's life into conversation.

Therapists do not float like pieces of driftwood in a stream of meaning. Therapeutic skill involves identifying therapeutically significant issues that clients cannot yet talk about. Mutually reflective conversation between therapists with a patient, with a family listening, is a method in which therapists take into conversation difficult but important issues and make them less threatening to the family. Vygotsky's (1992) concept of the zone of proximal development in education is similar to the idea of potential "discourse in therapy" (Haarakangas, 1997) or speech that is created by therapists in "reflective dialogue."

In reflective dialogue, members of a treatment team engage in mutual dialogue about the observations, thoughts, and images that are raised in the treatment meeting and, in reflecting, address their words to other team members rather than to the patient and family. The patient and family are thus afforded the opportunity to listen to the therapists' conversation without taking part in it, taking a stand, or responding to it. From the standpoint of the patient and family, the conversation between therapists can be a therapeutic context within which they clarify their own experiences and meanings. The therapeutic skill of team members finds expression in their ability to maintain respect for the patient and family, carefully balancing their comments so as not to offend or gravely disagree with the observers (Andersen, 1991). At its best, reflective dialogue is flexibly connected to other conversations to assure that the patient and family do not experience it as foreign or embarrassing. By reflecting subjective images, team members help shape the treatment meeting conversation into a form that the patient and family understand as personal opinion and thought—not fixed and final psychiatric truth.

Questions from therapists to the patient and family can also be reflective concerning their goals. Some therapeutically effective questions suggested by Tom Andersen are: If your fist that is ready to strike could speak, what would it say? What would your tears want to say? What other feelings does the pain you mentioned contain? Family members can also be asked about the thoughts aroused by conversation or asked to comment on the opinions of other participants.

Conversation in treatment meetings is a continuous reflective process where inner and outer dialogues alternate. A therapist should maintain inner dialogue with their own minds and bodies during the process by checking in with themselves asking, for example: Why do I think and feel like this right now? Why do I feel so uncomfortable now? Is it because of this conversation or is it because of my background or assumptions? A therapist can move their inner dialogue or emotional experience into conversation with other members of the therapy team during the treatment meeting. In a reflective dialogue between therapists, differences and similarities in observations and experiences can be explored. As manifested and modeled in the thinking and behavior of the therapists, reflectivity seeks to arouse in patients a reflective relationship to their situation.

Closing Thoughts

Since the early 1980s, we have been developing our work toward open dialogue. In the process, we have evolved from being "experts" to becoming "dialogicians." This present stance allows us more flexibility, thus increasing our options. The open dialogue method has also transformed the patient into coworker and therapists into active listeners. In the Finnish language, we would call the work of supporting of families caught in a mental health crisis "walking together."

References

Aaltonen, J., Seikkula, J., Alakare, B., Haarakangas, K., Keränen, J., & Sutela, M. (1997). Western Lapland project: A comprehensive family- and network-centered community psychiatric project. *ISPS Abstracts and Lectures October 12–16, 1997.* London.

Alanen, Y. (1997). *Schizophrenia. Its origins and need-adapted treatment.* London: Karnac.

Alanen, Y.O., Lehtinen, K., Räkköläinen, V., & Aaltonen, J. (1991). Need-adapted treatment of new schizophrenic patients: Experiences and results of the Turku Project. *Acta Psychiatrica Scandinavica, 83,* 363–372.

Andersen, T. (1991). *The reflecting team: Dialogues and dialogues about the dialogues.* New York: Norton.

Anderson, H. (1997). *Conversation, language and possibilities: A postmodern approach to therapy.* New York: Basic Books.

Anderson, H. & Goolishian, H. (1988). Human systems as linguistic systems: Preliminary and evolving ideas about the implications for clinical theory. *Family Process, 27,* 371–393.

Anderson, H. & Goolishian, H. (1992). The client is the expert: A not-knowing approach to therapy. In S. McNamee & K. Gergen (Eds.), *Therapy as social construction* (pp. 25–39). London: Sage.

Bakhtin, M. (1981). *The dialogic imagination: Four essays.* (M. Holquist, Ed., and C. Emerson & M. Holquist, Trans.) Austin, TX: University of Texas Press.

Bakhtin, M. (1984). *Problems of dostoevsky's poetics.* (C. Emerson, Ed., and Trans.) Minnesota: University of Minnesota Press.

Bakhtin, M. (1986). *Speech genres and other late essays.* (C. Emerson and M. Holquist, Eds., & V. McGee, Trans.) Austin, TX: University of Texas Press.

Berger, P. & Luckmann, T. (1966). *The social construction of reality: A treatise in the sociology of knowledge.* New York: Doubleday.

Bohm, D. (1996). *On dialogue.* (L. Nichol, Ed.) London and New York: Routledge.

Ellinor, L. & Gerard, G. (1998). *Dialogue: Rediscover the transforming power of conversation.* New York: John Wiley & Sons.

Gergen, K. (1985). The social constructionist movement in modern psychology. *American Psychologist, 40,* 266–275.

Graumann, C. (1990). Perspectival structure and dynamics in dialogues. In I. Markova & K. Foppa (Eds.), *The dynamics of dialogue* (pp. 105–126). London: Harvester Wheatsheaf.

Haarakangas, K. (1997). Hoitokokouksen äänet. The voices in treatment meeting: A dialogical analysis of the treatment meeting conversations in family-centered psychiatric treatment process in regard to the team activity. English summary. *Jyväskylä Studies in Education, Psychology and Social Research, 130.*

Holma, J. & Aaltonen, J. (1997). The sense of agency and the search for a narrative in acute psychosis. *Contemporary Family Therapy, 19,* 463–477.

Isaacs, W. (1999). *Dialogue and the art of thinking together.* New York: Doubleday.

Jackson, C. & Birchwood, M. (1996). Early intervention in psychosis: Opportunities for secondary prevention. *British Journal of Clinical Psychology, 35,* 487–502.

Keränen, J. (1992). The choice between outpatient and inpatient treatment in a family centred psychiatric treatment system. English summary. *Jyväskylä Studies in Education, Psychology and Social Research, 93.*

Lehtinen, V., Aaltonen, J., Koffert, T., Räkköläinen, V., & Syvälahti, E. (2000). Two-year outcome in first-episode psychosis treated according to an integrated model: Is immediate neuroleptisation always needed? *European Psychiatry, 15*, 312–320.

McNamee, S. & Gergen, K. (Eds.) (1992). *Therapy as social construction.* London: Sage.

Seikkula, J. (1991). Family-hospital boundary system in the social network. English summary. *Jyväskylä Studies in Education, Psychology and Social Research, 80.*

Seikkula, J. (2002). Open dialogues with good and poor outcomes for psychotic crises: Examples from families with violence. *Journal of Marital and Family Therapy, 28*, 263–274.

Seikkula, J., Aaltonen, J., Alakare, B., Haarakangas, K., Keränen, J., & Sutela, M. (1995). Treating psychosis by means of open dialogue. In S. Friedman (Ed.), *The reflective process in action: Collaborative practice in family therapy* (pp. 62–80). New York: Guilford.

Seikkula, J., Alakare, B., & Aaltonen, J. (2000). A two year follow-up on open dialogue treatment in first episode psychosis: Need for hospitalization and neuroleptic medication decreases. [In Russian, English manuscript from the authors] *Social and Clinical Psychiatry, 10*, 20–29.

Seikkula, J., Alakare, B., & Aaltonen, J. (2001a). Open dialogue in psychosis I: An introduction and case illustration. *Journal of Constructivist Psychology, 14*, 247–265.

Seikkula, J., Alakare, B., & Aaltonen, J. (2001b). Open dialogue in psychosis II: A comparison of good and poor outcome cases. *Journal of Constructivist Psychology, 14*, 267–284.

Voloshinov, V. (1996). *Marxism and the philosophy of language* (6th ed.). MA: Harvard University Press.

Vygotsky, L. (1992). *Thought and language* (6th ed.). (A. Kozulin, Ed.). Cambridge, MA: MIT.

Yankelovich, D. (1999). *The magic of dialogue: Transforming conflict into cooperation.* New York: Touchstone.

CHAPTER **15**

The Development of a Collaborative Learning and Therapy Community in an Educational Setting: From Alienation to Invitation

SYLVIA LONDON AND IRMA RODRÍGUEZ-JAZCILEVICH

I came looking for recipes and I found a new way of looking at the world, where I feel more accepted, less anxious, and more capable of seeing and using resources.

A participant (2001)

We would like to invite the reader to share with us our experience of creating and recreating a collaborative learning community intended to introduce postmodern and social constructionist ideas into a school setting. This community included the facilitators, the organizers, and the participants, who were teachers, school administrators, and Montessori guides. All these voices are present in this chapter.

Members of Our Collaborative Learning Community

The Facilitators

For the past 15 years we (Irma and Sylvia) have been practicing, teaching, and living with postmodern and social constructionist ideas in therapy and education. Through our shared interests we developed a close collaborative relationship with the Houston Galveston Institute (HGI) and Harlene Anderson. Our base is Grupo Campos Elíseos (GCE), a free standing postgraduate institution in Mexico City dedicated to using and spreading postmodern ideas in training, consultation, and therapy.

The Organizers

Olga Dantus and Julie Rivera Rio are Montessori guides who codirect an institute focused on training teachers in Montessori philosophy. Their institute is known within the Mexican Montessori community as a place that constantly invites new and novel ideas. Influenced by a long-term friendship with Irma, who had been their psychology consultant for 15 years, Olga and Julie participated in a year-long training at GCE.[1] We mention this to highlight the relationship of trust and understanding that existed among us before this project started, and which allowed for negotiation and flexibility in the design and implementation of the program.

After their training, Olga and Julie were enthused and impressed with the influence postmodern ideas had on their lives and work. They felt, for instance, they were better able to appreciate and work within differences, and to invite and use the expertise of those they worked with. They also felt that they were able to be more flexible and more creative in general. They thought the openness, multiplicity, and freedom they experienced in the GCE program would be useful to their students in the same ways.

The Participants

There were 15 participants; all were teachers and most of whom worked as Montessori guides with preschool children in private or public schools. Three of the participants were school principals or school owners. About half the participants had college degrees, mostly in education or psychology, but others had degrees in disciplines like dentistry and business administration. Their ages were diverse, ranging from the late twenties to the late fifties, and the number of years of teaching experience varied as well.

Developing Our Collaborative Learning Community

The Challenge: Live the Talk

Olga and Julie approached us looking for ways to incorporate postmodern ideas into the Montessori community. At first we thought that the task would be rather simple, drawing from our years of experience as teachers and facilitators working with therapists in universities and private institutes. We could transfer our experience and knowledge by offering an externship for Montessori guides.

Given the newness of the ideas for the institute trainees, we thought a one-day introductory workshop would be the best way to introduce concepts to the participants and to create excitement and curiosity about postmodern ideas and the training program. With Olga and Julie participating through their Montessori Training Institute, we organized a beginner's workshop entitled "Modern and Postmodern Ideas." This workshop was planned to (a) give participants an overall view of different paradigms and their implications in psychology and education, (b) allow participants to become familiar with our style of teaching, and, (c) generate interest about the externship.

Following the workshop, we felt so confident and excited that we proceeded to design the externship program, including exercises and readings. Then we met with Olga and Julie to talk about our planned program. To our surprise the feedback we heard from them was far from what we expected; they had learned from the participants that the workshop had been a distant and alienating experience. Olga and Julie shared some of the students' responses with us. They said that the students found

> ... the language they [Neca and Sylvia] were using to present the postmodern ideas was too foreign and difficult to follow and understand. "I do not want to be part of a training program where I do not feel I belong."

This was an eye-opening experience for the four of us; we had not lived our talk. We had moved too fast within our own framework without taking into account the needs and knowledge of the participants. This reminded us of Bateson's phrase cited in Anderson (1997) "in order to entertain new and novel ideas, there has to be room for the familiar" (p. 157).

As we listened to Olga and Julie talk about the participants' experiences we realized that we were facing the challenge of translating postmodern ideas to simple texts and exercises. We could not solve this problem alone; our experience as university teachers and supervisors was not proving useful in bridging the contextual and academic differences we were encountering. We looked to Olga and Julie, their lifelong experience in the Montessori community, and their recently acquired knowledge of postmodern ideas as the natural guides to help us achieve this difficult endeavor.

Our postmodern philosophical stance, which values and respects multiplicity and experience regarding conversations and relationships, helped us slow down, listen, and codesign together, step-by-step, the content as well as the process of the training program. We were reminded of Anderson's (2000) words:

> I think of my approach to therapy as a philosophy of therapy rather than a theory or model. Philosophy focuses on questions about ordinary

human life: self-identity, relationships, mind, and knowledge. It involves ongoing analysis, inquiry, and reflection, rather than a scientific search for truth. The philosophical stance becomes a worldview that does not separate professional and personal. . . . This refers to a way of being: a way of thinking about, experiencing, being in relationship with, talking with, acting with, and responding with the people we meet in therapy (p. 3).

Anderson's (1999) ideas in this article "Collaborative Learning Communities" offered a welcome platform for our postmodern philosophical stance and the concept of a Montessori community. The goals of a collaborative learning community include: (a) to access every members' creativity and resources and foster the kind of environment in which each participant feels comfortable, open, and part of the conversations, and (b) to create spaces and relationships in which each person has a sense of freedom and belonging, spaces in which everyone can voice their ideas, ask questions, and express concerns, without feeling blamed or judged.

Taking into account these overall goals, the wishes of Olga and Julie, and the participants' voices, we developed the following beginning learning goals: (a) to help participants gain an understanding of a philosophical stance based on postmodern and social constructionist ideas and the implications of this stance for psychology and education, (b) to provide participants with multiple new frameworks and languages to describe, face, and solve problems in their daily classroom activities, and (c) to offer space in which participants could talk about their everyday dilemmas and challenges in the classroom.

The Content

Once we felt comfortable with our shared learning goals, our next challenge was to find suitable readings that would address our philosophical stance in a language that was suitable and accessible for our students. We decided to start the program with Anderson's (1999) article to introduce the participants to our ideas regarding the learning/teaching process. Over the course of training, we introduced other readings in the following order and for the following reasons. We followed the first reading with Gergen's (1991) *The Saturated Self* to acquaint participants with postmodern social constructionist ideas as part of society. We chose this text because it is written from a broad perspective for the general public, and it challenges the predominant beliefs in society regarding health, normalcy, and diagnosis. We next invited the participants to read O'Hanlon and Weiner-Davis' (1989) book *In Search of Solutions*. Though some might challenge its inclusion, we felt that its simplicity and clarity provided a springboard to introduce participants to changes in psychology and offered a practical guide to thoughts about resources and possibilities. Andersen's (1987) article "The Reflecting Team: Dialogue and Meta-Dialogue in Clinical Work," a reading we used at the end of the program, gave the group a theoretical explanation for the consultation format we used during the training.

Given the nature of the selected readings and the participants' characteristics and prior training, we were very careful and moved slowly through the texts. We continually connected theory with examples and exercises to bridge the gaps between the familiar and the unfamiliar and to respond to the participants' questions. We focused mostly on the "doing" so that participants could learn from their own experiences and relate them to the philosophy of the approach.

The Richness of Diversity

The group's diversity or heterogeneity enriched the collaborative learning experience. Questions were posed from many varied perspectives. The more experienced teachers were respectful of the beginners' needs and dilemmas and made themselves available to consult and offer their knowledge, both within the training format and outside it. The younger teachers' constant questions and dilemmas helped create a learning atmosphere characterized by curiosity and excitement. We were reminded of Anderson's (2000) bias regarding the usefulness of diversity in learning communities

> Diversity among participants enhances the quality and quantity of learning that is produced. Each person brings differences in terms of age and life stage, personal and professional experience, degree and discipline, theoretical orientation, work and educational setting, learning style and agenda, or any of the diversity "isms." Varieties of voices provide a richness of perspectives and realities (p. 7).

The Format and Process

The format and process were similar to our clinical externship at GCE. We met with the group for three hours weekly for 15 weeks. We started each week with an hour to hour and half theoretical seminar in which participants conversed with each other and the facilitators about their questions, reflections, and experiences of the week's reading. The remaining time was used for consultations during which participants shared their dilemmas and were able to live the richness of multiple voices and years of experience in the room.

At the beginning of the externship, each week was assigned to a different student or group of students as their day to consult with the group. To create a consultation process in which everyone could participate and to help the participants reflect and focus their consultation, we designed a questionnaire that presenters completed before the class. A copy of the completed questionnaire and its answers was distributed to each participant prior to the presentation. The consultation questionnaire requested the presenters' reflections on the following:

1. Describe the situation you would like to talk about and the people involved in it.
2. Share a brief description of the history of the problem situation.
3. What have you done to try to solve it?
4. Why are you choosing to present this situation?
5. What are your goals for the consultation?
6. What questions do you have for the group?

We asked the participants to read the questionnaire in silence and think about questions they might have for the consultees. Then one of the facilitators conversed with the consultees in front of the group while the other participants watched and listened in silence. As the conversation unfolded, the facilitators initially recommended which reflecting format could maximize the number and variety of ideas for the situation at hand. Some of the reflecting formats we used were inspired by Andersen's (1987, 1992)[2] ideas regarding reflecting processes (see Appendix 1).

Our basic guidelines were:

1. Talk about what you hear and see in the conversation.
2. Be brief, tentative, and conversational with your fellow team members.
3. Choose ideas that you think might be useful for the consultee and that are related to the consultee's goals.
4 Be careful and respectful. Talk with the same care and respect you wish someone would talk to or about you.

We also used Anderson's (1987) "as if" exercise,[3] in which participants listening to the conversation were invited to listen as if they were one of the relevant characters in the situation (see Appendix 2). Once the interview was over, conversational clusters were formed based on the different characters. Using a "fish bowl" format, each group had a conversation from the character's perspective in front of the larger group.

These reflecting processes proved very useful in providing the richness of multiple voices, as well as familiarizing participants with the polyphony of postmodern and social constructionist ideas. As time went by, participants became very excited about the richness of the process and spontaneously become part of the interviews as well as design of the reflective processes.

We also believe reflection is a powerful learning tool, as espoused by Schön (1983) in his book, *The Reflective Practitioner*. Schön invites professionals to reflect upon their activities and the impact those activities have upon themselves and their professional practices. As facilitators we were very interested in following our students' learning processes. To access participants' ideas in a written format, we asked them to write weekly reflections to describe their experiences, including their reactions to the readings, the class, and the consultation processes. These reflections also gave us an opportunity to follow the participants' learning experiences and helped us change and adjust to their learning needs as their beginning learning agendas shifted.

Experiencing Our Collaborative Learning Community

Some Examples

During the first meeting participants signed up for consultation time. Jana's turn was scheduled for the tenth meeting. She expressed in the first meeting that she had a very difficult situation with a child in her class, and though she did not think we could help her change it, she could not wait to present her dilemma. Over the first weeks, she often said that her dilemma was much more difficult than the situation presented in the session; she would say, "Wait until you hear my story." Somehow, during the fourth or fifth meeting we started to notice a change in her discourse and her attitude. She reported that after listening to the conversations and participating in the reflecting teams, she was able to see her own situation, and the child's, in a different light. She talked about the changes she was making in her classroom, including different ways of relating to this particular child and his parents. By the time it was her turn to consult, the description of the situation with this child and his parents was less problematic: she seemed less anxious and, instead of talking about the problems in her classroom, she talked about the changes she had already made and emphasized her sense of competency. During the consultation interview, she expressed a strong sense of surprise regarding how useful the readings and the experience of listening to the interviews and participating in the reflecting teams had been for her. In her own words: "I can't believe how much my life has changed."

Soco, Yanira, and Olga, three Montessori guides who work in the same school, decided to consult about Ana, a five-year-old girl whom they described as having uncontrollable behavior in the classroom. Ana would hit, bite, kick, spit, and destroy the other children's work. Ana was medicated and in therapy. The guides expressed a negative view of Ana's behavior as well as her parents' attitudes toward her and the school. During the presentation we heard the language the guides were using to describe Ana and her parents as very negative; they seemed very frustrated, angry, and stuck in their own recursive descriptions. We thought that using Anderson's "as if" exercise could provide an open framework to invite multiple voices and perspectives. We described the "as if" to the guides and the group and invited them to join us in an "as if" exercise. We asked each member of the group to choose to listen to the conversation as if they were one of the following characters in the story: Ana, Ana's parents, the guides, the classroom parents, and the students.

After the interview, one by one, each group of characters was invited to the center of the room. In a fishbowl format they talked among themselves from a first-person voice about the thoughts and feelings they were having while listening to the consultation conversation. The richness and variety of reflections gave the guides an opportunity to listen from a different stance and to open their hearts and ears to the complexity of the situation.

The guides were very moved by Ana and her mother's voices. In the "as if" voices, Ana felt hurt, misunderstood, lonely, and alienated. The mother's "as if" voices expressed her sense of being criticized, not validated, and judged by the school personnel, and incapable of meeting her child's needs.

After listening to the "as if" voices the guides said they had never thought about the impact of their behaviors and attitudes on Ana and her mother. Instead they had been too busy thinking about their own classroom situation and looking for management solutions. The information provided by the "as if" voices helped them think about other ways to conceptualize and approach the situation that included understanding and compassion for the feelings of Ana and her mother. In following seminar sessions the guides asked for time to give follow-up reports to the group on Ana's situation. We were surprised to witness how the guides had incorporated the information they had heard, how they had changed their perception of Ana, and how that "change" translated into a different way of relating to her. In turn, the guides reported that Ana's behavior "changed." This difference in Ana's behavior and attitude had an impact on the rest of the children in the classroom. The guides said that the children were surprised to see that Ana was not misbehaving in class anymore and was not the one to blame for everything that went wrong. In addition, the guides reported being better able to understand Ana's mother's difficulties in dealing with her. The guides excitedly shared the news of Ana's changes in the classroom with her mother who had a hard time believing it. Ana's mother wondered what the guides were doing differently. The guides invited Ana's mother to join them in their different way of perceiving and relating to

Ana, a position based on confidence in Ana and emphasizing the exceptions to her disruptive behavior.

Participant's Voices

"We look at differences instead of problems ... "

A participant (2001)

At the end of the 15 weeks we had a meeting to ask the participants to reflect with each other aloud about the overall training experience. We invited them to talk about the process, their learning, their feelings, and their likes and dislikes. We had a lively conversation with the group during which they discussed their favorite readings, the style of the class, the richness of the consultation and reflective processes, and the impact of these new ideas in their personal and professional lives.

The participant's voices provided us with a very rich description of the development of a collaborative learning community and the introduction to postmodern and social constructionist ideas. To present these findings in a workshop (Anderson, London, & Rodriguez, 2001) we organized the participants' verbatim responses in three different categories:

1. The learning experience. "The training was a place that provided a relaxed, safe and caring atmosphere that opened possibilities, new visions, and ways of achieving goals". "The consultation was a different and new way of working, a process among us that fostered listening to others and invited the freedom to think about anything we want with a fresh and positive attitude towards people and problems that values differences, multiple realities and curiosity."
2. The learning process. "During the process we were developing a working team that listened without judging, trusting the possibilities of change and inviting self awareness". "It was hard dealing with uncertainty and incorporating new ideas, but as time went by, I was able to trust the others and their resources in order to develop my own potential and increase my abilities, but I still need more time and practice to feel secure."
3. Personal and professional implications. "As a person and in my work I am discovering that there are different views of the problem, that differences can exist without conflict. The invitation to action reduced my anxiety. I realized that what happens in my school happens in other schools. I saw lots of changes in my behavior. I was able to try new things with confidence in my abilities. I feel more comfortable not centering on problems, this change has had

an impact on my personal life; sometimes I can bring the ideas to the school, but I am still not able to apply them."

Our Voices

The process of creating this collaborative learning community became an opportunity to appreciate the type of collaborative professional and personal relationships we build in our lives. One of the most important factors that made this experience possible was the relationship of trust and commitment between the organizers and us. It was clear to us that we were visitors, invited guests, and that we must be open to learn and value every voice and opinion. We learned to slow down and engage in a process of asking questions, listening, designing, and redesigning the contents and processes according to the needs and styles of the participants.

> To invite and maximize collaborative learning I must act and talk consistent with my philosophy. I must live it, being genuinely and naturally collaborative. This includes respecting, inviting and valuing each voice, being flexible and responsive, and creatively doing what the occasion calls for on the spot. Foremost, this includes trusting the other and our process. (Anderson, 2000, p. 8)

This philosophical stance based on valuing and respecting multiplicity of thoughts, relationships, and ideas has become the cornerstone of our work. Based on this foundation we invite and define the types of relationships and conversations we choose to foster with and among people. In the spirit of a collaborative learning community and ourselves as lifelong learners, we must remember that the process began a long time before this story, and it will never end. It is a small part of ongoing conversations and relationships that build upon each other in the constant creation and re-creation of meanings through dialogue.

Endnotes

1. GCE offers a year-long training in postmodern/collaborative therapies. The goal of this program is to introduce postmodern and social constructionist ideas to help participants incorporate a different philosophical stance into their ways of thinking and working. The training consists of theoretical seminars and clinical consultations, during which participants have opportunities to use postmodern ideas with clients in various conversational arrangements, including the use of listening and reflecting processes.
2. For more details on Tom Andersen's guidelines see Appendix 1.
3. See complete description and guidelines for this exercise in Appendix 2.
4. Anderson's "as if" exercise recovered directly from http://www.harlene.org, 12/04/2005.

References

Andersen, T. (1987). The reflecting team: Dialogue and metadialogue in clinical work. *Family Process, 26*, 415–428.

Anderson, H. 1992. *C* Therapy and *F* Word. *American Family Therapy Association Newsletter, 50*(winter):19–22.

Anderson, H. (1997). *Conversation, language and possibilities: A postmodern approach to therapy.* New York: Basic Books.

Anderson, H. (1999). Collaborative learning communities. In S. McNamee & K.J. Gergen (Eds.), *Relational responsibility: Resources for sustainable dialogue* (pp. 65–70). London: Sage.

Anderson, H. (2000, Fall). Supervision as collaborative learning community. *American Association of Marriage and Family Therapy Supervision Bulletin,* 7–9.

Anderson, H. (2002*). Broadening the possibilities of clients and therapists.* Handouts presented at The International Summer Institute: Conversation Language and Possibilities, Cuernavaca, Mexico.

Anderson, H. & Levin, S.B. (1998). Generative conversations: A postmodern approach to conceptualizing and working with human systems. In M.F. Hoyt (Ed.), *Handbook of constructive therapies: Innovative approaches of leading practitioners* (pp. 46–67). San Francisco, CA: Jossey Bass.

Anderson, H., London, S., & Rodriguez, I. (2000). Postmodern supervision in two countries. Presentation at the Texas Association for Marriage and Family Therapy annual conference, January 27–30, 2000, Houston, TX.

Anderson, H., London, S., & Rodriguez, I. (2001*).* Challenging beliefs in supervision, consultation and education. Presentation at the Texas Association for Marriage and Family Therapy annual conference 2001, Dallas, TX.

Friedman, S. (Ed.). (1995). *The reflecting team in action: Collaborative practice in family therapy.* New York: Guilford Press.

Gergen, K. (1991). *The saturated self.* New York: Basic Books.

Montessori. M. (1966). *The secret of childhood.* New York: Ballantine Books.

O'Hanlon, W. & Weiner-Davis, M. (1989). *In Search of solutions.* New York: Norton.

Schön, D. (1983). *The Reflective practitioner: How professionals think in action.* New York: Basic Books.

Reflective Process: Tom Andersen's Guidelines (Andersen, 1987)

- I talk from something I saw or heard in the family's talk with the therapist and in a question manner avoiding statement.
- I feel free to talk about all I hear but not all I see.
- If the team is in the same room with the family, I ask them to speak among themselves without looking at or addressing the family.

Harlene Anderson: "As if" Exercise[4]

Aim of Exercise

The "as if" exercise provides participants with an opportunity to experience:

- Participating in generative conversations
- Creating space for the other person and listening to what the other wants to talk about
- Accessing inner silent thoughts and putting them into spoken words; the multiple angles from which any information, event, or person can be experienced, described, and explained
- The richness of different voices, and that a person may hold multiple, and often contradictory thoughts simultaneously about any one situation or person
- Talking about a person in their presence
- Conversations that invite the other person into them
- That it is not necessary to strive for a product
- The shifts, transformations, and possibilities (i.e., in meanings, perspectives, actions) that emerge from the process are spontaneous and endless.

Format

The format combines several phases to create a process toward accomplishing this opportunity. The format includes presentation, "as if" listening, reflection, and discussion. The "as if" can be individually tailored to a particular participant group: the group's size, the group's agenda, and the presenter's agenda. It may be used with any number of participants, from groups as small as two students or a six-person staff to one of conference size. The following is an example of one format.

Guidelines for the Presenter

1. Tell us the list of characters in this story. For instance, who are the members of the system in conversation with each other, and with you, about the situation? (The facilitator records the presenter's words.)
2. Tell us your hope, agenda, or goal. For instance, what do you hope will happen in the process of presenting your situation? Do you have a particular question that you would like us to address? Are you looking for fresh ideas? In other words, what are your expectations of us? The aim is not to have a content agenda but a general sense of the presenter's beginning expectation. (The facilitator records the presenter's words.)
3. Tell us what you think we need to know to help you with the above. For instance, what do you think is important for us to know?

Guidelines for the "as if" Listeners

1. Select a member of the story; listen to the presentation from that member's position.
2. Listen silently; hold questions, comments, and suggestions. Let the presenter tell us what (s)he thinks we need to know.
3. Offer reflections (may include questions, comments, and suggestions) from your "as if" position after the presenter has finished.

Presenter's Reflections

1. Presenters reflect on their own experiences of the process.
2. Facilitators may interview presenters on their experiences of the process.

General Discussion

1. The "as if" listeners reflect on their experiences of the process.
2. The facilitators reflect on their experiences of the process.

Variations

1. If the facilitator and the participants keep the aim of the exercise in mind (e.g., to create a generative process), then they may improvise to meet their needs and will find that the "as if" exercise takes on a life of its own and becomes unique to each group and their situation.
2. With a small group the facilitator may give each listener an opportunity to offer his/her reflections in the "as if" voice.

3. With a large group where two or more people are listening from the same position, the facilitator may give each "as if" voice cluster an opportunity to share reflections with each other. Each cluster may select one member to share reflections in the "as if" voice.
4. The presenter rotates through each "as if" cluster and listens to the reflections. The presenter and the "as if" listeners are asked not to talk with each other.
5. The variations for "as if" in the therapy arena are endless. For instance, with families, one member may be asked to speak while the others listen and reflect from an "as if" position.
6. With a single client a therapist listens and reflects, while the client listens, as an "as if" member of his or her story.

CHAPTER 16

Collaborative Therapy and Supervision in a Psychiatric Hospital

SYLVIA LONDON AND MARGARITA TARRAGONA

In this chapter we share our experiences as university faculty serving as trainers and supervisors for graduate students in a family therapy practicum in a psychiatric teaching hospital in Mexico City. As we began to reflect on our experiences we realized that at the start we were both very apprehensive. We had little experience in psychiatric settings, we were anxious about working with people who might be so "different" from our clients in other contexts, and we were concerned about how the hospital doctors and psychologists might perceive our work. Here, we share our supervisory experiences using a postmodern collaborative approach over a 2-year period, including our initial apprehensions and how they dissolved. We present a description of the setting, our approach to the clinical work, and the supervision format. As this was both a clinical and a training experience, we include supervisee accounts of their learning process, a clinical example, and clients' descriptions of their therapy.

The Setting

The hospital had recently become a practicum site for students in the master's degree in family therapy programs at the Universidad de las Américas (UDLA) and at the Universidad Nacional Autónoma de México (UNAM), in which we taught. The setting offered students the opportunity to work with young people diagnosed with psychiatric disorders and their families. The students, in turn, would support the hospital's need to expand its family therapy services. As a public institution, the hospital had limited economic resources and space. We were assigned as the family therapy team in two programs: Inpatient Adolescent Girls Unit and Outpatient Children's Services. The girls in the inpatient unit were hospitalized for suicide attempts. Clients in outpatient services presented a wide range of difficulties such as enuresis, school problems, couple's issues, family violence, and psychosis, among others.

Our Initial Reactions

Being invited to provide a practicum program in the hospital was both exciting and intimidating. Though we both had substantial experience as teachers and supervisors, neither of us had worked in a psychiatric hospital. We felt the weight of responsibility for both the clients and our students as well as the awareness that we were representing our universities. Here is an account of our shared inner dialogue and the transformation of it as we settled into a collaborative process.

Our Apprehensions

Margarita: Even though I had been practicing and supervising from a postmodern, collaborative approach for many years, I was scared that this work would be very different from the work I usually did. I felt I didn't have the specialized training required to work with severe psychiatric disorders. I thought "I don't know enough about these kinds of clients," and I was very worried about how I would go about my work in the hospital.

Sylvia: "Mental illness" was also an issue for me, but I was more worried about the politics of the institutions involved. I felt the responsibility of representing the universities and their psychology departments and was concerned that the ideas and practices we would bring to this traditional hospital setting would be too different from their usual ways of working.

In my experience in other practicum sites, I had sometimes sensed a tension between the university faculty and the site clinicians. We came from different professional discourses that seemed to have the potential to fuel competition over who had the better ideas and best practices. Avoiding this potential dichotomy was very important to me. We were not alone in our apprehensions. Our students, Alma, for one, shared similar feelings:[1]

> Today when they took us for a tour of the hospital, they took us to the pavilion for the severely disturbed. I had never been there, and

the truth is that I just couldn't go inside; it made me very anxious. I hope you can understand.

What helped us face our initial apprehensions was a network of interpersonal and professional relationships and our philosophical stance about therapy and supervision.

Sylvia: As a postmodern approach values a multiplicity of perspectives and voices, I began inviting colleagues to join me in the university classroom and other clinical sites as guest faculty and clinicians before beginning the practicum. This format initially seemed awkward for the students; however, over time, the visitors became so important to the learning process that students missed their contributions and asked for their presence.

As this visiting colleague format had proved so useful in other settings, we each invited close colleagues who were experienced supervisors to join us as cosupervisors[2] in the hospital. Having a team of trusted colleagues and being familiar with our students from previous classes helped us feel more confident about the work we were about to do. The presence of more supervisors also made it possible to work with trainees in separate units of the hospital simultaneously. They also provided the students the rich opportunity to experience variety in clinical and supervisory styles.

Once we started working at the hospital we realized it was not such an unfamiliar place after all. We discovered that many students had a colleague, friend, or acquaintance among the hospital staff. These relationships became very important in paving our way into the institution. As the Mexican saying goes "Siempre es bueno un conocido en un baile." ("It's always good to know somebody at the dance.") Through these relationships we were beginning to bridge the distance between "insiders" and "outsiders."

Following Andersen (2002) and Anderson's (1997) ideas about the way to meet and greet people, it was very helpful to think about ourselves as visitors or guests. Our hosts, the hospital staff,[3] were very gracious and gave us and our students a tour of the hospital on our first day. We continued the informal conversations of the tour in a meeting where we and the hospital staff oriented ourselves to each others' contexts and work. We also took note of the administrative policies and procedures, including office assignments, schedules, and record keeping. This may seem trivial, but for us it was part of taking the necessary care to build collaborative relationships between the individuals and the institution.

How We Worked

Our postmodern/social constructionist approach was foreign to the hospital staff. They were, however, familiar with systemic family therapy and reflecting teams, so we used this common language to describe our work. We made ourselves accessible to other clinicians at the hospital and invited them to visit our sessions and participate on our teams if they so desired. We worked with a team in every session, and used the "reflecting team" process introduced by Tom Andersen (1987, 1990) and his colleagues in Norway to our Mexican context.

As we were on a university academic schedule and the hospital had a long waiting list of clients, we had to limit the number of sessions for each family. We offered families seven sessions, usually held every other week. This format allowed each student to be the therapist for at least one family and to maximize the number of families that we could meet.

The team met once a week for 4 hours, allowing 1 hour for discussing readings and 3 hours for seeing clients. As part of the supervision process, students were required to write their reflections[4] after each meeting and develop case reports.

Working with Reflecting Teams

A central feature of our work was the use of reflecting teams in all sessions. We adapted the "original" reflecting team format described by Tom Andersen (1987, 1990) to better fit our culture. Given the space constraints, we used a one-way mirror with some discussions behind the mirror; others, we held in front of the family where team members were invited to share their ideas with the clients.

The families often became attached to and related in a very friendly and familiar way to the team members. The team sometimes spoke directly to the family members or to the therapist. The team listened carefully to the clients and honored their requests when they wanted a specific team member to participate in the reflections. The families cared about the therapist and their learning situation and sometimes expressed their interest about whether they were being useful, because "we were all learning together in front of this team." They often expressed a desire to be able to contact our treatment team in the future if they felt they needed therapy again.

Clients and supervisees reported that they found these sessions with the team helpful and enjoyable. In the beginning they had some reservations, but in time they found that listening to the team's conversations helped them think about the problem in new ways.

Though students had learned about reflecting processes in the classroom, the reflecting team in action was new for most of them. Like the clients, the students also expressed enthusiasm for this format and described it as helpful in their learning process and clinical work:

> I felt uncomfortable during the session, nervous by the presence of the reflecting team since I am not used to having so many people

observe me . . . made me lose my concentration, and I felt I couldn't work the way I would have liked to. (*Ignacio*)

Despite initial misgivings, Ignacio's later sentiment was shared by most students:

I feel very comfortable working as a team and I would like to do it like this always. Sometimes in my work outside the hospital I think of the advantages of having a team and I would like to have it there.

Many reflections echoed Anita's:

I definitely see all the benefits this type of work has for the group, for the therapist and, for the family. It is a tremendous learning experience!

Our Philosophy of Therapy and Supervision

Our anxieties about working with the unknown world of inpatient psychiatry started to subside when we reminded ourselves of the ideas that had been helpful in our previous supervision/practicum sites. Our postmodern and social constructionist approach emphasizes that experienced reality can be described in many different ways, that language is generative, and that therapy is a conversational process. As suggested by Anderson and Goolishian (1990), we conceptualized therapy and supervision as dialogic activities or joint explorations.

From this perspective, both therapy and supervision are language- or meaning-generating systems in which participants attempt to make sense of their and each other's experiences and may create new possibilities through their conversations. Anderson and Goolishian (1990) point out that the supervisor's goal is to create a context that allows the development of new meanings, learning, and change. The supervisor's responsibility is to facilitate a process in which trainees may broaden their ways of understanding and dealing with the difficulties they face.

The key elements of the "philosophy of therapy" that guided our work have been summarized by Anderson (2000) as the "three C's": connection, collaboration, and construction.

In the following sections we illustrate how we implemented this philosophical stance.

Margarita: For me it was very helpful to think "How would Harlene deal with this?" I remembered conversations with her, videos I had watched, and stories that I had read about her and Harry Goolishian. I remembered the work of other colleagues—Tom Andersen, Michael White, Melissa Elliott and James Griffith, Jaakko Seikkula and Marianne Borgengren—who have described their experiences working with people struggling with psychoses. It was reassuring to remember that many of the therapists I admire and respect have worked in psychiatric settings. I actively tried to keep them present in my mind while working in the hospital.

Sylvia: I just tried to forget I was in a psychiatric hospital! I did not want the seriousness of the situation to limit my creativity, freedom, and sense of humor, which I think are important assets in my everyday work. I decided I would give privilege to the importance of conversations and relationships over the overwhelming weight of diagnoses and illnesses.

Taking a "Not-Knowing" Approach

We decided we would approach each of our clients and their families as we would normally do: trying to avoid preconceptions about them, being curious about their lives and experiences, attempting to understand their dilemmas, and striving to have a productive dialogue with whoever was involved in the conversations. We encouraged our students to position themselves in the same way.

We invited our students to use their "not-knowing" as a way to get to know people. We wanted to help them feel free to go beyond the impact of working with "psychiatric patients" (as categories) and to be interested and curious about these patients as people.

We link the notion of "not-knowing" proposed by Anderson and Goolishian (1988; Anderson, 2005) with Shotter's ideas of "withness thinking" and "aboutness thinking" (2005). Traditionally, the training of mental health professionals emphasizes knowing *about* people: what patients with certain disorders are like, how they are likely to behave, and the best ways to treat them. *Knowing about* usually precedes the encounter between client and therapist, and it can color their interaction, once it happens. On the other hand, *knowing with* refers to a joint exploration between client and therapist in order to understand together the clients' experiences, meanings, and possible solutions to their dilemmas.

We believe that both kinds of knowledge are useful; what is important is "what you do with what you know" (Anderson, 2004). What we know *about* clients can be brought into the conversation and enrich what we can know *with* them about their lives and experiences.

We think that the "not-knowing" stance used in Collaborative Language Systems (CLS) therapy refers to not letting what we *think* we know about our clients take more space than the knowledge that can be created in the relationship and conversations with them. As Anderson has stated, "not-knowing" does not mean that the therapist does not know anything:

> Not-knowing refers to the attitude and belief that the therapist does not have access to privileged information, can never fully understand

another person; and always needs to learn more about what has been said or not said … not-knowing means the therapist is humble about what she or he knows (1995, pp. 34–36).

Adopting a "not-knowing" approach in our work at the hospital allowed us to dissolve our fears, have "normal" conversations with clients, and foster students' curiosity and confidence as therapists.

Living and Working with Uncertainty

An idea that goes hand in hand with "not-knowing" is "uncertainty." Uncertainty was pervasive in our work and colored every aspect of it: the settings, the logistics, the students' learning processes, the therapeutic processes, and the lives of our clients and our own. We often did not know if we would have an office to work in, if clients would show up (depending on if they could afford the bus fare), if we would make it there on time through the heavy Mexico City traffic, or if the microphones would work, and so on.

Uncertainty in Learning

Uncertainty was also an element of our students' learning process. It was expressed in their requests for clear guidelines that would tell them what to do. This echoes Anderson's (1997) observation:

> In our pragmatic Western world, most therapy students begin their study with a need and a quest for certainty. . . . We have come to expect therapists to be experts in human behavior and to expect teachers of therapists to tell them how to do therapy. Students want skill and techniques and are eager for foolproof recipes. Skills and techniques, like certainty, are often confused with competence. When students expect certainty and predictability, there is always a period of discomfort with a process that entails uncertainty and randomness. (pp. 250–251)

In the beginning of our work together, our students told us, for example:

> About the session with Anita, I think it was OK, but I feel that we need some guidelines, I feel there is no direction, I don't know if this is normal or if there should be more direction about where to head our work. (*Mariana*)

> I think we should put more emphasis on strategies to ask questions that can inspire families to create options or alternatives, as in "brief therapy." I think that we wander too much, and the more we wander, the less effective our contributions. (*Anita*)

> For me it would also be important if the supervisors would tell me what I could have done better in the session, or what could have been

different. . . . Maybe it is hard for me to think differently, because in my experience, learning has always been based on the dichotomy of what's well done or badly done, so maybe it would be interesting to learn this new way of being supervised. (*Sara*)

Anderson (1997) also describes how therapists' quest for certainty tends to change over time:

Moving toward comfort occurs slowly as they experience a collaborative and connected way of constructing meaning and thus learning with others. As students experience and recognize their own voice and authority to generate knowledge, certainty becomes a non-issue and the need for it dissolves. (p. 251)

Later in the semester, as their work with families and the teams continued, students tended not to request guidelines. Their reflections were often along the lines of

Reading the article "Understanding our Relational Expertise" by Sophie Holmes [1998] gave me the possibility of seeing therapy in a different way. That is, it is not learning theories and putting them to practice in therapy but that we also have the possibility of handling it in our own style that does not necessarily depend on experience. I really liked that it mentions some research on experienced and inexperienced therapists. Learning about the results made me feel excited and gave me the confidence that I needed to be sure of myself, of what I know, and about the way I have learned to relate to others. The anxiety and uncertainty that I had been feeling were diffused. (*Sara*)

I feel that this issue about conversations is beginning to resonate inside of me, that I can understand it better. I have noticed this when I hear the families, and I see how the therapist develops thoughts and ideas from their own conversation. (*Ines*)

During the sessions in the hospital we have seen how each therapist imprints his own art when asking questions or making interventions. Each member of the group has his own virtues that they share and enrich the group and the families that visit us. . . . It seems to me that this way of working promotes a constructive or directed freedom, since all of us, students and supervisors, learn in an environment of cordial respect. (*Anita*)

Uncertainty in Therapy

The uncertainty of the therapeutic process was also evident for our students in the clinical practicum. Anderson (1997) reminds us that you never know where a conversation may lead, what turns it will take, or whom the client may want to include in the next session. Each therapy and each session is different and unique. Students frequently commented about this:

> I was thinking a lot about where the next session should go and I think that the best thing would be, as the readings say, to ask them what they want from this space. . . . About the session, it is amazing how you never know what is going to happen. Everything was so different from what I imagined. (*Mariana*)

> I suppose that many times, even if there is one presenting complaint or petition, this becomes broadened by the family. This session helped me learn that we can not know what each family or each patient will bring the next time and that the best attitude we can have is not to have a fixed idea about it, but to be open and curious . . . sticking to an idea or hypothesis may "blur" the new scenarios that each family or each person builds each day. (*Violeta*)

Uncertainty in Life

Families at the hospital constantly put us in touch with the painful uncertainties of life, facing questions like, "Will my daughter recover from anorexia?" "Will she try to kill herself again?" "Is she going to be safe at home?" "Will he ever be able to live independently?" "Should I have this baby?" The struggle and pain that so many of our clients lived often seemed overwhelming for them and for us. We felt humbled and honored that they trusted us and let us into intimate corners of their lives. As David, one of our students, expressed, "The greatest personal learning for me has been to listen to the families telling their stories and sharing their experiences."

Different Realms of Knowledge and Expertise

Considering the hospital's context of "expert knowledge" and hierarchical structure, it was important for us to honor the diversity of expertise that coexisted there. We often wondered how we could include the various "experts," voices in the system: the clients as experts in their own lives (Anderson, 1997), the psychiatrists' medical and pharmacological knowledge, the nurses' and social workers' knowledge of clients' day to day lives, and the supervisee's and supervisors' ideas. The different points of view that each of us brought were often contradictory. The challenge was to try to build a respectful context in which there would be room for the tension and the coexistence of these knowledges.

The issue of knowledge, for instance, about diagnoses and medications, became evident. From some perspectives, particularly in medicine, an accurate diagnosis is the basis of all treatment. This is also true for many forms of psychotherapy. As Anderson, Gergen, and Hoffman (1995) have pointed out, there are limitations to the medical analogy for therapy, particularly if we think of psychotherapy as a linguistic process in which meaning is coconstructed by its participants. For example, when we see a diagnostic code in a client record, we often make judgments about the person and the kind of work we might do together, possibly imagining "This will be very hard," "Will I be able to connect with this person?" "How can I talk with someone who is depressed, suicidal, borderline, and so forth?" The preconceptions with which we enter the conversation influence how the conversation emerges.

To avoid such preconceptions, we decided to meet with the clients and families before reading their charts. Students had to review the charts after their initial meeting with the family. By doing this we encouraged therapists to have a first-hand experience with clients and to develop "inside knowledge" through conversation with them and then to enrich it with other information that comes from other perspectives. We then discussed how we could keep all of those perspectives present in our future conversations with the clients.

Some of the students, like Ignacio, seriously questioned the role of diagnosis in therapeutic practice:

> How does this trend towards evaluation and diagnosis influence our daily practice? How has it influenced our idea of psychology, psychotherapy, and most of all, of our clients? And how does it influence the view that clients have of us? Has it contributed to reinforcing the image that clients have of us as experts? Has it also contributed to us believing that we are? It is an important issue to consider, especially when it is so widely used in institutions. . . . The fact that I think that traditional evaluation is not as useful as interviewing clients does not mean that I am totally discarding the use of instruments. Tests can have a specific context and can be useful in certain situations.

Others, like Giselle, felt more comfortable with diagnosis, but reported changes in the way they saw them:

> I realized that beyond whether mental disorders exist or not, what is important is that we do not focus on them or lose sight of the person, her story, and her pain. . . . I feel that mental pathologies do exist, but what changed for me is that even those pathologies that may seem strangest or abnormal are "normal" deep inside, in that they are the way that our organism reacts when facing "abnormal" situations like abuse, violence, loneliness, and extreme pain.

As they saw different clients with various medication regimes, many students appreciated the usefulness of medication in treatment. Mariana explains:

I liked that Pilar (client) looked much better; she had a very nice attitude towards her parents. It made me think a lot about how moods can change with medication. When I got home and my husband asked me how things went, I said very well, that it was a very moving session, but the success was not mine, that I owed it to the medications. I was impressed by the radical change in her mood.

Identifying Resources

The readings for the practicum emphasized two areas: the importance of building a relationship and focusing on strengths. Several students were enthusiastic about this emphasis and found they made a difference in their work, as illustrated by the following student comments:

> Seeing people as competent and capable, and a therapy based on what's right and on resources, opens countless possibilities. I see this in my work with families, particularly with the one I am seeing now. I am surprised by the changes that can come about just by validating people, giving them space to feel capable and focus on their resources. This seems very helpful in my work. (*Ignacio*)

> I loved the following phrase (from the readings[6]): "Let's work with the family because they are the most powerful solution." It's beautiful! It leaves behind the idea that the family is or has the problem. (*Sara*)

> I really liked that the reading (and many others we've read) talked about the importance of believing the client's story. I think this is a basic point of departure to be able to work. After reflecting about this I felt more relaxed. There is nothing underneath to be discovered, no need to protect oneself from the client. If we don't trust what clients' tell us, how can we work?' I will try to be more open and trustful when I listen to the client's story. (*Mariana*)

Working with What You Have

Anderson (1997) often mentions the importance of being flexible and working with the resources that you have available. We found that under the special circumstances of the hospital and our city, with limited space, time, and resources, we had to be flexible and resourceful. For instance, when no offices were available for us to see clients, we often held sessions in the garden, which we amusingly referred to as "garden-variety therapy." We sat on the grass and when the ants attacked, the team worked standing up and ended up looking more like a Greek chorus. Therapy sessions were also conducted walking in hallways and in an ob/gyn exam room. Challenges such as these helped the therapists tap their creativity to overcome obstacles and to make do with what they had. For us, one obstacle that became a resource was the time that we had to spend driving. As is commonly known, Mexico City traffic can be terrible, so we often carpooled, spending a couple of hours in the car on the way to and from the hospital. We found that our best conversations were always in the car. Riding together gave us the uninterrupted time and space to process and brainstorm, as well as wonder about our work together, our students, and our clients.

Clinical Example: "The Shapeless Got Some Shape and Form"

Our team was invited to participate in the hospital's grand rounds, where we presented our work with Teresa and her family. As those attending the meeting were mostly psychiatrists, nurses, and social workers, we presented the case using the hospital's required and familiar format, making it inviting for them to listen and participate.

Identifying Information

Teresa was a 16-year-old Mexican girl, who had been admitted to the adolescent girls unit for a suicide attempt and was referred to the family therapy team. The doctors thought that, given her history of conflict with her mother, both could benefit from family therapy.

Presenting Situation

After a long fight with her mother—one of many—Teresa overdosed with prescription pills with the intention of killing herself. She was taken to the hospital and then admitted to the adolescent girls' inpatient unit for psychiatric and psychological assessment and treatment. She and her family were referred to the family therapy team on the unit.

Teresa was sexually abused by her maternal grandfather from the age of 6 to 12; he, along with her maternal grandmother, lived with the family at the time. At age 12, Teresa disclosed the abuse to her mother, after which her grandfather disappeared and, three months later, her grandmother died of diabetes. Teresa had a history of drug abuse, and when she entered the hospital she was using cocaine.

Treatment: The Clinical Process

We saw the family every other week for seven sessions, for approximately 1 hour each. These were conducted by two therapists[7] (male and female) in the room, assisted behind the mirror by the team that included colleagues and supervisors.

Though our clinical preference, in keeping with a collaborative philosophy, is to have all conversations about the client with them present, for learning purposes we sometimes find it useful to have discussions without them present. We, however, let the families know of these conversations and their content. In this situation the students and supervisors had a conversation in which they discussed the previous meeting. We then asked students about their needs for the session, with questions such as, "What do you need from the supervisor and the team today?" and "How can we be useful?"

The therapists began the session with the family, and after about 40 minutes the members of the reflecting team were invited to join in the conversation with the family and the therapists. This was accomplished in a number of ways: having a conversation among themselves, with the clients and therapists listening; having a conversation with the therapist, with the clients listening; and having a conversation with the clients, with the therapist listening. All variations aimed to invite reflective processes and elicit different ideas from the members of the therapy team.

Our Ideas

In this clinical instance, therapists chose to use some ideas and techniques from solution-focused therapy, narrative therapy, and brief therapies that had been part of their previous training, though the therapists and team both work on the assumption that conversation and dialogue are transformative and create possibilities for change. We believed that this family wanted to change and that they had the resources to do so.

During our initial meeting we learned that Teresa lived with her mother, her 17-year-old brother, and an uncle who was described as disabled and alcoholic. Her mother, Teresa, and her brother attended the first meeting. Although Teresa's parents had been divorced for sometime, the children maintained some contact with the father. Teresa had not returned to school after she was admitted to the hospital for the suicide attempt. We also learned that Teresa and her mother had already been in group therapy at an addiction center for treatment for her cocaine use, and they were both in individual treatment as well.

Teresa's brother described her as "stubborn, spoiled, aggressive, angry, and irresponsible." Mother believed that Teresa's behavior was the result of the sexual abuse she had suffered as a child. Though the abuse was a dominant theme, the therapists decided not to dwell on it, based on the idea that it is not necessary to understand the cause or origin of a problem to create possibilities. Instead, they chose to focus on resources and positive experiences. They learned about Teresa's strengths: her love for animals and her dream to be a veterinarian. When Teresa and her mother talked with the therapists about their relationship, Mother said that she trusted her daughter despite everything, and Teresa expressed that she trusted, loved, and respected her mother. She also saw her mother as a very strong, positive influence in her life and someone she could always count on.

Teresa directed the conversations in therapy toward many different issues, including her sexual abuse as a child, her school situation, her grandfather's running away, her grandmother's death, and the grief it caused the family. She also addressed the drugs, partying, family members' roles, parenting issues such as negotiation and discipline, future plans, and vocational choices. We were able to combine storytelling that had to do with their past as well as stay focused on their hopes for the future. Although it may seem hard to believe, we often laughed and joked in the sessions.

During the third session Teresa announced to the therapist that she had made the decision to stop using cocaine and start working. She had missed the school term, so she found a job as a veterinary assistant. She stopped using drugs and, week by week, she and her family continued to make changes. Teresa said that she was tired of "wasting her life" and she wanted to do something productive to make up for the time she had lost.

Therapists' and Clients' Perspectives on Therapy

A letter[8] that illustrated some of the family's achievements was written by the therapists and given to Teresa and her family in the last session:

> Let's finish with you, Teresa. First, we would like to tell you that we are very impressed by all the changes you have made in such a short time. This is quite unusual, young lady, to be able at age 16 to leave drugs behind, to acknowledge and recognize the risks along the way, and to know what works for you and what is useless, and what will help you build your own life project. It looks like nobody knows your resources better than you do. You have found a job that suits your professional interest, and you have found a way to create a team with your family. You know that your way of solving your life dilemmas has changed. In the past you used to direct your anger towards yourself or others, but now you have realized that everything takes time and that words can help you face any situation even if it appears difficult at first.

At the end of the last session, the therapists asked the family to share their thoughts about their therapy with the team. They are summarized in the following statements:

> The surprise was to have a different view. . . . When you entered the room and talked among yourselves in front of us . . . [it] is a different system, but it works like a mirror. (Mother and *Teresa*)

> We felt we had more support. Therapy is sharing with other people, it's not being afraid to be exposed. (Mother)

> There were more people listening to me . . . I liked it. (*Teresa*)

In the last session, the mother shared that she saw the therapists' youth as an asset. She also valued their curiosity and genuine concern in their story and dilemmas.

It is important to know that we are in the presence of people whose work is not to tell us what to do or how to do it, but to provide other views and ways to understand our attitudes, actions, and solve our problems in the best possible way. (Mother)

The decisions were made by me. (*Teresa*)

We learned to have conversations and to give ourselves time to think and reflect. Together we built this path and it will be very difficult to get us off it. (Mother)

When the family members described what the therapeutic process had been like for them, they said:

Something that arrived here shapeless got some shape and form through the trust and the atmosphere; it's something that we slowly built together. (Mother)

They remarked that this experience had been different from other therapies they had had:

The way you ask questions . . . the first psychologist I went to see, I did not like to go. . . . She had an ugly way of asking . . . not here . . . psychology is cool! (*Teresa*)

When we asked them what advice they might have for therapists working with families like them, they responded:

It was great . . . we slowly became sure of ourselves. Keep the freshness you have, this possibility to develop trust, to be with us, to compliment us, to be part of the team, to be close to our problems and dilemmas. From the first day I did not feel that you were out there, like therapists; you were right here, like people. (Mother and *Teresa*)

Some Afterthoughts

In writing this chapter we were able to revisit our experiences at the hospital and reflect on the challenges we faced and how we approached them. Despite the limitations of space and resources at the hospital, the flexibility of a postmodern approach allowed us to work productively.

After rereading the quotes from our clients and students, taken from session notes and therapists' written reflections, we were struck by what we saw as similarities in the experiences of clients and therapists. These include, for example, the development of a sense of personal and professional agency, the importance of being part of a team, the usefulness of reflective processes, and the value of a trusting and respectful atmosphere both for therapy and for supervision. This drives home Anderson's (1997) idea that a collaborative approach is a philosophical stance that can be applied to therapy, supervision, consulting, or training. It is a way of being in relationship with the other person.

Writing this chapter together made us realize, yet again, the importance of making time to nurture our relationship and have conversations about our work and ourselves. We close with this quote from one of our students which also reflects our sentiments:

Thank you for this opportunity to learn from everyone! (*Eugenia*)

Endnotes

1. Pseudonyms are used to preserve student's privacy. These are the authors' translations from the students' original, written reflections in Spanish.
2. Nora Rentería, Irma Rodríguez-Jazcilevich, and Conchita Quiroz were the supervisors who were extremely generous sharing their time and knowledge.
3. We would like to thank everyone in the hospital who welcomed us and supported our work there, especially. Special thanks to Dr. Sylvia Becerril, Dr. Armando Gutiérrez, Mtra. Ana María Ramírez, Dra. Miriam del Valle, and Dra. Rocío Chávez for their collaboration and support.
4. By "reflections" we mean their reactions, thoughts, feelings, and questions about the readings and the sessions we had that day. The quotes from students in this article come from those reflections.
5. See Madsen (1999).
6. The therapists in this case were Rocio Martinez Zaid and Alberto Díaz. The authors thank Rocío for the transcript and notes of the sessions.
7. This is a translation to English from the Spanish original.

References

Andersen, T. (1987). The reflecting team: Dialogue and metadialogue in clinical work. *Family Process, 26*, 415–428.

Andersen, T. (1990). *The reflecting team*. New York: Norton Books.

Anderson, H. (1995). Collaborative language systems: Toward a postmodern therapy. In R. Mikesell, D.D. Lusterman, & S. McDaniel (Eds.), *Integrating family therapy: Family psychology and systems theory* (pp. 27–44). Washington DC: American Psychological Association.

Anderson, H. (1997). *Conversation, language and possibilities: A postmodern approach to therapy*. New York: Basic Books.

Anderson, H. (2000). Supervision as a collaborative learning community: Supervision bulletin. American Association of Marriage and Family Therapy.

Anderson, H. (2004a). Collaborative therapy: Revitalizing therapists and broadening possibilities. Taos Institute.

Anderson, H. (2004b). Personal Communication. International Summer Institute. Playa del Carmen, Mexico. June 2004.

Anderson, H. (2005). Myths about not-knowing. *Family Process, 44*, 497–502.

Anderson, H. & Goolishian, H. (1990). Supervision as collaborative conversation: Questions and reflections. In H. Brandau (Ed.), *Von der supervision zur systemischen vision*. Salzburg: Otto Muller Verlag.

Gergen, K.J., Hoffman, L., & Anderson, H. (1995). Is diagnosis a disaster? A constructionist trialogue. In F. Kaslow (Ed.), *Handbook of relational diagnosis* (pp. 102–118). New York: John Wiley & Sons.

Holmes, S. (1998). Understanding our relational expertise in food for thought and dialogue, Houston Galveston Institute. Galveston VII Symposium, Paradise, TX, January 1998.

Madsen, W. (1999). *Collaborative therapy with multistresed families*. New York: Guilford Press.

Shotter, J. (2005). Goethe and the refiguring of intellectual inquiry: From "aboutness-thinking" to "withness-thinking" in everyday life. *Janus Head, 8*, 132–158.

CHAPTER 17

Women at a Turning Point: A Transformational Feast

DEBBIE FEINSILVER, EILEEN MURPHY, AND HARLENE ANDERSON

Believing . . . that man is an animal suspended in webs of significance that he himself has spun, I take culture to be those webs, and the analysis of it to be therefore not an experimental science in search of law but an interpretive one in search of meaning. It is explication I am after, construing social expressions on their surface enigmatical.

Clifford Geertz (2000, p. 5)

The provision of culturally appreciative and sensitive services unique to participants' expressed needs has increasingly become a priority for therapists, educators, and researchers. This is our story of a project in which we sought to access the voices, unique experiences, competencies, and needs of women identified as "homeless"—most with histories of substance abuse and domestic violence that included prison, prostitution, and poverty. We wanted to learn about the women's lives, self-identities, and histories from their first-person narratives. Specifically, we wanted to learn about their experiences of prior treatment, and use what we learned, along with them, to cocreate personalized tailored counseling services to maximize the opportunity for successful outcomes. Our story highlights and interlaces how we used our collaborative and conversational approach to position ourselves as learners to invite the women's expertise, understandings, and meanings concerning their lives—past, present, and future. Through the relationships and process, the women moved from a deficit discourse to one in which they found new possibilities for their identities and their lives. Our story is based on the collective memories of our experiences and relationships with the women.

The women in our story came from many walks of life—with diversity in color, language, socioeconomic class, and culture, and with differences in resources, educations, and aptitudes. They were able to transcend and use the richness of these differences to create an intercultural community. In the broadest sense, we have used "culture" to denote the varying systems of meaning and frameworks of reality, which have informed and maintained our identities and how we have lived our lives. Throughout the project, we thought of ourselves as a multiplicity of cultures encountering other cultures—a psychotherapy culture meeting a lay public culture, an organizational culture meeting another, one ethnic group meeting another, one religion meeting another, the so-called privileged and underprivileged meeting each other.[1] We did not want to obscure the fact that, within different contexts in our society, individuals have been subjected to varying amounts of privilege and penalty based on their category of identity and the people with whom they have related. Nevertheless, we wanted to avoid and minimize our participation in maintaining, exacerbating, or creating similar differentials in our work.

We consider this project to be an example of research-as-part-of-every-day-practice in which therapists and clients join in a participatory inquiry to mutually explore the task-at-hand and use what they learn to create local knowledge that will be useful to both therapists and clients in their joint endeavors. This kind of as-we-go-along-together "insider research" differs from an after-the-fact "outsider research" in that the latter then proceeds to transfer the learning across similar subject populations. In other words, we define our "insider research" as a collaborative process in which the persons that we want to learn about fully participate with us and with each other in an inquiry that is both theirs and ours.

In this chapter, we will walk the reader through the narrative of a transformational feast. We describe—though condensed because of space—our collaborative process, sprinkling in our comments and the women's voices while noting that it is impossible to capture the richness of a conversation or to give justice to others' words, sentiments, life experiences, and wisdom. In and through a relationship created by a conversational process embedded with local knowledge and new meanings, we hope to demonstrate how new identities and futures can develop.

Invitation to a Feast: Collaboratively Creating the Recipe

The new executive director of a nonprofit organization that served homeless women, mostly with histories of substance abuse and domestic violence, asked Harlene to develop a counseling project. Founded by two Roman Catholic nuns, the organization's mission was to provide homeless women with a safe and supportive rehabilitation environment that made it possible for them to become economically and emotionally self-sufficient. The organization's mission included the broadly accepted cultural norms of learning to live within the parameters of society by working, paying rent, supporting families, and remaining drug free. There were explicit rules—based on the organization's values—aimed at achieving these norms and that served as evaluation criteria for success. Women entered the program as a cohort and remained in it for 6 to 8 months, continued participation in the program (which required educational or vocational training), membership in a 12-step group, maintained attendance in a life-skills group, and volunteer work in the community. Individual and group counseling were sometimes offered or required. The women we worked with lived in what were called "scattered sites," literally living separately in their own apartments scattered around the city.

The founders and the organization had a local and national reputation for their dedication, resourcefulness, and excellence that was substantiated by a visit to the program from Oprah. Though there were many miracle stories, the staff was ever aware of some residents' failure to complete the program or succeed afterwards. Though the staff consistently strove to make a difference in the women's lives, they were ever mindful of the daunting undertaking they set for the women and themselves. Given high rates of recidivism and relapse in their target population, they believed that these women were very "troubled" and needed "intensive" counseling to achieve norms indicative of success. Hence, the director, who was one of Harlene's former students, hoped that the collaborative approach would offer new possibilities to help the residents become successful while in the program and afterwards.

In response to the director's invitation to meet with Harlene for an initial planning session, Harlene wondered with the director about who else might attend the initial planning meetings as well as who would serve as conversational partners. The director suggested the program's social worker and Harlene suggested three colleagues at the Houston Galveston Institute (HGI).[2] One goal of the initial planning meeting was to brainstorm and explore options for the counseling project, including delineating and understanding the needs of the organization and the women. Another goal was to determine how to include the residents' voices and to maximize their participation in the project. Although the organization and we both shared a desire to champion successful outcomes, we were historically different in our approaches to them. Whereas the organization placed an emphasis on the value principles that informed the in-place program structures essential to its mission, we placed an emphasis on the self-determined needs equally identified by both staff and resident. Our inquiries were designed to identify specific areas with which they wanted our help (and those with which they did not). We wanted to know what their perspectives were on how we might be helpful or how we might make things worse. In this vein, we felt that it would be important to recognize that the women were mandated clients and that, similarly, we were mandated therapists.

We brought our bias and a collaborative spirit about the importance of belongingness, participation, and ownership to the table. We knew that if we wanted the women to accept us as intruders into their lives and to maximize their contribution to the project, we needed to include them in the conversations about the project's design. With this in mind, an idea emerged in the initial planning meeting that we needed to start with a pilot project in which we would learn about the women, their expressed needs, and their perspectives regarding an ideal counseling service. We had the staff's blessing, and we now needed the women's.

Our[3] next step was to initiate a meeting with the executive director, the staff, and a cohort of eight women. In this meeting we introduced ourselves and our intent. We highlighted the importance of their input in determining what services were needed and what they should look like. Following the meeting's general introductions and the usual agenda items, we convened smaller groupings with the therapists, the staff, and the women, which afforded the residents and the therapists the opportunity to become acquainted with each other and to talk about the project.

Toward our goal of collaboration, we strived to become aware of the preunderstandings that we brought to our clinical and research endeavor, and the risk that these understandings may unduly define, form, or contextualize the client sitting in front of us, as well as what the client might say. We also strived to learn about the preunderstandings that our clients had about us and about counseling and therapy, including the way that they identified us and their expectations of us. We wanted to genuinely invite their participation as a right and respond to its value in creating knowledge that may affect them. In this vein, we wanted to position ourselves with the women, similarly as we had with the staff, as collaborative conversational partners rather than as experts on their lived experiences or their destinies. In our experience, this positioning encouraged less hierarchical and more egalitarian relationships, and the relationships among all participants in the process became more human and intimate rather than mechanical and distant. We were ever reminded that we were dialogically intertwined living beings.

As we learned about the women, three significant points emerged. First, the women were at yet another crossroad in their lives, and while seeking employment, furthering their education, and living on their own were exciting and gratifying, they felt at the same time uncertain and lonely. A noteworthy observation by one participant highlighted how the scattered site design unwittingly fostered an isolation and alienation that they had already experienced: "I have no one to talk with and feel safe with. No one understands where I'm coming from." Second, the majority of the women were worried and vexed about finding time to add counseling to their schedules and finding transportation to it as well. Yet, they expressed an overwhelming desire for emotional support to deal with their struggles and loneliness. And third, they were surprised and pleased that we wanted their opinions.

Although described by the staff as women with similar histories of substance abuse and domestic violence, we learned that the women had diverse backgrounds and experiences. Culturally, they broadly identified themselves using our words—African-American, Middle Eastern, Latino, and Caucasian. Cautious that labels can confuse the person with the types and categories of people that labels convey, we wanted to learn about each woman, to hear her unique story. We always heeded, however, our reality that there was never one story to tell and that there were countless versions of each. Influenced by our bias that the client was the expert on her lived experience, and based on what we had learned from the staff and women to this point—especially that each woman had been in and out of various treatment programs—it was important to hear everyone's unique story and self-description. As one woman poignantly said, "We wouldn't be homeless if it had helped us."

We suggested to the director and staff, based on the conversations above that included the women, that the project continue in two phases. In Phase I, we would meet separately with each woman in her apartment. In Phase II, we would meet with the women as a group at HGI. The combined goal was to continue to learn about the women, their previous counseling experiences, encounters with other "helpers," and to access their ideas about the design and preferred ingredients of a counseling program that would best fit their unique circumstances. In addition, we wanted to continue building positive relationships with them. As we had found that it was sometimes less difficult for people to first speak and express themselves when the conversations were more or less one-on-one, we hoped that the comfortableness attained in Phase I would transfer to the larger group conversations of Phase II. Equally important, we hoped that the conversations initiated in Phase I would continue in Phase II and foster the generative process.

Kitchen Sensibilities and Listening as Learners: Phase I

There was no one to talk with and feel safe and to understand where I was coming from.

Marla,[4] age 35

We go to work, and they don't know our situation and we don't tell them our situation.

Leticia, age 28

In-home conversations. While remaining sensitive to the women's concerns about time and transportation, we were eager to begin the intimate conversations of Phase I, and while desiring to develop positive relationships, we offered to meet with each woman in her apartment. Six of the eight women made appointments. We respected the other two women's insurmountable schedule difficulties and did not interpret or describe them as "resistant" or "unmotivated," as some might be tempted to do when working with people sometimes designated by others as "treatment failures" or "revolving-door" clients.

We designed a format for the in-home conversations that we hoped would replicate the relationship-building that had presented itself in the initial planning meeting. We invited their first-person descriptions that we hoped would become the beginnings of a dialogical storytelling process. We wanted to hear the telling of a first-person narrative in which the women could express their self-determined identities and meanings. It was important that the process not simply be a retelling of a single account of reality, but rather in this instance, the telling of an account through a dialogical experience in which both parties would become conarrators. We wanted to maximize the opportunity of continuing to learn more about the women by using our curiosity that, in turn, would invite them into a joint inquiry with us and that would be inherently generative. We described our suggested format with each woman and all agreed.

The format of the in-home conversation included client and therapist talking with each other while two other therapists served as reflective listeners. One of us engaged in a conversation with the resident, beginning with a spoken general interest: "What do you think might be important for us and other professionals to know about you and your life experiences?" We did not bring any other questions with us. Rather, subsequent questions such as, "What gave you the courage to seek help this time?" came from within the conversation with the intent to understand the women's stories and meanings as best as we could from within their realities and frameworks. After approximately an hour, the talking pair paused and listened to the reflective listeners as they shared their inner thoughts and curiosities about the pair's conversation. The reflectors then paused and invited the pair to respond to their reflections. Though each pair addressed the reflections, their response often led their conversation in unexpected directions and sometimes back to an earlier part of the conversation. With reflecting processes, we kept in mind that some utterances would strike the listener, inviting them into conversation while others would not; all utterances would be parts of the natural twists and turns that conversations take.

The in-home conversations were originally scheduled for 1.5 hours, but most lasted 2 hours. The women became deeply involved in talking about their lives. They frequently expressed amazement at being comfortable with talking and felt that the therapists were truly interested and not judging them. In our experience, a person can sense when an inquirer may truly be interested vs., for instance, when an inquirer may merely be collecting facts or asking questions for which they already "know" the answer. Learning and exploring how each woman arrived at this point in her life—her strengths, shadows, experiences, and relationships—provided a window into the lived experiences that were familiar and meaningful to them.

At the close of each in-home meeting we discussed the proposed Phase II group meetings, including practical matters such as days and times, as well as reiterating our intent. Each woman wanted to attend the group meetings, though some wondered about the benefits and worried about logistical concerns.

A key to the project was creating an environment forged in partnership—inviting the women's voices and letting them express themselves in their own manner, acknowledging them as experts in their own lives, and respecting the fact that they alone knew what was important for them to discuss. Basically, we wanted to communicate through our words and actions that we valued them and appreciated what they had to say. Traveling to their worlds—literally and metaphorically—created an opportunity for us, albeit temporarily, to be guests in their lives (Anderson 1997). We were sharers of the human experience rather than fixers of broken objects in need of repair. As the collaborative relationships took shape and the generative conversations grew, the women became more forthcoming and seemingly more self-confident as they experienced the freedom to express themselves in an environment where respect was the paramount principle. The process was a lived example of how when a therapist takes a learning position with these attitudes and actions, the client could spontaneously begin to join as a mutual inquirer, and how new and different possibilities could emerge where none seemed to exist before (Anderson, 1997).

Breaking Bread and Breaking Cultural Barriers: Phase II

You have to go through some tough stuff to come out the other end differently. Everything is a process . . . from the period of stepping back—it brought me a different awareness of life, and with a different awareness of life comes new goals and new directions.

Shalla, age 30

In consultation with the staff, and with respect for the women's unanimous preferences, we agreed to meet as a group once a month on a Saturday for 4 hours over a 4-month period at HGI. In planning, we kept several things in mind. With busy work and school schedules, as well as transportation and childcare concerns, most participants would require great efforts to attend. Being ever mindful of the challenges that faced us and wanting to maximize the possibility that the women would show up for the group meetings, we extended our invitation to the first group meeting and followed up with reminders by mail and phone. Four reminders were presented in person as four of the six women requested an additional in-home session.

In planning for the first Saturday, we imagined that there would be little chance of subsequent groups if the first one did not meet and exceed the women's expectations as well as diminish any apprehensions, foster a meaningful experience, and prove worth their time and trouble. Importantly, we carefully considered how to best welcome the participants and reciprocate the warmth that they had afforded us in their homes.

The greeting. As they were coming on their Saturdays off from work, we scheduled the meeting at 11 a.m. so they would not have to get up too early. We imagined that some might arrive late because of demanding bus schedules, perhaps taking at least 2 hours' worth of travel time. We wanted a welcoming that allowed those coming late to easily fold into the occasion. We wanted to avoid, if at all possible, the dilemma of starting without full attendance as well. Guided by these matters and by our host–guest metaphor and the belief that relationships and conversations go hand-in-hand, we began the meeting by serving lunch on the veranda for the first half-hour. As an expression of our creativity and personalities, we served Mexican and Latin American dishes from a nearby favorite restaurant, using platters and bowls from home and an antique wooden ironing board bedecked in a Guatemalan *reboza*. We wanted to put forward an ambience that spoke "We want you to feel welcomed and special." The ambience we believed was paramount to the kinds of relationships and conversations that we wanted to privilege. As the ritual of "breaking bread" can serve as a cultural metaphor for the beginning of a mutual understanding and the dissolving of interpersonal hindrances, we believed that a lunch on the veranda would serve in establishing our egalitarian objective.

We learned at our first introduction (the meeting with the staff, the therapists, and the women) that the women barely knew each other, so lunchtime gave them an opportunity to meet each other and us again in a relaxed setting. We were ever careful not to assume that we had known any person no matter how long or short our acquaintance had been, and that each time we gathered represented an opportunity to position ourselves to learn differently. Following Anderson's (1997) suggestion, we always met each person as if for the first time. Unquestionably, the women were pleasantly surprised and pleased by our hospitality.

Partner interviews. After lunch, we reconvened inside. We once again reiterated our intent and described our ideas for the day. Informed by this and what we had learned from the apartment interviews, and influenced by the notion of questions as not searches for answers but as invitations to dialogue, we created three sets of conversational "starter questions." (*See* Appendix 1) We referred to them as starter questions because they were a way of introducing our inquiry interests and indicated their provisional nature. With the first set, we asked the women to interview each other in pairs, or what we called partner interviews. Partner interviews seemed a gentle way of inviting intimate conversation. Keeping in mind that though the women seemed to like us, but also had little reason to trust us or to predict our words and actions, we imagined that those less inclined to talk or who might be uncomfortable in larger groupings might be more at ease and willing to talk in smaller groups. We reiterated that our questions were to serve as a conversation starter and that we wanted them to follow their own interests and intuitions and using their own questions. Each of us joined a pair as a silent listener; we always kept in mind that it would be impossible to capture the experience, fullness, and richness of any conversation. To enhance the capture, we gave each pair a flip chart and markers on which to record elements of their conversation. We were strikingly reminded of the risk in making assumptions when one pair did not want to record because one of the women could not read nor write very well, and the other one did not quite know what to do in response. In this instance, one of us carefully offered to record. Because all were deep in conversation, and at their request, we expanded the originally allotted time for this exercise from 30 to 45 minutes.

An unlikely pair. We were amazed at the women's engagement with the questions and with each other. We were equally amazed that some of them naturally seemed to hold the stance of a collaborative therapist. An example was Donna's partner interview with Janice. They were an unlikely pair on several accounts. Donna came from a poverty background and to the program directly out of prison where she had received her high school diploma. Janice, one of the two women who initially declined a request for an in-home conversation, had a master's degree in social work and came to the program after a discharge from a psychiatric hospital. Janice kept to herself during lunch and said very little in the introductions, other than that someone had followed her to the meeting. Janice sat stiffly, looking frightened and ill-at-ease. Donna on the other hand, was cheerful, friendly, and assertive, and took the lead in the partner interview. In response to Donna's first question, Janice talked of being scared of a woman who had been "stalking" her for 20 years. She told of reporting the woman numerous times to the police, adding that neither they nor anyone else had ever believed her or offered protection. With each question thereafter, though she initially responded to it, she always returned to the stalking. Donna never challenged the validity of Janice's story. Instead of trying to steer Janice back to the question, she began to ask her more about the long-term stalking situation. Janice seemed to relax ever-so-slightly. When it was Janice's turn to interview Donna, she went through the list of questions, methodically one-by-one. Though Janice's questioning might have been described as routine-like and unemotional, she seemed touched by Donna's scarred life and her spiritual awakening while in prison.

Bringing the partner conversations into the group. When we reconvened as a group, the women introduced each other to the entire group. Donna was the first to introduce her partner. With seriousness and no indication of disbelief, she shared what she had learned about Janice, emphasizing her social work career and at the same time compassionately sharing the stalking story. Observably, Janice physically relaxed her body and facial expression as Donna continued to introduce her. Janice, in turn, told Donna's story in a considerate and supportive manner and without any hint of judgment regarding Donna's past.

As the paired story sharing continued, the women became very interested in each other's stories, wanting to know more and to talk more about some of the issues that emerged in the sharing process. As they asked questions of each other, they found and discussed similarities in their lives as well as differences. We took a facilitative role in helping to ensure that the curiosities did not prevent any member from completing the introductions of their partner. We also helped them keep track of what they wanted to learn or talk more about by tagging the topics and questions, recording them on a flip chart in their words. These included such things as dealing with past mistakes; feeling guilt and shame; fearing not having a future; finding God; their divergent paths to spirituality; hope; staying in recovery; recognizing unhealthy choices; communication; procrastination; needing encouragement; listening; and choices. We often inserted our own curiosities which facilitated clarity and expansion. For instance, we might have asked "What do you mean by the word—?" or "Would you mind telling us a little more about—?"

Continuing the Conversations

What evolved was unexpected. Initial partner interviews generated lively and bountiful conversation, full of information and enthusiasm. After such a rich conversation, turning to our second set of questions seemed unnecessary; we questioned whether they would disrupt the flow currently unfolding and become out of sync with the conversational trend and the evolving interests that each of the women felt for others. So, with the women in agreement we shelved our next starter questions and focused on what was of interest to them. We divided them into two trios and one pair and asked them to simply talk rather than interview each other about the topics and questions that most interested them. After this round of conversation, the group reconvened for general discussion. They appeared even more animated and friendly with each other and continued to talk about what surfaced in the smaller groups. Our sense at the time was that this was the beginning of a shift or a kind of transformation. We later learned that the women felt that this first group meeting was a safe environment and that they could express themselves and talk about difficult things without fear of being judged by the group members or by us. Even though the women carefully guarded their privacy and safety—not wanting any identifying information to go outside the room for various reasons—they had already begun to speak of how much they missed a sense of community in their lives.

Time flew and the group ended; though we had planned for one more round of small and large group conversations, we stayed in-sync with the women's pacing and interests. We always kept in mind, however, that conversations do not end. Each of us would leave the meeting and participate in inner dialogues with ourselves and in outer dialogues with others. At the end of each meeting, the women unanimously expressed a desire and anticipation for next month's Saturday meeting. They were already participating in and beginning to take ownership of what was being created. For instance, two of the women approached us and asked if they could schedule a counseling session before the next group; one was Janice who had initially declined the "in-home" sessions. And, since they were now engaged in "their" inquiry, we perhaps no longer needed our other sets of starter questions as possibilities for inquiry so we set them aside.

Key Ingredient: Philosophical Stance

Something else I think about, too. I've noticed the past couple of years that children, babies, are being carried in carriers. The whole personal relationship with these babies has changed. They see the world at the knees. They don't have the rhythm of the voice, the heartbeat, the warmth. When they get older, they're going to be different than those that were carried around in their mother's arms.

Donna, age 45

More and more, mental health professionals have placed an increasing premium on the provision of culturally appreciative and sensitive services. By its very nature, the philosophical stance of our collaborative[5] approach has satisfied this provision. By definition the client has been viewed as the expert imbued with qualities that are unique to each human. Said differently, our collaborative approach has challenged its adherents to practice appreciation and sensitivity and to avoid the assumption trap in which a person can be labeled, categorized, or typed. Inherent in this assumption trap has been the risk that any singular identity can become the sole, limiting descriptor for a person or a group of persons. Our collaborative approach avoided what may be seen as the "freezing" of a person's identity. Our experience with these women overcame this caveat. In addition, as evidenced in our experience, opportunities to listen have allowed us to learn more when we have chosen not to make assumptions or filtered the conversation with preconceived ideas about its participants as categories or types of people. We do not suggest that we believe we can be, or that we have pretended to be, blank slates. Instead, our approach has emphasized that, as ever-interpreting beings, we can and must become aware of the multiple influences impeding our interpretations. In other words, how we describe a person can influence how we construct and deconstruct that person, and influence our limitations and possibilities as well as theirs.

Interestingly, we noticed that the women were beginning to think of themselves and each other in new and different ways that were evident in new fragments of meaning emerging in their voices. For instance, Donna expressed the idea of synchrony—a way of being with others simultaneously. She referred to it as a "rhythm" functioning within a relationship—integral to its formation and transformation. Just as a baby carrier might impede the relationship between mother and child, preknowledge, such as categorizing and typing people based upon their life situation, history, race, culture, socioeconomic class or gender, might obstruct the developing relationship, detracting a therapist's ability to relate to the uniqueness of each person and each situation. We have not assumed to know a client's self-descriptions, or the meanings of those descriptions, or the kinds of services they wanted or needed. Nothing could have replaced the process of learning from the clients themselves—they were the experts in their own lives. This did not mean that we did not "know" anything about particular cultures or groups of people. We did not, however, want to generalize this "knowing" or unwittingly have it interfere with getting to know the person sitting in front us and their situation from their perspective. We wanted to appreciate and experience each person as unique, and as mentioned earlier, as a person or life situation that we have not met before. We wanted to learn continuously about, for instance, their multifaceted identities without the expectation that these identities would remain predictable or constant or that our "learning" would reinforce them.

As collaborative therapists, we have sought to minimize and avoid taking advantage of power differentials among members as well as between facilitators and members (Anderson, 1997). We have illustrated this by inviting clients to share responsibility and in unexpected and subtle ways such as encouraging the client's voice, honoring it, and letting it influence the development of the conversation. Importantly, when we have allowed our clients to talk *with* each other and rather than *to* each other us and engage in a mutual inquiry, they have developed a sense of participation, engagement, and ownership. It has been in the merging of the conversation and relationship that participants have began to feel that their stories were worthy of the telling and valued on many levels without judgment. Conversation as shared inquiry became a joint activity of exploration that, in turn, led to new meaning, understanding, knowledge, and possibility. Thus, our clients naturally experienced a sense of belonging that led to further participation. Participation encouraged engagement, and engagement encouraged a sense of shared responsibility for the task-at-hand, including the relationships, the process, and the outcome.

Savoring the Ideas: Subsequent Saturday Conversations

> It's like you go into this house and in this house there's a room and in the room there's a closet and in the closet there's a dresser and in the dresser there will be some drawers, so you just start looking.
>
> **Donna, age 45**

At the women's request, the next three Saturdays continued the rituals that we were creating together. Each meeting began informally with a few minutes for the women to check-in with each other and catch up on their lives in between the meetings. We then collected the items that the women wanted to talk about that day. Topics introduced in the first meeting continued to be focus of the subsequent groups and new ones emerged as well: validation, children and their needs, family, the women's special needs, and community. We continued, at their liking, to move between smaller conversational groupings and the total membership.

The nature of the group members' relationships and conversations was transformed over time. You might say that the women appeared to blossom right in front of our eyes. We noticed, for instance, how the women subtly began to shift from a culturally driven dependence on the others and us to a delicate balance of independence and interdependence with each other, fostering a sense of shared responsibility among themselves and thus a sense of community. Notably, the women became more talkative and forthcoming through the companionship and support of their peers.

Coinciding with these shifts, the women became more and more active in facilitating their own process. Though initially we tagged the agenda topics that they wanted to keep track of on a flip chart, they naturally and increasingly joined in naming the topics as well as facilitating the discussion as their senses of competency came forward. We continued to offer our comments and questions, though always from our preferred tentative posture, being ever sensitive to their responses to us so as not to dominate or steer their agenda. The conversations became conversations among all of us, with each of us participating in form and direction. This shift from the culturally identified experts as leaders and facilitators to the membership sharing in these responsibilities was typical in our experience. We have found that when collaboration is demonstrated through our words and actions, others seem to spontaneously collaborate with us and with each other.

Drinking It All In

It's a maturing and bending of my mind to be able to think beyond circles of what you see and hear about a person.

Felicia, age 30

Positioning ourselves as learners allowed us to enter into the women's worlds in ways that were previously blocked when we took an expert's position. We, as well as the participants, attentively listened to each one's story about her family and relationships colored with their trials, disappointments, sadness, and frustrations. Participants, however, heard each other's stories differently than they might have in the past for what seems like the simple reason of making room for and allowing ample time for each voice. Making room for and inviting the women's humor, strengths, and resiliencies heightened their sense of agency. Not only did we embrace these views, they also became critical to the participants as they learned to listen to each other in an expanded way. Just as the women had experienced the reflecting listening dimension during the in-home conversations, they likewise became reflectors of each other's experiences in the group settings. Here they provided the storyteller the joy of being heard without judgment or assumption, while at the same time, experiencing that their voice had worth and import. It was as if the more they became familiar with each other, the more they questioned and let go of their preassumptions. As they did this, they began to notice what they referred to as each other's previously unacknowledged "inner strengths." As we continued to position ourselves in a more egalitarian manner, as we continued to demonstrate a lack of commitment to a pre-set content agenda, and as we continued to make room for the women's voices and expertise, the women increasingly took the lead. In turn, the dialogues became more multifaceted and resources leaped forward.

The Feast Continued: Their Mission Statement

> So when this is over with we can look back and say, okay, I remember when we said those thoughts and how we felt about the support we got from each other.
>
> **Janice, age 54**

Participation in this project reminded us that sometimes the best things that have happened in life were also things that were unplanned. Though we facilitated the individual and group meetings to provide for the inclusion of all voices, including room for the spontaneity of their voices and space for the familiar and the new, the final group meeting took on a life and spirit of its own. In keeping with our bias and intent—to access and learn from the women's expertise—we provided ample time at the last meeting for wrap-up conversation and (e)valuation. We used a conversational format rather than traditional survey and evaluation methods to glean the heart and nuances of the women's thoughts and ideas. We introduced our preplanned questions: "What did you like about the project?" "What would have made this project more valuable to you?" "What might we do differently if we were to start anew?" and "What might you do differently if we were to start anew?" We also invited them to compose their (e)valuation of the project and us. The women, however, did not want to talk about the project or us. They wanted to talk about themselves and their successes. We sat back and listened with amazement as one participant went to the writing board, taking one of our places, while the rest of the women sprouted ideas, thoughts, and feelings.

A sense of community. The women wanted to say who they were, what they were about, and how they had changed. They wanted "witness" to their words, to where they had traveled and where they intended to go. They also wanted acknowledgment for their journeys. Through the fellowship, through sharing of life experiences, through trying to understand each other, through becoming a part of each other's lives, and through the strength and understanding fostered by this, they formed and called their collective selves a "community." They built a network that included a sense of belonging and the support that came from it; this became, for them and their families, important elements for "healing" and "growth." They concluded that when they were not supported by healthy, positive environments, they often found unhealthy and unsafe ways not to be alone. At the same time, they felt that balancing independence with interdependence was a key to self-efficacy. They did not want what had happened among them to be forgotten. Janice's words above captured their sentiments. We were not surprised when they concluded that they wanted the group meetings to continue and that they felt strongly that other women in the program would benefit from the groups. Their hastily written words on the tablet that day grew and bloomed. What follows, in their exact words, was a testament to what that these women created and embraced regarding themselves and their families.

> We, the participants of Building Safer Families,[6] agree to be responsible for building better lives for ourselves and our families. We will do this through prioritization, acceptance, and respect for our uniqueness with unconditional love, lack of judgment or criticism, and living our values for our families and ourselves. We will recognize and maintain the objective that we know what is most important. We will continue to build and maintain strength by moving forward in order to grow. We hope to maintain independence and interdependence through this group. We will remember this group for appreciating the common bonds as well as the uniqueness of one another.

We congratulated the women on their remarkable accomplishments and, in our enthusiasm, we told them that they had created a "mission statement." In hindsight, their words did not need a name or a description. Their inspiration to write these final words was perhaps the most meaningful experience for us. The words became a paragon not only for community at work but for us as well and symbolized the true significance of client expertise.

Freedom and Hope

> You never really master anything. You know as much as you know until you find new information.

Stella, age 27

Just as we did not assume that you can create the whole story or know a person from a piece of it, we did not assume that these participants' experiences were universal to all women. We only wish to share what we have learned from them. As Anderson (1997) noted in her report of interviews with clients about their experiences of successful and unsuccessful therapy, clients told her that they wanted to be listened to, heard, and believed. They wanted to feel safe and to be accepted without judgment for their choices—both good and bad. They want to be valued for who they were and who they have been and are becoming as well. They wanted a sense of "hope" and "freedom." (*See* Appendix 2).

We have found that establishing and fostering the conditions for collaborative relationships and dialogical conversations has naturally invited transformation. An interactive process that has included inviting a client's voice, seeking their expertise, and continuing efforts to understand another's view have made possible a deeper meaning and understanding of life to emerge and expand that have yielded new senses of agency. Through the women's ability to participate and contribute, they experienced respect, acceptance, and a sense of personal worth. Though from diverse cultures, backgrounds, and experiences, the women were accepting and supporting of their differences and willing to learn from one another. Not being marginalized by us or by each other helped create relationships and processes in which the fullness of each woman as a person and their unique lives could be seen, not just the dysfunctional aspects. These women exhibited incredible strength; they were proud of having been alone and having survived. They acknowledged mistakes but wanted to make things better. Spirituality impacted their lives tremendously as did the need for community, and they all validated how powerful the groups were in answering both these needs. The therapists and the clients learned about the likeness of people while appreciating the differences. Over time, the initial deficient labels and identities such as "homeless," "substance abuser," and "victim of domestic violence" gave way to expanded and more useful notions of self and made room for each woman's unique goals as well as common collective goals such as independence, self-efficacy, and honoring a sense of one's female identity. In and through their spoken conversations with each other and with us, and in and through their silent ones with themselves, they established a sense of freedom from the past and hope for the future.

Acknowledgement

We thank Christine Zunker for her participation in the stimulating conversations about the meaning of "intercultural" and for her help with an earlier draft of this chapter.

Endnotes

1. The colleagues are coauthors Debbie Feinsilver, Eileen Murphy, and Judy Elmquist. We dedicate this chapter to our beloved colleague Judy who died of cancer November 10, 2002.
2. Harlene served as the Project Leader and attended the initial meeting with the executive director, social worker, and therapists; also present during the first group meeting in Phase II. Debbie, Eileen, and Judy jointly facilitated all Phase I and Phase II meetings.
3. We have changed the women's names to protect their privacy.
4. See Anderson (2003, 1997) and chapters 1–4 of this volume for a full discussion of a collaborative language systems approach (collaborative therapy) and its philosophical stance.
5. The project had been named Building Safer Families.

Reference

Anderson, H. (1997). *Conversation, language and possibilities: A postmodern approach to therapy.* New York: Basic Books.

Three Sets of Starter Questions

Set I: Partner Interviews

1. Introduce yourself to your partner.
2. What are your strengths?
3. What are you most proud of about yourself?
4. What are the most important things that you would like others to know about you?
5. If you have been in counseling or treatment programs, what was your experience like?
6. What was your counselor like?
7. What would you most like to understand about yourself and your life?
8. What questions would you like to ask each other or us?

Set II: Small Group Conversations

1. What did your counselor understand about you?
2. What did your counselor not understand about you?
3. What do you wish a counselor would understand/know about you?
4. What would you have liked to know about your counselor?
5. Among family and friends, who understands you the most? How do you know they understand you?
6. Who understands you the least? How do you know they don't understand you?
7. What questions would you like to ask each other or us?

Set III: Small Group Conversations

1. Describe a counseling program that would best suit your needs.
2. Describe your ideal counselor.
3. Describe the kind of relationship you would have with your counselor?
4. How would you know if the counseling was helpful?
5. What questions would you like to ask each other or us?

What the Women Considered Important for Therapists to Remember: Using Their Words and Ours

- The importance of "loving oneself first in order to take care of children."
- The "tendency to think of everything negative and miss the positive."
- The need for "help with making decisions, not someone else making them for you."
- Going to the shelter (Wellsprings) was viewed as "a sign of strength."
- Women did not think of their previous drug abuse counselors as counselors but rather as their "leader to sobriety"; the counselor role was more expanded than the label suggests.
- The "hindrance when AA focuses on the past rather than moving forward."
- "Recovery implies that you are going to get something back that you once had. What about women who never had much to begin with? Do they need something different?"
- The importance of the "spiritual" component in one's life.
- The importance of client and professional being mindful that there are multiple ways to identify a person. "Labels and words such as drug user or homeless are limiting."
- The importance of acknowledging and expanding multiple self identifies; although identified as drug user in recovery, "Keep in mind we are also others, such as friend, good listener, respectful, resourceful, student, hard worker, et cetera."

- Women's "individual differences" and "individual needs require different problem solutions."
- Recovery was often based on "faith."
- "A woman has to be ready for counseling; no one can make her ready."
- "Wanting to change has to come from within."
- "Talking to someone who really listens is helpful in contemplating recovery"; it can help to "bring out our thoughts and perhaps motivate you to get ready."
- "Women need healthier relationships—need to have boundaries in order to forgive, accept, and to be humble."
- "Feeling the feelings helps so they no longer have the power over you."
- "Success comes from admitting you have a problem, believing in a higher power, turning your life over to God."
- "Women feel alone with their problems."
- "The importance of a real friend."
- "The importance of a community.

CHAPTER 18

Dialogues in a Psychiatric Service in Cuba

KLAUS G. DEISSLER

Working in the fields of family, systemic, and finally postmodern therapies since the mid-1970s, I have many of my closest professional friends outside of Germany and Europe. With increased globalization, one might find oneself sharing more philosophical and therapeutic assumptions with those who live far away than those nearby; at least, this has been the case for me. In this chapter, I share the history and development of my relationship with my Cuban colleagues.

I begin the story by sharing a dream that lead me to where I am today. Earlier in my career, when I worked routinely as a psychotherapist, I would dream about working for a couple of years in South Africa, a couple years in Argentina, and a couple of years in the United States. South Africa fascinated me because of the opportunity to transform apartheid into a multiethnic community; Argentina, because of its strong European influence, especially the Spanish language; and finally the United States, which I found attractive because it was less history-bound and more open to the future than Europe. Having these simple ideas in mind, I dreamed from time to time of leaving Europe for six years to tour the world. However, I always felt bound to Europe because earning a living long-term would be restricted elsewhere.

Given these dreams, in the late 1990s, I had several opportunities to spend time with a close friend, Dr. Siegfried Schulz, a veterinarian at the University of Marburg and a painter. One day Siegfried suggested that I go with him on his next trip to Cuba. He had been doing research on ozone treatment of tumors in rats, and he suggested I could come along with him for some holiday time. Although Siegfried painted a beautiful and colorful picture of Cuba and his work at the research institute in Havana, I was reluctant and skeptical: I did not know anyone there, I could not speak Spanish, and what would I do while Siegfried was working? I rejected his offer, but Siegfried persisted in trying to convince me. The more I resisted, the more insistent he became. Finally I said, "Okay, next time you go to Havana, bring me an invitation to teach in the university's department of psychiatry. This will allow me to work, too; then we can spend some free time together." I was skeptical about the possibility, but I hoped the idea would successfully end our conversation about my visiting Cuba.

However, Cuba continued to appear in my life in other contexts. I soon learned of rock guitarist Ry Cooder's engagement with Cuban music and the Buena Vista Social Club music group. Coincidentally, around that time, my colleague Astrid Wortmann gave me some novels written by a Cuban author, which I read with great enthusiasm.

When Siegfried returned from his visit to Cuba, he greeted me with a bright smile. "Here is your invitation," he said and handed me an invitation from the director of the university's psychiatric clinic,[1] Prof. Dr. Reina Rodriguez.[2] I could not say no any longer. Siegfried spoke about Reina with enthusiasm. She had received her doctorate at the Humboldt University in East Berlin in 1984 and could, of course, speak German.

Siegfried and I started planning our trip to Cuba. I had an e-mail exchange with Reina, and we agreed upon the seminar topics and the time of my visit. In this process, Siegfried guided me in what to expect and how to plan my visit. However, shortly after I finalized the agreement with Reina, Siegfried told me that he had changed his plan and would be postponing his visit to Cuba. I felt disappointed by Siegfried, who had pushed me to go to Cuba when I did not want to; and now that I wanted to go, he withdrew. I felt trapped; I really wanted to go but felt insecure because I did not know the country or anyone there. However, I did not want to postpone my visit because I could not anticipate the future. I finally decided on a compromise: I would go only for a week. If it was bad I only had to suffer for a week; if it was good, I could return.

I ordered my tickets and thought I could calmly plan my visit to Cuba. Then, about 3 months before I left for Cuba, Reina asked me to bring some psychotropic medications because they needed them and could not afford it. I said, "No!" to myself: "All these years I have worked to construct alternatives to psychopharmacological treatment—especially dialogical approaches to therapy, consultation, and supervision. I am not an M.D. I am a psychologist. Three times, no!" But I was not sure how to tell her.

So I consulted friends and psychiatrists about the situation. They did not see a problem at all and counseled that I should not make it a question of principle. So I made the resolution: "Okay, as a guest, I will take them as a present to honor their request, but I will tell them immediately that my work will present alternatives to psychopharmacological treatment." I got psychotropics and put them in a rucksack in my office, and every day I looked at this strange thing waiting to be transported to Cuba.

Just as I had made peace with my plan to bring the medications, Siegfried showed me documents from Cuban customs stating that importing psychotropics is illegal. I felt desperate and did not know what to do. I decided I would request special permission from the Cuban embassy. I phoned the embassy and spoke with a friendly man who seemed to understand my problem and said he would call me back with answer. I waited and called several other times, but no answer. So the day before I left, I decided to smuggle the medications to Cuba. Strangely, after all these intense feelings of rejection, doubt, hope, desperation, I did not feel much passing the customs controls: just a little insolence.

After going through customs, among the many people waiting and waving, I saw three people laughing and waving warmly toward me. They had a little board with "Dr. Klaus" written on it. They seemed to recognize me, maybe from a picture that Siegfried had shown them; at least I recognized Reina that way. We drove to Reina's home for a long night of talking and drinking. It was "love at first sight" (metaphorically speaking): we immediately liked each other and felt strongly that we could work together.

Two days later, I started my seminar with a little story about how I was invited to Cuba. While talking I thought of my dream working in South Africa, Argentina, and the United States. I wondered: "Maybe in Cuba, a Spanish-speaking, multiethnic society with European traditions that is a stone's throw away from the United States, some of the things I have wanted to learn in these other places I can get here?"

Process and Content of the Seminars in Cuba

I believe that my work in Cuba is best described in my Cuban colleagues' words (see below). Nevertheless, I would like to identify the main influences of my work as, in historical order, the Milan systemic approach, Tom Andersen's work, Harry Goolishian's and Harlene Anderson's work, social constructionist theory (e.g., Gergen, Shotter), and postmodern philosophies (e.g., Bakhtin, Lyotard, and Derrida). Although personally I prefer the term "dialogic,"[3] for pragmatic reasons when teaching I refer to it as "reflexive systemic therapy and consultation" (RST) (Deissler, 1997).

Before I share the perspectives of my Cuban colleagues, I will briefly outline my work in Cuba. I have visited Cuba 9 times within 7 years

(1999–2005) and have done more than 10 seminars there, including several conferences. My Cuban colleagues have enthusiastically embraced the forms of practice and the ideas I presented and quickly put them into their daily routines and psychiatric practice. I have also been part of official and unofficial meetings at the university, including participating in the inauguration of the doctorate in medical sciences and serving on the morning shift at the psychiatric clinic. Most participants in the work of these seminars were associated with the university and many worked in its inpatient and outpatient psychiatric clinics that serve individuals and families.[4]

When teaching, I present ideas and practices in a narrative, colloquial, and dialogic manner: mainly I tell stories and intersperse theoretical ideas and concepts, and I do practical exercises and presentations. This becomes an intense way of dialoguing about and experiencing these ideas. Topics that I presented in Cuba included the following, with some formally planned and others improvised:

- History of family therapy, systemic therapies and postmodern variants
- Epistemological/poietological[5] (Deissler, 1989) ways to understand what therapists/consultants do
- Objectivism/realism/rationalism
- (Radical) constructivism, (social) constructionism, postmodern ideas
- The classical way to work with a "reflecting team" (Andersen, 1990)
- Reflexive systemic therapy (Deissler, 1997)
- Postmodern practices, e.g., "as if position" (Anderson, 1997) and "improvisational role-play" as reflecting process and as a form of self-reflecting for collaborators in psychiatric contexts.
- Therapy, consultation, and supervision as "forming dialogical ways" to dissolve "problems" (Deissler, 2000).
- Philosophical stances/attitudes of therapists and consultants (Anderson, 1997)
- "Appreciative organization"[6] (Anderson et al., 2001).

In each seminar I did three to five "reflexive live consultations" (Deissler & Schug, 2000) with clinical situations presented by my Cuban colleagues. These occasions offered the opportunity to demonstrate how different ways of talking simultaneously imply different ways of listening. I talk about these different ways to talk and listen as "polyphonic ethics." This means that this dialogical approach is "multivocal and multiaural," creating a new form of collaborative ethics, which opens up a space for new understanding and possibilities.

An important contextual factor in these visits was that in Cuba there is no pharmacological industry, so medication is a minor part of the practice of psychiatry. From my perspective, in Cuba the field of psychiatry and mental health is in a fortunate position: they have to think about and use different treatment approaches other than medication. Perhaps this necessity is why Cuban psychiatrists have been more receptive to dialogically oriented forms of therapy and consultation than those in other countries. This is in marked contrast to psychiatric contexts in Germany, where patients often seem to be reduced to packages of data that get analyzed, stored, and sometimes treated (the data, not the patients[7]). What is lacking are therapists who feel touched by the stories of the patients. The professionals often seem to be in the position of "untouchable knowledge." What I saw in Cuba was an extremely cordial, warm, and understanding way to relate to patients. Maybe if we learn from Cubans cordiality and they learn from us the philosophical stance of "not knowing" (Anderson, 1997), we will both arrive at what Anders Lind seth (2005), a Norwegian philosopher, calls "not knowing, being touched."

Interview with My Cuban Colleagues

Recently, I interviewed four of my Cuban colleagues[8] to learn about their experience of the seminars and the work that I had been doing with them and their clients. Such interviews are part of reflexive work, allowing me to better understand how my work and ideas have been helpful or not. The interview took place at the university hospital in September 2005.[9] Rather than present the interview in chronological order, the text of the interview is organized by theme to facilitate easier reading. Dingbats indicate a new section of the interview about the same topic.[10]

Changes in Approach to Treatment

Klaus:	What were the main theoretical and practical changes in your daily work [since my visit 7 years ago]?
Maria Eugenia:	Theoretically, our work has been based on Marxist social psychology.... I think that your work has allowed us to take new aspects of communication into consideration and work with greater depth. For instance, the interventions we have used with families in group therapy have been very helpful for the families, the groups and for ourselves.

⨳

Maria Eugenia:	This style of therapy has been very useful; it has allowed us to improve the quality of our work, to continue to develop our own theoretical perspectives, and the practice has positively caught the attention of our professional colleagues, bringing more patient and family referrals.

Elsa: The influence of the RST has permeated all our areas of service. We are working from this approach with individuals, couples, families and groups and with a variety of very difficult problems such as addictions and psychosomatic disorders. From a practical aspect, it is comfortable and much easier to work without the pressure of feeling that we must have answers for everything. Instead, there are constant surprises in almost every session. We have gotten used to listening, to being open to the "new." As therapists, we feel more comfortable with sharing responsibility for the process, enjoying the conversations, and above all, collaboration with patients and coworkers. From the theoretical aspect, we have been able to connect with various perspectives such as constructionism, constructivism, postmodern ideas, and narrative therapies.

❧

Isabel: Maria Eugenia said earlier that we came from a Marxist psychology orientation. Elsa says that we Cubans have been intrusive and directive. Without denying this, I want to stress that in recent years there has been an evolution in our country. Of course, many still practice psychoanalysis, but more recently some psychiatrists have become interested in systemic therapies. Some had moved from an interpretative to existential perspective (working with emotions in the here and now). As these shifts were already underway, it was natural that we were receptive to Klaus's RST approach.

Affect on Personal Lives of Therapists

Klaus: Is there anything you want to say about the effect these changes had on your personal life?

Maria Eugenia: Sure. For instance, I feel that the communication with my daughter, a teenager going into adulthood and struggling with the all the complexities of that stage of life—intra-familiar relationships in general and all the trials common to living with others—has improved. I realize that approaching things from a more conversational position proves to be useful, beneficial, lowers tensions, and makes relations flow easier.

෨

Elsa: Well, my personality and style have changed dramatically. I used to be very incisive, very intrusive, very directive, very impetuous. Now I am much more relaxed, soft, open to change and tolerant— these are changes noted by my coworkers and me.

Patient Response

Isabel: I would like to add that our clinic . . . has always tried not to have patients feel that the therapist is in a position of having the absolute truth. When we started the seminars with Klaus, we began to apply it with patients who had experienced prior treatment, both group and individual, and had complained of lack of problem resolution. We explained to them that it was not because the treatment was good or bad that there was a lack of progress but because the therapists put them in a position of resistance (using psychoanalytic terminology) or, in our terms, "a position of no change." The experience proved very interesting, the patients felt different.

Klaus: In what sense did they feel different?

Isabel: In the first place, they felt accepted. They felt that they could agree or disagree with us because ours was not the only truth. They could choose to accept our premises; having that choice made them, in our eyes, nonresistant. Instead, they were exercising a choice.

Ethics of Respect

Maria Eugenia: One of the reasons I think this technique was well received . . . has to do with the ethical component. Patients and families felt they were treated with respect. It is very important for people to feel respected. I think it was also useful for them because it involved a learning process; as they strove to be heard, they learned to hear themselves.

෨

Isabel:	Following Maria Eugenia's line of thought, the patient's relatives almost always feel guilty for what is going wrong with the patient or treatment, which affects the communication, its quality, its flow. Now, when we use Klaus's approach, the relatives feel comfortable, are cooperative, and often when the patient completes treatment, one of the relatives goes into treatment for his/her own development.

✎

Elsa:	Definitely we Cubans had a way of doing therapy. We were very intrusive, incisive, and directive. Our therapy has changed to a more colloquial language, to a relationship where the consultee feels highly respected. We do not impose dialogue, we share it; this extends to our relationships with colleagues and at home.

Perception of, and Working with, the Patient's Family

Maria Eugenia:	The only thing I would add is that the perception a therapist has of the patient is not the same as the perception he or she has of the patient's family. That is, we try to keep in mind that each family member is different from the others.
Klaus:	How do you see them as different?
Maria Eugenia:	When we have a patient, we now say this person has a "perception" about the family. If, for instance, a patient describes her husband, we do not pass him through a filter to see if he has disorders based on her description. With the family, maybe due to cultural problems, we maintain much stronger affective ties. The perception is different; it is what we know as "catatimia," distortion of perception due to affection.

✎

Elsa:	I think it is much easier to dialogue with the family starting with tentative comments such as, "maybe" or "I might be wrong but I feel that. ..." Whereas in the past I might have closed off the possibility of dialogue if I began with words or attitudes that might have invited resistance or a fight with the family. Having doubt in the air, indicating that I am

not quite sure, or I do not have the "Truth," provides openings that promote the flow of dialogue not only in therapy but in our personal lives as well.

∽

Magalis: Working in this way has allowed us to incorporate relatives in the therapy that we otherwise would not have considered including. We used to work only with closest relatives: the spouse, a parent, and maybe one of the siblings. Now we have expanded our idea of the family; we talk with members that were never listened to before but who are definitely important in the patients' lives.

∽

Maria Eugenia: I am talking about perception, how one perceives the patient, the family, even how one perceives her own family. I think that this procedure with the family is a predictive indicator. For instance, many times it is not the identified patient who really needs the consultation. When the family interacts this way, that is, through conversation, where nobody feels guilty for someone else's disorder, as Isabel said, it helps us therapists to realize how and how much each family member contributes to things not working. Sometimes we realize that the "patient" is not necessarily the one most urgently in need.

Shifting Away from the Expert Position

Isabel: This way of dialoging has contributed to a richer dialogue between therapists because we do not have to demonstrate our expertise. This liberates us from having to be exact or say the correct thing. In other words, we do not contribute more than the patients and their families; we equally contribute to the dialogue, and it is a more human and richer one.

Applications in Training and Supervision

Isabel: We have used this approach not only with medical cases but also with students. It's a didactic tool that promotes communication with and among them.

∽

Isabel:	I think it is important to add that this form of therapy has also been used in our supervision. Our colleagues come to train in the modality of psychotherapy that we practice. This has allowed our colleagues to observe us and understand what we do. This has served as a kind of supervision for us. This experience has been very important because we do not have a practice of supervision here as they do in other countries.

Applications Outside of Therapy

Elsa:	Rosario and I used the technique to help improve the communication and reduce violence and stress among taxi drivers at a base near the zoo.
Klaus:	What do you mean by "technique"...? (Laughs)
Isabel:	The way of doing things.
Klaus:	Yes, but, the way of doing what? How did you do it?
Elsa:	The same way we do it here with the families ...
Isabel:	... Favoring the dialogue, so they can learn to listen, so all that is said, independently of who says it, is valid because it is an alternative. Because nobody has the absolute truth, but everyone always has something valid to say. And the way we have intervened or coordinated has facilitated the problem resolution.
Elsa:	For instance with the taxi drivers, first we created a group with the taxi base supervisors, another group with union members, and another one with the workers. We listened to each group; then we did reflections on each group's narrations. We acted as coordinators or moderators not expert problem solvers, and the workflow improved.
Isabel:	I think the situation undoubtedly has changed; it was enriched, and they discovered more possibilities for their situation.

Medication

Klaus:	What have been the main effects on patients in terms of medication, days of stay in the hospital, quality of professional collaboration? Do they like the new way of working?

Isabel:　　　　　In our group, our patients stay on medication the first few days then we suspend the medication. As the patient gradually gains the capacity to reflect and change, the need of medication diminishes. In our work, from individual to group, most people come to us more in search of psychological treatment than medication. I believe the same occurs to Magalis and Elsa. Most patients improve without medication; some resolve their problem after two or three sessions.

Elsa:　　　　　Rosario and I work mostly with families, and we have seen dramatic improvement in patients treated with RST allowing us to reduce medication dosage. I cannot give percentages nor establish clear causality, but the advantages are evident to us. We have been able in many situations to avoid the need of hospitalization and reduce or even eliminate medication.

Magalis:　　　　We have not done any research nor do we have quantifiable data, but, without a doubt, we have observed two phenomena: reduction in hospital stays and in use of medication. We work with patients in acute states, drug users, and suicidal persons. With the new technique, they are out and recover earlier.

Maria Eugenia:　　In my experience patients with neurotic or dystimic disorders need less medication [using this approach]. They also request the involvement of their families in therapy.

Klaus:　　　　　How do you understand the decreased need for medication and the request for family members involvement in treatment? Are the two related?

Elsa:　　　　　We have had patients to whom we have proposed this new dialogical way of working. We tell them it is a new way to converse and that it works better without medication so they can have clarity to listen to what is said. Because they become interested in this new way of conversing, many reduce their medication dosage. For instance, Rosario and I had a case of bulimia that we initially treated using traditional systemic therapy with the family; we had to hospitalize and medicate her. When we shifted to the RST approach, we no longer had to hospitalize her and reduced her medication to a minimal dosage.

Work with Children and Adolescents

Isabel:	Sometimes, due to special circumstances, we see adolescents and children although that is not common practice. Some of them we see not so much as patients but youngsters to coach for school issues, career orientation, or handling family conflicts. RST has been very useful for these cases; the youngsters have felt listened to. I do not have statistics on this issue but a strong and hard-felt observation.

Cuban Cordiality and Spontaneity

Klaus:	How does Cuban cordiality and spontaneity fit with dialogic therapy?
Maria Eugenia:	I think it [this approach] has been easy for us; it comes naturally. On the other hand, we are culturally impatient, trying to squeeze out words from patients' mouths, so we have to make an effort to let patients say and, more importantly, finish what they want to say. So we do train harder on the timing of interventions to fight that natural [cultural] impatience.
Isabel:	I know every therapist needs training in the technique he is going to use, to feel comfortable using it, to adapt his personal style to it. Now thinking as a Cuban as well as therapist, I think Cubans are naturally very communicative; talking comes easy to us. Listening, being open to others' thoughts, and appreciating others' truths are harder for us.
Maria Eugenia:	I agree, we do have listening as a common characteristic difficulty.
Isabel:	Maybe we have a hard time listening because we are so passionate, emotional, impulsive, and temperamental. But, of course, we can learn!
Magalis:	Cuban traits affect not only our approach as therapists but the ways of our patients and their families. For instance, when we meet an atypical [Cuban] personality or an outsider such as Klaus who is a figure of knowledge, it brings a sense of

fear and inhibition. However, despite these fears, the approach has been successful. It has opened us up, and our natural spontaneity and sociability have more than compensated for our also natural (but controlled through training) impulsiveness.

Compatibility with Communism

Klaus: How do dialogic, systemic, and social constructionist ideas fit with communist ideas?

Isabel: Reading this question, it seems to refer to the philosophical position underlying each psychotherapy approach. I don't think this is a question to tackle quickly; actually, I would propose it as "the subject" of our next seminar (laughs). I think a seminar about the theoretic constructs that inform this therapy and the philosophical position that informs our ways of acting would be a good subject.

Klaus: What I didn't say but assumed is that if you do not want to respond, then don't.

Isabel: Clear enough.

Klaus: This interview will be published in the United States, so it up to you to respond.

Isabel: That is not the problem—not the publication nor where it will be published. We know we have the option to respond or not. We are giving the question the importance it deserves; it is not a question to be taken lightly. Maria Eugenia talked about our professional background and our limited exposure to psychological theories. We are trained as medical doctors and have been feeding our need to learn about the field of psychology. We are interested in learning about the scientific and ethical issues related to this work. So for me, the question is interesting and important, tackling it would add to our theoretical knowledge, therefore the request to do a seminar (laughs).

Maria Eugenia: I completely agree with Isabel on our need for more knowledge on theory about constructionism. I think we have a grasp of the practical concepts but not as fully the theory that sustains them. We need to know more about social constructionism and postmodernism. However, I think I can respond to the question based on a reflection I made on the relation that could exist between dialogic, social constructionist, and systemic ideas and communist ones. I think the common link could be the social. This question relates to a prior one on how we adapt the new ideas to our culture. So I think the common link is, from an ideological point of view, the social aspect.[11]

Cuban Innovations

Klaus: What are your own contributions/transformations to the dialogic way of speaking and listening to patients? What are your perspectives and future projects?

Isabel: Well, as we were introduced to this form of therapy and applied it to our work, let's say we made some modifications or innovations, because we are using our patients to form the reflecting team. We train them in how to work with our therapeutic model, and this is a modification, and so far everything has gone well and has been very productive.

Klaus: I learned about your modifications 2 or 3 years ago. Have you brought in more than one full family so these families can form reflecting teams for each other?

Isabel: We invite them as a matter of course to our group. The families can, at a given time, form part of the reflecting team in relation to other families; even the patients join the reflecting team because the model allows for patients to function as co-therapists . . . it flows very well. This is something we did without the professor's permission (laughs)! But it has been a very good experience; at least the patients have said so. We will continue to work this way. We have to write about it; we need to leave a written record of this practice.

Klaus: I'm waiting for the article to be written and translated into German.

Isabel:	Well, it is being written, but it is not yet translated (laughs). We have it pending; actually, we are doing it with our pupils, and it is coming together. Now that I am changing jobs, I am thinking of taking it with me as a new modality there.

❧

Maria Eugenia:	A contribution that we have made is to take our new approach to working with families and bring it to our group work. When we work with families in a group, the patients, together with us, became the reflecting team; therefore, the reflecting team is made up not only of professionals. This not only contributed to the therapy process but also enriched our work and made it easier. We've also done individual sessions during the group and are trying to use theatrical improvisation with them. We hope in the future to do improvisational therapy with families.

Future Possibilities: Community and Beyond

Klaus:	What about other projects you plan to do? Do you want to answer this question? (Laughs) Then you can refer to it…
Isabel (interrupting):	… Is she going to do a doctorate on RST? (Laughs)
Klaus:	… On what you said about the taxi drivers as well as other applications. Could you also talk about the project of the "reference center"?
Elsa:	*Entschuldigung*?! [German for "Pardon me"?!][12]
Klaus:	I am not trying to correct you; I just want to insist a little …
Elsa:	As we explained, this was a job done for the taxi-cab company as part of our community service using the "appreciative organizations" approach we learned from you. We also applied this approach in a very tense, problematic situation at the women's center. The scope of our work is extending beyond traditionally working with only patients and their families. As part of my masters in clinical psychol-

ogy degree, I am studying RST with families and have used it with 22 families having various problems. We had very good results.

Klaus: Would you like to add anything you think is important for you?

Elsa: As part of this research, I plan to do a project with a larger sample of families over a longer period of time and introduce variables in the study such as the use (or not) of psychotropic medication, dosage, hospital stays, et cetera. I plan to use a control group so I can compare results. Additionally, I feel that the theoretical-practical training we have received from Professor Klaus has been very important, not only because of the personal impact on each of us but because it allowed us to develop a very useful tool. And in my case, having been working as a therapist for a long time in the acute unit and then alternating as a family therapist and now as a group therapist, I feel this is a tool useful in all circumstance and all forms of treatment. It is said that one does not really have the knowledge until one is able to verbalize it, and so we mustered the courage to give a course on family therapy where the "main dish" was RST. So we have been able to train other therapists from other institutions in this systemic modality. With this therapy, we are providing service of high quality and ethical value, and I think this is very important due to the demand for assistance in this population, not only in quantity but also in quality.

Maria Eugenia: I think we should mention something about the applicability of this therapy in the community. After the taxi company experience, we said why not use the dialogue approach with other community institutions? I think it has many applicable variants.

From a Medical to Psychological Perspective

Elsa: I definitely think this is a very new approach, not only in terms of quality of participation but also in terms of conceptualizing illness. As such, diagnosis has lost its ontological privilege.[13] The patient is no longer viewed as a sick person with pathology and instead is viewed as a person involved in a plot of family relationships and personal constructions. This is critical to me because, before, the dialogue was centered on the dysfunction and illness.

Maria Eugenia: I'm thinking that without our consciously trying, we have been moving from a medical model to a psychological one, that being the contribution that this therapy has done for us ....

Isabel: ... to the point that many people (not patients) who contact us do not think we are psychiatrists; they say we are psychologists, and they do so based on the discourse (laughs). We constantly have to say, well, we are a little of both, don't you think? The distinction is our way of conversing.

Magalis: Each of us has identified our future project because obviously an internal shift is occurring that is changing each of our perspectives. In order to involve the community, we need to involve our colleagues with a job profile that is fundamentally community oriented. The relationship and communication with our primary care areas is changing, and we are using new forms of dialogue with them, moving away from confrontation to collaboration. This in itself is a new project, even if it is not written on paper yet, and we have been doing so for years. Something new this time in the seminar is that we asked Klaus for what we wanted. Before he has come prepared with his ideas for the seminar. Now we are asking in advance; we are progressing.

Influence in Cuba

Isabel: We act as a "reference center" for this type of therapy. We continue to grow through this annual training with Professor Klaus. This service has opened a new form of treatment for families in the acute unit.

Magalis: This approach has started to move beyond our walls, and we have taken our experiences to international conferences in our country. Recently we attended one in which we and Klaus made presentations. Next March, we plan to present at the Society of

Child-Youth Psychiatry meeting which will provide another opportunity to share our group's work. We have to mention here our next meeting with Klaus will be different because we will have guests that will hear about what we are doing and will share what they do.

Klaus: Any additional issues?

Elsa: Beyond theory, when a treated family brings another and that one brings another and so on, extending the chain of families, this happens not because we announce ourselves but because the families appreciate and recommend us. This is the best proof of success and usefulness of this therapy. Meeting Klaus, in addition to the opportunity to meet an excellent human being, introduced us to a new modality of therapy, and the postmodern movement in psychotherapy and allowed us to delve into philosophical issues that we don't frequently address but should. This has also allowed us to work under his supervision, which we value highly.

Isabel: One more thing: we have participated in many events and learned from the experiences of our colleagues, but with Klaus we actually had the opportunity to experience the process with families under his supervision.

Elsa: Something that just occurred to me is the impression we made on visiting colleagues who were very positively surprised by the work we do. Let me share an example: We had a woman from a family of seven, a very neurotic woman. When we ended the session, I asked her what title she would choose for the story she had told about the family, like a movie title. She thought for quite a while and came up with a very long, very dramatic title, something like "My Family Going through Life's Diatribes with Me at the Center of the Storm." I responded, "That is a title worthy of a Soviet export film." This woman, who seemed very angered during the session, got quiet and thoughtful and stared expectantly at the rest of the family; the family broke into loud laughs, which ended with her laughing, too.

Isabel:	The question would be: Is it the title or the script?
Klaus:	What happened after they laughed?
Elsa:	I closed with that because of the symbolic force; so I said: "I invite you to have a new conversation in a month." And they did appear the following month. We have had five sessions with them so far. They have many, many issues. There are three generations in this family.
Klaus:	Let me thank you enormously …

Future Projects and Perspectives

That there is a demand for the continuation of the seminars suggests the inevitable deepening of the presented topics and that new and different topics will be added. For example, we may add questions of teaching, supervision, consulting with other institutions, research projects, publishing articles, and conducting seminars together; mutual visiting of the collaborators of the institutions are also intended. All this will be embedded into the collaboration between the Marburg Institute[14] and Servicio de Psyquiatria Professor René Yodú in Havana. A contract between the two partners is under way. Finally, the two partners will support the building and official sanctioning of a Reference Center for Systemic and Postmodern Therapies and Consultation, allowing the dialogue to continue for years to come.

Endnotes

1. Servicio de Psyquiatria Professor René Yodú.
2. Prof. Dr. Reina Rodriguez was the director of the Servicio de Psyquiatria Professor René Yodú until 2001. She is famous in Cuba for introducing new methods of group therapy in psychiatric institutions. Today she is working as a senior consultant at Servicio de Psyquiatria Professor René Yodú, Hospital Universitario Dr. Joaquin Albarran, Habana, Cuba.
3. The guiding question for my concept of dialogic is: How to do I construct useful dialogic contexts together with clients?
4. Servicio de Psyquiatria Professor René Yodú, Hospital Universitario Dr. Joaquin Albarran, Habana, Cuba.
5. How do we know what we know, how do we construct, what we construct?
6. Together with Karl-Heinz Kose (diploma in psychology), Braunschweig, Germany.
7. I do not want to do an injustice to people whom I know work differently . . . I am just describing a tendency.
8. The interview includes the following colleagues: Dr. Magalis Alejandra Martínez Hurtado, professor of psychiatry, specializing in social psychiatry and drug addiction, and director of the psychiatric clinic at Joaquin Albarran Hospital (successor to Dr. Reina Rodriguez); Dr. Elsa Araujo Pradera, professor of psychiatry, group therapist, and director of the day clinic (working on her master's degree in psychology at the University of Havana); Dr. María Eugenia Lánigan Gutiérrez and Dr. Isabel Caraballo Pons, clinical psychologists specializing in psychiatry and assistant professors in psychology working at the psychiatric clinic as group therapists. All four of these colleagues are teaching in the new course programming "Family and Family Therapy" at the clinic.

9. I prepared ten questions, which were translated by Maria Teresa Ortega Sastriques who was the translator in the interview and for the last six seminars conducted in Havana.

10. Gema Carbajosa (diploma in psychology) transcribed the interview in Spanish and translated it, together with me, into German. Julio Richter translated it into English.

11. John Lannaman asked the following question at a panel of a conference in Svolvaer, North Norway in 1993: "Why shouldn't we abbreviate 'socialconstructionist' and call it 'social(construction)ist'?"

12. One day when I came back to Cuba for a seminar again, I was surprised and felt touched when all participants stood up when I entered the room and they said something like: "*Guten morgen, Herr Professor Klaus!*" ("Good morning, Professor Klaus"). This was also a very funny scene because I never had such an experience before, but I was very impressed by the fact that all the members of the seminar took some German lessons.

13. What Elsa means by "ontological privilege of diagnostics" can simply be put like this: In classical medical thinking and practice there is a rule that says: "Before treatment, God put the diagnostics." In dialogical (communicational, social constructionist) contexts it seems to be different: the way you talk with each other creates the reality, for example, a diagnosis.

14. http://www.mics.de/

References

Andersen, T. (1990). *Das reflektierende team. Dialoge und dialoge über die dialoge.* Dortmund: Verlag modernes Lernen.

Anderson, H. (1997). *Conversation, language and possibilities: A postmodern approach to therapy.* New York: Basic Books.

Anderson, H., Cooperrider, D., Gergen, K.J., Gergen, M., McNamee, S., & Whitney, D. (2001). *The appreciative organization.* Chagrin Falls, OH: Taos Institute.

Deissler, K.G. (1989). Co-Menting: Toward a systemic poietology? Continuing the conversation. *A Newsletter of Ideas in Cybernetics.* Hortideas. KY: Greg and Pat Williams.

Deissler, K.G. (1997). *Sich selbst erfinden? Von Systemischen Interventionen zu selbstreflexiven therapeutischen Gesprächen.* Münster: Waxmann.

Deissler, K.G. (2000). "... ich, mein Problem und die anderen ...": Von Ich-Erzählungen, Beziehungsgeschichten, transformativen Dialogen und Gesprächen im Dialog. *Familiendynamik, 25,* 411–449.

Deissler, K.G. & Schug, R. (2000). Mehr desselben?—Nur anders! Reflexive Konsultation—ein Vorschlag zur Transformation herkömmlicher Formen der "Supervision." In K.G. Deissler and S. McNamee (Eds.), *Phil und Sophie auf der Couch* (pp. 64–75). Heidelberg: Carl-Auer-Systeme.

Lindseth, A. (2005). *Zur Sache der philosophischen Praxis.* Freiburg: Fermenta.

In Education, Supervision, and Research

Relational Practices in Education: Teaching as Conversation

SHEILA MCNAMEE

One of my mother's favorite stories about my childhood revolves around my first film experience. She took me, with my older brother and sisters, to see *Sleeping Beauty*. While my siblings were completely engaged with the film, I squirmed and sighed big sighs of discontent on my mother's lap. When the film was over, instead of quickly scrambling out the door as expected, my mother describes me as "coming to life." I was finally fully engaged; the audience was applauding, and by applauding, too, I was able to do something. She, of course, has managed over the years to turn this story into an illustration of my need to be involved, a participant of any activity. And after suffering through years of believing that this maternal observation was, in some way, a slightly veiled insult to my character, I have finally come to recognize the wisdom of my mother's story.

I believe that this story has a good deal to do with the topic of teaching and learning as relational (collaborative)[1] practices. I often think of that 2-year-old child when I look around my seminar table at my students' faces. How often am I guilty of conjuring up a bright and fanciful "show" in the classroom only to realize that I am putting my students to sleep? How often do I make unilateral decisions about how what I judge as important should be integrated into their lives? Am I allowing them into a process of learning when I prefigure not only what they should learn but how and for what purposes? Am I guilty of assuming there is one set of concepts or topics they must know, and deciding, myself, what will count as the best way to convey them? In these reflective moments I wonder how I might engage them, metaphorically, in lively applauds throughout our time together, rather than postpone such active collaboration until the class's grand finale.

I would like to propose, therefore, that we bracket the metaphor of teaching as a technique or method for conveying knowledge and consider the potentials opened by approaching teaching as a form of collaborative conversation. As will become clear in my argument, a relational approach to education requires that we abandon the idea that knowledge or information can be conveyed from one mind to another and, instead, I will describe knowledge as constructed in our conjoint activities with others—in what people do together. Here, conversation suggests a "turning" together. We require (and need) each other to accomplish conversation (the turning together). Thus, conversation is a relational practice and, by extension, teaching as conversation—the collaborative process of learning—is also a relational practice. It is a relational practice where participants, both teacher and student, engage in a process of making meaning together. Simply put, meaning is not the possession of one person. It only emerges in the interplay of people interacting with one another. We literally "make meaning" as we engage with others. From this stance, "meaning" is not transmitted from one person to another but emerges from their joint actions. To give meaning to a learning relationship, for example, requires coordinated actions of all participants. To know the meaning of good or bad, I must participate within a community where such standards and meanings unfold from what people do together. My own 2-year-old attentiveness to a lively film did little to engage me because, at that time, I did not feel I was fully participating in the central activity. When I finally could join in with enthusiastic applause, I fully appreciated the event. It had meaning for me. It was enlivening for me to realize I was part of making meaning in that moment.

How many of my students, I often wonder, feel as I did in that theater over 50 years ago? How many are watching, listening, attending but not really "engaging"? In my attempt to articulate how I understand and perform collaborative educational practices, I will shift between conceptual discussion and visceral illustrations of those practices from my own teaching experience. Some of my illustrations will be in the form of reflections on the interactions I have with those in my classrooms. My hope is to invite you, the reader, into an ongoing inner dialogue where I continually try to challenge my own tendency to fall into my professional "competency trap"[2]—a trap of being the expert who ignores the expertise of those with whom I am engaged.

As professionals—whether educational, therapeutic, medical, artistic, or any other kind—we expect ourselves to be experts, and those with whom we work also expect us to be experts. After all, it is our expertise that grants us the identity of "professional." I find that embracing a collaborative professional stance requires a critical examination of our expert positions. It ironically requires that we suspend any uniform or proven method of professional practice and, instead, entertain what sorts of actions might help construct us as effective professionals in the very specific relationships and contexts we find ourselves in at any given interactive moment. This requirement is ironic because it undermines any standard notion that, once trained or armed with experience, we can act with professional authority. Only when our attention shifts to the interactive moment can we question the relationship between education and expertise. This chapter scrutinizes the cultural belief that education and experience yield professional expertise. I will try to illustrate the ways in which the collaborative activities of professionals and clients (teachers and students, in this case) stand as resources for successful learning. In other words, our focus shifts from learning *that* to learning *how*. This requires collaborative efforts among all participants.

Distinctions between the Tradition of Education and Education as a Relational Practice

There are many illustrations of alternative forms of education. Despite a wide array of experimental programs and schools that employ various strategies—each departing in many ways from traditional education—teaching, learning, and education overall remain within the dominant individualist discourse of our culture. We need only look to the common and expected practices within education. The focus is on individual students and their individual comprehension, ability, and performance. Standardized tests help us gauge how each individual "measures up." These educational traditions emerge when the unquestioned focus of learning is on self-contained individuals (Macpherson, 1962; Sampson, 1993). We channel our efforts in education to the sole learner, and we judge knowledge and ability only of singular persons. When we look into the dominant activities that constitute what we call "education," we see forms of practice that are conducive to conveying knowledge, thereby providing mechanisms to support our already existing structures—specifically, our educational system and the political and economic aspects of that existing system. This tradition is predicated on the hope that education will serve as a stabilizing institution creating the sorts of people who will fit into our already existing world.

Institutionalized education should bracket the constructive possibility of education. The institution of education should be recognized as transformative—one that creates the world. We should educate children so that they can learn not only how to live in the world but how to create the future. We should educate adults so that they can provide children with resources for engaged citizenship. Yet, when we treat teaching and learning as a domain where knowledge is delivered or dispatched to the "unknowing mind," we imply that one "mind" has knowledge while another does not. My argument for the relational construction of knowledge and a concomitant transformation in educational practice draws support from Lois Holzman's argument in her book *Schools for Growth* (1997):

> … A model of human understanding that is based on knowledge, that is, on knowing x about y—is education's chief structural defect. Like other societal institutions in Western culture, schools are committed to the philosophical position that human life and growth require some way of knowing the world. This belief, thousands of years old, has rarely been challenged; indeed, it is taken to be as "natural" as our upright stance. …
>
> … Might it be that centuries-old philosophical biases about what it means to understand, to mean, to learn—to be human—have as much to do with how schools run as do politics, economics, and pedagogy? Might it be that the "overidentification" of learning and teaching with the production, dissemination, and construction of knowledge is at the root of school failure, teacher discontent, and school mismanagement? (pp. 5–6)

Holzman's argument hinges on a movement away from epistemological issues (i.e., issues of what knowledge is and what learning and teaching are) and toward "embodied activities." Embodied activities refer to the visceral ways in which we move others and are moved by them, in conversation. This refers to more than the verbal or nonverbal aspects of our interactions. It is about those bodily experiences that also shape and are shaped by our relations with others. I share Holzman's sentiments and would like to focus my own argument on how refiguring teaching—and consequently learning—in collaborative conversation might open new forms of practice. Might we find, if we play with the notion of teaching as conversation, that we can easily draw on the resources we have readily available for conversation, and thereby transform learning from something one has to "work on" into a very common, everyday endeavor—an activity with which we all have some degree of expertise? That is, can we invite others into generative and transformative conversations where we can create what counts as knowledge together?

There are several implications for learning and teaching when we speak of knowledge[3] as emerging within communities of people working together. There is no uniformly "right" way to learn or to teach. There is no universal codification of knowledge. Knowledge will vary from community to community. Various schools of therapy, as well as various psychological theories, for example, will generate different understandings of what counts as knowledge and, concomitantly, what counts as an adequate demonstration of learning (or teaching). These judgments, in turn, will have serious implications for professional therapeutic practice. And the conversations that take place in different learning contexts will vary, thereby expanding what counts as knowledge, as effective learning, or as good teaching.

Thus, education is not defined by a specific formula. With no predetermined formula to follow, how might we proceed in the "doing" of education? Can we begin to consider forms of teaching as relational performances (e.g., conversations) engaging both teacher and student? When we do, teaching can become a joint activity where new resources for action emerge. How can we engage in the activity of "teaching" so that we approach it as a form of practice—an activity and a conversation—rather than a technique for conveying knowledge?

One brief example may help clarify my point and will illustrate the difficulties we encounter when we give ourselves over to professional expertise. When I began teaching undergraduate students, I was only a graduate student myself. Given the nearness of my age to my students' ages, I was even more inclined to act "professionally" so that my students would see I was worthy of my teaching position. Yet, the more I acted as I imagined a "qualified" professor would act, the more alienated I became from my students. In those days, a "good" class consisted of one in which I felt I had successfully "delivered" the necessary information to my students and where they documented my success, as well as their own, by producing a set of scores on tests and papers that neatly fit into the tried and true bell curve. I carried this model for teaching with me as I started my position as an assistant professor.

These early teaching relationships are so markedly different from my teaching today. Rather than place my focus on the content of my courses, I am now more centered on building a sense of community in my classrooms. I enter into each course wondering how the students and I will connect so that together we can create a sense of learning, of knowledge generation, and of personal and social transformation. How do I account for my shift in focus as a teacher? I realize that my own learning and competence are enhanced when both the teacher–student relationship and the content of a given course are, in some way, connected to me. Additionally, as a teacher, I find myself excited about my courses when I am teaching material that excites me. I find that when I am excited about a topic, my students can share in my enthusiasm. However, my enthusiasm can be distancing if it is "serious" enthusiasm. I find that the use of play and humor, as well as an ability to laugh at my own overly zealous attitude, invites students into collaborative learning with me. For example, I usually begin my courses by introducing myself to my students. Instead of giving them the standard information about who I am, I tell them that they will probably come to find me a "little bit crazy." I go on to explain that how much I love the material we will be talking about might make me seem a "little bit odd" to them. I tell them that because I like it so much, I choose to read it in bed, on the beach, during my free time, etc. But, I add that this is not why I think they might come to see me as crazy. I tell them that what I imagine what will make them think I am crazy is that, because they have selected to participate in my course, I assume that they, too, are deeply passionate about the topic and the material. I imagine that they are eager to dive in to some fascinating readings and discussions.

This conversation is fun because university students often select courses based on the time and day the course is offered. For many, the topic is secondary. At best, the topic is of interest; but rarely do students define themselves as passionate about academic material. By poking fun at myself and suggesting that I imagine them to be like me, we are able to give meaning to enthusiasm together. It is no longer threatening or distancing but something we might view as sharing in common.

This combination of connection and excitement describes the high-points in my professional experience; it also describes the process of collaboration. I will give illustrations of how I have tried to construct these collaborative opportunities later in this chapter.

From Technique to Conversation

The collaborative or relational orientation I want to discuss emerges within a social constructionist discourse (Gergen, 2001; McNamee & Gergen, 1999). Social constructionism, as a discursive option, assumes that meaning is not private or locked away inside an individual. Rather, it suggests that meaning emerges in the joint activities of persons in relation. To talk of meaning as relational requires that we replace our emphasis on individuals and their internal motivations, intentions, and perceptions with an emphasis on the "coordinated" activities of people engaging with one another (i.e., people conversing with one another, where "conversation" is used in the most general sense to encompass all forms of bodily and verbal engagement). For example, when I decide to make a friendly gesture toward you, perhaps in commenting on how nice you look with the intention of having a warm conversation, it really does not matter very much what I "intend or plan to do if you respond cynically or sarcastically or even defensively to my gesture. It is my action and your response that grants significance to what we are doing. Thus, my action alone conveys no predetermined meaning nor do your responses control the meaning of our actions. Whereas we might be interested in understanding another's intentions, such understanding fails to alter the meaning of what has just transpired between us. Meaning is relational and evolves from the accomplishment of participants.

When we refigure teaching as a relational phenomenon (i.e., as conversation) and not as a private, individual ability (where some have more knowledge to impart or convey to those who have less knowledge and where some techniques or methods for teaching are more successful than others) we begin to attend to different features of teaching. Specifically, our attention is drawn toward the process of teaching as well as the teaching "relationship." We are less focused on the "proper" or "best" way to teach or provide information. Our focus, instead, is centered on the multiple ways in which teaching can take place. Further, our focus is centered on the participants engaged in the immediate moment and the wide array of both common and diverse voices, relations, communities, and experiences that each participant brings to the current learning context.

This is consistent with my earlier description of my evolution in teaching. Once I gave up my attempt to act like the expert professor, I focused my concerns on creating a learning environment where all voices could be heard. To do this, I had to throw away my objective determinations of students as being either "intelligent" or "less academically inclined." I had to give up my expectation that the only way to evaluate my own abilities as a professor lay in showing the nice bell-shaped curve of my course grades. These were radical moves. How could I argue that I was a competent educator if all my students (with all their varying reading, writing, testing, speaking, and creative abilities) were evaluated with top grades? I had to embrace the multiplicity that confronted me each time I gathered with my students. Could one person's critical and analytical abilities be on a par with another's immediate ease at seeing how course material could help in her daily relationships? How could these varying aspects of learning be compared, weighed against one another, and adjudicated so that, in the end, we all would know who "really" had knowledge?

The Need to Improvise

Emphasizing the teaching relationship and the multiplicity of voices, relations, communities, and experiences present in any learning context highlights not only the variation in what counts as excellence and what counts as knowledge, but also highlights the need for improvisation in education. Just as the jazz musician who improvises "in the moment" must be attentive to their fellow musicians, teachers, and students (all learners) must be attentive to each other in order to improvise.[2] The difference between an engaging seminar and a boring lecture is the ability of all involved to coordinate their activities together. I am reminded of the many seminars I am asked to give on a guest basis. In these contexts, I rarely know the participants, and I am not there long enough to build an ongoing relationship. I spend significant time preparing material that is responsive to the specific invitation I have received. Yet, once I begin to work with a group, the seminar takes it own shape. While I have more material to cover than time to offer it, I never know what will be used, what will be discarded, and what will be invented in collaboration with the participants. Traditionally, this might lead one to such self-deprecating evaluations of disorganization or lack of discipline. But there is a vast distinction between those moments of disorganization and moments of collaborative teaching and learning. One can only be disorganized and undisciplined against the backdrop of a correct structure or a correct set of knowledge. Being responsive to those I am working with, on the other hand, requires movement through our conversation in ways that create opportunities for our transformation. Delivering the information that I prepared in advance would be dismissive of the relationship we create in the moment of learning. Further, it would be dismissive of the questions, concerns, and specific interests of the participants. As I prepare, I can only imagine our relationship. And I have never yet adequately imagined an unknown relationship!

What Counts as Knowledge

For the constructionist, what counts as knowledge emerges through a process of coordination. Over time, as people come together and coordinate their actions, they develop rituals and patterns. These patterns generate standards and expectations which give way to broader belief systems complete with their unique moralities and ethics. If we recognize that this process of constructing knowledge (what counts as truth) is taking place in all human engagements, then we should be able to see the potential for multiple and diverse standards, realities, and truths. What counts as knowledge to some will not to others. This stance is quite different from our traditional, individually focused approach to education.

As an illustration of what "counts as knowledge," my university, like most, has a separate program—the Honors Program—for students who maintain a high grade point average. Eligible students are allowed to take advanced seminars where they purportedly cover material that is more academically demanding. As these courses are very small by design, they are very costly to the university, which prefers the economic strategy of aligning one professor with 300 students in designating a class. Therefore, for purposes of economic gain, honors students are allowed to enroll in regular seminars and contract individually with professors for advanced supplemental work.

I have many of these students in my classes. They are the ones each day who have done all the reading for a given class, prepared any written assignment, and are always ready with factual information regarding the material being discussed. What is interesting to note, however, is how difficult it is for these honors students to go beyond the text. When asked to contemplate how the material we are discussing might relate to a completely different context, or how it might inform their own lives, these students have little to say.

Additionally, when asked to collaborate with others in preparing course work, these highly evaluated students show disappointment fueled by their fearful anticipation that their collaborative efforts might be less than perfect, ultimately preventing them from achieving their typical outstanding evaluations. To remedy this situation, honors students who are required to work collaboratively tend to take charge and do most if not all of the work themselves, thereby gaining greater assurance of a positive evaluation while inadvertently sabotaging the professor's effort to nurture collaborative practices.

These students are not, in themselves, a problem. Rather they are victims of the institutional structure of higher education. Higher education has defined what counts as intelligence. Learning the facts that are provided in textbooks and lectures, and being able to identify these facts on tests, in papers, and in classroom discussion are what garner many students' outstanding grades and their resulting identities as honor student. And yet, the ability to improvise and go beyond the text is thwarted as is collaborative practice. Solo performance is rewarded while group activities are ignored, at best. Yet do not the complexity of corporate life, global interests, and community investments today demand precisely the ability to work with others, to be responsive to the moment-by-moment interruptions and changes in plan, and to collaborate in working toward an unspecified future? This is but one example of the way in which traditional images and descriptions of learning impair our ability to be the sort of professionals we hope to be—ones who are responsive to the moment. The very structure of a university's honors program actually can inhibit collaborative learning.

Kenneth Bruffee, author of *Collaborative Learning: Higher Education, Interdependence, and the Authority of Knowledge* (1993), suggests that conversations among teachers and students "create" knowledge. He describes the difference between an individual conception of knowledge and the notion of socially constructed knowledge in higher education. He says:

> Traditionally, professors believe . . . that their job is to "reach" students and fill their minds with what they believe fills their own. They ask themselves questions such as: What's going on inside my students' heads? How can I get in there and change what's going on? What's the best way to impart to them what I know? (pp. 72–73)

He goes on to describe professors who adopt a social constructionist understanding of knowledge. He argues that social construction

> ... implies that teaching is an entirely different enterprise. Instead of thinking about what to put into their students' minds and how to put it there, professors think of teaching as helping students converse with increasing facility in the language of the communities they want to join, and they think about doing that as creating social conditions in which students can become re-acculturated into those communities. (p. 73)

In what ways does a collaborative social constructionist understanding of knowledge and teaching refigure educational life? Practices emerging from a relational and collaborative sensibility differ from individualist practices. Is there something to be gained from developing relational forms of practice? Once we move from inside the self-contained person to the realm of performance—what people do together—entirely new questions emerge for examining education. Teaching and knowledge are dislodged from the private sphere of persons and described instead as achievements of joint performance. This move encourages us to question the hierarchies of competencies or knowledge that are left unexamined in most contexts. Specifically, why are some forms of knowledge more respected and valued than others?

Why is it deemed better for a student to get the definitions, dates, and formulas correct instead of engaging in reflexive critique? Why is the learner who has had a transformative experience in a learning context less competent (intelligent) than the student who has all the correct answers on tests? To be a competent person takes on a very specific meaning within our dominant tradition. First, there is an embedded assumption that, equipped with the proper reasoning abilities, a person will behave in an expected and appropriate manner. Within traditional education, we can expect to identify those who are intelligent or competent (or "knowledgeable") by virtue of their behaviors (what they do and say) which are actually reflections of their inner reasoning abilities. Furthermore, if we know what constitutes an intelligent person, we can manipulate both environment and person to insure production of a good individual. We standardize curricula and tests; we make invisible the politics of topic and method selection for each academic level because those choices, we believe, have greater potential to produce knowledgeable, competent students. This in fact is what the institution of education is all about: promising the delivery of intelligent and good citizens to our communities.

This latter feature can be seen in virtually all of our educational settings. Even educational contexts outside of academia—for example, postgraduate training programs in therapy—strive to mimic the "rigor" of our educational system. And when they do, these programs are duly rewarded with academic certification. In turn, those who have trained in such programs secure more prestigious professional positions, are sanctioned to charge a higher fee to clients, and are able to take third-party payments. The educational stamp of approval has little to do with living collaboratively with others or performing one's job with competence and has everything to do with issues of political economy.

Limits to Individualism

The limits to individualist discourse have been discussed at length elsewhere (Gergen, 1994; Rorty, 1979; McNamee & Gergen, 1999). Rather than reiterate these arguments, I will summarize some of the constraints of this way of talking.

Self-focus and self-interest. When we locate all reasoning abilities "within" individuals, a person's success or failure in a particular learning context is dependent upon his or her own abilities. When the self is our priority, participants in a learning context focus their attentions on their own success, their own achievements, and their own movement up the academic ladder. The emphasis on the individual builds competition and self-interest into the educational endeavor. Whereas competition might be useful in many situations (including many educational situations), it might not always be the most productive path for learning.

Little to no concern for community. If my educational history is imbued with a concern for me and my achievements, I might be less inclined to utilize participatory forms of action, relying instead on my well-rehearsed mode of self-sufficiency. This form of relating might serve me well but might deplete the resources or opportunities for my community, my work place and profession at large, my family, and so forth. There is little to no concern for community.

Neglect of alternative modes of learning. Individualistic discourse and its associated notion of what counts as rational, real, and appropriate disregards potential modes of teaching and learning that might be fostered in diverse communities and contexts. A simple exploration of the "acceptability" of alternative forms of education (Holzman, 1997) calls attention to the very limited range of educational options. Some forms of education, such as the Reggio Emilia Model (New, 1998) or the Montessori Method (Montessori, 1964) find their origins in Italian culture where emphasis is placed on family, community, and collaboration among children and adults. In the North American culture, these and similar educational innovations are the exception and not the rule. We can ask what sorts of values, ethics, and moral codes are being obliterated by limiting the availability of these alternatives within the broader institution of education with its priority on the ritual of self-celebration.

From Teaching Individuals to Teaching Relationships

My aim is to illustrate how individualistic and relational discourses in education are metaphors, each inviting different forms of social life. Within individualistic discourse, cognitive or behavioral metaphors are central. If all activity emanates from one's cognitive abilities, then mind becomes the focus of attention. Or, if social life is guided by behavioral responses, then behaviors alone become our focus. We see this in most learning contexts where an appropriate demonstration of learning yields some form of positive reinforcement—good grades, extra credit, gold stars—all attempts to "condition" our behaviors to fit in with expected norms. For collaborative practitioners, the relational metaphor places our attention on conversation, joint action, performance, and thereby improvisation. The effort is one of understanding language not as a device used to represent reality but rather as a necessity to construct reality. Wittgenstein (1953) offers us a use-embedded account of language. To him, we "do" things with our words—that is, we *make* realities. Words and their meanings are secured by participation in specific games of language. Thus, the central question: What can we do differently when we talk of teaching as conversation?

It is important to note that the transition to a conversational and "performative" metaphor positions the teacher differently from any of the individualist metaphors upon which we currently draw. With the metaphor of teaching as conversation, the expertise of the educator becomes his or her ability to "keep the conversation going" in Wittgenstein's sense. Harlene Anderson (1997) echoes this view of the teacher or the professional when she describes the notion of the therapist's expertise. She states that, "A therapist brings expertise in the area of process: a therapist is the expert in engaging and participating with a client in a dialogical process of first-person story-telling" (p. 95). She goes on to describe the therapist as an expert in creating and facilitating the dialogue space and practice. She says, "A facilitative position promotes a process that keeps all voices in motion and contributing" (p. 95). Additionally, the expertise of the therapist is illustrated in her position of "multipartiality" (p. 95).

How do these forms of "performative" conversational expertise translate into a teaching and learning context? How can we engage with others such that the learning process is open to the multiplicity of worlds that are present in any one learning context? How can students and teacher engage together in coordinating their many voices, their many realities, their many ways of knowing?

Learning as "Making a World" vs. Learning as "Knowing a World"

With our history of education, it is a bit absurd for us to assume that we can simply enter into an educational context and automatically create a relational, collaborative learning environment. Learners expect educators to assess their individual abilities. They expect that the focus of most educational contexts will be on cognitive abilities such as comprehension, expansion, and innovation. Academic administrators also harbor the same expectations. Learning spaces are primarily designed to facilitate individual learning, individual work, and individual evaluation. Most often, we seat learners at separate, individual desks. Chairs and desks face the same direction—forward, focused on the teacher.

Given these features, it is necessary to foster a different environment if we want to engage in relational practices in education. We cannot expect it to develop automatically. For example, we should not assume that seating learners in working clusters around a common table should automatically yield a collaborative learning environment. Crafting a collaborative environment can be achieved in a variety of ways. What I offer here is not intended to serve as a recipe for relationally engaged education; rather, I urge you to view any specific activity suggested here as one among many ways to engage "relationally" with learners. It is not so much an issue of what we do as educators but how we do it. In the present context, the "how" is relational. Being relational suggests inviting participants into the very process of collaboratively constructing how learning will take place, what learning will take place, and what standards will be used for evaluating that learning. Opening each of these conversations to all involved privileges the multiple standards for learning and teaching and determines what counts as knowledge.

Four Resources for Collaborative Educational Conversation and Relational Learning

I would like to suggest four interrelated resources we might draw upon to invite others into a collaborative educational conversation with us: (a) avoiding abstract principles, (b) privileging narrative forms, (c) fostering community, and (d) blurring the boundaries between the classroom and everyday life. These four resources are not discrete. In fact, they could be more fruitfully viewed as facets of the same stone. Their common resonance can be found in their attention to language, stories, and relationships. As an elaboration of these features, I would like to expose some of the nuances in which I attempt to create a relational learning environment in my own classes, not as models but as illustrations to speak to the engaged tenor of the relational, collaborative learning environment. They are, simply put, various ways of creating the conversational space where different and generative conversations can take place. To me, this is the very nature of education, learning, and the collaborative construction of knowledge.

Avoiding Abstract Positions

Education, in general, privileges abstractions. My interest in my own teaching focuses on what might be gained in a learning environment by exploring the very situated narratives of participants engaged in an educational context. In other words, rather than begin a course by listing the principles, as in my own case, about human communication or psychology, I find it engaging to initiate inquiry among the students about their own personal understandings of communication, psychology, or the specific topic of the course. Can we begin our collaborative conversation by privileging what learners bring to the educational context? Can we assume that from the very start of our relationship, students also have value to contribute? Traditional education, we should note, tends to operate on the principle that learners are present to "gain," not to give, and the commodity they want to gain is "knowledge." In a collaborative educational context, knowledge is neither given nor gained; it is "jointly constructed."

Sometimes, for example, I ask students to identify silently a difficulty they experience. I next ask them to think about what they would need to do in order to teach someone else to act as if she or he had this difficulty. What would the other person need to do? What would they need to say? How would he or she react to specific situations? What would convince us that the other had the same difficulty? Once each person has thought through this set of questions, they are paired with another. They go to a private space and "teach" each other to "perform" their difficulty. When the group reconvenes, each pair performs the difficulties they taught each other while the rest of the class guesses what it was they were enacting.

For example, one student might say that she is shy. Shyness is this person's major "difficulty" in life. She then might list the following things that someone would need to do in order to demonstrate shyness:

- Never look anyone in the eye.
- Move back and forth on your feet when you are talking with another.
- Wrap your arms around yourself whenever anyone asks a question.
- Always have a hint of hesitancy in your voice.

This may seem like an unusual activity, but I use it to illustrate the often-abstract idea that our problems, our characteristics, our traits, and our personalities are not really "inside" of us but, rather, are brought to life only in our "collaborative" engagements with others. For example, one cannot just portray shyness. If shyness is the difficulty identified, the question becomes how can one who suffers from shyness teach another person to replicate (i.e., to "do") it as it is demonstrated. The performance of any quality or state of being is always responsive to others. Thus, in my students' performances, they usually find that no matter how well "trained" they may be by their partner, they are not prepared to respond to the spontaneous questions or comments of others in the group. Each student has been "taught" his or her partner's difficulty by the partner. Yet when it is time to perform the difficulty in front of the entire group, each trained student must now "improvise" their response to the audience's questions and comments. This simple activity illustrates nicely how one cannot simply "have" a problem or difficulty. One needs others to construct collaboratively the reality of the difficulty. If we are not responsive to others and if they are not responsive to us, we fail to produce what we intend and are left creating something entirely different. Therefore, in the case of shyness, someone in the larger group might say, "You look excited because you can't stand still or focus." Another might offer, "You have a difficulty asking others if you can use the bathroom!" This is one small illustration of how I aim to avoid speaking from abstract positions. As we can see, the shift from individual problems to collaboratively performed problem "scenarios" is easier to grasp in situated activity than through abstract discussion.

Privileging Narrative Forms

One very effective way of avoiding abstractions is to locate the topic of learning within a personal narrative. Stories told by participants (both teachers and learners) in an educational setting provide many things. First, giving voice to all participants' personal interests in the subject matter at hand underscores the wide array of perspectives that different people bring to the same subject. As well, don't all who populate our courses come with a wealth of information about, for example, what is normal or abnormal behavior, what counts as effective communication, what works best in organizations or in families or in couples to help them develop and grow? Inviting these stories from all members gives voice to the complexity of social life and thereby opens new resources for engaging in that life.

As mentioned earlier, I always begin my courses with stories about my own interests and intrigues in the topic. I tell about my curiosity with the subject matter from the standpoint of my everyday life as opposed to the standpoint of pure intellectual pursuit. But the scholarly is always eventually integrated with the very local coherence that my own significant life stories lend to any set of material. I find that students become much more engaged in their education when they realize they have the conversational resources to make academic material familiar. They, too, have stories, both lived and imagined, about the academic issues they confront in their education. To give voice to these stories and to make them a significant part of learning is to approach teaching as conversation. Stories create knowledge. The lessons that emerge within a story are not separated into some set of abstractions; rather, they are embedded in the very common activities of those present.

The activity I described above—where I ask participants to talk about the best community or group they have ever been part of—is an illustration of speaking from lived narratives. When we can begin with our own stories, we create a space where different conversations and different forms of "learning" can take place. I can invite you and others into my story. You might not like my story, but you cannot tell me it is wrong. You can ask me questions and even encourage me to see the same details in different terms. But then my story ceases to be mine. It is ours. We are already collaborating in the process of understanding (i.e., of knowing). I encourage participants in my courses to offer their stories for others to investigate. I explain that the investigations are not judgments but are curiosities. The questions others ask, the observations they note, might provoke new understandings.

Harlene Anderson's "as if" activity (1997, p. 235) serves as a wonderful illustration of the use of narrative as well. By giving voice to all participants' questions and comments about another's narrative, we open possibility for new meanings to emerge. As Harlene says,

> We often forget that we and our clients carry other people's voices around with us and that these voices become part of who we are, part of our thoughts and actions. . . . The ["as if"] experiential activity and discussion provide a chance for all participants to experience making room for an other and its relevance to dialogue. Silently listening enables both "as if" members and presenters to hear differently than

when listening and speaking simultaneously. That is, when the "as if" members are prohibited from asking questions, sharing ideas, or making suggestions, they sense the difference between listening to what a presenter wants them to hear and what they think they should hear. ... The "as if" voices do not offer new "information" for the presenter; this is not the intent. The newness and future possibilities come from the fluidity of the ongoing, back-and-forth interactions as each conversation (within and outside the consultation room) becomes part of and leads to others. (pp. 241–242)

Fostering of Community

Sharing personal narratives also fosters the development of a relational community among the group. In place of a teacher "conveying" knowledge to individual minds, we have participants creating together what will count as knowledge. What is significant to some may not be to others. But does this mean that this student should "fail" or that the teacher has not adequately done his or her job? If we use the metaphor of conversation to talk about learning, we might begin to open up the notion of "success" such that all participants are seen as achieving a mastery of the topic in different ways. The mastery is not uniform or universal. It is multivocal. One student learning to write more effectively while another learns how to handle personal conflict and yet another learns to distinguish between different philosophical schools might be well considered as effective learning.

Blurring the Boundaries between Classroom and "Life"

Constructing a community of learners through the telling of personal narratives also provides relational resources for students to dissolve the boundary between their education and their lives. In dissolving the boundary, students take their classroom conversations beyond the walls of the classroom. I find that my students report talking with family, friends, roommates, and coworkers about course material. They do so because it has been made "familiar" to and by them. They no longer need to struggle with abstract concepts and theories. The theories and concepts they are confronting are "practical" theories and concepts. They are "generative" theories (Gergen, 1994). The course materials create the world rather than represent the world. This is a vitally important shift in the classroom, particularly if we accept that education is about the continual construction of citizens and citizenship.

In addition to the informal blurring of inside–outside classroom boundaries, students engage in significant course projects, activities that allow students to illustrate how the educational situation has meaning beyond the classroom. My own students have designed and facilitated dialogues about alcohol consumption and campus restrictions. One semester, we collaboratively decided that the major project for our course on transformative dialogue in communities would involve designing and facilitating a dialogical experience for a local group who were experiencing conflict. While students were struggling to come up with groups more meaningful to work with than conflicting roommates, our campus had what the national media labeled as "riots." (We have come to refer to these recurrent situations on campus as "celebratory disturbances"!) The disturbance occurred when a fraternity party grew in size and local neighbors alerted the police. Hundreds of inebriated students were met by police in riot gear, armed with pepper gas. Many arrests and injuries fed the situation. On Monday in class, my students—the same ones who had been studying how to move beyond conflict toward transformative dialogue—engaged in a heated discussion about the Saturday night events. Most students blamed the police, the neighboring residents, and, of course, the university administration. Their feeling was that these groups simply did not want university students to have any fun. As I listened to them talk, I began to see their passion for this topic and suggested it as a perfect forum for their class project. They jumped on the idea and organized multiple groups, each comprised of a diverse set of participants from the university and from the community and included students (from both inside and outside the fraternity system), parents, local bar owners, town residents, police, university administrators, faculty, etc. The students collaborated in organizing, designing, and facilitating multiple dialogue groups. The impact was astounding. Participants wrote moving notes to the students telling of the learning that took place during these dialogues. For their part, the students reported what they observed:

- The ("mean") chief of police crying and explaining that he just did not want to hold another dead body in the street
- The (out of touch) administrator who described his own wild university days and what he learned from those experiences
- The bar owners who were glad to make the money selling beer to students but feared a loss of livelihood and an impending threat for their families should their license be revoked for selling beer to minors

The stories were palpable. Participants took issues that students viewed as being "black and white" and introduced an enormous amount of grey.

Since this project, other classes have followed with similar dialogue groups. These dialogues have brought diverse groups together in a way that avoids the simple black-and-white understanding of what is "right" or "wrong." The complexities of the issue are voiced. These dialogues do not magically alter the way university students celebrate on weekends. Nor do they change policies and procedures by official bodies. What they do accomplish, however, is initiation of a "different" conversation and thus a different "relationship" among participants. Since these dialogues began, more and more students are invited into the policy-making discussions at the university. Most significantly, students here hosted a national gathering of universities convened for purposes of talking about "celebratory disturbances"—a challenge confronting campuses across the nation.[4]

My students have provided several other illustrations of this sort of learning. By challenging themselves to find a group to work with, they collaborate with not only their classroom peers but with a group of participants with whom they have chosen to craft a dialogic process.

An Example: Creating a Conversational Space for Learning
Engaging Relational Partners in a University Classroom

In an attempt to emphasize the need to create the conversational space where different conversations can take place and to further illustrate the four resources, I will draw on my experience as a university professor. I will describe some of the ways in which I enter into my courses, inviting my students to collaborate with me in the construction of our knowledge and learning. My hope is that my description of the university classroom will be valuable and applicable to a wide range of learning contexts. I use these practices in diverse learning environments myself—beyond the university classroom.

Acknowledging that collaborative learning cannot be taken for granted in a traditional context, I attempt to engage my students in my first meeting with them in a process of building relationships with one another and with me as well as building commitments as relational partners for the duration of our course. Thus, I invite them to collaborate in creating a very different learning context. One way I do this is to ask them to work in partner dyads or triads, first sharing stories of the best functioning groups or communities with which they have been engaged. Once they have shared their stories, I ask, "What strengths, values, and talents does your story remind you that you have?"[5] After sharing their strengths, values, and talents with their partners and making a composite list, I ask, "What characteristics of communities or groups does your story illustrate?" In other words, what are the features of a great community, based on their own story? Again, partners generate a list of features. At this point, I ask them to report to the entire group the lists they have produced of strengths, values, and talents they most appreciate in themselves by virtue of their reflections. I ask them not to identify who in their small group is associated with each item on their composite list. They also share with the entire group the central features of a wonderfully functioning group or community. This reporting generates a lengthy list of qualities, with much overlap and great variation as well.

With these features, values, and talents listed for the entire group to see, I ask, "If we, as a group, were to be like your best community experience, what would be happening? What would we look like?" This question, again discussed in the original dyads or triads, yields a long list of images. Students frequently identify images such as the following:

- Everyone will know each other's name.
- Everyone will feel comfortable to say what's on his or her mind.
- We will be working together for a common goal.
- We will be open minded.
- We will be genuinely interested and demonstrate a sense of caring about each other.
- There will be no cliques.
- We will use common communication links (e.g., e-mail).
- We will engage in open discussion.
- We will foster a sense of individuality balanced with togetherness.
- We will be comfortable with each other.
- We will create relationships outside of class as well as inside
- There will be a high level of participation

After posting these images for all to see, I ask a final question: "What will we need to do to make this happen?" I see this as a moment when all participants in the room begin to envision their centrality in making our learning environment successful, worthwhile, and collaborative. Common responses to this question include:

- We will not hold back.
- We will lead by example.
- We will learn everyone's name.
- We will be respectful of what everyone says even when we disagree.
- We will create our learning goals together.
- We will stop thinking "factually"—be more open.

Finally, to facilitate students' abilities to see their own part in making our course a success, I ask each student to write down three things that each is willing to make a commitment to do in order to contribute to our success. By the end of our first meeting, students already have a sense of their responsibility to coconstruct a relational environment where together we can create meaning and knowledge. As a group, we have collaboratively constructed a very different sort of learning environment and one unique to the participants. It is a context where we are all relationally responsible (McNamee & Gergen, 1999) for what we learn, how we learn, and whose standards are used to assess our learning.

With a beginning sense of ourselves as a learning community, each contributing to our success or failure, we begin to talk about the content and structure of the course. I suppose some might say I am lucky to be teaching "about" communication. The very topic of my courses neatly blends with the relational context we establish together. However, I feel that regardless of the course content, learning is enhanced by a collaborative, relational sensibility. When participants feel connected to one another, an ability to ask questions in a way that make us vulnerable is eased.

With a budding sense of community then, we begin to discuss the contours of our course. What will we cover? What will be required? I have tried, on occasion, to invite my students into crafting the answer to these questions together. One semester while teaching a seminar on organizational communication, I proposed, "We are all here, I presume, because the topic of organizational communication is interesting to us. If that is the case, then what would you like to know about it? How would you like to explore this topic? What would you like to do to demonstrate what you learn here?" I gave the group two weeks to work together to design a proposal. One of the options I made clear to them, as a viable proposal, was to say, "You are the professor. We want you to make these decisions." But I did not assume that I should.

During other semesters, I have offered a course syllabus as a way to "begin" our conversation. I tell students that this is my invitation to them. They are encouraged to amend, edit, delete, or add to the structure and content of our courses. The general response to these suggestions has been for students to ask me to determine the readings and the requirements (papers, exams, presentations, and so forth). However, by the middle of the semester, students begin to propose alternatives. I am always open to their proposals as long as they participate in the dialogue about how their proposal will illustrate what learning has taken place and how it should be evaluated.

It is interesting to note that not every detail is usually "up for discussion." Often, I find students prefer to have their professor make certain decisions. They also often request a "formal lecture" as opposed to an open discussion. All of these decisions emerge in the give-and-take of open dialogue. There is nothing inherently wrong with formal lectures or with hierarchical decision-making. The important point here is that these more traditional educational practices have been "collaboratively" agreed upon. Such a collaborative process yields a very different result than, for example, giving a formal lecture because that is the way a "good" teacher teaches.

This is one way I attempt to create a set of collaborative relationships and a conversational space in a learning context. I might also open discussion about the various reasons for participants' presence in a particular course as assuming that all learners are present for the same reason limits the range of dialogue and transformation that can transpire. Or, I might begin a course by inviting students to talk about the diversity of perspectives, rationales, identities, and standards they each bring to the classroom community. Identifying and sharing diversities begins to invite and celebrate difference as a richness and a resource rather than as a stigma or deficit.

Teaching as Conversation

The metaphor of "teaching as conversation" is useful because it makes the ritualized practice of education familiar in a different way. It shifts teaching and learning from a focus on a method for conveying knowledge to a process that is attentive to the ways in which participants create meaning together. It allows us to celebrate our collaborative activities. As we engage with each other, we not only create a sense of "who" we are but also a sense of "what" is valued. We create—we perform "together"—a world wherein a lived reality can emerge. And this reality will very likely differ from others that we, ourselves, populate. This reality will differ from the realities of others in the very same learning context. The metaphor of conversation provides the opportunity for us to engage in self-reflexive inquiry about the resources for action that are not being utilized but that might aid in creating new ways of going on together. If education is conversation, then we are free to pause and ask ourselves what other ways might there be to talk about the topic, the issue, or the problem. How else can I invite others to collaborate with me in creating "knowledge?" Conversation as a metaphor enhances self-reflexivity by legitimizing it. In so doing, we open ourselves to listening, reading, talking, and writing in more "generous" modes while remaining open to the relational coherence of diverse ways of acting. We thereby avoid speaking with a sense of certainty that the world is or should be one way. And in so doing we open possibilities for collaboration and the coordination of multiple ways of being human. In other words, create new ways of "going on together."

Endnotes

1. I use the terms relational and collaborative interchangeably throughout this text.
2. Frank Barrett (personal communication) talks about jazz musicians who play the same riff as they improvise because it has been successful in the past. This repetition, he argues, gets in the way of the creativity of improvisation and, instead, creates a "competency trap" that inhibits generative possibilities from emerging.
3. I want to note that I use the terms "knowledge" and "meaning" interchangeably here. When we create meaning with others in our interactions, we are in fact creating knowledge or "ways of knowing."

4. See http://www.unh.edu/studentsummit/summary.html for a summary of the national student summit.
5. I designed these questions using David Cooperrider's model of appreciative inquiry (Cooperrider, 1995).

References

Anderson, H. (1997). *Conversation, language and possibilities: A postmodern approach to therapy.* New York: Basic Books.

Austin, J.L. (1962). *How to do things with words.* New York: Oxford University Press.

Bruffee, K.A. (1993). *Collaborative learning: Higher education, interdependence, and the authority of knowledge.* Baltimore, MD: Johns Hopkins University Press.

Cooperrider, D.L. (1995). Introduction to appreciative inquiry. In W. French and C. Bell (Eds.), *Organization Development* (5th ed.). New York: Prentice Hall.

Foucault, M. (1973). *Madness and civilization.* (R. Howard, Trans.) New York: Pantheon.

Gergen, K.J. (2001). *An invitation to social construction.* London: Sage.

Gergen, K.J. (1994). *Realities and relationships: Soundings in social construction.* Cambridge, MA: Harvard University Press.

Gergen, K.J. (1994). *Toward transformation in social knowledge* (2nd ed.). London: Sage.

Holzman, L. (1997). *Schools for growth: Radical alternatives to current educational methods.* Mahwah, NJ: Lawrence Erlbaum Associates.

Macpherson, C.B. (1962). *The political theory of possessive individualism.* London: Oxford University Press.

McNamee, S. & Gergen, K.J. (1999). *Relational responsibility: Resources for sustainable dialogue.* Thousand Oaks, CA: Sage.

Montessori, M. (1964). *The Montessori method.* New York: Schocken Books.

New, R. (1998). Theory and praxis in Reggio Emilia: They know what they are doing and why. In C. Edwards, L. Gandini, & G. Forman (Eds.), *The hundred languages of children: The Reggio emilia approach to early childhood education* (2nd ed.). Norwood, NJ: Ablex.

Rorty, R. (1979). *Philosophy and the mirror of nature.* Princeton, NJ: Princeton University Press.

Sampson, E.E. (1993). *Celebrating the other.* Boulder, CO: Westview Press.

Wittgenstein, L. (1953). *Philosophical investigations.* (G. Anscombe, Trans.) New York: Macmillan.

CHAPTER 20

From the Theory to the Practice of Inquiring Collaboratively: An Exercise in and Clinical Example of an Interviewee-Guided Interview

SALLYANN ROTH

In recent decades, traditional hierarchical values in many professions have been challenged by the egalitarian values of working collaboratively and according primacy to people's expertise on their own lives. In the field of psychotherapy, its supervision and practice, theorists such as Andersen (1987), Anderson (1997, 2005), Anderson and Goolishian (1988), Gehart-Brooks and Lyle (1999), Hoffman (1990, 2002), and White and Epston (1990), among others, have emphasized the centrality of the client's lived experience while respecting the therapist's skill in creating " ... a space for inviting collaborative relationships and dialogical conversations." (Anderson 2005, p. 502)

Collaborative inquiry has at its heart the interviewer's commitment to serve the client's purposes and to this end recognizes the interviewee as an expert on his or her own experiences, desires, and ways of moving toward them. Essential to the interviewer's stance is being fully present, open about his or her own purposes, respectful of the shared and separate purposes of their conversation, and possessed of the readiness to lead by following while respecting and fostering the interviewee's sense of his or her agency in the process.

These developments in thinking about psychotherapy have sought to move the work of the client and the therapist toward a mode of greater and more equal partnership. This is a tall order. Although for many practitioners these are easy concepts to embrace, for most practitioners the concepts are more difficult to embody and put into practice, especially for those who have grown up in a largely hierarchical world and have been trained in models heavily influenced in content and form by top-down ways of looking at the world and acting in it.

Most of us have experienced and been trained in ways of inquiring that are shaped primarily by the inquirer's agenda. In this older way of working, the person asking questions selects a style, form, content, and sequence of questions for his or her own purposes, be they to investigate, influence outcome, serve organizational requirements, or whatever. The therapist who would practice collaboratively may need to unlearn what he or she has been taught in school and in life. In trying to practice in this less familiar way, we may fear that we will disappoint others (or ourselves) by not being and seeming "expert" about the dilemmas our clients confront and their possible resolutions. By definition, holding a collaborative stance and acting from it requires tolerating uncertainty about how even a small conversation will go.

As a therapist, supervisor, and trainer of therapists and of people who work with conflict, I have experienced and observed how challenging it can be for those who care deeply about embodying the values of collaboration, cocreation, and mutual inquiring to implement them. Collaboration (and avoiding imposition) does not dictate withholding our own thoughts and feelings; it involves finding ways to use them openly to welcome and invite others to surface their thoughts and feelings so to enrich the mutually enacted dialogue by building on what each of us brings to the conversation.

Some of us may not have experienced such relationships in our own lives and our professional training. Such a stance may not be prevalent or even valued in our work place. Many trainees I work with want to embody such a stance. They are committed to not imposing their ideas and values; they are dissatisfied with the "expert" stance their training invites them to assume, and yet they are stymied about how to enter deeply and fully into collaborative relationships. Trainees have told me that discrepancies they experience between their commitments and practices show up most intensely in traditional hierarchical relationships such as those of client and therapist and of supervisor and supervisee.

I also experience this dilemma. A collaborative stance does not always come readily to me; I struggle to keep myself on a path toward a collaborative way of being. It can take a dismaying amount of energy and attention to continue moving forward and not backward on that path.

In the course of providing training and supervision, I have become aware that a number of people have not experienced genuine collaboration across hierarchical differences in their lives—or, for some, any genuine collaboration at all. No wonder it is challenging for many to work from a collaborative stance, despite their intellectual commitment to do so. With these trainees and supervisees' concerns in mind, I developed a series of exercises intended to provide them with opportunities to experience and reflect on clinical and consultative collaboration at first hand.

The exercise[1] below was developed for use in full-day or multiday training programs, and in ongoing supervision, where its use is preceded by building-block exercises and collaborative demonstration as well as extensive exploration of collaborative values and hours of conversation. Its use is probably most effective and least confusing in a context where such preparation has occurred.

Exhibit

A Training Exercise in Inquiring Collaboratively: The Collaboratively Developed Interviewee-Guided Interview[*]

Purpose and Structure of This Exercise

The primary purpose of this exercise is to provide an experience of collaboration from the positions of both interviewer and interviewee with the ultimate goal of making collaborative inquiry more readily accessible. The exercise offers experience of and practice in the following:

- Developing collaborative, side-by-side inquiring relationships
- Evoking an inquiring stance in all who are in the conversation
- Trusting the interviewee's expertise about his or her experience and chosen directions; leading by following
- Attending to the effects of a collaborative stance on both interviewers and interviewees, the effects on their relationships with each other and on the kinds of developments that follow such collaborative conversations
- Shifting between action and reflection

In broad outline, as participants working in conversational pairs in the exercise, you will each describe one personal dilemma or concern (or even an event you want to celebrate) to your conversational partner as the starting point for an experience of collaborative inquiring. Each of you will alternately take the role of the interviewing person and the interviewed person after you have collaboratively developed some questions for each other. As you each take a turn as interviewer, you will be called upon to restrain any inclination you may have to take control of the process; then, in turn as interviewee, each of you will be called upon to bring your experience to the conversation and to make decisions about the form in which you will be interviewed and the interview's content.

Agreements and Time Allotments

People engaged in this exercise have found it useful to establish process agreements that they believe will support their feeling safe enough to speak personally and to experiment with ways of interviewing and being interviewed that challenge familiar ways of thinking and acting. Some agreements, also found to be useful, are listed by topic below.[2] Time allotments for each activity are given in brackets throughout the steps of the exercise.

The Exercise

    I. Specific preliminary steps for participants to prepare for the conversation. Read through this section, parts A through C, then carry out those instructions. [5 minutes]

        A. First, form pairs in which to perform the exercise.

        B. Then, enter into agreements in your dyad that will create a safe structure and process. Some examples are agreements to
            1. Protect confidentiality
            2. Observe time limits
            3. Follow exercise instructions
            4. Allow each person to decline without explanation to respond to anything he or she is not ready to respond to.
            5. Avoid interrupting one another

        C. Next, decide on a turn-taking order (Person A is the first interviewee, Person B the first interviewer, then the roles reverse).

    II. Individual preliminary steps. Read through this section, parts A. and B (1–4), then carry out those instructions. [6 minutes for steps A and B].

        A. Silently select a personal dilemma or concern (or, alternatively, a desired celebration) that you are interested in exploring with your conversational partner. This exercise is most effective if you select something that really matters to you. You won't be trying to find solutions but rather to gain greater clarity or other perspectives, to see more complexly, and so on.

B. Reflect silently on the dilemma. Consider the aspects specified in the items 1–4 below. Jot down a few notes that will enable you to describe the situation you want to work with.

1. A theme, title, or headline for your experience of the dilemma (e.g., "being demeaned in public," "anger and silence when a person tells me one thing privately and speaks differently in front of others")

2. The minimum essential facts a listener needs to know in order to grasp your specific dilemma in its context

3. Why the situation presents a dilemma for you (or why the thing you wish to celebrate matters to you), even if you think it is obvious (Include the meanings you hold about the situation as well as the facts.)

4. A specific experience, encounter, moment, or time when you experience the dilemma in a concrete, in-the-moment way (What actually happened? What are the actual, enacted details of your experience when you are in the heart of the dilemma? Note both visible and invisible aspects of your experience—what you did, what others did, what you felt, thought, imagined, feared, and so on.)

III. Collaboratively conversing about Person A's dilemma

A. Person A's telling of the story; Person B's listening to the story [4 minutes]

Person A: Tell Person B your story using the parameters above to help you stay focused, succinct, and also accurate about what matters to you. Rely more heavily on description than explanation.

Person B: Listen to Person's A story. Listen for what matters to Person A. This section of the exercise is not an interview; it is wide-open listening to heart-felt speaking. Soon you will rely on your having listened well to what was said and what was not said as you think of questions you might ask Person A with the purpose of evoking fresh reflections, questions that might open a window to experience the situation described with greater complexity and other perspectives. Make note of words or phrases that repeat, seem unusual, or are laden with feeling.[3] Stay connected with Person A, but only ask questions if you are confused and need clarification.

B. Codesign of the inquiry and inquiring [3 minutes for 1, 4 minutes for 2 through 5]
1. Silent reflection: Person A and Person B reflect separately and silently, as indicated below:
Person A: During this time think of a few questions you might like to be asked by Person B. Are there a few questions that seem as if they might be quite interesting to consider? Write these down.
Person B: During this time reflect on what you have heard, how it was said, and the words you heard. Think of a few questions that you believe would be interesting for Person A, questions that you imagine are likely to generate fresh reflections, a richer description, or greater complexity.
2. *Person A*: Tell and show Person B the questions you thought of and might wish to be asked.
3. *Person B*: Tell and show Person A the questions you thought of for him or her.
4. Work together to create a few more questions that you think might be useful for this exploration.
5. *Person A*: You (and only you!) decide which of these questions you would like to be asked, and in what order you want Person B to ask them. The only selection criterion is that you find them genuinely interesting.
C. The interview [15 minutes].
Person B: Begin the interview of Person A with the question or the first of the sequence of questions Person A selected after hearing and seeing both sets. Your goal is to promote reflection that might evoke a richer description of Person A's dilemma. As Person A responds, it may seem natural to move on to some version of the other questions he or she found compelling. As it seems right to you, use other questions that either of you or both of you developed, or ask questions that arise in the conversation. Check with Person A about how it is going and be ready to receive and act on the interviewee's suggestions.
Don't forget to—
• Stay in good contact with Person A.
• Accept every change that he or she suggests, whether it makes sense to you or not. Ask for specifics if you are in doubt about what, exactly, he or she wants you to ask.

- Seek to learn about and evoke conversation about developments the interviewee prefers or seeks.
- Take good enough notes to track, use, and elaborate on specific language (key words and phrases) that the interviewee uses.

Person A: This interview is for you and your learning and interest. What is most important here is that you only respond to questions that you find genuinely interesting, that you feel open to fresh thinking, feeling, or possibilities for action.

If a question does not engage you, don't answer it. Rather, use it as a prompt to notice what you would prefer to be asked and suggest the revised or totally different question to *Person B*, who will then ask it. No explanation is needed. You can do this at any time. Try not to worry about the interviewer's feelings (but notice if you do). By offering a correction or shift of the question you are giving a gift to the interviewer. It would look something like this.

- Ask about that again, but this time ask me about what I wanted to have happen, instead of what actually happened,

Or,

- I thought I was interested in my boss's views when we started, but as we are talking now I find I am bored by them. Ask me about what I do, think, and feel about my competence when my boss is not around;

Or,

- No, ask me whose views on me I respect and care about.

At the end of 15 minutes, bring this interview to a close.

D. Initiate mutual reflection on the effects on you of this inquiring process.

Reflect on your experiences with one another. [2 minutes].

IV. Collaboratively conversing about Person B's dilemma

Return to the start of the just-completed interview instructions and reverse roles. Person B becomes the interviewee and Person A, the interviewer. Follow all the steps of the interview, Section III, parts A through D. [28 minutes total]

V. Shared reflection following the two collaboratively developed interviews

Talk together about what you found challenging, invigorating, puzzling, satisfying, surprising, or otherwise notable in this process and what you will take with you from this experience.

VI. Large group reflections on this collaborative process that do not
reveal anyone's personal material
Talk in the larger group about your experiences of this process
and any questions it raised.

Comments from People Who Have Done This Exercise

Although people who have done this exercise and its variants often report
learnings connected with various interviewing practices—such as the power
of attending to the interviewee's specific words in moving the interview
forward or observing an interviewee's delight when the conversation has
opened fresh perspectives by veering away from solution-talk—others focus
on learnings that directly relate to inquiring from a collaborative stance.

Many people mention surprise at experiencing comfort in openly collaborating to develop the structure and content of the interviews. Some
have commented on how this exercise invites them to notice what and how
much they assume and how their assumptions can constrict what they
hear and see. Others reflect on provocative surprises they experience.

Some Comments Made from the Interviewer Position

- "Seeing the two sets of questions next to each other helped me
  think of questions I would never have imagined."
- "Wow, did I get some surprises when I followed the interviewee
  and not my assumptions about her!"
- "What a relief to not have to do it all—to not carry the weight of
  thinking I should know what I can't know. I hope I can keep it up."
- "I didn't feel exposed (something I often worry about)."
- "I felt that the work is about the person, not the story. I usually try
  to figure out questions to transform the story."
- "It was like having a reflecting team without having a reflect-
  ing team."
- "My interviewee's ideas about the situation transformed dramati-
  cally in only 15 minutes. Does this usually happen?"

Some Comments Made from the Interviewee Position

- "I loved being in charge of the questions. It kept me focused on
  what I cared about."
- "I didn't get annoyed when the interviewer asked questions that I thought
  were off the point; I just told her the questions I wanted to hear."
- "When I thought of questions for myself my story got bigger. The
  questions I finally wrote down were questions from a story that
  had already changed."

- "Picking where to start . . . helped me remember what is at the heart of my concern."
- "When I felt the interviewer's questions were 'off,' I realized I hadn't told what mattered most to me; I got clarity right there."
- "I never asked my interviewer to change one thing. She used the questions I selected. Then, as I responded I noticed new questions that I had for myself. After a while, she didn't have to do anything but be there with me as I answered my own questions!"

Difficulties Reported from Both the Interviewer and Interviewee Roles

Difficulties reported from both the interviewee and the interviewer roles are beyond the scope of this paper, but present important challenges in the development and use of collaborative stances and practices. I'll describe two of them here. Some interviewers experienced the very success of their having taken an openly collaborative working stance as challenging the sense of professional identity they held (e.g., "I didn't feel I was doing anything!"). Some interviewees felt uncomfortable asking the interviewer to change course or modify the questions asked. A few felt entirely unable to do so. Others simply forgot that they could ask—some because the process was unthinkable. Their difficulties were variously described as not wanting to be rude, not wanting to be seen as critical, and not wanting to hurt the interviewer's feelings.

These reported experiences invite me to reflect on ways that cultural and contextual expectations such as those connected with issues of difference (e.g., class, color, education, linguistic fluency) or with histories of abuse or marginalization, shape people's readiness to work collaboratively with us in what is, in its social form, a hierarchical relationship. What are safe enough conditions for those who have not been able to believe their voices and perspectives welcome to join fully in a process in which they are asked to correct our questions, and to value their experience as central? Thinking about ways to address these challenges is work for another time and place.[4]

Collaboratively Developing Questions and a Sequence for Asking Them: A Clinical Example

In developing the exercise above I relied on learnings from clinical work to design ways to teach. Recently I brought learnings from this training exercise directly into a clinical situation. In making the connection in the other direction, I experienced anew the generative effects of welcoming and inviting clients to join with me in a relationship of collaborative inquiry when the way forward is murky and confusion or paralysis threatens.

A 45-year-old woman ("Connie A.") with whom I met recently was distressed by the likelihood that life as she had known it and expected it to continue to be was not going to conform to her long-time expectations and that each day, if not each hour, would call for her to make frightening choices. Every choice-point seemed to invite moves toward fresh, unknown, and fearsomely unpredictable territory or toward painful, dissatisfying, but familiar places. When she took certain observations and feelings into account, she felt pushed toward all-or-nothing actions that did not seem right to her at the same time that they did. It was hard for her to stand firmly grounded in her own experience.

It was hard, she said, to feel anger in the moment, even though she had felt angry just an hour earlier. She said it was hard to refrain from dismissing what she wanted to do, to say, and to consider in favor of considering others' wishes and desires, and it was hard to linger on noticing and exploring the logistical and emotional complexities of her situation without deciding that maybe she was making a big deal out of nothing. As our conversation went on she paused, frowned, looked a bit perturbed and said a bit harshly, "This is not the right conversation. I know it isn't, but I don't know what is!" I said that I also did not.

In the few moments of silence that followed I thought of the exercise in this paper. I relied on its structure and premises in a proposal I made to Connie. I said, "Neither of us knows what might be a more useful way to go on. I have an idea that might help us get to a conversation that feels more 'right' to you. Let's each separately take a few minutes to think of and write down any questions you or I might have for you that might be interesting for you to be asked now. Then we'll tell each other the questions we thought of so you can see if any of them point our conversation in a direction that feels better to you. If they don't, once we've looked at them we'll work together to make up some more." She nodded in agreement. We each thought, we each wrote; she read her questions to me, and I read mine to her.

The questions Connie thought of, wrote down, and read aloud were the following.

- What do I need to remember or do to stay away from conclusion land (moving rapidly from thought to conclusions about what I should do)?
- What are some ways to psych myself that this is about me, my life, and not about anyone else—not my husband, not my kids, not my parents, not anyone else?
- Am I afraid I'll have to eat twigs and bark and lose my food, my cushions of comfort, if I let out my anger?
- How can I remember that there is always a possibility for choice?

- How can I keep from feeling that I am losing all control?
- How can I take on my fear of being watched and seen?

Following are the questions I thought of, drawing on information she had shared with me in our earlier work, then wrote down and read aloud.

- If you were to put Fear into an audience position, and not give it permission to be an actor in your life, what, if anything, in your experience of this situation do you believe might shift?
- Have there been times you believed that Fear was acting in your interests? That it was a good friend?
- What do you love about swimming in the open ocean?

We each read aloud the questions we had separately created—and each wrote notes on the other's questions. Then I asked, "Which questions, of those we've each written—or any others that might have occurred to you since—do you want me to ask you?" She replied without a moment's hesitation that she was intensely interested in being asked the following questions:

- How can you take on your fear of being watched and seen?
- How can you psych yourself that this is about you, not about anyone else?
- What do you love about swimming?

Then I asked, "Of these three questions, where would you like to start?" Again she responded without hesitation, "I want to start with the question 'What do you love about swimming?'"

We shifted our postures from the more-side-by-side orientation we had taken as we shared our questions and resumed more face-to-face postures. I noted to myself that she had shortened the question I had proposed, removing the phrase "open ocean" which shifted the focus of the question. In my speaking, I followed her lead, trusting that she had heard and chosen the language that was resonant with what she cared about. I asked it as she had stated it, "What do you love about swimming?"

She spoke at great length with few pauses. Each one of her statements and responses seemed to produce a cascade of others. It was as if each statement she made generated inner questions that she then answered. Her facial and body expressions became lively and fluid as she experienced her own responses and her curiosity and cascading additional responses. Somehow, her speaking seemed to include responses to the other two questions she wanted to be asked and even some that she had passed by.

As she spoke I took notes of her words. I recorded the following statements.

- "When I swim my legs do what they want to do; it is like fear poisons my muscles on land. That doesn't happen at all when I am swimming."
- "When the fear is in my muscles, it isn't *for* me. It is not there for me, to help me. It is to stop me, to make me more watery. This is about me. Fear distracts me from my legs, where my anger is. My legs have a job to do. This has happened; I won't let this happen again. I will kick; [my legs] can't do that job, kicking, when I worry that someone is watching. Fear stops the connection between the nerves and the muscles."
- "Different strokes feel different. I like the breast stroke; with that one I feel stretchy and flexible. I really like my legs then; I can feel them all the way to my crotch. They feel more a part of me, I have a sense of wholeness and connection. I feel whole. I have all of me."
- "When I do the back stroke I feel my hamstrings—in the back of my legs. My back! A dimension I usually don't know I have. When I am using the hamstrings I feel fuller, in better shape—it hurts after, it has longer effects, and I know I have really done something!"
- "With the side stroke I feel myself kicking to push myself forward; With this stroke my legs feel the longest they ever are, I feel all of me. I know it is my life, not anyone else's. I have my life then. Fear can't be in the pool; it can't come in. It doesn't float."

As she finished speaking she smiled. Her attitude had shifted: she was ready to take on the considerations that had stymied her earlier.

At a moment when Connie felt helpless to go on and did not trust her own perceptions and desires, she selected a question that could, through metaphor and body memory, provide a way to recall and expand her own resources, to notice both what felt good to her and her own ability to chose it. By the time she finished responding to the first question she had selected she again felt the possibility of being an active agent in shaping her own life. I believe, though I have not heard so from her, that this recall began at the moment she wrote out her own questions and was amplified at the moment she experienced herself choosing the question that was most likely to set her on a path to restoring her sense of, well, swimming.

Conclusion

This account from a therapy session is not meant to recommend or encourage the direct transfer of this training exercise to clinical work. In fact, this literal transfer is unusual. What is more usual is the experience trainees report that once they have had the experience of acting as both interviewer and interviewee in this collaborative mode and reflected on its effects on both roles and both participants, they more readily find ways to bring their practices and their commitments to work collaboratively closer together in startling and fresh ways. (See Stains, 2003, for an explication of the potentiating force of trainees' bringing clarity about their own purposes to training contexts.)

Where I have had an opportunity to observe trainees' ongoing work, I have found that trainees who participate in this exercise—whether they are engaged in mediation, facilitation, organization development, clinical work, or another field—show qualitative differences in their practice. For the most part, the transfer of learning from this exercise experience to their actual practice results in increased acuity in seeing assumptions as simply assumptions and not truths, in enhanced openness to action toward the joint shaping of the forms and content of the interview process as a mutually constructed enterprise, and indeed in greater courage and artistry in their work. Along with this movement there often comes another: the movement between action and reflection that helps them stay attuned to and inclusive of the reliable and generative tension between their own questions, assumptions, and beliefs, and those of the people with whom they work.

Acknowledgments

My thinking about exercise included in this chapter has benefited greatly from discussions over time with my colleagues Richard Chasin, David Epston, Peggy Sax, and Robert R. Stains, Jr. Carole Samworth has provided invaluable editorial support for this chapter.

Endnotes

1. The first version of this exercise, "An Exercise in Collaborative Inquiry: Inquiring in the Service of the Asked," was developed in 1999. This latest iteration has benefited from experience in using "Inquiring from a Side-by-Side Position to Generate Experiences of Purpose and Possibility," an exercise developed in 2005 with my colleague, Robert R. Stains, Jr., for the Public Conversations Project.
2. Chasin, Roth, and Bograd (1989) and Roth and Chasin (1994) include an account of using such agreements in therapy. Such agreements are also a core feature of preparing the ground for dialogue in the work of the Public Conversations Project (Chasin, et al., 1996).
3. See Roth and Weingarten (1991) for an exercise that aims to increase awareness of the effects of listening for, following, and working with clients' specific language.
4. See Madsen (1999).

References

Andersen, T. (1987). The reflecting team: Dialogue and meta-dialogue in clinical work. *Family Process, 26*, 415–428.

Anderson, H. (1997). *Conversation, language and possibilities: A postmodern approach to therapy* (pp. 25–39). New York: Basic Books.

Anderson, H. (2005). The myth of not-knowing. *Family Process, 44,* 497–504.

Anderson, H. & Goolishian, H. (1988). Human systems as linguistic systems: Evolving ideas about the implications for theory and practice, *Family Process, 27,* 371–393.

Anderson, H. & Goolishian, H. (1992). The client as expert: A not-knowing approach to therapy. In S. McNamee and K. Gergen (Eds.), *Therapy as social construction* (pp. 25–39). Newbury Park, CA: Sage.

Chasin, R., Herzig, M., Roth, S., Chasin, L., Becker, C., & Stains, R. (1996). From diatribe to dialogue on divisive public issues: Approaches drawn from family therapy. *Mediation Quarterly, 13,* 323–344.

Chasin, R., Roth, S., & Bograd, M. (1989). Dramatizing ideal futures and reformed pasts: Action methods in a systemic frame. *Family Process, 28,* 121–136.

Gehart-Brooks, D.R. & Lyle, R.R. (1999). Client and therapist perspectives of change in collaborative language systems: An interpretive ethnography. *Journal of Systemic Therapies, 18,* 58–77.

Hoffman, L. (1990). Constructing realities: An art of lenses. *Family Process, 29,* 1–12.

Hoffman, L. (2002). *Family therapy: An intimate history.* New York: Norton.

Madsen, W.C. (in press). *Collaborative therapy with multi-stressed families,* From old problems to new futures. New York: Guilford.

Roth, S. & Chasin, R. (1994). Entering one another's worlds of meaning and imagination: Dramatic enactment and narrative couple therapy. In M. Hoyt (Ed.), *Constructive therapies,* I (pp. 189–216). New York: Guilford.

Roth, S. & Weingarten, K. (1991). Two exercises: Attending to the other, attending to the word. In K. Weingarten (1998) The small and the ordinary: the daily practice of a post modern narrative therapy, *Family Process, 37,* 6.

Stains, R.R., Jr. (2003). Training on purpose. *Conflict Resolution Quarterly, 20,* 473–476.

White, M. & Epston, D. (1990). *Narrative means to therapeutic ends.* New York: Norton.

CHAPTER 21

Curious George: Interview with a Supervisor

GLEN GARDNER AND ANTHONY NEUGEBAUER[1]

George Pulliam is well known and revered in marriage and family therapy circles in Texas. George worked, collaborated, and argued with Harry Goolishian and Harlene Anderson while they were colleagues at the University of Texas Medical Branch in Galveston (UTMB) before they created the Galveston Family Institute (GFI), now known as the Houston Galveston Institute). After Harry and Harlene moved to GFI, George maintained a close relationship with them and continued his professional career at UTMB. To many of the trainees at GFI, George was like the "sage" uncle who came to visit from time to time. Although he was close to the action and ideas at GFI, he was also far enough away from the Institute to present some different perspectives to the trainees. George is legendary among his former trainees for his inquisitiveness, creativity, humor, energy, caring, and pragmatic approaches to therapy, and his willingness to change his mind on just about any subject.

We have supervised, taught, and trained students for many years. So, naturally we have been interested in what effective supervisors do in supervision. We wanted to study a supervisor who had a reputation as a good and effective supervisor and someone who made a difference in the lives of his/her trainees. George Pulliam's name came to mind immediately because of our professional relationship with him for 20 years, his reputation as a quality supervisor, and because of the many therapists who trained with George who have told us stories about his work. Everything we observed pointed to George as an exceptional supervisor. We asked George if he would be willing to be the focus of our case study of one supervisor who is considered to be a "master" supervisor. He immediately objected to the term "master" so we ceased to use the term to describe him in this study. He felt complimented that we would want to interview and study him.

Although we have introduced George Pulliam as a supervisor in the above paragraphs, perhaps the best way to introduce him is through his own words. The following are his comments on this chapter:

As I read this chapter about my supervision I thought what a very fortunate person I have been. I became a mental health professional by accident. Following 4 years in the Navy and 3 years of college with a major in psychology, I was ready to go to work and to get married. The only jobs available were as a salesman and in travel. Instead, I went to work at an institution for the mentally retarded, loved the work, was encouraged to go to graduate school, and the rest is history. I came to Galveston because I met a child psychiatrist, Gene Hornsby, in Ohio who came to UTMB. Gene an exceptional child psychiatrist who has great respect for other professionals, allowed me to develop however I wanted to while at UTMB. Harry Goolishian and I became friends and colleagues because he was there. The family therapy movement was in its infancy and Houston/Galveston was a nursery for developing it. I was in the right place at the right time to be a part of it. As the concepts and ideas emerged from this chapter [through] the efforts of Glen and Tony to pull them together from disjointed and incoherent conversations, I was so pleased to learn that most of the people I had supervised and trained had gotten the most important part of that which I believe, which is respect for every client, the lack of expertise for any individual or family, the absence of blame and efforts at empathy, and the search to find humor in most situations. I have never thought of myself as anyone special or as one who has special talents. To have my colleagues and trainees believe that I do a good job and that I have their respect is the greatest compliment I could receive. I have been doing this work for over 40 years. There is still much to learn and much to do. I hope that I have contributed a little here and there. Thank you, Glen and Tony. You have made me feel special and that feels very good, so I really don't mind if it is true or not.

GPP

Data Collection

We did four 1.5 hour interviews with George. The format of each consisted of 1-hour interviews between George and the researchers, and in the final 20 to 30 minutes of each interview, the faculty of the Houston Galveston Institute (HGI) added their questions and comments. At least two HGI faculty members were available for each interview. All interviews were audiotaped, videotaped, and transcribed immediately after each interview by a professional transcriptionist. The first interview was an unstructured interview in which we asked George to "tell us about your supervision." Immediately after each interview, we discussed our impressions based on our notes and memories of the sessions. General questions were then formulated for the next interview. When new information arose from our conversations with George, we pursued those that he found interesting or we were curious about. After the third interview, we gave George video copies of all three interviews for his review. We requested that George view the tapes between the third and fourth interviews and share his feedback with us at the final meeting.

Also, after the third interview with George, we conducted two focus groups with former supervisees. George gave us a number of therapists that he had supervised over the last 15 years including some with whom he thought he did not have a good supervisory relationship. Out of 20 names that we were given, 17 attended one of the two focus groups. The focus groups were structured similar to the first interview. We started each focus group with "Tell us about George's supervision." Finally, after viewing the tapes and reading the transcripts of the focus groups, we completed the fourth interview with George. During that interview we asked for his reactions to his first three interviews and asked questions based the content of the focus groups.

Data Analysis

The two researchers did independent analyses of the texts; areas of agreement and disagreement were identified throughout the analysis process. Formal analysis began with the two researchers reading and rereading the transcripts. Each researcher then separately developed meaning units line-by-line. Initial categories and codes were completed as the interviews were transcribed between the interviews. Categories were further refined with each interview until all interviews were complete. Subcategories under each major category were developed and are reported in this chapter. Categories remained flexible throughout the process.

George's Theory

How George views the process of therapy and supervision as intertwined was evident in our discussions with him about clinical theory. Before examining the specific details of how this process of supervision appears, we wanted to explore with him and his supervisees his ideas about the theoretical notions that inform his interactions with his trainees. George revealed a mixture of personal values/beliefs and experiences that revolved around formal clinical theory. These combined to form what we called "George's Theory." The following categories emerged from the content of our conversations.

Questioning Theory

George's natural curiosity and irreverent disposition makes him cautious of all the theories he has been exposed to from the beginning of his training. He told us how he began his struggle with psychodynamic theory during his early training. "A lot of it just didn't make sense to me. Still doesn't." There came a point in his development when he heard there were interesting and different approaches being used in the Galveston area: "There were some things happening in Galveston; people doing Multiple Impact Therapy." It was "just natural" that he would "bump into" Harry Goolishian in that context. He described Harry back then: "He always had an idea and was always looking at things a little bit differently than what was happening at the moment." George described their early interactions at the Galveston Family Institute: "So I fit in nicely with that because I always questioned the theories, and I always had a sense that this doesn't have it correctly; that it is not right yet." The impact of Harry's ability "to challenge your thinking" remains a profound factor in George's development as a supervisor.

George talked about how his initial experiences of training in Galveston involved "learning all the time and churning up ideas . . . being skeptical." That early influence continues today in his irreverence and questioning nature about theory

> George: I'm skeptical of theory . . . it can't have answers for people's problems. I used to kid about this, but I really mean it . . . despite our theories ad our training . . . we know if we've been in the trenches . . . that we don't [necessarily] do what theories say we do. . . I don't have one that I'm in love with . . . I'm not into teaching one theory. I want to open minds . . . there are many theories and there are many ways of looking at cases. The more resources you have, the more you know, the more possibilities you have.

We were curious about what these ideas look like, in general, when he is working with his trainees.

George: If they're seeing a case, I may talk about the narrative perspective, I may talk about the collaborative perspective. I'll say, hey, why don't you think about *this*? Now I still find it helpful to think about some structural concepts which I thought about long before it was called that... I'm a person who is very concerned about boundaries and developmental norms for instance in terms of where kids are in their development, where people are in their development as couples. And I don't mean in categories; I mean in terms of where they are and what they are up to right now. They have stories to tell, they have ways of thinking. Each has a different language and it conveys a different kind of meaning.

A bit later in the interview George clarified the point we were discussing above.

George: I'm an atheist as far as theory is concerned in terms of the purity of it. Yet I think all theories are good; there are no bad theories . . . . But to think that any one of them encompasses the truth or understanding is foolishness in my view.

Coaching

At one point in our interview about theory George stated that he preferred to view what he does with trainees as "coaching" rather than supervision. He talked about how everyone needs supervision, to talk with others about cases, regardless of how much clinical experience they have: "I can't think of any of us that are so good that we don't need that."

The idea of coaching is, as I see it, encouragement, trying to get them to reach their potential, to teach them some of the things that they are questioning, some of things that they are looking at . . . trying to get their own sense of beliefs. I often ask them, "Okay, you just saw this case. Which theory are you going to put it in?" And then I show them very quickly you can put it in any of them.

The Importance of Supervisee Theory

George always reminded us of his belief that "all theories can do good and all can do harm." But rather than the formal theory that trainees learn in a classroom, George is interested in the personal theories of his trainees and how these ideas evolve with the ideas of the clients. Again, the theme of how therapy and supervision is a very practical endeavor was prevalent in these conversations.

George: Well, you name it, and I've probably used some of it at sometime. I talk about theory. . . We talk about actual cases . . . What is the client saying is wrong? How are you making sense out of it? . . . They talk about how they are thinking about the case. They talk about what needs to be done. All that is coming out of a theory. But it's not coming out of one that is conceptualized like they learned it in the classroom.

He continued to describe how theory is taught in academic settings, from books and lectures, and how he prefers to explore the unique theory of his trainees.

George: Sometimes we'll try to put students' unique theories into the perspective of a formal theory as an academic exercise. It's an academic exercise because I'm not so interested in the theory they believe in as I am in how they are thinking about the people that they are dealing with, what they think is going to help, how can they achieve that help, and how do they see that process developing.

Another way George inquires about the individual theory of his trainees is through a writing assignment. He talked about how students come to him from their training programs with an assignment to write case studies from a particular theory. George says he hates to read those papers. Instead, George has them write their own "theory" paper. The nature of the assignment was described this way:

I say "I want to know what you think . . . you can include anything about theory or your own experience." I want to know how you make sense out of how people get way they are. I want to know how their problems developed and what helps them change and overcome them.

Theory about Expectations

George discussed with us how he viewed student's questions about theory as indicative of their "expectations" about the supervision experience. He explained how the expectations trainees bring to supervision influence the development of their ideas about theory and supervision and how having these expectations can result in a positive experience.

George believes that positive clinical experiences result if you manage the "expectation" aspect of therapy and supervision in a similar manner. If prospective trainees inquire about his "theory," he addresses this in the same way he would if the question came from a prospective client: "I tell them my supervision style is a lot of things, and why don't we just meet a few times and see how it goes. After that, [the interest in my having theories] usually never comes up again."

George summarized his ideas about the link between expectations and supervision in the following manner.

George: My reputation as a supervisor is part of the perception the trainee brings to the supervision context. So I say, well, we'll perpetuate the myth and that's all right (laughs) we'll keep it going. But if the myth is perpetuated, the fact of the matter is that it becomes a reality for some people, including me. I mean, it's not like it has to be the ultimate truth. They've got some expectations of the supervisor before they walk in the door. And if those expectations are even met a little bit, they think they've made a good decision.

In the Beginning

Beginning therapists (interns or trainees) are a constant challenge for George because it seems there is so much for them to learn, so much to understand about them, so much to adjust to, so much they think they "should" be. And, there are so many factors that determine whether an intern will achieve the full benefit of their time with George. "Success" in internship often depends on accidental occurrences such as working with the client who gets better in spite of the intern's initial awkward attempts to be helpful. Or, they may see the client that disturbs their comfort zone just enough that they have to do something different.

Beginning therapists are different from one another. Yet they have a great deal in common when they arrive at their first intern site. Throughout our conversations with George, we discussed various aspects of the "beginning therapist" as he sees them. What follows are our selective impressions mixed with George's ideas about beginning therapists:

George has numerous ways of understanding and describing new interns with whom he worked. He wouldn't go so far as to admit that he has stereotypes about beginning therapists. However, he did say that they have some general characteristics.

Tony: Do you have a stereotype of a beginning trainee?

George: I don't think so. I think there is a world of difference out there. I think they, most of the time, have some [similar] characteristics. Maybe they are a little bit afraid. They are concerned about doing well, which is one of the things that I try to get out of the way. They want to do it well right off the bat. They already want to have arrived instead of being in process.

Integration of Self

Another common characteristic that George sees in his beginning therapists is that they tend to think about themselves differently when they are in the therapy room and act differently as a result. George suggests that one of the things that beginning therapists need to learn is that they don't need to change themselves in order to be a good therapist. They simply need to use who they are in a different context, which is therapy.

George: They have an image about what they're supposed to be . . . this professional person who is someone different from who they are. My contention is that you're the same person [personally as well as professionally]. You just take what you have and use it in a different way. That includes all you tried to learn and all the experiences you've had and everything else, and put it in that perspective. So, when you're this therapy person, you're still the same person. I'm not so sure if I were doing supervision or we were having this conversation that I'm very different [in one role from the other]. My idea about what I'm up to is very different but I don't think that I'm a different person at all.

Life Experiences

One issue that is examined from time to time in the literature is the relationship between the beginning therapist's personal life experiences and their effectiveness as a therapist. Intuitively, it makes sense that someone who has lived longer may have gained more insights about life, be less surprised about unique situations, and therefore work with clients from a more informed position. George says "not necessarily." Simply having experience doesn't necessarily predict a broader view of the world. He further reflected

George: If I were to create the perfect world, for the most part I would want a person who was going to be doing therapy with me, or anyone who was dear to me, to have had some world experiences themselves. That means that I want somebody who's past 25. Just as soon as I mention that to you, I [recall that I] had a trainee last year who was 24 years old who was one of the most brilliant trainees I've ever had. She was great. There was just no question about it. She was exceptional. There are others who come in at age 50 who probably never will improve any more. So having said what I said, I think world experiences are good but it doesn't mean that that's going to do the trick. Maybe the language I'm looking for is not age but maturity, whatever that means.

Relationship with Trainees

As alluded to earlier in the core ingredients of supervision, George thought that good relationships with his trainees were essential to doing good training. Without the relationship, supervisors do not have the level of trust required for good training.

George: Probably the most important ingredient across all good teachers and supervisors regardless of what theory they have, is the relationship they have with the student, and the respect and trust that grows out of it. . . . I feel it's my responsibility to find a way to connect. . . . If I don't have a chance to spend that time and [instead] I'm only hearing about cases and about theoretical notions, [I will] never get a chance to really get beyond that. So, it's part of the supervision process that I foster a personal relationship, that I want to know about that person. I respect that person. I want to encourage the positive and I want to see if they have any glitches that I need to straighten out a little bit. But it's all done more personally. I don't know how else to say it.

Time

Perhaps something that is not considered enough in supervision is the amount of time that we spend with a trainee. Too often supervision is a brief scheduled encounter with one or more trainees that focuses on the theory or pragmatics of therapy, there is little time to go beyond the professional relationship to a greater understanding of the whole person. George believed that the supervisor needs to know his/her trainees very well, and he is frustrated when he is unable to have the time he needs with them. The key ingredient in developing the relationship that he prefers is a lot of time with the trainees. It is very difficult to develop an in-depth relationship with trainees unless you spend a significant amount of time with them. George called it "leisure."

> George: When you've got the leisure, you can talk about other stuff. You can talk about interests. You can talk about your family. You get to know the person as a person, not just as this object of supervision.

Personal Impact

Many of the participants commented on the personal impact that George had on their professional lives and their personal lives as well.

> Trainee A: Even though it's on a professional level, he makes a completely personal impact which is what I think you were trying to get at earlier, not by being personal necessarily, though he sort of plays the Wizard of Oz. He gives you the gifts you already had but you didn't want to own, somehow.
>
> Trainee B: It's real easy to get dug in and get real comfy [with George] when you are around him.

One of the more poignant descriptions of George's impact on his trainees was the following.

> Trainee C: It's interesting because we had a luncheon . . . and I got the time wrong, and [before I arrived] you had all stood up and said something about your supervisor and that relationship. And so I got there, after that was over, they gave me an opportunity to speak, and I just sat there and wept. I couldn't say a word. Just sat there and wept. 'Cause . . . he's meant so much to me, and he's been such a major support and just really kept me going, and has been such a role model . . . one of the most positive role models that has ever stepped into my life. And I was thinking all these things I wanted to say to George and all that came out was tears. And I just couldn't say a thing.

Being Real

Another aspect of his relationships with his trainees and with others was the idea that he was the same wherever you found him. George doesn't believe in playing roles. That is, he didn't act differently at work and another way in a social situation. Harlene Anderson commented to George during one interview, "You are George in whatever context I meet you. And *that* George is a certain George that is always there." George responded to Harlene's comment that "As a supervisor or supervisee, you've got to be yourself. And what you said is true. I mean, it's the nicest compliment I can have; I'm George. And that's what I'd like to be. It fits in nicely because this is my profession and it even makes it more wonderful."

George further contended that you should not have different personas in different contexts. For example, if you are doing therapy, you shouldn't have a "therapist" persona and if you are doing supervision, you shouldn't have a "supervisor" persona and so on. He thought that you should be the same wherever you are. George said more than once in our interviews, "What you see is what you get."

> *George:*   I don't know anybody that I've supervised ... that I've spent any time with ... that would see me just having a professional relationship with them. . . . I try very hard to get past the notion of what one should be.

Interestingly, this way of being seemed very reassuring to his trainees because they didn't have to guess about what George was thinking. He would tell them.

> *Trainee:*   So that, for me, was what made George distinctive from other supervisors ... that he was the same no matter what context I saw him in. And it was very reassuring to me that it wasn't a pretend strategy. It was who he was.
>
> *George:*   Yeah, I think being the same person in all contexts and having permission to be a variety of people in all of the contexts helped me more than anything ... to be real with trainees and yet be clear about who's the supervisor and not be confusing or mystifying about that.

Supervisory Behavior and Process

Although we were very interested in the theoretical notions underlying George's interactions with his supervisees, we were also interested in specific behavioral aspects of his supervision that exhibit his theoretical ideas.

Differences between Supervision and Consultation

As we discussed with George his supervisory experiences in different contexts, he wanted to make sure we understood how he conceptualized his role as a "supervisor" vs. a "consultant." He told us about the agencies he has contracted with over the years, where he comes in for an hour or so a week. "People bring cases in. They present them and we talk about them. And I give them 16 ideas about how I might address these kinds of cases." George referred to these types of interactions as "my fantasy cases."

> George: They present a case, and I have this fantasy therapy. I talk about how it may go and what might happen and what they should be looking for. So that is consultation. It is brainstorming about possibilities, and they take whatever they can use of that.

Ideas/Offerings/Nudge Supervision

We spoke with George about how we had heard that as a supervisor in his "earlier years" he had been "very authoritarian" and tended to tell people what to do. He replied, "People still accuse me of that. It's probably true. I have a lot of ideas, and I like to give them out. But I offer them in therapy and in supervision as [they are requested] rather than teach you how to do them." He always described this act as presenting an "offering." "Sometimes I tell trainees I have an idea that could be worth a nickel, or maybe a quarter, or it could be a really good five-dollar idea." Another practical "offering" described by George and his former supervisees included: "You can ask any question as along as it's without judgment. . . . If you avoid asking a question that might upset somebody you may be avoiding bringing up the stuff they really need to talk about." Still, he related the importance of the perception of the offering to the trainee.

> George: I have this practical side. If it doesn't make sense to them, no matter how strongly I feel about it then I'm willing to abandon anything like (snaps fingers) that. I call it nudge supervision. I nudge people. But I'm willing to give it up if they're not giving a little bit.

Putting Supervisees at Ease

George assumes his trainees can only be receptive in supervision to his "offerings" and feedback if he can put them at ease. "They are concerned tremendously about what you think about them. They are worried about how they are doing. I spent all this time and effort does it really work? What am I doing?" When we asked him what he does to create an atease environment he answered:

George: Well, I do it in a number of ways. I say things like "If you are going to screw up, this is the time to do it because you're never going to have a chance to talk it over like we are going to have now. You know they are going to mess up and come out feeling badly and sometimes they come out feeling good. I try to do the same kind of accepting of where they are as I want them to be with the clients they are seeing. I want to keep it open enough that they feel "safe."

A few minutes later in our conversation George returned to the theme of having a sense of safety and comfort in the supervisory process again and summarized his thoughts.

George: I think this is true of anyone in training with any supervisor. They are concerned tremendously about what you think about them. When we are teaching and helping them develop as trainees, managing that piece, which is very fragile for some, is so important in how they secure confidence in what they think they will be able to do eventually. I think it might be the most important thing we do.

One former trainee concisely described this thought when we asked the group if they could put into a few simple words what they received from George in their training. "I think certainly the positive regard with the supervisee's mistakes ... the sense of humor about [mistakes] and the belief, the faith in the person."

Getting What You Need from Supervision

One of the ways George addressed that "fragile part" mentioned above is consistently checking with his trainees about their experience with him in supervision.

George: I don't want you to think that I am always tuned in because I'm not. I ask for feedback. I ask regularly, "Are you getting what you want or is there something else you would be rather talking about? I try to ask it every week. What are you getting here? Are you getting what you need? What are we missing? Is this helpful?"

George believes asking questions such as these is the only way students are going to obtain the maximum benefit from his supervision. In our conversation with the former trainees they reflected several thoughts. "What I chose to focus on he would go with. I think George allows you to define the agenda." Another added, "I think he adjusts to whatever I would bring in. I think he does that with just about everybody."

These trainees emphasized George's openness to their agenda in supervision. Other supervisees highlighted George's tendency to insert his ideas into the supervisory process. Two former trainees described their version of this dynamic, in a particularly humorous exchange that described interactions with George that were obviously familiar to many in the group.

> *Trainee*: George is brilliant and quick in his creativity. He always had a thousand things to talk about and a briefcase of stuff to give us. . . . And they would be the most fantastic topics and we would get into the greatest discussions. But in the end, you wouldn't have got to the case (laughter) that you were dying to talk about. And so you really had to take a stand there.

He admitted that it is not always easy to blend his need to offer ideas and the trainee's needs to participate in setting the agenda.

> *George*: Sometimes it is way down the road before they tell me and I'll say "okay, shut me up." And I do. But then they ask some question and the next thing I know I'm over here somewhere running down a trail they're not interested in (laughs). It is something I have had to learn how to manage over all the years.

Self-Disclosure/Personal Dynamics

In talking with George about how to make sure they get what they need from supervision, we talked about how supervisees, particularly new trainees, seem to have an inclination to self-disclose.

> *George*: There is something interesting about that word "self-disclosure." People in social work and marriage and family therapy seem to be more open about themselves and what they are up to and about their life in general—and sometimes improperly. I was talking to one of my favorite supervisees just the other day and I told her, "Look, I don't really care about your life [laughs]. Let's talk about what is happening in the room!"

He added later:

George: Some people are taught to self-disclose a lot, which I think is a mistake. Again, it's the pragmatics. I have to turn them away from "Oh, that reminds me of my family" to getting back to taking care of *this* family. And if it is interfering, I will deal with it. I tell them, "After you have 30 years of experience, maybe you can self-disclose in the therapy in the therapy room." Self-disclosure has so many possibilities for problems. I tell them if they feel they have to say something then do it by using a third-person reference, one way to refer to something and not create a problem.

George strongly believes personal issues can be a valuable opportunity for trainees and clients. He calls it "facing the monsters" and described it this way.

George: I don't go into the trainee's personal dynamics unless they bring it up or unless something is happening with a case where I can see that something is not working that ought to be. And then I'll ask them about it: "What's up?" And sometimes you get into their personal life and their personal history. And sometimes they tell you, "I have this problem, [or] I came from a family with this problem." And I say, "Gee, what a wonderful opportunity to work on some of your stuff."

Many former trainees shared stories about how their exposure of personal information was used in a beneficial way in their training with George. One of them put it this way:

Trainee: I think that was part of the getting to know us and because he learned a lot, and I think learning how we coped with certain stressors helped him discover how we were going to be as a therapist; how we were going to relate to other clients in their situation. If you are falling apart inside you can't be there for your clients.

Fun

George also thought that it was important to have fun both in the therapy room and in supervision. Responding to a comment from Sue Levin about how training with George was fun, George commented:

George: You mentioned [that] you remembered supervision being fun, and I think that is the greatest compliment I've had because I like to have fun. I don't think supervision has to be grim. You can laugh about the most serious issues, and we can figure out ways of dealing with them and still go into the room and be very respectful of people we are seeing.

Summary and Conclusion

George identified several aspects of clinical supervision that are important features to his supervision style. First, George stressed that the most important ingredient in supervision was getting to know his trainees as persons. Second, George thought that it was very important that neither he nor his trainees be something other than "who they are." He asserted that students should not be a "different person" just because they are doing therapy. And, according to his former trainees, George practiced what he preached; he was the same in whatever context you found him. Third, it is imperative to address the specific needs of beginning trainees in a supportive and sensitive way. Beginning trainees are different from seasoned therapists in terms of the way they are supervised. Fourth, a heavy dose of humor and fun makes the most serious situations tolerable. And, finally, George emphasized the importance of the practical application of theory to practice. There is no good theory or bad theory; it is all in the way we "practice" them.

Our goal in undertaking this project was to examine how George Pulliam was an example of "a good clinical supervisor." We wish we could capture the richness of the interview experiences that we had with George and his former trainees. However, the reader cannot "live" our descriptions and, therefore, a great deal is lost in the translation. We can only hope that our telling of the many stories about George conveys the essence of who George Pulliam is as a person and as a supervisor.

Acknowledgment

1.   We would like to thank the faculty of the Houston Galveston Institute including Harlene Anderson, Sue Levin, Diana Carleton, Jamie Raser, Susan Swim, and Paul Burney for participating in the interviews with George. The interviews were enriched by their time and effort. We also thank Monte Bobele and Joan Biever for their willingness to spend their weekends editing this chapter. And, finally we would like to thank George Pulliam for allowing us to tell his story and for enriching our lives both professionally and personally.

CHAPTER 22

A Collaborative Approach to Research and Inquiry

DIANE GEHART, MARGARITA TARRAGONA, AND SALIHA BAVA

Collaborative therapy (Anderson, 1997; Anderson & Goolishian, 1992) is a therapeutic approach grounded in a postmodern–social constructionist perspective of knowledge. In this perspective, postmodernism's skeptical stance toward universal knowledge and dominant discourses and its preference for local knowledge and social constructionism's view of knowledge as cocreated in relationship and dialogue go hand-in-hand. This approach to knowledge informs a dynamic way to conceptualize and conduct research, offering a counterbalance to academia's pervasive preference for research grounded in logical positivism (i.e., the scientific method). This chapter details how we draw from the philosophical stance and dialogical approach described in collaborative therapy to think about, design, and conduct a research inquiry. We present the philosophical background of this approach, discuss its characteristics, and give examples for putting it in action.

This is not an approach we developed in joint projects; rather it has evolved through our relationships with each other and those who work with these ideas. Each of us works in different places and contexts, yet our work shares a commitment to collaborative practices that include participants' voices in the process of research inquiry. Diane Gehart has conducted research primarily in "teaching" universities in master's level programs with minimal financial or other support; in this context, smaller, qualitative, community-based research projects in on-campus clinics have been most viable. Her research has focused on the client's lived experience of therapy (Gehart & Lucas, in press; Gehart & Lyle, 1999, 2001), which is scarcely represented in professional literature, as well as qualitative research more broadly (Gehart, Lyle, & Ratliff, 2001). Margarita Tarragona is in a very similar situation at the universities where she teaches in Mexico City. She and her colleagues conduct their interview studies of clients' and therapists' experiences of therapy and fund their own research at Grupo Campos Elíseos, a small private training center. Saliha Bava has research experiences in various community and academic settings, currently working primarily in the academic setting with master's level students and master's and doctoral level students at the Houston Galveston Institute, where there is also minimal funding for research.

We would like to add that many of our colleagues who work from a collaborative perspective in therapy conduct research using many of these same ideas. Many describe their collaborative research projects in this volume, including Klaus Deissler; Sue Levin; Glen Garnder, and Tony Neugebaur; Debbie Feinsilver, Eileen Murphy, and Harlene Anderson; Sylvia London and Irma Rodríguez-Jazci-Levich; Marsha McDonough and Patricia Koch; Kauko Haarakangas, Birgitta Alakare, Jukka Aaltonen, and Jaakko Seikkula.

Philosophical Background

The collaborative research or inquiry approach we describe is a continuation and evolution of the turn-of-the-century debates about the differences between natural and human sciences and the respective goals of explanation (*Erklären*) vs. understanding (*Verstehen;* Schwandt, 2000). Proponents of the neo-Kantian *Verstehen* tradition argue that the goal of social sciences is foremost to understand human behavior rather than predict it. This pursuit for understanding human behavior has been at the heart of social science endeavors for over a century and has been the driving force behind most forms of qualitative research.

Phenomenology and interpretivism were two of the earliest methods used by social scientists to understand human behavior, with the former focusing on the understanding of an individual's subjective reality and the latter on the meaning of human action (Schwandt, 2000). The aim for these researchers was to "understand the subjective meaning of action (grasping the actor's beliefs, desires, and so on) yet do so in an objective manner. . . . Both the phenomenological observer and linguistic analyst [studies human behavior using detailed transcripts of verbal and nonverbal communication] generally claim this role of the uninvolved observer" (pp. 192–194). In these approaches, the researcher brackets or suspends biases as much as possible to allow for accurate rendering of the subject's experience and lived reality.

The possibility of a bracketed or an uninvolved researcher was questioned in the philosophical hermeneutics of Gadamer (1960/1994), inspired by the work of Heidegger. In philosophical hermeneutics, understanding is considered an act of interpretation; it is produced in dialogue rather than discovered or reproduced. Departing from phenomenological and interprevist traditions, sociocultural prejudices are not regarded as something the interpreter can separate from in order to gain a "clearer" understanding. "The point is not to free ourselves of all prejudice, but to examine our historically inherited and unreflectively held prejudices and alter those that disable our efforts to understand others, and ourselves" (Garrison, 1996, p. 434, cited in Schwandt, 2000, p. 195). Only through dialogical encounters with what is different from ourselves can we identify, test, and redefine our prejudices. Thus, understanding is a lived and embodied experience that simultaneously shapes one's sense of personhood and one's experience of life itself. From this hermeneutic perspective, the researcher is no longer a detached observer but rather a dynamic participant who shapes and is shaped by the process.

Social constructionists share much in common with philosophical hermeneutics but depart on the issue of truth, which the latter asserts is arrived at through interpretative practice. In contrast, social constructionists are more skeptical. A moderate or "weak" (Schwandt, 2000) form of social constructionism, developed in the feminist philosophy of science, is attentive to the subtle ways that the researcher's sociocultural biases inform the research process. This model embraces objectivity and attempts to reduce bias by identifying and critiquing the researcher's background assumptions in order to arrive at communally shared standards of evaluation. In contrast, a "strong" (Schwandt, 2000) constructionist approach (Gergen, 1999) maintains that even observational descriptions cannot escape sociocultural bias because they are conveyed through language, which is always embedded in broader culturally defined language games (Wittgenstein, 1978). This strong social constructionist approach maintains that there is no single framework that can be identified as "better" outside of its communal or cultural context. Such a view gives rise to *relational hermeneutics* (Anderson, 2005), which emphasizes the interpretive stance that occurs socially in language. Thus, a research methodology grounded in a strong social constructionist perspective takes into account the immediate relational and broader social contexts that shaped the knowledge which emerges from the research endeavor. Collaborative therapy draws heavily from this social constructionist perspective or relational hermeneutics, thus creating a theoretically harmonious research option for therapists working in this tradition.

Overview of Collaborative Therapy

Collaborative therapy, also known as "collaborative language systems [CLS] therapy," is a postmodern, social constructionist approach to therapy developed by Harlene Anderson and Harold Goolishian (Anderson, 1997, 2001; Anderson & Goolishian, 1988, 1992). As its name suggests, language and collaboration are central in this way of conceptualizing and doing therapy. Language is viewed as the medium through which people construct and express meaning and lived reality. Collaboration refers to a "stance," a way of relating with clients and with conversational partners in general.

Collaborative therapy proposes that human systems are "linguistic systems" (Anderson, 1997; Anderson & Goolishian, 1988). People are intertwined in relational networks that are built in and through language and are constantly taking part in multiple conversations. These can be "internal" within ourselves and "external" with other people. Through these conversations we make sense of our experiences; therefore, language systems are also "meaning-generating systems" (Anderson, 1997). From this perspective, language is not just a "tool" that human beings use to describe the world and themselves. Rather, language builds or constitutes lived reality.

Anderson (2005) places the collaborative therapy view of language in the postmodern tradition of hermeneutics and social constructionism, influenced by the ideas of theorists like Wittgenstein, Vygotsky, Bakhtin, Gergen, and Shotter. She also describes CLS as a postmodern approach referring to a broad critique that takes a critical perspective, challenging "fixed meta-narratives, privileged discourses, and universal truths" (1997, pp. 35–36) and emphasizing the importance of local knowledge. Furthermore, Anderson (n.d.) says that although the "postmodern family" has many branches, they share the notion that knowledge and language are relational and generative.

Anderson (1997) advocates integrating research into the daily work of therapists by continually reflecting on ideas and actions that emerge in therapeutic conversations, becoming what Schon (1991) calls a "reflective practitioner." Rather than separating therapy, consulting, teaching–learning, and research, Anderson views these as similar dialogical processes that are distinguished mainly by their purpose or intent. Their content and outcome may differ, but the relationship between the participants and the process of collaborative inquiry, exploring together the familiar and constructing the new, is essentially the same.

Anderson (2001) states that the central question of collaborative therapy is, "How can therapists create the kinds of conversations and relationships with others that allow all the participants to access their creativities and develop possibilities where none seemed to exist before?" (p. 20). Applying the question to collaborative research, we ask ourselves: How can researchers create the kinds of conversations and relationships with others that allow all the participants to access their knowledge, create knowledge, and develop understanding where none or little seemed to exist before?

Assumptions and Characteristics of Collaborative Research and Inquiry

Rather than a single methodology or model, collaborative inquiry represents a way of conceptualizing and approaching the research endeavor. Just as the collaborative stance of the therapist is the heart of the therapeutic approach, the stance of the researcher is the defining feature of collaborative inquiry. For this reason, the term *inquiry* is sometimes preferred to *research,* with the former emphasizing that participants join the researcher in the research process, and the latter more traditionally implying that only the researcher's intentions define the process. However, in many contexts it is advantageous to expand the traditional concept of research to include collaborative approaches to generating knowledge. Therefore, in this chapter we use inquiry and research interchangeably.

Researchers have many options for implementing collaborative ideas in research. Table 22.1 provides a brief overview of a continuum of differences between collaborative and traditional research methods grounded in the scientific method. Although collaborative research projects can take many forms, the informing assumptions are the same. Following are considerations for designing collaborative research endeavors.

Coconstruction of Knowledge or "Data"

Collaborative inquiry focuses on the relationship between researchers and participants and is grounded in the assumption that knowledge about their experience is constructed between them through linguistic processes. This view contrasts with research practices in which, as Paré and Larner (2004) comment, data is seen as something the investigator "gets" from participants; such a view fails to "capture the ways in which the researcher's contribution is integral to the participants' experience" (p. 213). Paré and Larner succinctly state what we believe is the most important concept in collaborative research: "Research is not simply an act of finding out but is also always a creating together process" (p. 213). Bray, Lee, Smith, and Yorks (2004) define a collaborative inquiry process as "consisting of repeated episodes of reflection and action through which a group of peers

Table 22.1 Comparison of Noncollaborative and Collaborative Inquiry Methods

Along a Continuum …	Differences from Our Perspective(s)
Noncollaborative approaches	Collaborative approaches
Paradigm/Philosophical Orientation	
Discovery model (mining)	Exploratory model (traveling)
Knowledge is discovered	Knowledge is socially constructed
Positivist	Hermeneutic, social constructionist
Positioning of Researcher	
Expert	Partner
Knowing	Curious
Hierarchical	Lowering hierarchy
Predetermined agenda	Evolving agenda
Objective and independent	Contextual and critical
Research Process	
Fact oriented	Construction oriented
Representational	Reconstructive
Observable/countable data	Includes stories/meanings
Directional	Expanding
Replicable	Unique
Questions are diagnostic	Questions are conversational
Meaning interpreted by scientist	Meaning coevolved
Singular truth of meaning	Multiplicity of meaning
Findings are universal/meta	Findings are localized

Note: We see these differences as existing along a continuum.

[researcher and participant] strives to answer a question of importance to them" (p. 6).

Tom Strong (2004), a discursive practitioner–researcher who draws on social constructionist ideas, describes his work as "a 'poetic process' in which 'respondents' are as active in their meaning-making efforts" as the researcher is" (p. 214). Strong notes that research questions can be an invitation into a joint meaning-making process and that this has ethical and pragmatic implications. He describes a difference between a "forensic quest for facts" and an invitation to get accounts or opinions from people. The former is about "'getting things right' whereas other forms of conversation welcome subjectivity" (p. 214). Influenced by dialogue theorist Bakhtin, Strong skeptically approaches research conversations, questioning whether they have a "tilt" that gives the researcher greater influence over the process than the respondents, whom he refers to as "our reciprocators," emphasizing the interdependence between researchers and participants.

Generative Process

When research participants are no longer viewed as containers for information but interactive participants, research becomes a generative process. In such inquiry, the interviewer does not simply elicit or get responses that are already formed inside the "subject" but participates in the creation of these responses. Anderson's notion of the "not yet said" (1997) refers to how meanings are articulated in the process of conversation and that most ideas are not stored inside the person, but emerge in the dialogue between people. Harry Goolishian expressed this succinctly when he stated: "I never know what I mean until I say it" (Anderson, 1997, 2005). Strong (2004) encourages researchers to "accept our participation in the yet-to-be spoken" and to ask themselves, "How does my participation in conversations of inquiry shape what I am told?" and "What happens when asking clients to make distinctions in previously unarticulated areas of their lives?" (p. 217). He adds that questions are *performative*; they can evoke, construct, and invite positions and experiences from which generative dialogues can emerge. This is similar to William Madsen's statement (1999) that "evaluation is intervention" because, even if the interviewer's intent is to gather information, the interview itself generates experiences for the participant; it can evoke memories, trigger emotions, and question or strengthen ideas. For example, in Gehart and Lyle (2001), participants were asked to describe their experiences of working with male and female therapists (working with both was part of the selection criteria). The research topic itself inspired new insights and perspectives for many participants because they had never put the comparison into words prior to the research interview.

Conversational Partnership

The assumption of collaborative research as joint action blurs the boundary between the researcher and the participants, who are considered conversational partners (Anderson, 1997) or peers (Bray et al., 2000); the research is being performed in partnership with the participants. Researchers must consider many factors when identifying and inviting participants to become active architects of their lived experiences while attempting to create a level playing field. First, researchers must be sensitive to the organizational politics and/or academic discourses, where much of the research is performed (Bava, 2005), which may affect participants' choices to become involved and how they may interpret the process. For example, in attempting to do a Web-based dissertation that would be presented outside the normative parameters of a linear text, I (SB) had to recruit the graduate school's dean, the Electronic Thesis and Dissertations (ETD) Committee, the dissertation archiving team, and the computer sciences research team, which used my dissertation process to test their ideas for developing an ETD language. Thus, in the traditional sense, these people would not be identified as research participants, yet they were very instrumental in orchestrating the organizational politics and in the creation of the academic discourse. All three groups were attempting to expand the parameters of traditional research so as to create space for nontraditional electronic dissertations, thus sanctioning my research as legitimate. Thus, all those in dialogue about the project were considered conversational partners in the study.

Additionally, researchers must consider the broader disciplinary and organizational discourses regarding what constitutes research and how the research will be perceived by various consumers, including the participants, the professional community, and the broader social community. For example, when considering the perspectives of various constituents, a researcher may choose to interview therapists, in addition to clients, to solicit descriptions of the process from more than one perspective; alternatively, family members or employers may be included in the study as well to broaden the discussion. Including multiple voices is not to establish greater accuracy but rather to create space for the many realities and voices in a given situation. This approach honors the *polyphony* of voices, which are typically preserved and presented in the final report rather than analyzed or otherwise "smoothed over" by the researcher.

Researchers must also consider the endeavor from the participant's perspective, even on seemingly mundane matters. Some of the issues that they identify include time requirements for participants who, unlike the researcher, are generally not paid, resulting in expenses such as travel and babysitting. Creating an informal and inviting setting for participants reduces the stereotypical sterile "research" context, thus lowering the hierarchy contextually and making the context more conducive to collaboration (Anderson, 1997). Communication is also a factor: participants should be kept informed throughout the process and a recursive loop set up such that they continue to shape the research product. Lastly, funding agencies often define the research from a generic set of guidelines, often limiting the participants from informing the research program at a local level. To address this issue, Lister, Mitchell, Sloper, and Roberts (2003) suggest setting up "user consultation groups" for the research project, who can continue informing the policy and research production. We believe that doing research from a collaborative stance minimizes the risk of exercising "relational violence" (Willig & Drury, 2004) toward research participants.

Mutual Inquiry: Joint Construction of Research Questions

A collaborative research approach is appropriate whenever there is a desire or need to understand how people are experiencing (have experienced) and understanding a circumstance or phenomenon from their first-person narrative. This approach is particularly well suited for arenas of new inquiry in any discipline; psychological and social researchers have an ongoing need to answers these questions. In these disciplines, most research projects include at least one research question that addresses how people experience the phenomenon being studied.

What is unique about collaborative inquiry is that the researcher and participants inquire *together*. Thus, the participants share in developing research questions and finding ways to explore them. The process is one of *mutual inquiry*, similar to that of collaborative therapy (Anderson, 1997). Participants are invited to share in developing and refining the research questions throughout a study. This is particularly important when the researcher is an "outsider" to the community, group, or situation being studied.

A collaborative approach always involves participants in defining what questions need to be asked and identifying processes that might be useful in answering those questions. In one instance, I (DG) had a client approach me about what she believed therapists needed to know more about: client advocacy (Gehart & Lucas, in press). In this instance, the idea for the project, along with the primary research question, came from the participant rather than the professional.

Collaborative inquiry is particularly useful for informing action that will impact the participants' lives. Participant informed process for social action leads to research questions that the participants identify as pertinent. Participant informed social action can also lead to research questions that require quantitative data collection.

Curious Stance of the Researcher

As in collaborative therapy, the researcher is a "nonexpert" in the participants' lived experience and therefore takes a "learner" position (Anderson, 1997). As a learner, the researcher's intention is to learn from the participants: What should be studied? Which questions are most important? How best do we answer these? How do we make sense of the answers? This learner position, developed originally as a stance for therapy, transfers well to the research arena. Curiosity and "not-knowing," two of the hallmarks of collaborative therapy (Anderson & Goolishian, 1992; Anderson, 1997), provide a refreshingly simple and clear description of researcher positioning, whether one is investigating new or familiar territory. A position of curiosity and not-knowing requires that the researcher acknowledge the limitations of any position or opinion, professional and personal, knowing that any single view of reality is one of many and has been constructed within the relationships and institutions with(in) which one, historically and currently, interacts. Curiosity fuels the research process: a desire to understand how others are experiencing a particular phenomenon. For example, in psychotherapy, collaborative research often explores how clients are experiencing the therapeutic process, providing a counterbalance to the dominance of therapist and researcher descriptions of therapy in professional literature. This shift in the role of researcher and research participant is often represented by choosing to avoid the use of the traditional research term of "subject," with a preference for terms that denote a more active role, such as participant, interviewee, or coresearcher.

Insider Research

The researcher's relationship to the subject matter, context, and participants is different than in traditional research. A collaborative approach does not strive toward objectivity, recognizing that all linguistic descriptions are inherently biased, revealing the assumptions and worldview of the speaker. Instead, collaborative researchers strive toward negotiating a coordinated understanding. In this approach, the detached position of the researcher, which characterizes the scientific method, is no longer a nonnegotiable necessity. Describing collaborative research using reflecting team practice conducted by Tom Andersen and his colleagues in Norway, Anderson (1997) explains:

> They have found that this collaborative and inclusive approach to research has enhanced professional–professional and client–professional relationships. Most significant and with far-reaching implications, this collaborative approach brings the practitioners to the forefront of research and challenges the convention of research performed by "outsiders" in the academy. Evaluation and research performed by "insiders" [practitioners] becomes a learning opportunity for practitioners and useful in their future practice. (p. 102)

As examples of this type of inquiry about psychotherapy, at Grupo Campos Elíseos there is currently a project in which a client and a therapist were interviewed by a researcher, and the three of them together are analyzing the transcripts of these interviews. In another project, a therapist is writing a piece together with her clients about their experience in family therapy with her.

The researcher's insider perspective can be a resource for understanding the phenomenon being studied. Whether an insider, outsider, or somewhere in-between, the researcher's position always affects the development, implementation, and outcome of a study. Therefore, researchers make *public* (Anderson, 1997) their positioning in relation to the participants and phenomenon studied by sharing information that has typically not been included in research reports: this may include the researcher's age, gender, ethnicity, professional background, assumptions, experience with the research population, et cetera. In research reports this may be identified as locating the researcher or researcher's subjectivity. In this way, both sides of the research relationships are visible to the reader, which, paradoxically, may move closer to providing a clearer description of the research study than conventional research. For instance, Bava (2001) in her dissertation interwove stories of herself as a researcher and her research process throughout the nine sections on "research narratives." In a section titled "What Am I Creating?" she states:

> As I developed my dissertation web, I was asked the question "So what are you doing?" "What is your thesis?" Each of these questions is embedded with certain epistemological assumptions. But, rather than deconstruct them, I have chosen to create a story of what I think I am doing. I view my dissertation as a "cultural ritual performance" (Gergen, 1999) within the doctoral research "language game" (Wittgenstein, 1978) located within the academic community of Virginia Tech and postmodernism.
>
> In my effort, to honor the tradition of the language game and to further the generative discourses (Gergen, 1999) of doctoral dissertation, I write and talk in ways "that simultaneously challenge existing traditions of understanding, and offer new possibilities for action" (Gergen, 1999, p. 49). I do so by using hypertext, that is, chunks of text which are linked to each other in a narrative structuring that is at times circular and at other times linear. I assume that you, the reader, bring to this text your context and meaning frames as you participate in the performance. Since I view dissertation as a production of a performance, I invite you to the interactive unfolding stories of my internship experience and the research process (Bava, 2001).

Interview as Conversation: Inquiry as Construction

Qualitative interviews are one of the most frequently used options for accessing participant perspectives because they allow for interviewees to use their own words to describe their experience rather than the researcher's predetermined categories. Consistent with other qualitative interviewing approaches in the *Verstehen* tradition, we do not conceptualize interviews as one person asking questions and another responding. Instead, we conceptualize interviews as a dynamic and organic dialogical process. Both the designated researcher and the invited researcher jointly participate in a dialogical process. They are in conversation about the topics of inquiry, and each can contribute to its focus, which is usually informed by the conversation itself as it unfolds.

In qualitative research, researchers have many options for structuring interviews from ones highly structured by the researcher to ones that record participant voices with minimal influence from the researcher (Fontana & Frey, 2000). A researcher can structure interviews in various ways, depending on the type of knowledge a research team hopes to generate. For example, the research team may decide to not develop any questions at the beginning other than: "What do you think we or identified constituents need to know about the identified topic?" In another study, the research team may develop a preliminary set of questions or what Feinsilver, Murphy, and Anderson (this volume) refer to as "starter questions" and ask for participant input on the appropriateness and usefulness of the questions as the study evolves. As well, from the initial contact they invite the participants to lead the inquiry conversation with their voice and their interest.

Research interviews are organized around the same principles that guide therapeutic conversations, and they share similar goals: to generate knowledge and understandings that are useful to the participants. However, in marked contrast to therapy, it is typically the professional (i.e., the researcher) who begins the conversation with the greater need. Therefore, it is often less challenging for researchers than therapists to assume a curious and *not-knowing* perspective.

Similar to conversational questions (Anderson, 1997) in the therapeutic process, collaborative research questions emerge from the research dialogue, from inside rather than outside the conversation. The questions emerge from what is being said as the researcher strives to *maintain coherence* with the participants' descriptions of their experience (Anderson, 1997) rather than try to fit what the participant is saying into the researcher's paradigm. Therefore, questions are based on what the participant is saying, rather than a rigid script, common in other forms of research.

The interviewer uses conversational questions to clarify and check if she is understanding what the participant wanted to convey. For example when a client being interviewed about his therapy process said that this therapy is "a therapy for grown ups," the researcher asks "What do you mean when you say a therapy for grown ups?" The client goes on to explain that in this therapy she felt she could make her own decision, and the therapists were respectful of these.

Though a set of preformulated questions may be used to initially guide the interview, conversational questions are always used to facilitate an understanding of the participant's response. When preformulated questions are used, they serve as a guideline or starting point; if the interviewee wants to discuss things in a different way or address the topic from a different angle, the researcher respects this, only returning to the original questions if they are later still relevant. In maintaining coherence, collaborative researchers do not assume meanings of specific words, phrases, or stories, and frequently check to see if what they have heard is what the participant has intended for them to hear.

A series of interviews conducted at Group Campos Elíseos in Mexico City (London, Ruiz, Gargollo, & MC, 1998; Tarragona, 1999, 2003; Fernández, Cortés & Tarragona, this volume) provides an example of one way to conduct a collaborative interview process. The aim was to capture clients' "voices" and explore what they have to say about their therapeutic experiences. The participants were viewed as experts in their own therapeutic experience, and the interviews were conducted in a collaborative way: the researcher states the general purpose of the conversation (to understand therapy from the perspective of the clients) and from then on follows the participant's lead in a dialogical conversation. For example, one interview began as follows:

> Nice to meet you. We are grateful that you are willing to talk with us.... We are very interested in understanding the client's perspective of therapy, your experience, what it's been like for you, what has worked for you, what has not worked. I don't have a prepared list of questions; I am interested in knowing about your experience: how would you describe your experience in therapy with [her therapists]?

The client responded that in order to describe her experience with these therapists she had to talk about a previous treatment that she had had elsewhere (in another country) and goes on to describe it in detail. Even though the researcher was interested in learning about the client's current therapy, she listens carefully to what the client wanted to discuss about her previous therapy and how understanding her previous experience is necessary to understand what her more recent therapy had been like for her.

Making Meaning: Data Analysis

Data analysis, the process of making meaning, is a practice of a discourse community that occurs recursively through–out the research process rather than just post-data collection. All meaning making is a social activity (Lemke, 1995). The process of meaning making starts when one is deciding to delimit and define the research problem, when one is gathering and reviewing the "pertinent" literature, when one is gathering data and through out the process of writing. Each interaction in the research process is a decision point in which we make sense of the data we have at hand. Thus, in collaborative research, data analysis cannot be separated from the data gathering process itself. Collaborative inquiry generates new meanings and new understandings (Anderson, 1997). Knowledge is generated at several points in the process.

Analysis in this approach contrasts sharply from the conventional conceptualization of data analysis performed solely by the researcher. Instead, the emphasis is on a coconstruction of meaning between the researcher and participants. Understanding begins with the collaborative inquiry process, participants sharing their experiences and generating new understandings through the telling. This parallels the collaborative therapeutic process of shared inquiry, which allows clients to hear themselves differently: "We talked in here about the same things we talk about at home over and over again. But somehow talking about it in here was different. After we talked about it in here, things changed" (Anderson, 1997, p. 160). These shifts are often identified in dialogue with statements such as, "I am just now realizing ... "; "As we've been talking, it occurred to me ... "; or "I've never described this to someone before, and now that I say it ..."

New knowledge is also generated in the interview process by researchers being *public* (Anderson, 1997) with their understandings and interpretations as they emerge during the interview. While listening, researchers must take in what is being said and compare it against personal preunderstandings (Gadamer, 1960/1994); this is the point where the researcher's influence is inevitable because each person lives in uniquely constructed linguistic and experiential worlds based on prior history and experience. Researchers can lessen the chance of their preunderstandings overshadowing that of the participants by *maintaining coherence* with the client's story (Anderson, 1997). Researchers maintains coherence by using the participant's words and language, staying in sync with the participant's way of talking (speed, volume, tone, etc.), and frequently inquiring about how pieces of the story make sense together rather than making logical assumptions or interpretations. For example, when clients were describing their experience with male and female therapists in Gehart and Lyle (2001), the interviewer was careful to not "fill in the gaps" with logical assumptions about gender stereotyped behaviors; instead interviewers asked clients to describe in their own words what they meant when they said "female therapists are more caring" or "male therapists made us think more."

Somewhat paradoxically, as the researcher tries to maintain coherence with and understand the participant's story, new understandings are created because the researcher's questions are imbued with the researcher's preunderstandings. The seemingly innocuous process of researcher and interviewee trying to understand each other is where new meanings, understandings, and realities are created. Thus, the researcher is not getting closer to the participant's "true" meaning but rather working with the participant to negotiate new understandings.

An experience and emphasis of our collaborative inquiry is that, through the joint inquiry process, new meanings are negotiated and emerge for both the participants and the researcher. In most cases, the researcher chooses to further clarify the emerging descriptions by transcribing the interviews and organizing the themes that emerged across interviews. Ideally, researchers do the transcription themselves, creating maximum familiarity with the text and ultimately allowing for a more thorough and efficient analysis. Anderson (personal communication, October 24, 2005) not only recommends that researchers transcribe themselves but that they also carefully listen to the tape at least one time without taking notes or transcribing to encourage fully attending to the participant without the distraction of being in the conversation, typing, or coding.

Qualitative researchers have the option of using computer programs to assist with analysis by creating virtual versions of the traditional cut-and-paste index card method. The researchers' interface inevitably shapes their relation to the text of the interview. Although there is little research to indicate the exact effect, I (DG) have found that the computer version encourages the identification of more subthemes because most programs use a tree structure to track themes.

If the researcher generates an initial set of written themes, it is important that they are then presented to the participants for their comment and clarification to produce a final set of themes or to continue in an ongoing reflective process of refining descriptions and understandings. For example, Gehart and Lyle (1999) used a series of three interviews to trace clients and therapists' "lived experience" of change over the course of therapy. Participants reflected and commented on the emerging themes, each time adding new understandings about how their perspectives evolved since the prior meeting. The process of data gathering and analysis became a single harmonious and organic process.

Several researchers have developed specific forms of collaborative analysis and data presentation. One of the authors, Bava (2001, 2005), presents alternative data analytical methods referred to as aesthetic forms of data presentation (Piercy & Benson, 2005). Emphasizing the process of writing as inquiry (Richardson, 2003) and analysis, Bava (2001, 2005) identifies the following as ways to analyze:

1. *Stories as interpretations:* All stories about the inquired experience or subject are interpretations, i.e., relational hermeneutical texts. In the art of "reporting" the researcher is weaving a story together which is embedded in his or her discourse of knowledge and research. For instance, in telling about my story of internship, I (SB) was creating a relational hermeneutical text.
2. *Stories about stories:* Narrative about the production of stories is an important aspect of analysis and reflexivity. It is the researcher's story about how he or she made sense during the "sense-making"

process. Another way to understand this is to view it as production narratives.

3. *Interwoven reflexive narratives:* Reflexive texts that are interspersed
   among the above narrative practices such that they question the built in
   assumptions of the relational hermeneutical texts (interpretations).
4. *Decentering texts:* Boldfacing or highlighting certain words or
   phrases in the texts, draws the reader's attention from the content of
   a lexia to the boldfaced/highlighted texts thus shifting the emphasis. Electronically this is done by hyperlinking, thereby creating
   a more dynamic process, as the reader might chose to follow the
   link, thus shifting the context and content of the interpretation.
5. *Afterwords:* Richardson (1997) utilizes the notion of "afterwords"
   as reflexive epilogues thus building further reflexivity on all of the
   above layers.

Similarly, Kvale's (1996) postmodern approach provides a model for
data analysis that includes six overlapping steps (p. 189):

1. Subjects describe their lived experience.
2. Subjects themselves discover new meanings during the interview.
3. Interviewer, during the interview, condenses and interprets meanings and "sends" the meanings back for confirmation or discon-
   firmation of the description; a "self-correcting" interview.
4. The interviewer interprets the transcribed interview either alone
   or with others.
5. Reinterview subjects for their feedback, corrections, and
   clarifications.
6. New action on the part of participant and/or researcher in personal and/or social world.

Establishing Trustworthiness: Validity and Reliability

Similar to many forms of qualitative research, collaborative research does
not produce results that conform to traditional standards of validity and
reliability because, quite simply, that is not the goal of constructionist
research. Instead, the goal is to produce useful responses to research questions that fairly reflect the lived experience of research participants. Validity and reliability are primarily associated with quantitative data, which is
not always preferable for capturing lived experience: "When our language
of description is converted to numbers, we do not thereby become more
precise. Numbers are no more adequate 'pictures of the world' than words,
music, or painting. They are simply a different translation device" (Gergen,
1999, p. 92). Thus, in collaborative inquiry, validity and reliability become
living processes embedded in communities and relationship.

Collaborative researchers, like Denzin and Lincoln (1994) prefer the term *trustworthiness* and *authenticity* to reliability and validity to remind themselves and research consumers of the differences between results produced using positivist vs. constructionist approaches to knowledge. A variety of methods have been used in marriage and family therapy research to establish trustworthiness and authenticity (Gehart, Ratliff, & Lyle, 2001), including:

- Participant verification of results: participants review and verify that results fairly describe their experience.
- Multiple coders and peer debriefing: multiple researchers code transcriptions and/or peers review coding to reduce subjective bias of a single researcher.
- Triangulation: multiple data collection techniques (e.g., interviews and surveys) and/or multiple data sources (e.g., interviews with clients and therapists about same therapeutic process) are used to generate knowledge of phenomenon being studied.
- Reading against interpretation: during analysis the researchers read against the current interpretation to identify deviant examples and possible biases in the interpretation.

All of these methods potentially can be used either to seek a singular truth or to enhance the collaborative spirit of the project. Thus, the method used is determined by the researcher's intention and is contextualized by localized research performances (Bava, 2005). If the researcher is intending to use any of these methods to capture the studied phenomenon, then he or she is more likely situated in a positivistic paradigm and is seeking proximity to truth. However, to a researcher who is seeking polyphony and believes that every "reading" is a new reading, the above methods lead to multiple versions of the studied phenomenon with each being no more or less "accurate." Rather each version is a "new" version informed by the current conversation and relationships that one is involved in at that given moment. Often we are able to use the temporal context to situate research in a historical context, especially if there are years or decades separating two studies of the same phenomenon. However, one loses the perspective of time in an inquiry that involves participant verification, triangulation, or reading against interpretation. All of these methods happen along the dimension of time, thus introducing historicity and other contextual factors to the texts being created. Each version, then, is a new version rather than a closer version of the truth.

Of the above method, participant verification is most closely aligned with collaborative and postmodern research and is included as a standard part of analysis in Kvale's (1996) analysis procedures. However, it is important to note that similar to the therapeutic process, every retelling is a new experience. Thus, "verification" is another lived experience or emerging meaning of what has been told rather than the notion that the second telling is more accurate than the first. Participant verification was used in Gehart and Lyle (1999) who employed collaborative inquiry to explore clients' and therapists' lived experience of change in collaborative therapy over the course of 4 months. Kvale's (1996) analysis process (described above) was used to develop a recursive analysis process over a series of three interviews with each participant. "Verification" was an organic process in which participants were invited to comment on emerging analysis of the prior interview while simultaneously adding new experiences and perspectives since the last interview (spaced approximately 1 month apart). The emerging analysis became a strand of dialogue introduced into the next research conversation. Additionally, in this study, a type of triangulation was used. Triangulation in collaborative inquiry is not used to verify or come up with the "truest" description, but rather to describe the multiple realities in a given situation. In this case, there were certain aspects where putting the clients' and therapists' descriptions together painted a "fuller" picture and certain aspects where each voice remained distinct, describing a unique reality.

Additionally, being public (Anderson, 1997) or reflexive (Gergen & Gergen, 2000) about the researcher's position socioculturally, theoretically, and personally provides accountability by situating the researcher and the research process: "the act of reflexivity asks the reader to accept itself as authentic, that is, as a conscientious effort to 'tell the truth' about the making of the account" (Gergen & Gergen, 2000, p. 1028).

Although the researcher is responsible for addressing issues of trustworthiness and authenticity, Atkinson, Heath, and Chenail (1991) point out that in postpositivist qualitative research, the burden to legitimize knowledge is shared communally with stakeholders in the research endeavor. Research consumers must ask for whom it is valid and reliable and for what purpose. To answer this question, Kvale (1996) prefers the criterion of pragmatic validity: "Truth is whatever assists us to take actions that produce the desired results" (p. 248). The effectiveness of the knowledge produced is the criterion. Kvale identifies two types of pragmatic validity: knowledge accompanied by action and knowledge that instigates action. In the first, the research identifies whether the participant's verbal statement is supported by actions consistent with the statement. For example, if the participant describes a particular change in behavior, this change should be evident in the interview or live events. In the second type, knowledge instigates actual change in behavior. In the case of collaborative research, results are considered "valid" to the degree they inspire the participant, researcher, and/or consumer to develop new understandings and meanings that generally inform new ways for people to better go on together.

Space for Quantitative Approaches

Although we have mostly discussed examples of quantitative research, a collaborative approach can be taken when conducting quantitative studies as well. Quantitative research can capture information of which participants may be unaware. For example, based on their observational study, Werner-Wilson, Price, Zimmerman, and Murphy (1997) found that male and female therapists interrupted females three times more often than male clients. This quantitative information provides a description that most likely would not be generated through dialogue with therapy participants; thus, it is invaluable in the broader discourse of gender in psychotherapy. Similarly, large scale outcome studies provide information that no single client or therapist could provide. Collaboration refers to a stance that can be adopted in different ways and at different points of the research process. A quantitative survey, for example, may be constructed based on the input given by possible participants in the study.

Often qualitative and quantitative research work best together. For example, in my (DG) training clinic, we used a pre- and postmeasure of symptoms as part of a grant program. In one case, after 3 months of therapy, the client's score indicated she had become clinically much worse. When the therapist interviewed the client about the change, she explained that when she came to therapy, she did not want to admit that she was having problems, especially on paper; she was an immigrant from China and felt that she would lose face by doing so. When she was asked to fill out the form a second time, she had developed enough trust in the therapist to more honestly answer the questions. This situation clearly illustrates how important it is to have participants help researchers make sense of the numbers.

Further Thoughts

Likened to collaborative therapy, collaborative inquiry is a way of practicing a philosophical stance of respect, curiosity, polyphony, and social meaning making. More than the methods used, it is the intention and the assumptions that inform the research process that constitute the collaborative nature of inquiries. On paper, two researchers may have used similar "methods," yet it is the stance of the researcher that creates a process that is collaborative or not. There will be as many possibilities as there are participants (including the researcher) about the construction of research as a collaborative inquiry.

References

Anderson, H. (1997). *Conversation, language and possibilities.* New York: Basic Books.

Anderson, H. (2001). Becoming a postmodern collaborative therapist: A clinical and theoretical journey. Part II. *Journal of the Texas Association of Marriage and Family Therapy, 6*(1), 4–22.

Anderson, H. (2005). Myths about not knowing. *Family Process, 44,* 497–502.

Anderson, H. (n.d.). *A postmodern collaborative approach to therapy: Broadening the possibilities of clients and therapists.* Retrieved August 21, 2005 from http://www.harleneanderson. org/writings/postmoderncollaborativeapproach.htm.

Anderson, H. & Goolishian, H. (1988). Human systems as linguistic systems: Preliminary and evolving ideas about the implications for clinical theory. *Family Process, 27,* 157–163.

Anderson, H. & Goolishian, H. (1992). The client is the expert: A not-knowing approach to therapy. In S. McNamee & K.J. Gergen (Eds.), *Therapy as social construction* (pp. 25–39). Newbury Park, CA: Sage.

Atkinson, B., Heath, A., & Chenail, R.J. (1991). Qualitative research and the legitimization of knowledge. *Journal of Marital and Family Therapy, 17,* 175–180.

Bava, S. (2001). Transforming performances: An intern-researcher's hypertextual journey in a postmodern community. Doctoral dissertation, Virginia Polytechnic Institute and State University, Blacksburg, VA. Available at http://scholar.lib.vt.edu/theses/available/ etd-01062002-234843.

Bava, S. (2005). Performance methodology: Constructing discourses and discursive practices in family therapy research. In D. Sprenkle & F. Piercy (Eds.), *Research methods in family therapy* (2nd ed., pp. 170–190). New York: Guilford.

Bray, J.N., Lee, J., Smith, L.L., & Yorks, L. (2000). *Collaborative inquiry in practice: Action, reflection, and making meaning.* Newbury Park, CA: Sage.

Cortés, A., Fernández, E., & Tarragona, M. (this volume). You make the path as you walk: Working collaboratively with people with eating disorders. In H. Anderson & D.R. Gehart (Eds.), *Collaborative therapy and beyond.* New York: Routledge.

Denzin, N.K. & Lincoln, Y.S. (1994). *Handbook of qualitative research.* Thousand Oaks, CA: Sage.

Fontana, A. & Frey, J.H. (2000). The interview: From structured questions to negotiated text. In N.K. Denzin & Y.S. Lincoln (Eds.), *Handbook of qualitative research* (2nd ed., pp. 645–672). Thousand Oaks, CA: Sage.

Gadamer, H. (1960/1994). *Truth and method* (2nd ed.). New York: Continuum.

Gehart, D. & Lucas, B. (in press). Client advocacy in marriage and family therapy: A qualitative case study. *Journal of Family Psychotherapy.*

Gehart, D.R. & Lyle, R.R. (1999). Client and therapist perspectives of change in collaborative language systems: An interpretive ethnography. *Journal of Systemic Therapy, 18*(4), 78–97.

Gehart, D. & Lyle, R. (2001). Client experience of gender in therapeutic relationships: An interpretive ethnography. *Family Process, 40,* 443–458.

Gehart, D.R., Ratliff, D.A., & Lyle, R.R. (2001). Qualitative research in family therapy: A substantive and methodological review of the research literature. *Journal of Marital and Family Therapy, 27,* 261–274.

Gergen, K.J. (1999). *An invitation to social construction.* Thousand Oaks, CA: Sage.

Gergen, M. & Gergen, K. (2000). Qualitative inquiry: Tensions and transformations. In N.K. Denzin & Y.S. Lincoln (Eds.), *Handbook of qualitative research* (2nd ed., pp. 1025–1046). Thousand Oaks, CA: Sage.

Kemmis, S. & McTaggart, R. (2000). Participatory action research. In N.K. Denzin & Y.S. Lincoln (Eds.), *Handbook of qualitative research* (2nd ed., pp. 567–605). Thousand Oaks, CA: Sage.

Kvale, S. (1996). *InterViews.* Thousand Oaks, CA: Sage.

Lemke, J.L. (1995). *Textual politics: Discourse and social dynamics.* Bristol, PA: Taylor & Francis.

Lister, S., Mitchell, W., Sloper, P., & Roberts, K. (2003). Participation and partnerships in research: Listening to the ideas and experiences of a parent-carer. *International Journal of Social Research Methodology, 6,* 159–165.

London, S., Ruiz G., Gargollo, M., & M.C. (1998). Client's voices: A collection of client's accounts. *Journal of Systemic Therapies, 17*(4), 61–71.

Madsen, W. (1999). *Collaborative therapy with multistressed families.* New York: Guilford.

Paré, D. & Larner, G. (Eds.). (2004). *Collaborative practice in psychology and therapy.* Binghamton, NY: Haworth Press.

Piercy, F. & Benson, K. (2005). Aesthetic forms of data presentation in qualitative family therapy research. *Journal of Marital and Family Therapy 31,* 107–119.

Prilleltensky, I. & Nelson, G. (2004). Research and solidarity: Partnerships for knowing with community members. In D. Paré & G. Larner (Eds.), *Collaborative practice in psychology and therapy* (pp. 243–258). Binghamton, NY: Haworth Press.

Richardson, L. (1997). *Fields of play: Constructing an academic life.* New Brunswick, NJ: Rutgers University Press.

Richardson, L. (2003). Writing: A method of inquiry. In N.K. Denzin & Y.S. Lincoln (Eds.), *Collecting and interpreting qualitative materials* (2nd ed., pp. 499–541). Thousand Oaks, CA: Sage.

Schon, D. (1991). *The reflective practitioner: Case studies in and on educational practice.* New York: Teachers College Press.

Schwandt, T.A. (2000). Three epistemological stances for qualitative inquiry: Interpretivism, hermeneutics, and social constructionism. In N.K. Denzin & Y.S. Lincoln (Eds.), *Handbook of qualitative research* (2nd ed., pp. 189–214). Thousand Oaks, CA: Sage.

Strong, T. (2004). Meaningful moments as collaborative accomplishments: Research from within consultative dialogue. In D. Paré & G. Larner (Eds.), *Collaborative practice in psychology and therapy.* Binghamton, NY: Haworth Press, pp. 213–228.

Tarragona, M. (1999). La supervisión desde una perspectiva posmoderna. *Psicología Iberoamericana, 7(3),* 68–76.

Tarragona, M. (2003). Escribir para re-escribir historias y relaciones. *Psicoterapia y Familia, 16(1),* 45–54.

Werner-Wilson, R.J., Price, S.J., Zimmerman, T.S., & Murphy, M.J. (1997). Client gender as a process variable in marriage and family therapy: Are women clients interrupted more than men clients? *Journal of Family Psychotherapy, 11,* 373–377.

Willig, C. & Drury, J. (2004). "Acting-With": Partisan participant observation as a social-practice basis for shared knowing. In D. Paré & G. Larner (Eds.), *Collaborative practice in psychology and therapy* (pp. 229–241). Binghamton, NY: Haworth Press.

Wittgenstein, I. (1978). *Philosophical investigations.* (G.E.M. Anscombe, Trans.) New York: The Macmillan Company.

Never-Ending Possibilities

Collaboration without End: The Case of the Positive Aging Newsletter

MARY GERGEN AND KENNETH J. GERGEN

Lance Armstrong realized his dream of winning his 7th Tour de France the summer of 2005, breaking all records for victories in this historical bicycle race. The newspaper photos showed a triumphant Armstrong holding high the golden trophy—a lone man against the blue skies, with his children below him, his son reaching high trying to touch his father's trophy. This story flowered amidst a summer of heroic deeds, from Tiger Woods' win at St. Andrews golf classic to Barry Bonds' record-breaking home run spree. The world loves stories of champions. Vicariously, we walk in their shoes. But, let us ask, where would Lance have been without his team leader who gave him advice via the microphone he wore in his helmet, or without his teammates who protected him from the pack, or his mechanics who repaired his bikes, or the coaches who helped him train his body, or the doctors who treated him for testicular cancer? Where should we terminate the list of collaborators? Should we not also include the competitors, the French culture, and the news media? Nor does the list end with human helpers, either. Where would he have been without the road, the mountains, the air, and the water? The more one contemplates the victory, the more the glory spreads, until it runs from the Champs Elysses to Armstrong's childhood paths through the fields of Texas. Collaboration came first; the champion emerged from it.

Breaking with Individualism

Traditionally, we view collaboration as involving two or more people as independent entities, coordinating their efforts to bring about some desired endpoint. In this sense, collaboration is a secondary process in a world where independent entities are fundamental. In this chapter, we wish to reverse these commonplace assumptions. We propose that the relational process of collaboration is fundamental and that it is only within relational processes that what we take to be entities come into being. This is to say, collaboration is not a secondary process that must be mobilized only when an individual strives to protect or improve his or her condition. Rather, without collaborative relationships, there is no individual who deliberates on gains for the self. More dramatically, we might say that individuality is an illusion, brought about by the failure to appreciate the fundament of process.[1] And when we allow these illusions to become our realities, we place impediments in the way of appreciating the positive power of the collaborative process.

To explore these potentials of this perspective, we shall first describe a sea of collaborative processes that help bring forth what we might otherwise consider a specific *thing in itself.* The object in focus is one on which we have worked for countless hours, and in which we have a substantial investment: *Positive Aging Newsletter.* This freely distributed electronic newsletter came into being in April 2001. Its goal was, and continues to be, to replace the traditional stereotype of aging as decline with one that emphasizes aging as an unparalleled period of enrichment and growth. The newsletter features summaries of relevant research, news, book reviews, Websites, conferences, and more.[2] After describing the collaborative processes essential to bringing the newsletter into being, we shall consider several conceptual resources that we find pivotal in our approach to collaboration.

The Collaborative Matrix

As we begin our initial level of analysis as to what constitutes the collaborative matrix from which the *Positive Aging Newsletter* emerges, we do not so much disclose the unknown as acknowledge the often suppressed. That is, when we consider the collaborative processes from which the newsletter draws its existence, we primarily illuminate a domain that we well understand but typically disregard. Consider, then, the following:

The Authors

Most obvious in this case is the fact that the existence of any written document depends on its author(s). We might say that the entity is an emanation of a relationship that only seems independent by virtue of its physical separation from that of which it is a part. In the same way as we may objectify "the building," "the film," or "the criminal," we obscure the architect, the director, or the network of others to which a criminal belongs.

The existence of the newsletter depends on an ongoing process of coordination between us. One of the topics of conversation that is never far from our lips is the question of what will be the theme of our next editorial. It is here that we organize central ideas about aging and often draw in the research and news items that we are also gathering as we go. We continuously discover and share resources, such as books, research articles, Websites, videos, and listserves. Often the merits of the materials are unclear.

Are the ideas important, interesting, and relevant or are they too complex, marginal, or whimsical? These and other questions are raised as we encounter such materials. Discussions are thus set in motion and without mutual graciousness of response between us, there is no movement. The quality of the newsletter is imperiled. Negotiating these matters requires close attention to framing; a language of possibility proves more effective than a discourse of declarations. That is, if Mary says, "We must have this article on the sex lives of older women in the next issue," it is less well received that if she says, "What do you think about including this piece in the next issue?" Polyvocality is required of both of us, as we "try on" various voices that might respond to a given idea. This is to say, it is more helpful to obtaining a high quality in the newsletter, as well as in our relationship, if Ken responds in a variety of ways. He might say, "Well, it might spice up the next issue, given our last one on bereavement practices," and he might also add, "Isn't there anything on sex lives of older men, just to be fair?" And he might inquire, "Where did this piece come from? Do you think it is a respectable and trustworthy source?" Each of these provides another template against which to judge whether or not to include a piece of research in the newsletter. Mutual respect must prevail, even when there are distinct differences in proclivity. Mary might well respond, "Thanks for thinking outside the box on this one. I know I'm overly concerned with getting women to feel more comfortable with their bodies, especially sexually, so I might have not worried as much as I should have about the credibility of the source. Maybe we could put this material in the news section as opposed to the research section; this way we can expose the ideas, but not stamp them with authority."

The Authors' Authors

We write about ourselves as if we are the originary sources, coming together as independent beings to collaborate on the newsletter content. But the vision of independent authors is an illusion. We come together as beings deeply wedded to a history of relationship. Where would either of us be without a collaborative relationship with our parents? (And, of course, we could go back to their relations with their parents, and their parents' parents, until we would discover that there is indeed no originary moment of authorship.) We could also move through countless relationships with family and friends; all leave subtle marks on our relationship with each other. Most directly instructive are our relationships with those who precede us in the life course. From them we learn so much about the potentials of positive aging. In certain respects, they are our mentors. We could make a similar case for our relationships with various teachers and colleagues in the social sciences. The collaborative process of education has left us with a particular standpoint in understanding and writing about positive aging.

Yet, in order to collaborate as authors, we must also develop a form of collaboration with those whose work we write about. Our writing is absolutely reliant on social science journals, news reports, recent books, Websites, and more. Yet, the form of our collaboration with these materials is specialized. These texts supply a wealth of words or, one might say, a wealth of possibilities. We do not wish to copy the material, but rather, to provide easy access to a range of useful material. Our readers may follow up on details if they wish. In addition to reducing the size of the offerings, we are also interested only in what these materials may contribute to a positive orientation to life. Thus, we dance only with those ideas, findings, practices, and opinions that enable us to make such a contribution. At times, this requires rewriting materials so that what might not have been central to the original article becomes highlighted, or research findings are placed in a different conceptual context. For example, many research articles feature correlates of negative behaviors such as depression, incapacity, or suicide. An entirely different and more promising story may be told if we reverse the emphasis of the research and write about the correlates of optimism, abilities, and survival.

Because we take a social constructionist perspective toward our work, we are also careful to look at the labels placed on cognitive abilities, physical and social skills, personality traits, attitudes, and other variables that might be derogatory or demeaning to aging people. For example, the term *rigidity*, which has a negative connotation, is often used as a descriptor of older people's modes of responding. We may point out that terms such as *consistency*, *faithfulness*, or *principled* could also describe the same activities. In effect, collaboration in this context is essentially a form of fusion.

Sometimes we get into trouble when we take liberties with a text. In this case, our collaborative efforts become sabotaged. For example, one day we received a very angry e-mail from an author who told us that we had misrepresented his article in a professional magazine, and he wanted us to remove it. Of course, it is not clear how one might remove an electronic newsletter message that has already been sent out, but he was clearly upset. The article had a positive theme, which suggested that people who have disabilities and poor health may not be as unhappy as one might imagine, nor are people without similar life-limiting qualities as happy as disabled people might think they are. In general, people feel about the same, reacting to the minutia of daily life as it comes to them, not to the Big Picture. At least that was the positive idea we took from the article. It counteracts the view that many younger people and caretakers of older people have that a serious physical limitation or disease makes people constantly depressed or unable to experience happy moments. This is not the case, as this article helped to show. Mary wrote to the author and offered him space in our next newsletter to respond, thus giving him an option to collaborate with us, and to have a voice in our newsletter. We never heard back from him. Sometimes people just don't want to play.

The Readership

Without a collaborative relationship with our readers, we do not qualify as authors. Without readers, we are effectively mute. Readership often begins with an invitation from us. To send potential subscribers a copy of the newsletter and offer them an opportunity to accept or decline, we are effectively asking if they would like to join us in bringing the newsletter into full being. Most people do enjoy it when we send a copy to them. However, most subscribers find us and ask to be put on our list.[3] Many subscribers also share their copies of the newsletter with colleagues, friends, and family. In this way, they now join in the collaborative process. The result has been the continuous expansion of the newsletter, which now reaches over 20,000 readers.

In writing the newsletter, we also act collaboratively with our readers in other ways. This collaboration first requires an act of imagination on our part. We must consider the audience—their likely interests, needs, level of sophistication, and so on. Writing is collaborative when the text already bears the contours of the reader's being. At the same time, readers are not just passive recipients. They write to us with their reactions, and these help us to respond more fully with them. Through their e-mails, we gain a feeling that we are serving people in ways they value and that is an important part of a collaborative effort. In a certain sense, many of them also become writers. Our readers send suggestions for books and videos to review, announcements to make, and personal experiences to share in our "Readers Respond" column. Our newsletter is far richer for their participation in our mutual venture.

Interestingly, our newsletter is read by editors of various periodicals, including other newsletters, and they in turn use our materials to reach their readers. We have decided to give away all of our copy to anyone who asks, without any obligations. In this sense, we are collaborating with those who are editors and facilitators of adult and aging services across the world. The collaborative energy sends out waves of activity that far surpass our knowledge of how it travels and where. It is exciting for us to discover that various publications for older people are featuring the newsletter's contents.

The Support Network

Beyond these collaborative contributions, there is an extended network of people, without whom the newsletter would not exist. It would be difficult to determine where the list begins and ends, given the shifting world of Webmasters, apprentices, assistants, supporters, students, translators, technicians, and the like. However, by far the most significant member of our support network has been Charles Studer, a longstanding friend and a resident of Basle, Switzerland. Our earliest acquaintanceship extends back to when *The Saturated Self*[4] was originally published, and the general thesis of the book caught Charles' eye. Later, when Charles became director of the Novartis Gerontological Foundation, we entered into a process of creative collaboration together, and it was this relationship that gave birth to the vision of the newsletter. Since that time, Charles has been an ardent supporter and continuous source of wise counsel. Without him, there would be no newsletter. Through Charles, we also came to work with the staff of an independent firm, Boomerang, Inc., that provides the technical services for converting our drafts to an electronically satisfactory vehicle for mass distribution. Here we were fortunate enough to work with Stephanie Dorr, who edited and formatted our materials, stored and repaired the continuously altering mailing list, and supervised dissemination.[5] We have never met Stephanie face to face, but her buoyant good will and depth of knowledge were essential to our collaborative venture.

When the Novartis Gerontological Foundation shifted its mission away from disseminating health and well-being information to the aged and those professionals who work with them, financial support for the newsletter was terminated. At that point, we came to rely on two further organizations: The Health and Age Foundation, headed by Dr. Robert Griffith, which helps to advertise the newsletter and collect subscribers,[6] and the Taos Institute. Both of us serve on the executive board of the Taos Institute, a nonprofit organization devoted to dialogue between social constructionist theory and collaborative practices. This institute has also provided resources for archiving the newsletter and featuring its recent editions on their Website. Our close relationship with Dawn Dole, the executive director of the institute, has ensured an effective working relationship with a Webmaster and facilities for communicating with subscribers from France and Germany.

One of the most amazing stories in the collaborative history of the newsletter is how it has become international and multilingual. We were aware that for many people who have English as a second language, reading the newsletter might be difficult. For example, we knew that in the United States, there would be several language communities that would miss it altogether. We were then approached by our friend, Dr. Cristina Ravazzola, a Buenos Aires therapist, who was willing to collaborate with her brother, Mario, to translate the newsletter into Spanish. We then proposed the idea to Charles Studer, who agreed to sponsor the Spanish edition. On the heels of this venture, our good friend and translator, Alain Robiolio, volunteered to translate the newsletter into French. Now the newsletter was becoming truly international. The thrills did not end there. Two German colleagues, Syliva Roderburgand and Thomas Friedrich, had found great sustenance in social constructionist ideas in therapy and volunteered to create a German language edition. With the collaboration of the Taos Institute, we were then able to offer the newsletter in four languages. Virtually all this activity takes place on a strictly voluntary basis.

Extending the Collaborative Process

Our account has thus far described numerous individuals who have collaborated with us either directly or indirectly to bring the newsletter into being. Yet, why should we suppose that these various individuals function as independent beings? Do they not live within an extended matrix of relationships that make possible their contributions to the ultimate publication of the newsletter? To take but one example, our friend Merrell Clark, on whom we depend for thinking-through funding sources, contributes in this way precisely because of a history of collaborative relationships with nonprofit institutions. (Not to mention that Ken and he were bosom buddies at Yale.) Such an account could be furnished for virtually everyone we have mentioned. Their contribution to the newsletter is intricately woven into their relationship with others. And this surrounding cast of characters is, in turn, representing a still further expanse of relationships.

It is also important to note that our account of the collaborative matrix has focused entirely on human participation. Yet, this is most inadequate. The functioning of all these people is enabled by a world of material. Most immediately is the computer technology that sweeps information, articles, manuscript draft, and the newsletter itself through cyberspace each month. And virtually all this technology depends for its contribution on still other technologies, which in turn depend on human designers. Broadly speaking we should also pay homage to the environmental elements—food, temperature, oxygen, plant growth, and the like. All are essential to nourishing the agents who employ the technology to achieve outcomes such as the newsletter. We take so much of this for granted, scarcely noticing our enmeshment, but the extent to which our silent partners are essential to the collaboration is truly remarkable.

From Entities to Process

At the beginning of this chapter, we pointed out the longstanding tradition by which we understand the social world to be made up of independent beings. In certain respects, we have sustained this tradition in our writing by referring to others and ourselves as individuals. We have described the way in which the two of us relate, the contribution of friends, colleagues, readers, translators, and so on. Even our account of technology referred to a world of separate entities—computers, Websites, archives, and the like. Yet, we also view our reliance on this language of independent units as an occupational hazard. We are forced to write in this way because nouns—which create a world of discrete units—make up a major part of our descriptive discourse. To abandon nouns would be to exit the house of sense making.

Yet, our hope is that the unfolding logic of our narrative serves to deconstruct the unitizing of the world. What we have tried to demonstrate in each instance is that there is no act possessed by any individual alone. To act meaningfully or intelligibly on any occasion is necessarily to give expression to the matrix of relationships in which one has lived and to the relationship in which the expression occurs. Thus, we may refer to each other as individual beings, and we may see before us biological entities that seem to be independent of their surrounds. But such references and perceptions are illusory. There is first relational process, and from this process we develop the very intelligibility of singularity.

Implications for Collaborative Action

We wish to complete the analysis presented in this chapter with several lessons from which will we draw from our work on the newsletter in understanding the collaborative process and in rendering it more effective. Three of these deserve special attention:

1. *The tension between flexibility and continuity.* Collaborative relationships invariably require mutual adjustments. Seldom do preferences, abilities, proclivities, or points of view make a perfect match. Flexibility is an absolute requirement for effective outcomes. One must often sacrifice a particular goal, value, preference, or favored way of proceeding. At the same time, to approach relationships with openness to the other's ways is to sacrifice the matrix of relationships

from which one emerges. For example, if we agree with what our technician might say about efficiency in format, we relinquish our histories of relationships from which we draw our sense of aesthetic taste. Similarly, if our technician allows our aesthetic preferences to dominate, efficiency flies out the window. We have no overarching rule for dealing with these continuous tensions. However, we do find it useful to remain sensitive to them and to the values embedded in both our own favored ways as well as those with whom we work. As always, it is useful to call on our social constructionist heritage, in that we are able to declare that there is no one right way to do anything, but rather it depends upon the language game that is dominant in any particular context.[7]

2. *Creativity and the appreciative core.* There is a tendency over time to treat smooth and continuous processes of collaboration as a ritual. That is, we understand that this is what we do together; each person has a part to play and if we continue to perform our parts, the newsletter will successfully be published. Yet, we also find it essential to resist this tendency. Dance is a useful metaphor here. If we become very skilled at performing a particular dance—swing, rock, two-step, etc.—it can become ritualized. We also stop learning new ways to dance together, and the familiar can become a bore. We know that when the production of the newsletter becomes simply a familiar chore—done "the way we do it"—the joy will slowly vanish. We find both in dancing and in publishing the newsletter that the best antidote to ennui is in appreciating our moments of serendipity and in welcoming creative encounters. We also find that frequent expressions of welcoming, gratitude, admiration, and pleasure are essential to sustain the vitality of the collaborative relationship. Remembering and appreciating the positive core of our mission is a morale booster even when deadlines seem overwhelming.[8]

3. *The multiplicity of skills.* There is a strong tendency to view collaboration as a unified or singular process, one that can be transposed from one situation or relationship to another. In contrast, we find it more useful to think of the particular conditions confronting us in the moment and then to consider what kind of skills or moves are essential to bring about a positive end. As we noted earlier, certain collaborations require a careful interweaving of opinions and ideas—a form of dialogue from which innovation may spring.[9] Other collaborations depend on imagining the other and trying to take into account their needs and values in our own actions. In still other cases, we listen with rapt attention to the advice we

are receiving, understanding that we must ultimately sift out that which is most useful. In our relations with our technologies, we often rely on knowing friends who can coach us through complex maneuvers. In effect, we may say that the collaborative process is an adjustment of adjustments.

In Conclusion

We began simply, by introducing an electronic newsletter on positive aging. Yet, as we have attempted to demonstrate, the newsletter as an independent entity is an illusion. Not only does its existence depend on the collaboration of its authors but on their collaboration with many others. Further, the newsletter fails to be an entity of any kind until readers collaborate with its content, until they invest it with meaning and significance. We then expanded the vision of the collaborative practices required to bring the newsletter into active existence and soon found that we could extend the network almost indefinitely, both in terms of people and material. The newsletter may be viewed, then, not as a "thing in itself" but the common intersection of an enormous process of relationship. In this sense, perhaps the newsletter is but a symbol of what is the case for all manner of people and things and events.

Endnotes

1. We wish to thank editor Diane Gehart for pointing out the similarities between this view and the teachings of Buddhism, which also considers individuals as deeply and irrevocably relational.
2. The interested leader may view both past and present newsletters at www.positiveaging.net.
3. One may subscribe to the newsletter by sending an email to Mary Gergen at gv4@psu.edu
4. The *Saturated* Self by Kenneth J. Gergen was published by Basic Books in 1990 and again as a new edition in 2000.
5. Stephanie has recently been replaced by Heather Force, who now takes on the same responsibilities.
6. www.healthandage.com
7. See Gergen & Gergen, M. (2004).
8. We are indebted to our colleagues and friends who have created and sustained the appreciative inquiry movement and who have made a difference in the way consultants engage in organization behavior change. Three books among the many that describe this popular grass-roots movement are Anderson, H. et al. (2001), *The appreciative organization.* Chagrin Falls, OH: Taos Institute Publications; Watkins, J. & Mohr, B. (2001), *Appreciative inquiry: Change at the speed of imagination.* San Francisco, CA: Jossey-Bass Pfeiffer; Whitney, D. & Tosten-Bloom, A. (2003), *The power of appreciative inquiry: A practical guide to positive change.* San Francisco, CA: Berrett-Koehler.
9. See Gergen, Gergen, & Barrett (2004).

References
Gergen, K. (1991). *The saturated self: Dilemmas of identity in contemporary life*. New York: Basic Books.
Gergen, K.J. & Gergen, M. (2004). *Social construction: Entering the dialogue*. Chagrin Falls, OH: Taos Institute.
Gergen, M., Gergen, K.J., & Barrett, F. (2004). *Appreciative inquiry as dialogue: Generative and transformative*. In D. Cooperrider & M. Avital (Eds.), Advances in appreciative inquiry (Vol. 1). Bristol, England: Elsevier Science.

CHAPTER **24**

Collaborating as a Lifestyle

SALLY ST. GEORGE AND DAN WULFF

Much has been written about therapeutic collaboration (Anderson, 1997; Gilligan & Price, 1993; White & Epston, 1990) as a way that not only respects clients in the general sense of the term but that consistently privileges their points of view in therapy. Therapeutic collaboration is a stance that implicitly and explicitly opens therapy decisions and other activities to the client for participation on a par with the therapist. We believe that a collaborative approach also has great potential to enhance our professional relationships with colleagues and students. Harlene Anderson (Malinen, 2000) talks about collaborative work as a demonstration of a philosophy of life. She states that, "there is a natural coherence between the way you are in the world and all of your life roles" (p. 70). The hierarchical leveling that therapeutic collaboration offers can similarly stimulate new generative relationships in other professional encounters. Therefore, in this chapter we focus on collaboration as a professional lifestyle, a way to conduct one's life across the board rather than as a preferred stance only in the therapy room, and use as illustrations examples from our experiences.

We have found that approaching the daily interactions of our professional lives collaboratively with others (a) enhances and produces greater satisfaction within those working relationships, (b) supports and deepens our collaborative efforts with our clients, and (c) has the potential to stimulate change on other levels, including larger systemic levels. In the following pages, we will explore the collaborative lifestyle in the arenas of relating with our colleagues and with our students.[1] We will examine how collaborative ideas and practices are effective, generative, and transformative when they are generously and broadly incorporated within and across our professional worlds.

Our Professional Context

Our professional world includes directing a master's-level family therapy program in a department of social work at a university, teaching and supervising students in the program, working within an academic environment with colleagues from other related disciplines, and practicing family therapy in private practice. We both work collaboratively with our clients and teach collaborative clinical work to our students. In recent years, we have been experimenting with using a more collaborative approach in our interactions with our students. Now we are taking it further and trying to live it daily with our fellow professionals.

As we taught our students about collaborative approaches with clients, it became increasingly apparent to us that there were significant parallels between what we advocated student clinicians use with clients and more satisfying teacher–student interactions. This led to reflections on our practices as teachers. We see a fundamental inconsistency between teachers who promote a collaborative stance for their students to use with clients, but who also are unwilling to employ those same collaborative principles in their interactions with students in the classroom. Proposing that students adopt a collaborative stance with clients is a difficult position to maintain seriously if the person making the proposal does not actively represent that collaborative posture in their professional conduct. The content says one thing, whereas the delivery of that message sends another. The consequences of this for teachers of therapy seem particularly problematic because what they tell students to do seem to be remembered less than how they relate to students and colleagues. We believe that living and performing, or the professional modeling of, the collaborative approach is an essential ingredient in teaching collaborative work. We will be fairly scrutinized for the degree to which we "walk our talk."

In our positions, we have had many opportunities to observe and/or work with seasoned, as well as with new, therapists. In recent years, we have witnessed the work of many therapists who have described their clinical work as *collaborative*. What we observed was that collaboration for some clinicians seemed to be a term used to describe a "kinder and gentler" approach in interacting with clients, while remaining focused in moving the client in the theory-informed direction they set. We have also noticed that the use of the word *collaboration* has become commonplace.

Who would claim to be against collaborating with clients? *Collaborative* is a term embraced by many to characterize their work but can represent many diverse practices, some of which may bear little resemblance to the core ideas embodied in the term.

"Walking our talk" is not just a cliché for us. We often use the phrase as the yardstick of credibility when viewing master therapists, teachers, economists, politicians, and writers. We think that people behave in accordance with principles, spoken or unspoken. If their behavior is not congruent with their announced principles, the disconnection makes us suspicious of how much they are committed to their own espoused ideas. In those cases of perceived incongruity, the actions trump the verbal claims.

Out with Relationship, in with Technique

Our popular and professional cultures have created a climate whereby outcome is the gold standard of success. Process goals of respectful and collaborative interaction are not valued as highly as reaching a specific desired end-state. The allure of therapies that claim to produce significant behavioral changes within short time frames has led to simplistic understandings and immediate (as well as shortsighted and premature) solutions. Perhaps even more regrettably, it has tempered therapists' curiosity and inventiveness in copursuing new and generative solutions with their clients. Financial stressors can pressure therapists and their agencies to be more focused on production levels (hours invested or number of clients seen), limited and tightly targeted measurable goals, or documentation that offers protection from legal culpability should a client not improve (or worsen), all of which can distract therapists from the heart of their work. All these entice the therapist to center on therapeutic change more as a commodity or product (outcome) rather than as a relationship or process.

The conditions described above influence how collaboration is introduced into clinical work. Because working collaboratively suggests that clients will be respected and become more centrally involved in therapy, the political correctness of this position leads many therapists to select the collaborative label for their work. However, a closer look at how collaborative work is sometimes enacted and described reveals serious divergences from client valuing. We hear the term *collaboration* invoked while downplaying or outright dismissing the inherent power differentials between a therapist and a client, a position that masks structural inequalities in the therapeutic encounter. It has come to our attention that collaborative practice is at times only reserved for use with those clients or colleagues with whom we already share a like-mindedness. In the name of collaboration, therapists relate to clients in ways that appear to give voice, while, in fact, that voice is not substantively included in the ongoing work; the client's ideas carry little or no weight in directing the therapeutic agenda. Some elect to act collaboratively when the outcome is assured. To be collaborative in this situation risks nothing. It is when the outcome of the work together is not known that our collaborative process is measured. Finally, some choose to be collaborative intermittently, only when it is convenient or expedient.

Collaborative Work as Relationship

Our view of collaborative clinical work is based upon mutual agenda setting and a fundamental trust in clients' ideas about what is best for them. It includes holding a client's views in the highest esteem and using them as the cornerstones of our work with clients.

This respectful joining of people to pursue common goals or interests is a significant element in the development of community. It means neither that everybody does the same thing nor does it mean that everyone thinks alike. Collaborators come together in mutual endeavors such that each person's contribution is validated and used to generate even more possibilities for action or change that will result in some benefit for all involved.

Our belief is that collaborating is an attitude, a spirit, a way of being and interacting in this world. It is a stance or a tone that we set as therapists, teachers, and colleagues. It is from these beliefs that we became attracted to and influenced by Harlene Anderson's (1997) therapeutic work. An assumption we hold is that working collaboratively will not always produce specified behavioral outcomes nor is it the only way of relating with others to accomplish good things. We believe that working collaboratively is not merely a strategy to reach a predesigned end. We assume that our collaborative efforts will not always be understood or appreciated or that collaboration will look the same all the time. It has a fluidity and freshness to it that defies easy defining or locating.

We have found, however, that operating from a collaborative stance allows us to feel good about what we do, allows us to more effectively join with others, and shows a consistency between word and deed. Behaving collaboratively does not require that all the interacting partner(s) be equally collaborative; in fact, collaboration often starts unilaterally.

Collaboration comes in variations and in degrees. Collaboration can be just acting in a coordinated or cooperative way with others—nicely getting along, friendly, and polite. We prefer to define collaboration according to Bray, Lee, Smith, and Yorks (2000) in their work with collaborative inquiry:

Collaborators can engage in inquiry together for divergent reasons and can hold somewhat divergent assumptions about what constitutes knowledge, as long as they agree to the essentials. These essentials are the need to engage in a process of collaborative discovery marked by democratic participation in all phases of the inquiry process, authentic reflection on the interests that motivate their participation, and the honoring of a holistic perspective on the construction of valid knowledge. (p. 6)

Even though Bray et al.'s description is focused on the process of inquiry, we believe that their "essentials" hold true in the arena of daily professional living. Behaving with our colleagues and students in ways that privilege them as much as we do ourselves generate more effective and transformative possibilities than without such relationships.

Although it may seem ironic or misplaced to discuss hierarchy and privilege in a paper about collaborative work with colleagues and students, we would be remiss if we did not address this question: Can collaborating be achieved if the initiating party has a position of authority or responsibility over the potential collaborative partner? In a therapy situation, it seems that a collaborating relationship could develop if the therapist initiates that type of interaction. Even so, how can we know if those behaviors that look collaborative are genuine or perhaps just evidence of the client just following or acting in compliance with the therapist's lead?

On the flip side, if a client or student prefers a working relationship with their therapist or instructor that is collaborative in nature (but the therapist or instructor has not initiated it), what is the likelihood of success in attaining this relationship? How will the therapist or teacher respond to the request or effort? If they refuse the idea of collaborating, their superior power position in the interaction will likely stall the collaboration. What is the likelihood of collaborative work between and among equals or at least supposed equals, such as between professors in a department? Does the equal positioning in a hierarchy improve the chances of developing a collaborative relationship?

Collaborating Elements

Collaborating as a professional lifestyle includes the following key elements: valuation, manners, critical self-reflection, appreciation and responsibility for community, and creative action.

Valuation (not Evaluation)

A common misconception about collaboration is that it requires the collaborating parties to have equal roles or assignments. Collaboration does not necessarily mean "the same." There are significant and desirable differences among people, their roles, and their ideas. Often, as we face such differences we are tempted to mark these differences according to evaluative, oftentimes dualistic, criteria (e.g., good/bad, right/wrong). Evaluations judge the worthiness of some differences over others, whereas valuing seeks to acknowledge and utilize the potentials among all the differences. In collaborative work, we try to move toward a stance of valuing, which is characterized by appreciating, learning about, and honoring differences and uniqueness. If we can listen for the goodness and viabilities that differences provide, we can add to our knowledge and understanding. Although the familiar and the similar may be more comfortable for us, the possibility of experiencing aspects that are new and different in our lives provides us with the chance to learn and grow beyond our individual reach.

Child Care 101. The following example highlights this valuing process. During a spring college semester, DW was organizing summer practicum experiences for three students. Three months prior to the summer term, two of the students inquired about the progress that was being made regarding their specific practicum arrangements for summer. They mentioned to DW that their interest to know quickly was fueled by their need to arrange for childcare for the summer well in advance. Given DW's hectic work schedule at the time, he was slow in finalizing these arrangements; other matters kept taking precedence. He was not deliberately trying to delay or complicate these students' lives, but in effect, he was not attending to their request for speedy resolution so they could make the needed childcare preparations.

The students were placed in an awkward yet necessary position of repeatedly reminding DW of their request with increasing urgency in their voices each time. When the arrangements for summer practica were finally finished, the timing was sufficiently late and the students' childcare plans were very hard to arrange. The students were upset and let DW know how they felt about how their conscientious requests had been consistently overlooked or dismissed. DW was initially reluctant to hear their critical comments, choosing rather to consider the situation as regrettable but not as his fault. There was a marked lack of understanding regarding the import of the students' concerns; consequently, their requests had not activated DW to privilege their requests.

DW's codirector of the program, SSG, who was also his wife, was contacted by the students toward the end of this period and apprised of their feelings of being discounted. SSG mentioned her concerns—which were in line with the students'—to DW who continued to discount the import of the past and current circumstances, noting that the practica had now been successfully arranged and that the students had secured their childcare. DW believed the complaint was not significantly relevant at this point— perhaps the oversight had been unfortunate at the time, but in the end, everything had worked out.

SSG insisted that DW consider that what had happened (and what was happening now) was an indication of a patterned inattentiveness to what the students had been saying (and what they were still saying). She presented this point of view with an intensity that strongly urged DW to listen more carefully to what she was saying. SSG suggested that DW's gendered perspective might have prevented him from truly listening and responding in kind to the students' requests. As DW replayed in his mind the events that had led up to the current moment, he could see how, at each request from the students, he had placed their requests behind other activities and priorities. He also realized that he had been in charge of prioritizing his roles and responsibilities and had had the power to place their concerns high on his list if he had had the will to do so. He privileged other activities instead.

Being unaware and unappreciative of the urgency of the students' request was an example of failing to value their position, needs, and voice. Even once the practica and childcare had been arranged, the discounting of the students' emotions and anger were further examples of DW's "not getting it." SSG's persistence to have DW see how the situation was challenging his commitment to his own espoused beliefs—whether or not he could "walk his talk"—combined with his willingness to consider another viewpoint allowed a "valuing" process to occur. In stepping outside of his customary perspective in order to hear the "other," DW netted an awareness of the students' points of view. One of the key ingredients in this process involved DW resuming a collaborative posture of being nondefensive regarding his own point of view, and in particular, being open to alternative viewpoints. Once he was prepared to not stand up for his view against all others, he was able to examine carefully other viewpoints different from his own.

When DW understood the students' perspectives better, there was a bit of embarrassment in realizing how he had appeared to the students. He spoke directly with the students regarding how he had regretted his dismissive behavior, how the experience had opened his eyes, and how they had played a key role in the process. He thanked them for their courage and honesty in pushing him to see how he was coming across to others. So, too, was SSG a key player. Using the "argument" of an importance of living according to your principles, she nudged DW to see himself from another viewpoint.

This example highlights how relationships are fluid and subject to continuous maintenance and alteration. It is probably inevitable that judging and devaluing behaviors will occur, often without intent. What is crucial is an interest in and an ability to "catch" oneself as it happens—pause—and then respond in a different manner, for instance, with careful listening, listening to hear, learning, and understanding. In response to the students' anger, DW could have evaluated the students, their requests, and their reactions in ways that characterized them as out-of-line, as selfish, or wrong in ways that would have rejected their claims and feelings. In addition, the students could have adopted evaluative positions in ways that characterized DW as a disrespectful and noncaring person, but they elected to value him as a person who might be able to see things differently and maintained a dialogue that allowed for a new interpersonal arrangement that was more satisfying.

Related to the notion of valuation and empowerment, another significant piece of collaborative logic questions the degree to which the "other" is capable of defining and representing their own self (Sampson, 1993). Just as a client is empowered to name and outline their experience in therapy, our students are similarly empowered in their interactions with us, including any defining differences that may be expressed in our relationships with them. This does not preclude us from giving our opinions or reflections; both students and we are charged with helping create contexts that integrate our ideas with each other. Actually, we prefer to think in terms of multiplicities or multiple alternatives rather than singularities or privileged views. Our ideas as therapists and teachers and supervisors ought not to prevail simply due to hierarchical superiority. Valuing alternatives goes beyond appreciating points of view and opinions and include how problems are constructed and how goals are set. As if appreciating alternative and multiple points of view were not enough, joining with others to define problems in an inclusive fashion and establishing goals for joint action are very challenging endeavors.

Faculty meetings are oftentimes the site of devaluing or evaluative interactions. All too often, ideas are mentioned or positions stated that are summarily ignored or glossed over by others. Conversations are not threaded to value each person's contribution. Personal agendas frequently supersede a genuine interest in what others have to say. It is easy for us to presuppose what another person is going to say, and then to make pre-judgments or decisions based on our presuppositions that prevent us from attending to, learning more about, and discussing, their voiced statements or suggestions. When such devaluing situations occur, they may appear inconsequential because they are so commonplace; we become conditioned to accept them as a natural occurrence.

Instead, what if we behave in ways that truly value what each person has to say. Rather than frame interactions as "in agreement with mine" or "against mine," what if we become genuinely interested in views that are different from our own for the sake of their creative potential? What if we approach views that are different or even contrary to our own with a sense of novelty and attraction? What if we adopt a stance that places value on the unusual and encourages development of ideas outside of our comfort zones or preferred views? Perhaps we might even see the novel and unusual as potential areas of development or growth—a site of fresh thinking. If this approach could be adopted by conversational partners in a faculty meeting, it is likely that each point of view would receive more attention and appreciation. Occasions of defending one's view from the criticisms or expected criticisms of others would be minimized, leaving more space and time for ideas to be stimulated and developed. This would also capitalize on the breadth of diversity present among the participants to generate new ideas to problems or issues under consideration.

Acting Mannerly

We probably cannot say enough about manners even though it seems like such a simple and basic concept. Whereas manners are subject to, and derived from, our larger systems of culture, ethnicity, gender, and context, and therefore not a singular notion, we are referring to the specific behavioral ways that we communicate our respect and regard for others. Manners help us convey to others that we are connected to them and they matter to us. Using manners reaffirms our basic human connectedness and interdependence despite the hierarchies that compose so much of our professional and personal lives. Therefore, manners are a crucial part of the behavioral repertoire of the collaborative lifestyle.

Though infrequent, when manners are discussed in the family therapy literature, authors typically focus on their strategic uses rather than their value in and of themselves (Zingaro, 1988), once again demonstrating the overvaluing of outcomes as compared to process. In both the psychotherapy and family therapy literature, it is very common for relational dynamics to be characterized as objects, commodities, or internal characteristics that then can be added or subtracted relatively easily, rather than as moving interacting moments. It is probably more appropriate to refer to this idea as "acting mannerly" rather than as a set of "manners." Using manners as a noun may inadvertently suggest that they are composed of a discrete checklist of behaviors whereas using the phrase "acting mannerly" creates the image of a more fluid process.

Respecting others is widely viewed as a core ingredient in successfully working with clients. So, too, is it a vital element in all the relationships of our lives. Bill Madsen (1999) has said that much good and lasting work can be accomplished in our professional interactions simply by our mannerly decorum. People often do not remember the specific content of working together, but they often remember how they were treated.

Although our society seems to be largely unconcerned with the absence of consistent mannerly behavior in general, it seems that each of us is aware when disrespectful discrepancies occur and consequentially we usually are offended. It seems that the missing piece here is not a lack of understanding of what mannerly conduct is, but it is in "minding our manners" or enacting those behaviors in relationship. We also believe it likely that everyone at times behaves mannerly but we are far too selective in exhibiting these behaviors. In roles or relationships in which we are hurt, rushed, confused, or threatened, we find it exceedingly difficult to bring mannerly behaviors forward. Many professional contexts are understood as competitive sites with the primary objective of personal gain, so mannerly conduct may not be a valued activity. Educational contexts reflect larger cultural narratives that privilege individualism as a prime goal with the resultant emphasis placed upon competition and individual gain and accomplishment (Cushman, 1995).

The little things. Some illustrations of teacher and student interactions in which manners were lacking highlight our point. Communications between teacher and student often convey relational expressions and meanings. A student once reported that when she called an instructor's office, she was greeted with "Yeah, what do you want?" She reported feeling intimidated, put off by this very unwelcoming phone greeting, and consequently did not finish her business with the instructor, figuring the instructor would likely be unresponsive to her. We have had students report that when they communicate via e-mails to various instructors and university offices, their e-mails are not answered for many days and sometimes never. In terms of face-to-face communications, learning students' names quickly and remembering to address them by their preferred names is another arena where manners can be demonstrated. These examples may be considered incidental or minor events, but they are often the exact location where mannerly conduct is revealed or shown to be absent.

Demonstrations of behaving mannerly show up in our language, in our interpersonal responsiveness, and in our dependability. The academic and business worlds are fraught with opportunities for feeling brushed off and unappreciated; the risk of miscommunications with others is likely. But if we can graciously, rather that patronizingly, take the time to talk about and understand what has transpired, get back to people in a timely manner, acknowledge their suggestions and contributions, and greet those we see, we will have a greater chance of getting things accomplished with greater efficiency and effectiveness as well as enhancing our world of relationships.

In the fast-paced world of academia, we often only relate to our professional colleagues around tasks to complete or in official meeting contexts. We notice faculty walking through office areas without any obvious awareness that others are around. They do not respond with friendly greetings to those they pass in the hallways or those who may be working in their offices with their doors open. They may not answer voicemail messages, e-mail, or respond to invitations, even after repeated overtures. For some, the carefully circumscribed delineation of job duties and responsibilities provides the rationale for declining requests to participate with colleagues. These missed opportunities or indiscretions are usually not noticed or highlighted—we have become used to them. Nevertheless, they can represent a pervasive discounting behavior, no matter how routine or unremarkable they may be. Taking time to greet and speak with professional colleagues— especially when the time is not scheduled or when only for an instrumental purpose—is a mannerly and valuing interpersonal behavior.

We are provided with opportunities to behave mannerly in every interaction throughout our day: talking with prospective students, talking to colleagues with whom we often disagree, talking with students about their classroom performance, receiving feedback, or working with staff members. In those relationships in which we work with others regularly or in those relationships that have long histories, we cannot assume that overlooking mannerly behavior will not take a toll. As we have seen in working with many couples over the years, taking for granted manners and courtesies has much to do with relational decline (Stuart, 1980).

Critical Self-Reflection

Critical self-reflection refers to a process of carefully examining our behavior with the goals of (a) maintaining positive behaviors and (b) generating improved or enhanced behaviors and relationships. Critical self-reflection includes valuing abilities and capacities and communicating the results of such inquiries in respectful ways. It does not refer to a process of developing negative attributions.

The process of critical self-reflection involves asking questions of our behaviors, assumptions, and effects on others. It may involve asking questions of ourselves such as: Am I being true to what I believe? Is what I believe been checked lately to see if it still is meaningful and useful for me? Am I sure that I am taking everything into consideration that I need to? How does my behavior look from a variety of positions? What ideas do I consistently edit out?

Diagnosing our view of the DSM. Here is an example of critically examining one of our strongly held positions that relates to our roles as teachers as well as colleagues. The place of the *Diagnostic and Statistical Manual of Mental Disorders (DSM-IV)* in our curriculum is an ongoing issue with our students as well as with our faculty and community colleagues. We have concluded through different means and experiences that the DSM-IV is not a useful framework with which to organize our clinical work in family therapy or in social work. Our position on this matter is quite dogmatic, and we have made this bias public. We also know, however, that our students must learn the *DSM-IV* in their roles as practitioners within the various mental health delivery systems (Wulff, St. George, & Chenail, 2000). So how do we come to understand the place of the *DSM-IV* in graduate education for family therapists and social workers?

We must put our strongly held biases in this regard up for examination and reflection just as we ask of our students. We ask ourselves, "Is our position becoming 'automatic'—without regular reexamination? Are the reasons on which we base this view valid? Are our views shifting in any way? What justices and injustices are we exerting on our students, our academic programs, and our reputations by holding the opinion(s) we do?

Our reflections on these questions are leading us to include more information about the *DSM-IV* and its workings than we had previously included. We are continually accommodating requests and guidance by students and field supervisors by providing additional attention to the *DSM-IV* in our curriculum. Rather that assuming a defensive position, we are attempting to spark our interest in the possible utility of the *DSM-IV*. Listening for the justifications professed by others that support its inclusion in academic curriculum is giving us a broader vantage point to understand better those who advocate its usage. This reflective position does not indicate a lessening of our concerns about the *DSM-IV*, but we find ourselves in a better position to study, discuss, and generate ideas about its inclusion in our practices than we did before when our energy was more devoted to using our power and position to battle forces bent on including it. This shift of position also has the effect of allowing the proponents of the *DSM-IV* to listen to our alternative viewpoints.

What is illustrated above is that we need to be critically reflective with ourselves and open to receive feedback from others. We instruct our students to be critically reflective and for us to do otherwise is to behave hypocritically and unwilling to "practice what we preach." Critically examining our positions models a willingness to challenge our own beliefs and creates room for other ideas to emerge.

Community

In order to live collaboratively, we need to understand that our so-called individual thoughts and actions can always be considered a part of a larger picture and acting within this larger context view can lead to new ideas and positions. We can entertain the idea that the advancement of our preferred ideas and actions can likely be inextricably linked to our larger community and therefore can have consequences for our larger networks. We are not islands. This view is centered on a stance of relational responsibility and accountability (McNamee & Gergen, 1998)—from us to others and from others to us. Therefore, limiting our thinking to how decisions and behaviors only affect our immediate situation can cut us off from considering and understanding our wider communities.

Identifying ways with which we keep community in mind is to ask consistently of others and ourselves the following questions: Is this decision, suggestion, or proposal a beneficial choice for each of the individuals involved and is it beneficial for our group, faculty, student cohort, or administrators? Who might be hurt or disenfranchised by this action? What are the possible consequences? How might others view it? Do we appreciate others' views as much as our own? Doherty and Beaton (2000) remind us that "civic mindedness" is a key part of our professional role as family therapists: "We call for a new kind of community practice that is driven less by therapist-defined problems and professional expertise, and more by community-defined problems and families' own expertise" (p. 149).

Tamasese, Waldegrave, Tuhaka, and Campbell (1998) relate this community-mindedness to processes whereby the privileged or dominant groups in their setting monitor and rectify, as needed, abuses of power within organizations and communities. Rather than expecting those that are harmed within a community to grieve instances of abuse (which is the typical process in Western countries), the stockholders of power and privilege within a community shoulder greater initiative in locating the harmful excesses that result from the power and privilege they are afforded. This does not reapportion "blame" to another group or individual but, rather, broadens the understanding and responsibility for adjustments to those conditions that harm some in our world more than others. This attention to others in one's community has enormous implications for how communities can address issues of diversity and marginalization.

Being neighbors. In our educational program, we seek to encourage a sense of community within our student cohorts as well as among the faculty and students. Beginning with the initial interview, we accentuate the importance of caring for the collective unit and other individuals as much as we do for our own selves. Students are encouraged to help one another on projects, lend support to one another, and value the other students' progress through the program as much as their own. Faculty members arrange cookouts at their homes for faculty, administrators, support staff, and students and their families. Being there for one another in fun and celebratory moments enriches the relationships and increases the likelihood that serious or problematic issues can be safely discussed among students and faculty. Oftentimes, casual and social gatherings are considered outside of our professional or academic roles. Our notion of living collaboratively considers all relationship building—even outside of the formal or official work setting and time frame—as valid and valued.

In another example, SSG was chosen to serve on an ad hoc committee on diversity to create a plan that would address the racial tensions that were rising in campus life as well as recruitment of minority (particularly African American) students and faculty. This committee chose to focus on racial issues as experienced in our department and to develop recommendations or action plans to address any concerns that were noticed. The committee was comprised of seven women, three of whom were black and four white, and had the potential for a positive impact on our departmental community.

With this committee assignment, SSG faced some of the challenges of embracing collaborative work, namely the need to take a collaborative stance whether or not others would approach the committee work collaboratively, valuing differing views, and being accountable to the committee as a whole. The committee was tense in its discussions surrounding the many differing perceptions of racial issues in our department. Opinions that were expressed mirrored our larger community and included the following: "We have no racial troubles," "We, as a committee, are too small to change racial divisions," "Racial problems are not our fault," "If we address these issues there will be reprisals against us." And, "We need to be courageous and try new ways to raise awareness of the troubles we have in our department." For SSG, who held the idea that the committee should seriously risk trying to make changes that could be controversial, the collaborative challenge was to consider carefully each person's view, especially those opinions that she fiercely disagreed with, including those that denied the presence of racial discord and insisted that nothing could be done to alter things.

Early discussions focused on ways to address a controversial topic without upsetting anyone. This trend in the conversation was discouraging to SSG, which prompted her to ask if the diversity committee should work in "name only," suggesting that such actions were considered by her to be shallow and insufficient to the import of the task given to the committee. She also indicated that if the committee members were on that track, then she would probably be of little value in their efforts. SSG was not attempting to strong-arm the committee toward her position; rather, she stated as clearly as she could her point of view and her commitment to the committee's work.

Committee discussions continued to focus on how the committee would define its presence and function and what they would recommend and ultimately execute. SSG continued as a vocal participant, often refuting or glossing over any talk that she interpreted as not acting in the service of change. Luckily, the other committee members were also persistent and kept repeating their cautions and fears. Similarly, in therapy when clients repeat themselves, SSG sees it as a sign that they are "not getting it" and adopts a position of curiosity in order to learn more and different things from what she currently knows or thinks she knows. Applying this same reasoning to her fellow committee members, SSG became quiet herself in order to listen and let their cautions and fears accompany her own views so as to create a more complete picture of the complexity of the committee's work. When SSG used her energy to listen and privilege others' voices, she heard stories that reiterated themes of fear and punishment. She recognized how, in some respects, her position as a white, experienced faculty member blocked her from validating the potential risks as necessary wisdom in designing a collaborative forward movement. Clearly in this group she was the "privileged," the majority, and therefore subject to the blindness of power and "rightness"—the perfect formula for thwarting community effort by deleting or overlooking important aspects and views in order to let one's own views take priority.

The committee continued to work together on different plans and came up with several innovative and generative experiences for the faculty, staff, and students of the department. The committee members were challenged to develop a sense of community within their ranks that was in a sense the diversity issue in a microcosm. The threats to collaborative professional interacting were present in this committee, and the committee worked to find ways to privilege each committee member's views, thereby upholding their collective sense of community.

Creative Action

Talking, describing, and planning are not enough. We must combine those steps into a way of coordinating with others to take action that maximizes the benefits that can accrue from collaborative ways of understanding. Certainly talking with others is a form of action, but by action, we mean to take collective behavioral steps to secure structural and relational changes for the benefit for all involved. The emphasis on action involves understanding how to act in the world to effect change while cognizant of both positive and negative consequences of any action. It involves joint responsibility, without individuals or groups taking over (Shotter, 1993). It necessitates valuing, using manners, critically reflecting, and incorporating respect for community.

As teachers, we have the responsibility of making decisions in our classrooms. With this responsibility comes a desire to be successful that might entice us into doing it "our" way. Giving in to this pressure may directly work against collaborative efforts. There are many situations that may not seem to be collaborative opportunities: grading, disciplinary actions with students, or carrying out tasks that seem mundane. Grading is a teaching task that invites teachers to act hierarchically, without participation of students other than providing the raw material that is to be graded. It is a prototypical example of "evaluating" another's work rather than "valuing" it. Teachers decide whether students have mastered the material. Inviting students into the process of deciding what will be evaluated, how, and by who, opens the door to collaboration, and ironically, may produce superior results in estimating a student's performance and capability while at the same time enhancing it.

Disciplinary actions are often handled by formal procedures and, at times, legal means that place students in responding positions where they only follow preset procedures. They have precious little to say other than to answer specific questions put to them. Decisions about them are adjudicated and consequences meted out to them. Allowing students to address the issues raised by their behaviors in ways that provide the students with more responsibility enhance their accountability for their actions and what they learn.

A second chance. DW had a student who was overall a good student but who had failed a key component of the course resulting in a grade of "C"— typically, a failing-type grade. In some ways, the student had achieved most of the course's objectives, but some specific graded elements were not successfully met. DW believed that giving the student the "C" was not reflective of his abilities and wondered whether the course design was flawed in not recognizing this student's mastery of the material. DW met with this student at the semester's end to discuss the student's performance and wondered if there were other acceptable options on how to proceed other than to give the "C," perhaps altering the grade after some reconsideration and reevaluation of the student's performance. DW and the student imagined the possibility of giving a grade of "incomplete" which meant that the two would engage during the summer semester in a series of meetings to continue the student's learning of the course material. Such a continuance would likely improve the "C" grade, but the student had the choice to pursue this option or not. The substance of these meetings would be primarily the responsibility of the student (with the instructor's agreement) to ensure that the course continuance would be a substantive learning experience. Therefore, the student was asked what ideas he had to manage this situation. Recognition that charting the course of action was somewhat ambiguous for both DW and the student invited both into creating a plan that would meet the needs of each. The student opted to work together with DW over the summer. These meetings yielded extremely valuable conversations for both the student and DW, extending the course material even further than had been the case during the course proper.

Opportunities for creative action are abundant with respect to collegial work. In academic institutions (as well as other institutional settings), faculty are often in positions where it could be efficient and logical for them to consider some tasks mundane or routine (e.g., making copies, answering phones, delivering mail to offices) that could be just as easily handled by students or staff. Some faculty consider such tasks as "beneath them" or too menial for someone of their rank or salary. However, there are occasions when going the "extra mile" to help someone with their task would be precisely the collaborative thing to do. In these situations, maintaining those functions as "not my job" would be not facilitative of a collaborative stance. Volunteering to help with a problem or task outside of your immediate set of responsibilities can boost a sense of community within one's group.

Creative action works on multiple levels simultaneously, including personal as well as larger, social levels. Such action includes a "process which involves investigating the circumstances of place; reflecting on the needs, resources, and constraints of the present reality; examining the possible paths to be taken; and consciously moving in new directions" (Smith, Willms, & Johnson, 1997, p. 8). The paths we take in working creatively and collaboratively have implications for what we accomplish now, the consequences for relationships that result from the work, the impact on our larger communities, and the directions we take.

Looking Back and Looking Ahead

We have contended in this chapter that living a collaborative professional lifestyle involves a view of collaboration that values relationships and refuses to see them as merely a means to an end. We have also said that living according to collaborative principles affords us greater success in our work with clients as well as in our work with our students and our colleagues.

Deliberately reflecting upon and practicing collaborative behavior across multiple contexts in our lives (e.g., in therapy with clients, in class with students, and at work with our colleagues) supports an overall collaborative style of being and interacting. To apply the collaborative elements and practices of valuing, acting mannerly, critically self-evaluating, building community, and enacting creative changes in multiple contexts reinforces and expands our vision of what collaborative is and generates more ideas on how we might increase its impact in our own lives.

We have experienced how adopting collaborative ideas and principles positively influences our clinical work and our wider professional circles. These principles do not present themselves as structured behavioral scripts that one must scrupulously follow. Rather, they appear as guideposts to consider creatively.

Just as we have presented our ideas on ways we have found to expand collaborative work into our professional lives, we also can envision extending them into one's personal life. How do we live the collaborative lifestyle at home with family, close friends, and neighbors? Is it appropriate with these relationships? Is it in some ways natural and expected? Is it for adults only? Does its practice require total dedication in order to perfect? What are the downsides of taking such a stance in our personal lives? Are there areas that "a little collaboration" might be helpful in, and total dedication might be harmful? Collaborative relationships are rich with potential far beyond their usefulness within the therapeutic context. In addition to examining collaborative stances in our personal lives, we can expand the question upward to consider their application on the national or international level. How might these ideas influence our world?

Endnote

1. We originally planned to discuss collaborative living in our personal daily lives as well as professional, but that arena is so interesting in its own right we will save that discussion for another work.

References

Anderson, H. (1997). *Conversation, language, and possibilities: A postmodern approach to therapy.* New York: Basic Books.

Bray, J.N., Lee, J., Smith, L.L., & Yorks, L. (2000). *Collaborative inquiry in practice: Action, reflection, and meaning making.* Thousand Oaks, CA: Sage.

Cushman, P. (1995). *Constructing the self, constructing America: A cultural history of psychotherapy.* Boston, MA: Addison-Wesley.

Doherty, W.J. & Beaton, J.M. (2000). Family therapists, community, and civic renewal. *Family Process, 39,* 149–159.

Gilligan, S. & Price, R. (Eds.). (1993). *Therapeutic conversations.* New York: W.W. Norton.

Madsen, W.C. (1999). *Collaborative therapy with multi-stressed families: From old problems to new futures.* New York: Guilford.

Malinen, T. (2000). The wisdom of not-knowing—a conversation with Harlene Anderson. *Journal of Systemic Therapies, 23,* 68–77.

McNamee, S. & Gergen, K.J. (Eds.). (1998). *Relational responsibility: Resources for sustainable dialogue.* Thousand Oaks, CA: Sage.

Sampson, E.E. (1993). *Celebrating the other: A dialogic account of human nature.* Boulder, CO: Westview Press.

Shotter, J. (1993). *Conversational realities: Constructing life through language.* London: Sage.

Smith, S.E., Willms, D.G., & Johnson, N.A. (Eds.). (1997). *Nurtured by knowledge: Learning to do participatory action-research.* New York: Apex Press.

Stuart, R.B. (1980). *Helping couples change.* New York: Guilford.

Tamasese, K., Waldegrave, C., Tuhaka, F., & Campbell, W. (1998). Furthering conversations about partnerships of accountability: Talking about issues of leadership, ethics and care. *Dulwich Centre Journal, 4,* 50–62.

White, M. & Epston, D. (1990). *Narrative means to therapeutic ends.* New York: W.W. Norton.

Wulff, D., St. George, S., & Chenail, R. (2000). Searching for family therapy in the Rockies: Family therapists meet a paleontologist. *Contemporary Family Therapy, 22,* 407–414.

Zingaro, J. (1988). Manners and family therapy. *Journal of Strategic and Systemic Therapies, 7,* 25–26.

Subject Index

A

aboutness (monological) thinking, 45, 51
  aboutness thinking (Shotter), 53,
    69, 256
  as monologue, 51, 53
  vs. withness thinking, 45, 69
abstract position, 326
abstract principles, avoiding, 326–327
acting mannerly, 411–413, 419. *see also*
  Manners
action, 14, 16, 18, 34, 43, 54, 243, 319,
  339, 349, 415
  action-sensitive cell (Damassio), 72
  causality and, 10
  collaborative action, implications
    of 398
  "Collaborative Action Plan", 76
  collaborative inquiry and, 375
  coordinated, 185, 314, 319, 320
  creative, 407,417–419
  human action and meaning, 368
  joint, 12–13, 54, 314, 324, 334,
    373, 410
  knowledge and, 384
  meaning-making through, 185
  narrative and, 16
  participatory forms, 323
  possibilities for, 343, 377, 406

  research, 143
  reflection and, 349, 371
  self-agency and, 17–18
  social, research questions and, 375
  theories and, 43
  verbal, 12
actions, 33, 185, 247, 319, 399, 416
  accountability for 418
  answerability and 211
  attitudes and, 27
  constructing effective professionals, 315
  coordinated, 185, 314
  dialogically or responsively linked,
    12–13
  knowledge and, 9
  meaning and, 10, 18
  MIT, 30. *see also* Multiple Impact
    Therapy
  research and 370, 384
  researcher's 115
  therapist, 38
  thoughts, 328, 414
  words and, 7, 25, 40, 275, 277, 282
action-sensitive cell (Damasio), 72
agency, 47, 224, 265, 338
  client, 54
  self-agency, 7, 16–18, 53, 168, 172,
    176, 180

self-competence, 181, 195, 257
   sense of, 282, 285
   students', 54
aging, 151, 165, 393
   labels on, 394
   students' reflections on 164
   stereotypes of, 392
Aging Well (Valliant), 154
agreements
   establishing, 340, 349n
   building, example of, 178–179
"answerability" (Bakhtin), 211–212, 214, 215
appreciative
   audience, 67, 159
   core, 399
   culturally, 269, 280
   inquiry, 335n, 400n
   organizations 294, 305
"appropriately unusual" (Andersen), 87, 186, 188–189
"As If" exercise, 131
   examples of, 177, 240, 242, 244, 247–249, 328–329
   language, 65
   position, 294
   position, speaking from, 177
assumptions, 2, 48, 349, 392, 406
   accepted, blind trust in, 12
   antithetical, 96
   beyond therapy room, 55
   collaborative research, and characteristics, 371–385
   dialogue and, 230
   interpretation and, 13
   knowledge and 406
   meaning and language, about, 88–91
   researcher's, 369, 377
   risk of, 53, 277
   theories and 82
   therapists' 124, 169, 171, 216, 231, 280, 344, 419
   postmodern, 7–8
assumption trap, 280

B

battered women vs. "women who have been battered", 114
battering 112
   assumptions about, 113
   couples therapy, 122–123
   generative conversations about, 124
   participants' definitions of, 112–113
   words and terms, 113, 114
being public, 50–51, 384. *see also* Public
   inner dialogue and, 39
   MIT actions and, 30n
   private thoughts, inner talk and, 50
bond 84, 89. *see also* Circle of life
   relational bond, 84
   social bond, 89–90
boundaries, 53, 115, 154, 212, 227, 290, 355
   classroom and everyday life, blurring of, 326, 329–331
   team and therapist-in-the-room, 28
breathing, 70, 84–87, 90, 212
bullying, 12

C

category, xix, 444, 49, 114, 256, 273, 280, 355. *see also* Aboutness thinking; Diagnosis; Labels, Problems; Typologies
   abstract, 68
   category-based (and unit to be treated) populations, 96
   diagnostic, 35
   of identity, 270
   labels on aging, 394
   pre-determined, 115, 377
   research, 112, 353–354
   risk of, 49
   stereotypes of aging, 392
change, 10–11, 23, 90, 228
   action and, 417
   certainty and, 258
   constant state of, 29–30, 90
   dialogue and, 174
   felt sense vs. codifed rules of, 77
   context for, 123, 255
   epistemological error, 11, 29–30
   meanings and, 229, 230
   MIT and, 23
   not-knowing and, 228
   observer punctuation of, 30, 188

predictability of, 35
process as, 405
reflecting talks and, 206
relationship or process vs.
   commodity or product, 405
research and, 353–354
research, participants' lived experiences, 381, 384, 385
resources for, 188
social and political, 48
supervisor, 241, 351
system, culture, 64, 226, 403
therapist and, 11, 49, 297
trusting possibilities of
vs transformation/ing 10
uncertainty and, 52
words, 230
Childhood Years, 149
children
   artistic reflections, 194–195
   board games, 191–192
   constructing meaning with, 185–191
   creating a dialogical space, 186–187
   curiosisty and nonexpertise with, 188
   inner talk of, 190
   not-knowing, 187–188
   parents and therapy (*see* Chapters 7,
      11, and 12)
   play and, 85–86, 186, 187, 189,
      190–194
   puppet and play enactment, 192
   puppet reflecting teams, 193
   reflecting teams with children, 194
   Vygotsky on, 81, 85
   words and beyond, 190–191
chronification, meaning of, 75
circle of life, 84, 164
client/s, 33, 67, 74,
   accounts of therapy, 56
   advice to therapists 283
   challenging, 23
   as expert and expertise, 46–47, 48,
      134, 136, 188, 273, 280,
   freedom and hope, 55, 284–285
   knowledge, 26, 38, 50
   listening, speaking, and hearing,
      35–39
   language, 24, 26

mandated, 56
story/ies, 25, 27, 47, 123, 129,
   as conversational partners, 45–46
   therapist in mutual inquiry and, 26,
      47–48
   perception of therapy, 36, 130, 133,
      144–145, 376, 378, 379, 385,
   as therapist's teacher, 46
   voices, 33, 57, 143–145
client and therapist transforming
   together, 51–52
CLS (*see* Collaborative Language
   Systems)
coaching, 55, 355
coherence, 16, 403
   with client's expertise, 25
   local, 328
   maintaining, 16, 25
   relational, 334
   researcher and, 378, 379, 380,
collaborate, 44, 54, 173, 213, 282, 321,
   394
   definition of, 115,
   students and, 331, 334,
   team and, 172,
collaborating, 328, 344, 406. *see also*
   Collaboration; Collaborative
   elements of, 407–419
collaboration, 142–143, 282, 338, 392,
   394, 395, 396
   avoiding imposition, 338
   defined, 115
   demonstrated, 282
   in education, 318, 320, 334
   empathy and compassion and,
      106–107
   hierarchical differences and, 339, 374
   intentional, 136
   interviewee and interviewer, 339–345
   language and, 370
   learning exercise, 339–244
   misconceptions, 407–408
   physiotherapists with, 86–88
   preunderstanding, 272
   process, extending, 397
   professional, 225, 307
   relational process of, 392
   stance, as a, 385

understanding and, 115
values of, 336
withness and, 57
collaborative
    action, implications of, 398–400
    approach, 21, 22, 23, 57, 131, 137,
        142, 151, 184, 205, 251, 266,
        269–270, 280
    colleague/s, 173
    conversation, 314, 316
    creation of questions, 339
    dialogue, 34
    ethics 288, 294
    inquiry, 24, 56, 109,
    interview/s 105, 111, 114–116
    invitation to, 199
    language systems. (see Collaborative
        Language Systems)
    learning. (see Collaborative learning)
    orientation, 318
    partners, in research, 115
    practice/s, 335, 336, 321
    practitioners and relational meta-
        phor, 324
    process, 124, 130, 270, 333
    relationship/s, 44, 45, 47, 48, 51, 52
    research. (see Collaborative research)
    shift to collaborative inquiry, 24–27
    stance, 50, 142, 315
    style, 75
    therapist, 46, 48, 52, 57. see also Col-
        laborative therapist; Therapist
    therapy. (see Collaborative therapy;
        Therapy)
    work as relationship, 406–407
"Collaborative Action Plan"
    (Kinman), 76
collaborative approach and MIT, 22–24
Collaborative Language Systems, 56,
    103, 150, 256, 370. see also Language
    systems theory
collaborative learning, 314, 318,
    321–322, 325, 326, 331
collaborative learning community/ies
    developing, 236–241
    diversity in, 279
    experiencing, 241–244

*Collaborative Learning: Higher Educa-
    tion, Interdependence, and the Author-
    ity of Knowledge* (Bruffee), 322
collaborative relationships and dialogical
    conversations, 198
collaborative relationship/s and genera-
    tive conversation/s, 44, 45, 47, 48, 51,
    52,54, 132, 133, 134, 174, 235, 236, 285,
    334, 337
collaborative research
    conversation, 117–121, 377–379
    as conversational partnership,
        373–374
    curiosity, 375–376
    data analysis, 379–382
    as generative process, 373
    as insider research, 376–377
    knowledge construction, 317–372
    meeting, 217
    mutual inquiry, 374–375
    researcher relationship and role, 109,
        115, 116, 374, 375–376, 377
    validity and reliability, 382–385
collaborative therapist, 168, 173,
    176, 177
    knowledge and, 48–50, 179
    and not-knowing, 48–50
    being public, 50–51, see also Public
    position, 46
    power differentials, 281
    uncertainty and 52–53
    stance, 277
collaborative therapy, 43, 44–57, 131
    being public, 50–51. see also Public
    characteristics, 44–54
    central question, 33–34, 57, 370–371
    children and. (see Children)
    child's perspective 180, 186–191
    client expertise, 46–47
    client knowledge, 46–47
    clients' perspectives of, 142–143,
        180, 384
    client position, 46
    curiosity and. (see Curiosity)
    distinctive feature/s, 54–57
    as dynamic, 54–55
    effectiveness, 56–57

evaluation. (*see* Evaluation)
(e)valuation. (*see* (E)valuation)
as everyday, ordinary life 53–54
future of, 57
hallmarks of, 18
heart and spirit of, 33, 43, 44, 54. *see also* Philosophical stance
improvisational, 52, 54, 294
language. (*see* Language)
learning, studying, 44, 53, 56. *see also* Collaborative learning
as nonformulaic, 44, 54–55
overview, 370–371
philosophical background, 368–370
philosophical stance, 44–54
premises 162, 168,
research and. (*see* Research)
as shared talks or trialogues, 203
therapist expertise, 46–47, 259–261, 325
therapist perspective of, 384
trialogues and uncertainty, 52–53
words, beyond, 190–191
compassion, 99
empathy and 100–101
listening and, 105–106
what defines (Nussbaum), 106
community, 8, 9, 11
members, 23, 29
professional/s, 22, 67
learning. (*see* Collaborative Learning Communities)
life-long learning, 54
competence
child sense of, 195
learner/student, 241, 257
skills, techniques, certainty, and, 25, 399
teacher, 318, 323
therapist, 46–47
competency, 17, 53, 54
client, 282
"competency trap" (Barrett), 315, 334n
constructionism, 296, 303. *see also* Social constructionism
constructionist 2, 113, 115, 320, 369
see also Social construction; Social constructionism

positivist vs., 383
research, 382
constructivism 12, 18n, 110, 294
constructionism, differs from, 12
radical, 294
consultation
format, 239
interview/s, 35, 129, 132, 241
"reflexive systemic therapy" and process, 239
questionnaire, 240
supervision and, 362
"user consultation groups" (Lister et al), 374
"consultation interviews", (Fernandez et al.), 129
conversation/s, 14, 15, 16 ,22, 27, 44, 49, 41, 50, 51, 123, 133, 134, 180, 240, 242. *see also* Dialogue; Talk
collaborative, 1150, 314, 316, 326
dialogic. (*see* Dialogic)
dialogical, 41, 44, 52, 131, 132, 134, 379, "dialogical conversations" (Yankelovich) 229
dialogue and, 34, 35–38
equality in, 170, 226
everyday, ordinary, 53
generative conversations about battering, 124
good conversation 203
guest in, 205
in-home, 274–275
inner, 48
interview as, 377–379
invitation to, 225
local 25, 52
multivoicedness and, 226–227
as mutual inquiry. (*see* Mutual inquiry and Shared inquiry)
overlapping conversations, 168, 169
partner, 278
"polyphonic" (Bakhtin), 75
relational conversations, 33
as relational practice, 314
relationship and, 43, 44, 45, 46, 47, 48, 49, 54, 142, 212, 281
research, 114

"rolling conversations" (Hoffman), 169, 179
as shared inquiry 275
shifting and overlapping 162
space, 146, 227
starter/s, 227–233
teaching as, 313, 317 316, 324, 328, 334
therapist knowledge and, 49, 260
transformational dialogue, 51–52
uncertainty and. (*see* Uncertainty)
overlapping voices, 70
"withness", 63, 64, 65, 67, 69, 70, 77, 78, (*see* Withness thinking)
"without rank," (Bakhtin) 74, 77
witnessed conversations, 215
words, beyond, 190–191
conversational
approach, 137, 150, 151, 269
becoming, 17
clusters, 240
dyad, 110
process, 27, 47, 270,
questions, 378
resources, 328
space, 326, 331–334
"starter questions" (Feinsilver, et al.), 277
therapy, 64, 77, 78, 132
therapy process, 23, 26, 27, 34, 35–41, 44–54, 144, 305, 378. *see also* Conversational partners; Conversational partnerships; Dialogic; Dialogue
conversational partner/s, 34, 45–46. 52, 168, 170, 173, 181, 271, 272, 340, 411
conversational partnership, 46, 173,
mutual inquiry and. (*see* Mutual inquiry)
research as, 373–374
shared inquiry and. (*see* Shared inquiry)
"conversational realities", (Shotter), 12
conversational therapies, 64, 77, 78, 132,
couples therapy and battering, 122–123
creativity, 23, 27, 51, 53, 55, 168, 173, 238, 261, 399

"Creatura" (Bateson), 64, 65
culture, 269
cultural barriers, 270
culturally identified experts, therapists as, 282
culturally appreciative and sensitive services, 269, 280
"culture of femininity" (Walker and Shaw), 138
individualistic discourse and, 315
local, 137
knowledge and, 8, 46–47
"polyphonic" treatment, 226
reality and, 9
as systems of meaning, 270
curiosity, 37, 38, 47, 123, 151, 168, 186, 274, 354, 405, 417. *see also* Not-knowing
in learning, 237, 239, 243
nonexpert position and, 188
researcher, 375

D

"definitional ceremony" (Meyerhoff), 151
description/s 13, 17, 88, 341
alternate, new, richer, 73, 76, 190, 342
congruent, 207
language and, 9, 382
diagnosis, 22, 35, 133, 168, 175, 223, 225, 238, 259, 260, 306–307. (*see also* Aboutness thinking, Categories, Labels, Problems and Typology)
Diagnostic and Statistical Manual of Mental Disorders, 413–414. *see also DSM-IV*
dialogic, 10, 14, 34, 47, 64, 66, 75, 223, 293, 294, 302, 331
"dialogic conversation" (Yankelovich), 229
dialogical conversation and collaborative relationship, 52, 133, 134
see also generative dialogue and collaborative relationships
dialogical equality, 225–226
dialogisms, 72, 75

dialogue/s, 10, 12, 13, 15, 34, 48, 64, 168, 224, 399, 410
  being public and, 51
  bodily activities and, 315
  children and, *see* Children
  colleagues and, 307
  defined, 34, 230
  enhancing possibility for, 40–41
  equality in, 218, 299
  distinctive features (Yankelovich)
  form of play, *see* Children
  generating, 228
  as generative, 34, 54, 224, 373
  inner, 39–41, 252, 315,
  inner, importance of articulating, 39
  inner and outer, 231
  as interpretations of interpretations, 40
  invitations to, 277
  knowledge and, 48–49, 367
  language, 14, 48
  listening, hearing, and speaking and. (*see* Listening, hearing, and speaking)
  meaning-generating process, 39, 255
  misunderstanding, missed-understanding and, 39
  monologue and. (*see* Monologue)
  mutually enacted, 338
  newness in, 13
  not-knowing and, 34–35, 48–50, 256–257,
  open dialogue. (*see* Open Dialogue)
  "reflective dialogue" (Haarakangas), 231
  relationship and, 33
  response and, 36–37
  research. (*see* Research)
  self and, 14
  self-agency and, 172
  space for, 34, 137, 179–180, 325,
  therapist inner, 39, 41, 51, 168
  transformation and, 34, 180
  as transformative, 263, 330,
  as transforming, 35, 54
  understanding and, 14–15, 38, 230, 369,
    uncertainty, 34–35
    "withness thinking" and, 51
    word/s and, 298. *See also* Conversation; Talk
differences, 47, 407. *see also* Diversity
discourse, 13, 64, 68, 75, 231, 270
  academic, 374
  authorative, 9
  individualistic, 323–324
  as narrative form, 15–16
  postmodern, 54
  professional, psychology, psychotherapy, 30, 170, 307, 381
  self and, 17
diversity, 168, 173, 215, 239, 259, 270, 334, 411, 415, 416, 417. *see also* Differences
Driftworks (Lyotard), 67

E

eating disorders
  acceptable change, 137
  action research and, 143
  biomedical aspects of 139–142
  client voices, 133–135
  client expectations, 139
  clients as experts, 134
  collaboration, 142
  dialogical conversations and space, 129, 131, 132, 133, 134
  generative interaction with clients, 133
  local knowledge and, 136
  medical risks, 134–137
  meaningful conversations, 132
  not-knowing and, 133–134
  biomedical aspects of, 139–142
  philosophy of therapy with, 142
  reflecting processes and teams, 313, 132, 133,
  sociocultural aspects, 137–139
education, 48, 55, 56, 231, 235–238.
  (*see* Learning and Teaching)
    alternate forms, 324
    avoiding abstract positions, 326
    conversational space, 331

examining, 322
expertise and, 315
higher, 321–322
improvisation in, 320
institution of, 323
institutional, 316
knowledge and, 320–323
relational approach to, 314
as relational practice, 315–318
of therapists, 24
Eighth Annual Open Dialogue Conference, 41n
elders. *see also* Aging, Elder Project, Positive Aging
"dis-membered" (Meyerhoff), 151
listening, 150, 152, 165, 166
loss and, 164
reflective process, 152
"re-member" (Meyerhoff), 151
opening space, 152
Elder project
context and modalities, 153–164
student reflections on, 165
empathy, 72
compassion and, 104–105, 106–107
listening with, 104–105
"traveling empathy" (Hoffman), 72
engaged, 313, 314, 319. *see also* Conversational becoming
in conversation , 215, 274
in democratic dialogue, 218
in education, 326, 328, 330
meetings, 74
relationally, 325
in story, 37
with, 24
with words,
engagement, 74, 281
Epistemology, Psychopathology and Psychotherapy Conference, 30
equal,
partners, 170
partnership, 338
positioning, 407
therapeutic conversation, 226
voices, 226, 228
equality, 227, 229

in client-therapist
relationship, 338
in dialogue, 218, 225–226
dialogical, 225–226
see also Hierarchy and Hierarchical
ethics
collaborative, 294
"polyphonic ethics" (Deissler), 294
of respect, 297
ethical
introducing, 214
listening 99
open space and, 214
"Exchanging Voices" (Hoffman), 70
expert. *see also* Expertise; Not-knowing
client as, 46–47, 48, 280
interviewee as, 337
position, away from, 299–300
therapist as, 46–47,
Expertise *see also* Expert; Not-knowing client
knowledge and, 259–261
relational, 258
therapist, 325
evaluate, 199, 319
coherency, 116
effectiveness, 222
expressions, 89
(e)valuate, 55
evaluation, 205, 217–218, 271
follow-up, 56, 217–218, 223
insider, 376
of outcome, 70, 73, 215–216, 217, 325, 376,
as part of everyday practice, 55, 96, 143, 270
positive, 321
shared standards, 369
of trialogue program, 217–218
(e)valuation, 4, 283
"evaluation is intervention" (Madsen), 373
everyday, ordinary life, therapy as, 53–54

F

flexibility
continuity and, 398–399

mobility and, 223
uncertainty and, 134
freedom, 27, 236
belonging and, 238
to express, 275
of expression, 50
and hope, 55, 284–285
learning and, 243
losses of, 215, 218, 219n
from past, 285
sense of, 54

G

Galveston Group, 21, 24. *see also* HGI;
Houston Galveston Institute
Galveston Symposium VII, 267
GCE. *see* Grupo Campos Eliseos
Gee's Bend Quilts, 77
Grupo Campos Eliseos, 57, 129, 142,
236, 368, 376

H

Health and Age Foundation, 396
Hearing, 33, 35–38, 39, 40, 44, 70, 71,
87, 103. *see also* Listening, hearing,
and speaking; Responsive-active
listening-hearing
the unheard, 111–112, 113, 115, 117,
123, 125
research and, 112–113
hermeneutics, 11, 13, 15, 24, 115, 369, 372
contemporary, 7
defined, 13
language and, 14
relational, 13–15, 18n
understanding and, 13–14
HGI, 236, 271, 273, 276, 353. *see also*
Houston Galveston Institute
hierarchy, 407. *see also* Equal; Equality
and dualism, 30
lowering, 372, 274
social, 72, 75, 76
Hogg Foundation, 30n
homeless women, 271
hope and freedom. (*see* Freedom and hope)

Hospital Universitario Dr. Joaquin
Albarran, 309n,
host-guest metaphor, 45, 95, 276
Houston Galveston Institute, 15, 150,
167, 236, 217, 351, 353, 368. *see also*
HGI; Galveston group
human systems as linguistic systems,
15, 30
Humboldt University, 292
Hundred Languages of Children, 167

I

Identities,11, 16, 17, 18, 215, 169,
270, 274, 281, 285, 321, 334. *see also*
Identity
identity, 10, 37, 43, 67, 137, 164, 270,
280, 285. *see also* Identities
as dialogical, 16
narrative, 16
professional, 167, 238, 315, 345
improvisation/al, 52
in education, 320, 324, 334n
theatrical in therapy, 305
improvise, 248, 320, 321, 327, 334n
"In the Pantheon", 160
In Search of Solutions, 238
individual
authorship vs. multiple/plural, 12
as autonomous, 8, 12, 28
family and, 29
knowledge, 8, 9, 322, 329,
language, 25
-in-relationship, 17, 29
person-in-relationship, 16–17
person(s)-in-relationship, 2, 55
relational
individualism
breaking with, 329
limits of 317
in-home conversations, 274–275, 276,
277, 282. (*see* Mobil crisis interventive
teams)
inner conversation, 41, 48, 50. *see also*
Inner dialogue; Inner talk; Inner
thoughts; Monologue
inner dialogical loops, 39

inner dialogue, 39. *see also* Inner talk;
  Inner thoughts
    articulating, 39
    monologue, 51
inner talk, 51, 85–86, 191. *see also* Inner
  dialogue; Inner thoughts
    bodily expression and, 89
    inner monologue and, 51
    being public and, 51
    spoken words and, 50
inner thoughts, therapist's, 39, 50, 51.
  see also Inner dialogue; Inner talk
inquiry ,17, 238, 407
    appreciative, 335n, 400n
    collaborative, 24–28, 56, 109, 337,
      338, 345, 349, 370, 371, 372, 375,
      379, 380, 382, 384, 385, 406
    as construction, 377–379
    joint, 274
    mutual, 26, 34, 43, 47–48, 52, 54, 281,
      475,
    participatory, 270
    research and. (*see* Research)
    self-reflexive, 334
    subject of, 17, 24
    shared, 47, 133, 168, 175, 281. *see also*
      Conversational partners
instructive interaction, 11
intent
    interviewer's, 370, 373
    therapist's, 40, 49, 50, 272, 274, 275,
      277, 283, 329, 370
intention, 49, 13, 165, 179, 209, 319
    of interviewing, 114
    meaning and, 14
    researcher's, 375, 383, 385
interactive moment, 315
interdependence, 282, 284, 322, 372, 411
interpretation, 10, 13
    dialolgue and, 40
    as interactive process, 40
    as relational process, 14
    in research, 369, 382, 383
interview/s
    as conversation, 377
    interviewee-guided 337
partner interviews 271–272

interviewing 108
    collaborative 105

J

joint action, 54, 324, 373, 410. *see also*
  Conversational partners; Mutual
  inquiry; Shared inquiry
joint activity
    conversation as, 281
    dialogue as, 35
    teaching as, 317
    understanding as, 14

K

knowledge
    client, 26, 38, 46, 131, 272
    collaborative, 114–116, 326, 371–372,
      407
    drifting and, 67
    education, teaching, and, 314, 315,
      316, 322
    "embodied-knowing" (Shotter), 65,
      68, 69
    first-person descriptions 268
    first-person lived experiences 9
    foundational, 8, 28
    individual, 8
    inside knowledge, 260
    lived experience 266, 267, 269
    language and, 8, 9, 10
    local knowledge, 8, 15, 136, 270, 370
      130
    local relevancy, 47
    "naïve knowledge" (Freire), 48
    "non-knowing" (Bachelard) 67
    not-knowing and, 8, 48–50, 228
    as objective reality, 8
    postmodern and, 43, 44, 370
    preknowledge, 25, 26, 280
    professional, 46, 179, 239, 259
    as relational and dialogic, 7
    research and, *see* Research
    social, 18n
    social construction and, 11, 12, 13,
      15, 322, 367, 369

stories and, 16, 328
student, 237, 258, 331, 332
tacit, 225
theoretical, 9, 205, 303
therapist, 26, 49, 50, 130, 140, 226
uncertainty and, 27, 52
"untouchable knowledge" (Deissler), 295
what counts as, 317, 320, 321, 325, 329. *see also* Expertise
knowing
    dialogue and, 40
    "embodied knowing" (Shotter), 68
    imaginary, 49
    inner dialogue and, 39
    knowing about and *knowing with*, 256
    preconceptions, 210, 229, 256, 260
    preknowing, 48–49
    preknowing vs. knowing with, 48–49
    relational, 8
    risks of, 40, 49, 67, 280
    therapist, 15

L

label/s, 12, 113, 114, 125, 210, 273, 285, 289, 394 405. *see also* Aboutness thinking, Categories; Diagnosis; Problems; Typologies
language, 7,8, 9–10, 12–17, 24, 25, 28, 30, 65, 228–230, 324, 370, 412
    "appropriately unusual" (Andersen), 87, 186, 188–189,
    assumptions about, 88–91
    being in language, 28
    children's, 176, 185, 186, 188. *see also* children
    client's, 24, 26, 27, 45, 107, 133,
    common, 64, 73, 74, 75, 205, 254
    communion, 212–214
    everyday ordinary, client, 24, 26
    expressions and, 9, 69, 72, 84, 88, 89, 90, 92, 186, 228, 347
    as generative, 255
    game (Wittengenstein), 68, 69, 79, 377, 399
    as a gift, 85

knowledge and, 7, 8, 10, 18, 28, 43, 44, 370
labels and categories of, 112. *see also* Categories; Labels; Typololgies
limiting and labeling, 107–108
local, 10
meaning and, 88–92
"power of language" (Freire), 48
professional, 26
research and, 110, 114, 380, 382
shared inquiry and, 168
systems, 15, 370. *see also* Collaborative Language Systems
therapist's, 4
transformation and, 10–11
understanding and. *see also* Words
language systems, 15
language systems theory, 109, 111
learning. *see also* Education and Teaching
    about other, 9, 35, 40, 45, 49, 280–281
    alternate modes of, 324
    client language, 24, 26
    collaborative, 239, 244, 318, 322
    as collaborative conversation
    collaborative environment for, 319
    collaborative learning community/ies, 235,–238, 241, 244
    collaborative therapy, 53, 57
    community, 146, 239, 333
    context, 317, 319, 323, 324, 325, 331, 334
    conversational space for, 331–334
    diversity and, 239
    as "embodied activities" (Holzman), 316
    as "making a world", 325–331
    mutual, 47
    as not linear, 167
    position, 123, 275
    process, 47, 48, 125, 241, 243, 251, 253, 254, 297, 314, 325
    as relational, 313, 314, 315–319
    resources for, 326–331
    therapist, 34, 47, 142
    undertainty in, 257–258
learner/s
    in education. (*see* Education; Learning)

therapist as, 142, 270, 274, 283
voices of, 57
listening, 35–41, 150, 152, 165, 166.
    see also Listening, hearing, and speaking
    compassion and, 104–105
    defined, 36
    differently, 25–26, 294
    empathy and, 106, 230
    ethical, 105
    healing and, 104–106
    "radical listening" (Weingarten), 105
    reflective, 269, 276
    response and, 36–37
    response-active listening-hearing, 38
        (Anderson)
    responsive listening (Shotter), 38
    therapist's inner thought and, 51
    therapist's inner voice and, 101, 104
    therapist manner, 26, 27, 28, 38, 45,
        49, 50, 53
    voices, 105
listening, hearing and speaking, 33, 35–41
lived experience, 9, 47, 48, 337, 368, 375,
    381, 382, 384

M

manners, 33 see also Acting mannerly
meaning/s, 7, 10, 12, 40, 314, 318–319
    child's approach to, 185
    as coordinated action (Gergen), 185
    construction, development, and
        generation of, 12, 13, 14, 34, 169
    as contextual, 12
    as discursive, 12
    in hermeneutics, 13–15
    inner dialogue and, 39
    intention and, 13–14
    as intersubjective, 115
    language and, 9–10, 14, 88–91, 111
    making meaning in education.
        (see Education; Teaching)
    meaning-generating process, 39
    meaning-making, 15
    meaning-making system, 15
    in research. (see Research)
    narrative and, 15–16

social construction and 12–13, 15
systems of, 110
transformation and, 10
understanding and, 13, 14, 34, 38, 50
words and, 10, 14, 110, 122. see also
    Words
Mental Research Institute, 24
Method, 67
    "onion theory" (Goolishian), 29
    theory and, 82
    theory and explanation, 88
Mexican Association of Eating
    Disorders, 130
Milan team, 204
mirror, one-way, 23, 28, 132, 152,
    157, 254,
misunderstanding 38–39. see also
    Missed-understanding; Understanding
missed-understanding, 50. see also Mis-
    understanding; Understanding
MIT, 21–24. see also Multiple Impact
    Therapy
monologic, 45, 51. see also Aboutness
    thinking; Monological; Monologue
monological, 41, 51, 69. see also About-
    ness thinking; Monologic; Monologue
    inner and outer talk, 51
    thinking, 51
monologue/s, 50, 51. see also Aboutness
    thinking; Monological
    dueling, 51
    inner conversation and, 41
    therapist-client, 69
    therapist, 39, 41, 51, 53, 57n
Montessori guides and communities, 235,
    236, 237, 238, 241
Montessori Training Institute, 237
MRI, 24
"multipartiality" (Anderson), 325
Multiple Impact Therapy, 21–24. see also
    MIT
    key assumptions and characteristics,
        23–24
    team/s 22–24
    collaborative therapy and, 23–24
multiple voices and perspectives,
    189–190

multiplicity, 17, 23, 28,
mutual inquiry, 26, 47–48, 52, 52. *see also*
  Inquiry; Joint action; Mutually explore;
  Shared inquiry
mutually explore, 47, 270. *see also* Inquiry; Mutually explore; Shared inquiry
mutual coupling, 227

N

Naming the Violence (Lobel), 239
narrative, 18n. *see also* Stories
    account, 17
    first-person, 274, 375
  identity, 16–17
    metaphor, 2, 15, 16
    mutually transforming, 51–52
    privileging narrative forms, 327–329
    reflexive, 382
  transformation and, 168, 180
Narrative and Psychotherapy Conference, 15
Need-Adapted Approach, 222. *see also*
  Open Dialogue
nonexpert, 225, 375
    curiosity and, 188
    expert dichotomies, 46
    position, 170. *see also* Not-knowing
not-knowing, 27, 34, 35, 133–134, 168,
  256–257
    approach, 115
    in learning and supervising, 256–257
    position, 53, 114, 115,
    in research, 96, 375, 378
    stance with children, 186, 187–188
    therapist, 48–50
    in treatment meetings, 128, 130
    uncertainty and. *see also* Not-knowing;
      Uncertainty
Novartis Gerontological
  Foundation, 396
not-yet-said, 14. *see also* Unsaid;
  Yet-spoken)
Number Our Days (Meyerhoff), 151

O

observer punctuations, 10, 30
ongoingness, 30

Open dialogue, 56, 64, 71–74,
  221–232, 333
    development, 221–223
    dialogical equality, 225–226
    "dialogicality", 228–230
    mobil crisis interventive teams.
      (*see* in-home therapy)
    multivoicedness, 226–227
    mutual coupling, 227
    "polyphonic treatment culture", 226
    safe atmosphere, 227–228
    in schools, 180
    seven key principles of, 223–224
    treatment meetings, 224–225
Open Dialogue conferences, 41
Organizations, 44, 55, 57
outer dialogue, 231, 279. *see also* Public
  "reflective dialogue", 231

P

participatory, 14, 36, 45, 218, 228
    belonging, 215
    knowledge, 8
    ownership, 270
Participatory Action Research, 217
pause/s, 40, 83, 211
    three kinds of, 92
Philosophical Investigations (Wittgen-
    stein), 64, 81
    philosophical stance, 43–44, 73– 74,
      170, 176, 237–238, 244, 255, 266,
      279–280, 294, 295, 385
  characteristics of, 44–54
philosophy, 8, 43–44, 56, 77, 83, 142, 228,
  236, 237, 239, 244, 255, 369. *see also*
  Philosophical stance
    multiperspectival, 176
    of life, 43, 403
    and theory, 43–44
multiperspectival, collaboration with, 70,
  85–87
play, 85–86
    in therapy, 176, 186–195
playfulness, 64, 192
"Pleroma", (Bateson) 65
positive aging, 154, 391, 392, 394, 400

Positive Aging Newsletter, 391, 392
Positive psychology, 11
  possibility/ies, 10, 13, 16, 26, 27, 34,
    40, 47, 53, 54, 57, 78, 124, 142, 151,
    185, 187, 207, 211, 224, 255, 263,
    275, 281, 295, 328, 377, 393, 406
  postmodern, 7–10, 15, 16, 21, 34, 43,
    57, 66, 68, 131, 186, 236, 237–238,
    243, 252, 253, 255, 293, 294, 367,
    370, 382
  collaborative approach, 7, 150, 151,
    167, 175, 185
  definition, of 8–10
  knowledge and language and, 8–10, 44
  psychology, 66
  transformation and, 10–11
  words and, 10, 190
"Postmodern Therapies List Serve Discussion Group", 68
problem/s, 22, 24, 25, 30, 38, 46, 69, 76,
  122, 141, 162, 165, 189, 194, 195, 224,
  240, 263, 290, 293, 297, 300, 327, 365.
  see also Aboutness thinking; Categories;
  Labels; Discourse
problem-created system, 90–91
problem-determined system, 30, 75
problem-determined/problem-organz-
  ing/problem-dissovling system, 30
problem-dis-solving system, 30, 75
problem-organizing system, 30
professional/s, 49, 156, 167, 238, 241, 243,
  315, 345, 358, 359, 376, 403–405
  actions that construct, 315
  knowledge, 46, 170, 176, 188, 252
  language, 26
  life, 54, 57, 243, 244, 360, 403
  what it means to be, 407–419
psychosis, 71, 141, 206, 221–223, 251.
  see also Open dialogue
  first-episode, 222, 224
  schizophrenia, 35, 222
public, 28, 50–51, 174, 376, 414. *see also*
  Inner conversation; Inner dialogue;
  Inner talk
  being public, 50–51, 380, 384
  personal vs private, 212
Public Conversations Project, 349n

Q

Questions, 25, 35–36, 38, 45, 64, 88, 101,
  114, 115, 171, 184, 189, 191–192, 206–
  209, 228, 231, 240, 265, 274, 287–288,
  338, 341–343, 364, 413
  collaboratively developing, 345–348
  conversational, 152, 378
  research, 373, 373, 373–375, 377,
    378–379, 380
  shelved, 279
  starter, 178, 277, 279, 287, 378

R

reality, 8, 9, 12, 16, 25, 28, 46, 82–83, 84,
  110, 111, 270, 274, 310, 324, 375, 419
  dialogical reality, 9, 69
  experienced reality 255
  lived, 194, 334, 369, 370
  multiauthored, 9
  sensing, 81–82
  subjective, 368
realities, 22, 51, 188, 274, 324, 334, 384
  conversational, 12
  multiple, 13, 243, 384
recipes, 235, 257. *see also* Techniques
reflecting process, 152, 193
reflecting teams, 64, 67, 123, 129, 130,
  151, 159, 193, 204, 240, 241, 254, 294,
  304, 344, 376. *see also* Team/s
  artistic reflections and, 181–192
  composed of families, 304
  puppet reflecting teams ,193–194
  with children, 193–194
reflection/s. *see also* Reflecting process;
  Reflecting teams
  in learning, 313, 314, 315–318
  as relational possibilities, 211–212
  therapist's written, 265
reflexive critique, 322
"Reflexive systemic therapy and consultation", 293, 294
Reggio Emilia Model, 324
relational, 12, 14, 15, 39, 40, 50, 84,
  315–318, 411
  approach, 314
  conversations, 33

knowledge, 7–11
  orientation, 318
  practice/s, 317, 319
  processes, 16, 40, 392
  responsibility, 33
  self(ves), 16–18
  systems, 23
  therapies, 68
relational hermeneutics, 13–15, 369–370,
  381–382
relationship/s, 11, 12, 16, 24, 29, 33,
  44–43, 55–56, 57 , 81, 142, 238, 244,
  253, 261, 270, 274, 339, 412. *see also*
  Relationships; Conversations
  collaborative, 34, 45, 52, 54, 132, 285,
    337, 392, 398, 399, 407
  collaborative work as relationship,
    34, 43
  egalitarian, 272
  hierarchial, 338, 345
  matrix, of 398
  nework of relations
  persons-in, 16–17, 29, 55
  research, 109, 115–116
  supervisory, 359–360
  teacher-student, 314, 317–318, 319,
    324–325
  vs. Technique, 38, 40, 41, 54
  web, of 12
relationships and conversations, 237,
  256, 371, 383. *see also* Conversations;
  Relationships
  hand-in-hand, 367
research, 367–388
  on collaborative therapy, 56–57, 222,
    225, 353
  collaborative, social construction
    research, 56, 110
  collaborative research meeting,
    114–116, 217
  conversation, 377–379
  co-research, 168
  data analysis as making meaning,
    378–382
  dialogical approach to, 56
  as generative process, 373
  hearing and, 112–113

insider, 9, 270, 376–377
  joint construction of research ques-
    tions, 374–375
  making meaning in, 379–380
  as mutual inquiry, 374–375
  outsider research, 9, 270, 376
  as part of everyday practice, 130, 270
  participatory action research, 217
  performing, 110–111
  qualitative, 56, 385
  quantitative, 385
  questions, 373, 373, 373–375, 377,
    378–379, 380
  relationship, 109, 110, 115–116
  traditional research relationship, 109
  trustworthiness and *authenticity* vs.
    reliability and validity, 382–385
researcher
  as learner, 375
  curious stance of, 375–376
  stance, 375–376
  as transcriber, 381
resources, 16, 23, 188, 223, 317, 393
  for collaborative educational conver-
    sation and learning, 326–331
  identifying, 150, 238–239, 261
  respect, 27, 34, 40, 46, 150–151, 168,
    211, 240, 259, 275, 297–298, 366,
    393, 411–412, 413
responding, 36–38, 47, 112, 114, 231, 394,
  409. *see also* Listening; Responsive
  active responding, 52
  to understand, 38
responsibility, 17, 105, 123, 169, 212, 223,
  227, 229, 252, 296, 407, 415, 417, 418
  relational, 414
  shared responsibility, 48, 55, 281, 282
  student's, 332
  supervisor's, 255
responsive. 37, 45, 50, 152, 320, *see also*
  Listening; Responding
  relational-responsive understanding,
    38, 50
  responsive-active listening-hearing,
    38
  responsive understanding, 50
rhizome connection, 75

S

schools, 236, 243, 316
Schools for Growth, (Holzman), 316
self/selves. *See* Identity; Identities
   conversational becoming, 17
   dialogical-relational self and agency,
     17–18
   individual-in-relationship, 17, 29
   multi-authored polyphonic self, 16
   narrative self, 18n
   person/person(s)-in-relationship, 2,
     16–17, 55
   relational self/selves, 16, 17
Servicio de Psyquiatria, Hospital Universitario, 309
"syllogisms of metaphor" (Bateson &
   Bateson), 65
Smilla's Sense of Snow (Høeg), 41
Smith School of Social Work, 64, 71
social construction, 7, 11–13, 15, 30, 68, 77,
   110, 185, 190, 221, 228, 239, 253, 294, 318,
   322, 367, 369. *see also* Social constructionist; Social constructionist dialogue
social constructionism, 11–13, 68, 110,
   228, 294, 318, 369, 370
social constructionist
   discourse, 318
   research, 369
social justice, 58
socially constructed
   communal construction, 11, 12
   multi-plural authorship, 12, 13
social constructionism vs. constructivism, 12, 110
socially created, 9, 16
Solution-Focused Therapy, 64, 78, 263
space, 27, 34, 168, 214, 216, 238, 326, 374
   conversational space and learning,
     325, 326, 331, 336
   creating, 54, 124, 142, 184–185, 247
   dialogical, 132, 179, 186
   dialogical space and process, 18, 51
   metaphorical space, 15, 34, 44
   opening, 152
   physical, 48, 186, 207, 252
   relational, 39
   "safe", 227

"Stages", 163
story(ies), 15–16, 26, 37, 46, 133, 150,
   327, 328
   dialogical, 13
   performance of, 206
   in research, 377, 381
   sense-making, 13
   story ball, 47
   story-telling, 325
   story-telling process in therapy, 341
substance abuse, women with, 269, 271,
   273, 285
synchrony, 280
system/s, 23, 109
   Collaborative Language Systems, 150,
     167, 256, 370
   cybernetic, 13, 15
   evolutionary systems, 29
   linguistic systems, 15, 30
   meaning-generating, meaning gener-
     ating, 255
   meaning systems, 110, 270, 320
   ongoingness, 30
   onion theory, 29
   participative, 214–215
   shared meaning systems, 110
   social systems metaphor, 17, 29
systemic family therapy, 13, 253

T

talk. *see also* Conversation; Dialogue
   effects of open talk on prison system,
     216–217
   egocentric talk, 86
   mutual talks, 215
   open talks, 216
   participatory talks, 215
   shared talks, 203, 204
"*Talk of the Nation*," National Public
   Radio 78
Taos Institute, 396, 397
Teaching, 27, 55, 237, 238, 294, 313–335,
   354, 404. *see also* Education; Learning
team/s, 22–23. *see also* Reflecting teams
   "after discussions", 131s
   host, 70–71

spirit, 172
team's role, 23
teamwork, 223
treatment, 131–132, 172, 222, 223, 227, 262
technique/s, 35, 38, 40, 41, 44, 54, 132, 142, 257, 263, 300, 314, 317, 318, 319. *see also* Recipes
The Art of Agape Listening 41n
"The Art of Lenses", 70
"The Greeting" (Viola) 46, 57n
"The Hundred Languages of Children Exhibit, 2000", 167
The Namesake (Lahira), 37
"The Reflecting Team: Dialogue and Meta-Dialogue in Clinical Work" (Andersen) 78, 146, 239, 244, 266, 349
The Reflective Practitioner (Schön), 241
The Saturated Self (Gergen), 238, 396
theory/ies, 21, 43, 88. *see also* Social Construction
    absence of theory and method, 43, 237
    expectations and, 356
    "good" vs. "bad", 366
    language systems theory, 109, 111, 216
    "onion theory", 29
    practice and, 205, 337
    supervisee theory, 355
therapist/s
    attitudes and actions, 38
    apprehension, fear, 225, 251, 252, 253
    blank slate/s, not as, 49, 280
    burn-out, 55
    "challenged", 56
    competence, 47
    from expert to "dialogicians" 232
    expertise, 26, 27, 44, 46, 47, 65, 225, 259, 324
    as experts, 225, 257, 282, 315
    knowledge, 26, 46
    as learner/s, 26, 40, 115, 124, 244, 274, 282
    learning position, 45, 47, 270
    nonexpert, 46, 186
    nonexpert position, 170, 186, 188
    not-knowing, 50, 114–115, 133, 168
    personal lives, 296–297

power differential, 40, 53
therapy. *see also* Collaborative Therapy
    as conversational process, 27, 47, 255, 270
    as everyday ordinary life, 53–54
    supervision as language- or meaning-generating systems and, 255, 370
    therapists' and client's perspectives on, 143, 180, 243, 261, 283, 295–309, 359
three Cs, 255
training, 23, 130, 151, 173, 236, 237, 299–300, 338, 359,
training exercise, 339–344
transformation, 10–11, 16, 34, 52, 168, 184, 270
transformation vs. change, 10
transforming, 10
transformative experience, 322
    change, 10
    client and therapist transforming together, 10
    inherent in dialogue, 34, 180, 263
    social, 318
treatment meetings, 73–74, 221, 224–231
    dialogical equality, 225–226
    "dialogicality", 228–230
    multivoicedness, 226–227
    "polyphonic treatment culture", 226
    reflective activity, 230–231
    safe atmosphere, 227–228
trialogues, 203, 206–211, 215
trust, 15, 46, 52, 122, 224, 228, 236, 243, 261, 359, 406
truth/s, 8–9, 11, 13, 15, 44, 65, 69, 110, 139, 225, 238, 297, 320, 349, 355, 357, 369–370, 384

U

uncertain, 179
uncertainty, 15, 27, 34, 50, 52–53, 134, 257, 338. *see also* Not-knowing
    in learning, 243, 257–258
    in life, 259
    in therapy, 52, 258–259
    tolerance of, 224
    trusting, 52

understanding, 13, 34, 40, 50, 69, 224, 230, 316, 328, 355, 417
  generative process, 34
  interpretive process, 13
  meaning and understanding, 7, 34, 45
  mis-understanding, 38
  mutually collaborative and dialogical, 110, 276
  never-ending, 40
  pre-understandings, 13, 43, 272, 380
  relational-responsive kind of understanding, 50
  responsive, 50
  shared, 230
  Verstehen vs. explanation (*Erklären*), 368
"Understanding and Relational Expertise" (Holmes), 258
Universidad de las Américas (UDLA), 251
Universidad Nacional Autónoma de México (UNAM), 251
University of Havana, 309n
University of Marburg, 291
University of Texas Medical Branch, 21, 351
University of Tromsø, 63, 205
unsaid,14, 38. *see also* Not-yet-said; Yet-spoken
Upheavals of Thought (Nussbaum), 106

V

valuation, 55, 283, 407–411
violent acts, 213
  prison system, 216, 218
visiting
  colleagues, 253
  therapists, 28
  visitors, 28, 227, 244, 253
voice/s, 23, 27, 35, 55, 75, 168, 175, 226, 244, 393
  children's, 184

client, 33, 57, 143
  client and eating disorders, 143
  inner voices, 66, 86, 104
  "listening voices", 105
  multiple voices and perspectives, 28, 47, 189, 239, 374
  multiplicity of voices, 67, 70
  social voices, 85
  women's voices, 111, 275, 283

W

wisdom, 57, 417
  "Local Wisdom of the Kids", 76
  "Local Wisdom of the Mothers", 76
  "Three Pillars of ", 66
with, 44
witness, 44, 45, 51, 64, 77
  "art of witness" (Hoffman), 57n, 63
  participatory
  witness practices of Tom Andersen, 64, 70–72
  witness process, 44
  witness (dialogical)-thinking, 45, 70
  witness thinking (Shotter), 45, 51, 69, 256
words, 10, 13, 74, 85, 87, 105, 112, 145, 152, 174, 211, 218, 227, 230, 343
  beyond, 190
  generative, 48
  meanings, 89, 185, 324
  receiving, 91
  spoken, 39, 50–51, 70, 91
writing, 84, 102, 159, 195, 334, 356, 376
  as collaboration, 212–213, 395
  letter written by therapists, 180, 264
  writing and letters, 84, 102, 103

Y

yet-unspoken, 39. *see also* Not-yet-said; Unsaid

Author Index

A

Aaltonen, J., 56, 222, 224, 368
Acevedo, G., 142
Alakare, B., 56, 222, 368
Alanen, Y.O., 73, 74, 222, 224, 224–225
Almeida, R.V., 122,
Andersen, T., 1, 3, 18n, 36, 37, 45, 58n,
  63, 64, 67, 68, 70, 71, 72, 73, 77, 88,
  104, 131–132, 150, 151, 167, 184, 189,
  190–191, 205, 206, 217, 230, 231, 253,
  254, 255, 294, 337, 376
Anderson, H., 14, 15, 16, 17, 22, 25, 29,
  30, 30n, 38, 39, 43, 50, 51, 53, 54, 55,
  56, 57, 57n, 64, 66, 75, 88, 95, 110,
  111, 114, 115, 123, 131, 132–133, 133,
  134, 137, 140, 142, 150, 151, 167, 168,
  169, 170, 171, 172, 173, 174, 175, 176,
  176–177, 179, 179–180, 184, 186, 187,
  188, 189, 204, 205, 224, 228, 236, 237,
  243, 244, 255, 256, 258, 258–259,
  259, 259–260, 261, 275, 281, 285,
  286n, 294, 295, 324, 337, 351, 361,
  367, 368, 369, 370, 370–371, 373, 374,
  375, 376, 376–377, 378, 379, 380, 381,
  384, 400n, 403
Andrews, J., 96, 150
Atkinson, B., 384
Austin, J.L.

B

Bachelard, G., 66
Bakhtin, M., 2, 15, 28, 45, 50, 63, 64, 68,
  69, 74, 75, 88, 215, 226, 228, 229, 293,
  370, 372
Barrett, F., 334n, 400n,
Bateson, G., 2, 24, 30, 64, 65, 66, 150, 204
Bateson, M.C., 65, 110, 112,
Bava, S., 18n, 56, 199, 368, 373, 377,
  381, 383,
Beaton, J.M., 415
Becerril, S., 266n
Beneviste, E., 18n
Benson, K., 381
Berger, P., 228
Berger, V., 191
Biever, J., 366
Birchwood, M., 224
Bograd, M., 349n
Bohm, D., 28, 229
Borgengren, M., 255
Boscolo, L., 30, 204
Boyd, G., 41n
Braatøy, T., 88
Bray, J.N., 371, 373, 406, 407
Bruffee, K.A., 322
Bruner, J., 18n, 185
Bryant-Waugh, R., 140, 146n

Bülow-Hansen, A., 70, 86, 87
Burney, P., 56, 366

C

Campbell, W., 415
Caraballo Pons, I., 309n
Carbajosa, G., 310n
Carlsson, J., 83
Cecchin, G., 30, 72, 204
Chasin, R., 349, 349n
Chávez, R. 266n
Chenail, R.J., 384, 414
Clark, D.J., 150
Clark, M., 397
Cooperrider, D.L., 335n
Cortes, A., 96, 379,
Csikszentmihalyi, M., 11
Cushman, P., 412

D

Damasio, A., 66, 72
Dare, C., 140, 141,
Deissler, K.G., 198, 293, 294, 368
del Valle, M., 266n
Dell, P.F., 29, 29–30,
Denzin, N.K., 383
Derrida, J., 2, 28, 88, 293
Díaz, A., 266n
Doherty, W.J., 415
Dole, D., 396
Dorr, S., 400n
Drury, J., 374
Durkin, T., 122

E

Ellinor, L., 229
Elliott, M., 255
Elmquist, J., 286n,
Epston, D., 337, 349, 403
Erikson, E.H., 165

F

Feinsilver, D., 286n, 368, 378
Fernández, E., 96, 379,

Fontana, A., 378
Force, H., 400n
Foucault, M.
Frankfurt, M., 213
Freud, 86
Frey, J.H., 378
Friedrich, T., 397

G

Gadamer, H.G., 14, 18n, 28,
  369, 380
Gardner, G., 198
Gargollo, M., 56, 379
Gargollo, M.C., 56, 379
Geertz, C., 269
Gehart, D., 56, 96, 96–97, 191, 199, 337,
  367–368, 368, 373, 375, 380, 381, 383,
  384, 400n
Gerard, G., 229
Gergen, K.J., 1, 8, 10, 11, 12, 15, 16, 17,
  18n, 88, 110, 111, 137, 150, 185, 199,
  228, 259–260, 318, 323, 329, 333, 369,
  370, 377, 382, 384, 400n, 414–415,
Gergen, M., 199, 293, 384, 400n
Gilje, N., 205
Gilligan, C., 111
Gilligan, S., 403
Gleick, J., 110
Goldner, V., 122
Goolishian, H., 11, 14, 15, 16, 17, 21,
  21–22, 23, 29, 29–30, 39, 51, 56, 57n,
  64, 66, 75, 88, 89, 90, 110, 111, 114,
  115, 150, 151, 167, 184, 186, 188, 224,
  228, 255, 256, 337, 351, 352, 354, 367,
  370, 373, 375
Granger-Merkel, L., 196n
Graumann, C., 230
Grayling, A.C., 88
Griffith, J., 255
Griffith, R. 396
Gutiérrez, A., 266n

H

Höyer, G., 205, 217
Høeg, P., 36

Haarakangas, K., 56, 197, 222, 224, 226, 227, 231, 368,
Hacking, I., 18n
Hare-Mustin, R., 18n
Harré, R., 18n
Heath, A., 384
Helms, S., 56
Heraclites, 90
Hermans, H.J.M., 17
Hesse-Biber, S., 137
Hoffman, L., 1, 2, 3, 15, 30, 57n, 167, 205,
Holma, J., 224
Holmes, S., 258
Holzman, L., 1, 324
Hoy, D.C., 13

I

Ianssen, B., 86
Isaacs, W., 229

J

Jackson, C., 224
Johnson, N.A., 419

K

Katz, A., 64
Kaufman, G., 122
Keeney, B.P.,
Kempen, H.J.G.,
Keranen, J., 56, 222, 225
Kinman, C., 64, 75, 76
Koch, P.K., 96, 180, 368
Kose, K.H., 309n
Kvale, S., 384

L

Lannaman, J., 310n
Larner, G., 371
Lask, B., 140, 146n
Lee, J., 371, 406
Lehtinen, K., 222
Lehtinen, V., 223

Lemke, J.L., 379
Levin, S.B., 38, 56, 112, 176, 365, 368
Levinas, E., 214
Lincoln, Y.S., 383
Lindseth, A., 295
Lister, S., 374
Lobel, K., 113
Locke, L., 122
London, S., 56, 243, 368, 379
Lowe, R., 64
Lánigan Gutiérrez, M.E., 309n
Lucas, B., 368, 375
Luckmann, T., 228
Lyle, R.R., 56, 337, 368, 373, 380, 381, 383, 384
Lyotard, J.F., 67, 293

M

MacGregor, R., xix, 23
Macpherson, C.B., 315
Madsen, W.C., 266n, 349n, 373, 411
Malinen, T., 403
Martin, D., 121
Martinez Hurtado, M.A., 309n
Maturana, H.R., 11, 28, 30, 110, 111, 150
McCollum, E., 122
McDanald, E.C., 23
McDonough, M., 96, 180, 368
McNamee, S., 1, 197, 198, 318, 323, 333, 414
Miller, D., 111
Mitchell, W., 374
Mohr, B., 400n
Morgan, G., 115
Morson, A.C., 88, 90
Murphy, E., 286n
Murphy, M.J., 368, 378, 385
Myerhoff, B., 149–150

N

Neugebauer, T., 268
New, R., 324
Niles, C., 56
Nussbaum, M.C., 106, 107

O

O'Hanlon, W., 238
Oakley, A., 115
Olson, M., 64, 71, 72, 73, 74, 75, 76
Ortega Sastriques,
Øvreberg, G., 70, 86, 87

P

Pantanleo, D., 196n
Paré, D., 371
Penn, P., 64, 86, 122, 167, 184, 204,
    205, 213
Piaget, 85, 86
Piercy, F., 381
Pipher, M., 137
Plotkin, S., 56
Polster, M., 152
Pradera, E.A., 309n
Price, R., 403
Price, S.J., 385
Pulliam, G., 351, 352, 366

Q

Queroz, C., 266n

R

Ramirez, A.M., 166n
Raser, J., 56
Ratliff, D.A., 368, 383
Ravazzola, C., 397
Reese, A., 56
Renteria, N., 266n
Richardson, L., 381, 382
Richter, J., 310n
Riikonen, E., 105
Ritchie, A.M., 23
Roberts, H., 56
Roberts, K., 374
Robiolio, A., 397
Roderburgand, S., 397
Rodriguez-Jazcilevich, I., 243, 266n, 386
Rodriguez, R., 292, 309n
Rorty, R., 9, 18, 28, 34, 323
Rosen, K., 122

Roth, S., 339, 349n
Rothblum, E.D., 138
Ruiz G., 56, 379
Räkköläinen, V., 222

S

Sampson, E.E., 88, 315, 410
Schön, D., 241, 370
Schug, R., 294
Schulz, S., 291
Schuster, F.P., 23
Schwandt, T.A., 368, 369
Seikkula, J., 37, 56, 64, 70, 71, 72, 73, 74,
    75, 76, 77, 222, 223, 225, 255
Seligman, M.E.P., 11
Serrano, A.C., 23
Shawver, L.,
Shaw, J., 138
Shawver, L., 66, 68
Sheinberg, M., 122
Shotter, J., 10, 12, 13, 15, 18n, 37, 38, 43,
    45, 50, 52, 64, 68, 69, 88, 150, 185, 256,
    293, 370, 417
Singh, L., 89
Skirbekk, G., 90
Sloper, P., 374
Smith, G.M., 105
Smith, L.L., 371, 406
Smith, S.E., 419
Smith, T. E., 193
Sonkin, D.J., 121
St. George, S., 55, 56, 57n, 414
Stains, R.R., Jr., 349, 349n
Stein, S.A., 165
Stith, S., 122
Strong, T., 372, 373
Stuart, R.B., 413
Studer, C., 397
Sutela, M., 56,
Swim, S., 56, 57
Swint, J. A., 56
Szmukler, G., 140, 141

T

Tamasese, K., 415
Tannen, D., 111, 112

Tarragona, M., 146n, 368, 379
Tinez, D., 56
Treasure, J., 140, 141
Tuhaka, F., 415
Tutu, D., 203, 219

V

Varela, F.J., 110, 115
Viola, B., 46, 57n
Voloshinov, V., 15, 73, 76, 228
Von Glaserfeld, E., 28, 110
Von Wright, G.H., 88, 90
Vygotsky, L., 15, 28, 73, 76, 81, 85, 86, 88, 90, 213, 231, 370

W

Wachterhauser, B.R., 14
Wagner, J., 205, 217
Waldegrave, C., 415
Walker, G., 122
Walker, L., 121
Warneke, G., 14
Watkins, J., 400n
Watzlawick, P., 110
Weeda-Mannak, W., 138
Weiner-Davis, M., 238

Weingarten, K., 105, 349n
Weisenburger, G.A., 56
Werner-Wilson, R.J., 385
White, M., 67, 68, 255, 337, 403
White, W.F., 217
Whitney, D., 400n
Willig, C., 374
Willms, D.G., 419
Winderman L., 17, 30,
Wittgenstein, L., 9, 10, 14, 15, 28, 34, 41, 43, 45, 50, 52, 64, 65, 68, 69, 79, 81, 83, 87, 88, 90, 324, 369, 370, 377
Woldt, A.A., 165
Wortmann, A., 292
Wulff , D., 55, 56, 57n, 414

Y

Yankelovich, D., 229
Yorks, L., 371, 406
Yodú, R., 309n

Z

Zaid, R.M., 266n
Zimmerman, T.S., 385
Zingaro, J., 411